Emerging Trends in Machine Learning Data Science, and Internet of Things

(Part 1)

Edited by

Manoj Kumar
Faculty of Engineering & Information Sciences,
University of Wollongong, Dubai, UAE

Sachin Kumar Gupta
Department of Electronics and Communication Engineering
National Chiao Tung University (NCTU)
Hsinchu, Taiwan

Navnath Kale
School of Computer Engineering, MIT Academy of Engineering
Pune, India

Pramod Ganjewar
School of Computer Engineering, MIT Academy of Engineering
Pune, India

&

Sandeep Pande
School of Computer Engineering, MIT Academy of Engineering
Pune, India

Emerging Trends in Machine Learning, Data Science, and Internet of Things *(Part 1)*

Editors: Manoj Kumar, Sachin Kumar Gupta, Navnath Kale, Pramod Ganjewar & Sandeep Pande

ISBN (Online): 979-8-89881-471-7

ISBN (Print): 979-8-89881-472-4

ISBN (Paperback): 979-8-89881-473-1

Published by Bentham Science Publishers Pte. Ltd. Singapore,

in collaboration with Eureka Conferences, USA.

First published in 2026.

Bentham Science Publishers Pte. Ltd.
No. 9 Raffles Place
Office No. 26-01
Singapore 048619
Singapore
Email: subscriptions@benthamscience.net

BENTHAM SCIENCE

CONTENTS

FOREWORD

The remarkable progress of artificial intelligence over the past decade has been driven not only by advances in algorithms, but by the creative application of these techniques to meaningful real-world problems. This volume is a compelling reflection of that progress. It brings together diverse research contributions that demonstrate how machine learning, data science, and intelligent systems are reshaping healthcare, security, automation, and human–computer interaction.

The chapters in this book highlight the expanding influence of deep learning and data-driven methodologies. From skin lesion classification and epileptic abnormality recognition to cancer gene detection and bacterial colony analysis, the healthcare-focused studies illustrate the profound societal impact that intelligent models can deliver. Equally noteworthy are the works on sentiment analysis, optimization strategies, and automated grading systems, which demonstrate the growing sophistication of computational approaches in understanding human language and behavior.

The inclusion of research on early-stage fire detection, AI-powered anomaly detection for cyber security, and conflict resolution in self-driving vehicles underscores the importance of reliable and trustworthy AI systems. These contributions reflect a strong awareness of the need for robustness, safety, and privacy in modern technological ecosystems. The chapters on IoT-enabled cloud security further emphasize that intelligent systems must be both innovative and secure.

What distinguishes this volume is its balanced integration of theory and application. The contributors not only explore advanced computational models but also present practical implementations that address pressing global challenges. Such interdisciplinary engagement is essential for the continued evolution of artificial intelligence.

I commend the editors and authors for assembling a work that captures the dynamic spirit of contemporary research in intelligent computing. This book will serve as a valuable resource for researchers, practitioners, and students seeking to contribute to the next generation of AI-driven solutions.

K. V. D. Kiran
Department of Computer Science and Engineering
Koneru Lakshmaiah Education Foundation
Guntur District, India

Preface

The unprecedented growth of intelligent computing technologies has opened new avenues for research, innovation, and societal transformation. The integration of Machine Learning, Data Science, Artificial Intelligence, Internet of Things, and Cloud Computing is redefining the landscape of modern technological development. This book is the result of collective scholarly efforts to present recent research advancements and practical applications in these rapidly evolving domains.

The primary objective of this volume is to provide a comprehensive platform for researchers, academicians, industry experts, and students to explore innovative methodologies and solutions addressing contemporary challenges. The chapters included in this book reflect diverse research perspectives and demonstrate how intelligent systems can enhance healthcare, security, automation, and human–computer interaction.

The Machine Learning section presents research contributions focusing on healthcare diagnosis, biological data analysis, sentiment analysis, sustainable food management, and gesture-based virtual interfaces. These chapters highlight the effectiveness of advanced computational models in addressing complex real-world problems and improving decision-making processes.

The Data Science section emphasizes the importance of data-driven methodologies in improving automated assessment systems, enabling cloud-based healthcare services, and strengthening network security through advanced artificial intelligence techniques. These contributions demonstrate the significant role of data analytics in building efficient and reliable digital infrastructures.

The Internet of Things section focuses on emerging challenges in autonomous systems and secure cloud communication. The research presented in this section addresses conflict resolution in self-driving vehicles and privacy-preserving frameworks for IoT-enabled cloud environments, emphasizing the need for secure, reliable, interconnected systems.

The editors sincerely acknowledge the valuable contributions of all authors who have shared their research work and insights in this volume. We also extend our gratitude to the reviewers for their constructive suggestions, which have helped maintain the academic quality and relevance of this book. Special appreciation is extended to the organizing team and supporting institutions for their continuous encouragement and assistance throughout the compilation process.

It is our sincere hope that this book will serve as a valuable reference for readers, inspire future research endeavors, and promote innovation in intelligent computing technologies. We believe that the ideas and methodologies presented in this volume will contribute to academic excellence and technological progress.

Manoj Kumar
Faculty of Engineering & Information Sciences
University of Wollongong
Dubai, UAE

Sachin Kumar Gupta
Department of Electronics and Communication Engineering

National Chiao Tung University (NCTU)
Hsinchu, Taiwan

Navnath Kale
School of Computer Engineering
MIT Academy of Engineering
Pune, India

Pramod Ganjewar
School of Computer Engineering
MIT Academy of Engineering
Pune, India

&

Sandeep Pande
School of Computer Engineering
MIT Academy of Engineering
Pune, India

List of Contributors

Areeba	Department of Computer Applications, PES University, Bangalore, Karnataka, India
Atharva Mahatekar	Department of Computer Engineering, Vishwakarma Institute Of Technology, Bibwewadi, Pune, India
Anju Sharma	Department of Computational Sciences, Maharaja Ranjit Singh Punjab Technical University, Bathinda, India
Arsh Swami	Department of Information Technology, Amity Institute of Information Technology, Noida, Uttar Pradesh, India
Asha Sunki	Computer Science and Engineering, Vardhaman College of Engineering, Hyderabad, India
Aditya Goutam	Department of Computer Engineering, MIT Academy of Engineering, Pune, India
Anita Mahajan	Department of Computer Engineering, Ajeenkya D. Y. Patil School of Engineering, Pune, India
Bandaru Vivek	Department of Computer Science and Engineering, Gokaraju Rangaraju Institute of Engineering and Technology, Hyderabad, Telangana, India
C. Satya Kumar	Computer Science and Engineering, Vardhaman College of Engineering, Hyderabad, India
D. Dileepan	Department of Computer Science and Engineering, Rajalakshmi Institute of Technology, Vel Tech Rangarajan Dr. Sagunthala R&D Institute of Science and Technology, Chennai, India
Dhruv Deshmukh	Department of Computer Science and Engineering, Dr. Vishwanath Karad, MIT World Peace University, Pune, India
Ganga Gudi	Department of Computer Applications, PES University, Bangalore, Karnataka, India
Harshitha Reddy	Department of Computer Science and Engineering, Vardhaman College of Engineering, Hyderabad, India
J. Kanimozhi	Department of Computer Science and Engineering, Rajalakshmi Institute of Technology, Vel Tech Rangarajan Dr. Sagunthala R&D Institute of Science and Technology, Chennai, India
Jyoti Kanjalkar	Department of Computer Engineering, Vishwakarma Institute Of Technology, Bibwewadi, Pune, India
K. Srinivasa Karthikeya Reddy	Department of Computer Science and Engineering, Gokaraju Rangaraju Institute of Engineering and Technology, Hyderabad, Telangana, India
Laxmi Kove	Department of Computer Engineering, Vishwakarma Institute Of Technology, Bibwewadi, Pune, India
Md. Sahilur Rahman	Department of Computer Science, American International University, Dhaka, Bangladesh

M. Chitra	Department of Computer Science and Engineering, Rajalakshmi Institute of Technology, Vel Tech Rangarajan Dr. Sagunthala R&D Institute of Science and Technology, Chennai, India
Md. Fahad Khan	Department of Computer Science, American International University, Dhaka, Bangladesh
M. Manikandan	Department of Computer Science and Engineering, Rajalakshmi Institute of Technology, Vel Tech Rangarajan Dr. Sagunthala R&D Institute of Science and Technology, Chennai, India
Mahesh Jadhao	Department of Computer Engineering, Vishwakarma Institute Of Technology, Bibwewadi, Pune, India
Manish Hakeem	Computer Science and Engineering, Vardhaman College of Engineering, Hyderabad, India
Monika Dangore	Department of Computer Engineering, Marathwada Mitramandal's Institute of Technology, Pune, India
N. Chaithra Reddy	Department of Computer Science and Engineering, Vardhaman College of Engineering, Hyderabad, India
Neeraj Kumar	Department of Computer Engineering, MIT Academy of Engineering, Alandi, Pune, India
Nausheen Aftab	Department of Computer Engineering, MIT Academy of Engineering, Alandi, Pune, India
Nehaal Pandey	Department of Computer Engineering, MIT Academy of Engineering, Pune, India
Pramod Kanjalkar	Department of Computer Engineering, Vishwakarma Institute Of Technology, Bibwewadi, Pune, India
Prathamesh Shirnath	Department of Computer Engineering, MIT Academy of Engineering, Alandi, Pune, India
Pallavi Nehete	Department of Computer Science and Engineering, Dr. Vishwanath Karad, MIT World Peace University, Pune, India
Priyanka M. Chovatiya	Department of Computer Applications, PES University, Bangalore, Karnataka, India
Priyanshu Paul	Department of Computer Science and Engineering, Dr. Vishwanath Karad, MIT World Peace University, Pune, India
R. Sanmugasundaram	Department of Computer Science and Engineering, Rajalakshmi Institute of Technology, Vel Tech Rangarajan Dr. Sagunthala R&D Institute of Science and Technology, Chennai, India
Rajeshwari Goudar	Department of Computer Engineering, MIT Academy of Engineering, Alandi, Pune, India
Ravula Arun Kumar	Department of Computer Science and Engineering, Vardhaman College of Engineering, Hyderabad, India
Sunit Trivedi	Department of Computer Engineering, MIT Academy of Engineering, Pune, India

Sunita S. Barve Department of Computer Engineering, MIT Academy of Engineering, Pune, India

Sampada Khopade Department of Computer Engineering, Vishwakarma Institute Of Technology, Bibwewadi, Pune, India

Soumil Jha Department of Computer Science and Engineering, Dr. Vishwanath Karad, MIT World Peace University, Pune, India

Sandeep Kaur Gill Department of Computational Sciences, Maharaja Ranjit Singh Punjab Technical University, Bathinda, India

Sai Aryan Sangam Department of Computer Science and Engineering, Gokaraju Rangaraju Institute of Engineering and Technology, Hyderabad, Telangana, India

Tallapally Uday Kiran Department of Computer Science and Engineering, Gokaraju Rangaraju Institute of Engineering and Technology, Hyderabad, Telangana, India

V. Srilakshmi Department of Computer Science and Engineering, Gokaraju Rangaraju Institute of Engineering and Technology, Hyderabad, Telangana, India

Vijay Varia Department of Computer Science and Engineering, Dr. Vishwanath Karad, MIT World Peace University, Pune, India

Vinith Koppera Computer Science and Engineering, Vardhaman College of Engineering, Hyderabad, India

Veeraj Goudar Department of Computer Engineering, MIT Academy of Engineering, Pune, India

Vivek Talnikar Department of Computer Engineering, Annasaheb Dange College of Engineering & Technology, Ashta, India

Vanita Kshirsagar Department of Computer Engineering, Dr. D. Y. Patil Institute of Technology, Pune, India

Vishal Borate Department of Computer Engineering, Dr. D. Y. Patil Colleges of Engineering & Innovation, Talegaon, Pune, India

Yechuri Srikar Department of Computer Science and Engineering, Vardhaman College of Engineering, Hyderabad, India

Yogesh Mali Department of Computer Engineering, G.H Raisoni College of Engineering and Management, Pune, India

Summary of the Chapters

Section 1: Machine Learning

Chapter 1: Skin Lesion Classification Using Data Efficient Image Transformer

This chapter presents a deep learning framework using data-efficient image transformer architectures for accurate skin lesion classification. It focuses on improving diagnostic performance with limited datasets, aiming to support early detection of skin diseases.

Chapter 2: Neurological Tests for Human Epileptic Abnormality Recognition

The chapter explores machine learning techniques applied to neurological test data for identifying epileptic abnormalities. It highlights feature extraction methods and classification models designed to enhance diagnostic reliability.

Chapter 3: From Tweets to Insights: A Diverse Classifier Approach to Analyze Sentiments on Twitter

This study examines multiple machine learning classifiers for sentiment analysis of Twitter data, comparing their effectiveness in capturing public opinion and extracting actionable insights.

Chapter 4: Unveiling Optimization Algorithms for Fine Tuning of Sentiment Analysis

This chapter investigates optimization algorithms to improve sentiment classification performance, emphasizing hyperparameter tuning and model refinement strategies.

Chapter 5: Comparative Analysis of Bacterial Colony Counting: YOLOv8 vs Blob Identification

A comparative study evaluating deep learning-based object detection (YOLOv8) against traditional blob detection techniques for bacterial colony counting and clustering in laboratory settings.

Chapter 6: Fire Detection at Early Stage Using Deep Learning through Real-Time Video

This chapter proposes a real-time deep learning-based fire detection system to enhance early warning mechanisms and minimize disaster impact.

Chapter 7: Enhancing Sustainable Practices in Food Management Using Machine Learning Approach

The study presents predictive models aimed at optimizing food resource management and reducing waste through data-driven decision-making.

Chapter 8: Cancerous Gene Detection Through Machine Learning Techniques

This chapter focuses on identifying cancer-related genes using advanced machine learning algorithms to support early diagnosis and precision medicine.

Chapter 9: Virtual Mouse Using Hand Gestures

An innovative human–computer interaction system that uses computer vision and gesture recognition to control cursor movement without physical hardware.

Section 2: Data Science

Chapter 10: Improving Automated Grading Systems

This chapter compares machine learning techniques for handwritten digit recognition to enhance the accuracy and efficiency of automated evaluation systems.

Chapter 11: Implementation of Cloud-Based Healthcare System

The chapter discusses the architecture and deployment of a scalable cloud-based healthcare management system for improved accessibility and data handling.

Chapter 12: Enhancing Network Security through AI-powered Anomaly Detection Using GANs

This study applies Generative Adversarial Networks (GANs) for detecting anomalies in network traffic, strengthening cybersecurity frameworks.

Section 3: Internet of Things

Chapter 13: Conflict Resolution in Uncertain Situations for Self-Driving Cars

This chapter addresses decision-making algorithms for autonomous vehicles operating in uncertain environments, focusing on safety and reliability.

Chapter 14: Security & Privacy Preserving in Cloud Computing Using IoT

The final chapter proposes secure IoT-enabled cloud frameworks that ensure privacy protection and secure data transmission in interconnected systems.

Section 1: Machine Learning

CHAPTER 1

Skin Lesion Classification Using Data-Efficient Image Transformer

Md. Sahilur Rahman[*,1], **Md. Fahad Khan**[1] and **Golam Rabbani Rafi**[1]

[1] *Department of Computer Science, American International University, Dhaka, Bangladesh*

Abstract: Skin cancer, especially melanoma, is the most common cancer globally and in the United States. About 10% of melanoma cases have a family history. In 2023, an estimated 97,610 new melanoma cases are expected in the US, with 58,120 affecting males and 39,490 affecting females. To enhance diagnostic accuracy, the DeiT (Data-Efficient Image Transformer) model was applied to the ISIC 2019 dataset, which comprises a diverse range of skin lesion images. Our Transformer model outperformed traditional CNN models, achieving a precision of 94%, a recall of 95%, and an accuracy of 93%, surpassing models such as EfficientNet and DenseNet169. This superior performance is attributed to the DeiT model's ability to capture complex image patterns efficiently. Its success indicates that Transformer-based models hold significant promise for improving skin cancer diagnosis, leading to earlier detection and better patient outcomes.

Keywords: DeiT, Melanoma, Skin Cancer, United States, Worldwide.

INTRODUCTION

The abnormal growth of skin cells, known as skin cancer, usually appears on skin that is regularly exposed to the sun. That being said, it's essential to remember that this common type of cancer can also develop in areas of the skin that are not typically exposed to sunlight. People of any skin tone can be affected by melanoma [1].

Melanoma frequently appears on the palms, soles, or under fingernails or toenails in those with darker skin tones [2]. With an expected 1.5 million new cases reported in 2022, skin malignancies are the most common group of tumours diagnosed globally. More specifically, the disease was blamed for almost 60,000 deaths in the same year that 330,000 new cases of melanoma were reported globally [3]. Generally speaking, machine learning-enabled early detection can

* **Corresponding Author Md. Sahilur Rahman:** Department of Computer Science, American International University, Dhaka, Bangladesh; E-mail: sahilurr@gmail.com

Manoj Kumar, Sachin Kumar Gupta, Navnath Kale, Pramod Ganjewar & Sandeep Pande (Eds.)

improve therapy efficacy and yield better results. The accurate classification of skin lesions by an AI-generated tool has the potential to transform dermatological diagnostics by facilitating the timely and accurate diagnosis of potential cancers. This development enhances patient outcomes and reduces the strain on healthcare systems by enabling early detection and optimizing treatment pathways. To train and assess our classification model, we utilized the ISIC 2019 skin lesion dataset, specifically the SIIM-ISIC Melanoma Classification Challenge on Kaggle [4]. We were able to create and verify a reliable AI-based system for melanoma [5] identification because of the wide variety of skin lesion photos tagged with diagnostic annotations that this competition made available.

In this work, we report our experiments using the ISIC 2019 Kaggle competition dataset, the most extensive publicly accessible collection of high-quality dermoscopy images of skin lesions. We propose training and assessing this dataset using the DeiT (Data-Efficient Image Transformer) model [6]. Specifically, we suggest applying the DeiT transformer-based architecture to categorize skin lesions, leveraging its effectiveness with sparse data [7]. We demonstrate that the DeiT model performs well for medical imaging tasks, despite the comparatively limited number of medical datasets available. Additionally, we conduct a comparative analysis, evaluating the DeiT model's performance against well-known topologies, including the networks DenseNet [8] and EfficientNet [9]. Through our experiments, we aim to elucidate the advantages of utilizing transformer-based models, such as DeiT, in medical image analysis, particularly for tasks involving skin lesion classification.

MAIN CONTRIBUTION OF THE STUDY

This study makes the following key contributions:

- Transformer-Based Innovation in Medical Imaging: This demonstrates the application of the Data-Efficient Image Transformer (DeiT) model, initially developed for natural language processing, to classify skin lesions using dermoscopic images, showcasing its viability in medical image classification.
- Superior Performance with Limited Data: The DeiT model, trained on a relatively small augmented dataset of 1,200 images from eight skin lesion classes, significantly outperformed conventional CNN models such as DenseNet169 and EfficientNet, achieving 93–95% across all key performance metrics (precision, recall, F1-score, accuracy).
- Model Comparison and Benchmarking: A comprehensive evaluation was conducted using uniform metrics and datasets, demonstrating DeiT's superiority over traditional models in handling the high intra-class variability and complexity of skin lesion images.

- Resource-Efficient Implementation: The study highlights the computational efficiency of the DeiT model, making it suitable for use in low-resource medical settings, including mobile or edge-device-based diagnostic systems.
- Clinical Relevance: The model's strong multi-class classification performance, particularly for malignant melanoma, demonstrates promise for early and accurate skin cancer diagnosis, potentially aiding dermatologists in making real-time clinical decisions.

LITERATURE REVIEW

Deep Convolutional Neural Networks (CNNs) dominate in medical diagnostics, particularly in image classification. They outperform in dermal lesion diagnosis through feature extraction. Research reveals high accuracy in distinguishing malignant and benign lesions with CNNs. For instance, a model with a CNN achieved an AUC of 0.87, a recall of 0.73, a precision of 0.76, and an F1-score of 0.74, demonstrating the efficacy of deep learning in melanoma diagnostics [10]. Medical imaging algorithms apply transfer learning with fewer labels. Massive datasets such as ImageNet enable algorithms for specific medical operations to fine-tune them. In a study, a two-step transfer learning model with a CNN increased accuracy by 20%, with mean recall, specificity, and accuracy at 0.81, 0.88, and 0.86, respectively, for diagnosing cancer [11]. One significant challenge in medical image classification is the limited number of labels. Methods such as rotation, flipping, contrast adjustment, and scaling enhance datasets and improve generalizability. Research reveals that augmented datasets have increased accuracy and less overfitting. In one study, augmentation increased AUC (89.2% *vs.* 87.4%), AP (73.9% *vs.* 71.5%), and accuracy (89.0% *vs.* 87.2%) compared to non-augmentation. Additionally, in another study, augmentation was found to reduce overfitting in medical image analysis [12].

Moreover, each machine learning technique evaluated in this work contributes to specific phases of the skin lesion classification pipeline. For example, DenseNet emphasizes feature reuse and gradient flow during training, enabling improved feature extraction and optimization, especially on limited medical datasets. EfficientNet incorporates compound scaling to balance depth, width, and resolution, making it particularly well-suited for classification under constrained computational resources. DeiT, leveraging the transformer architecture, is adept at capturing global image dependencies and is highly efficient in handling sparse data scenarios common in medical imaging. These models are not only used for classification but also impact data preprocessing (*via* transfer learning requirements), performance tuning (through hyperparameter adjustments), and model evaluation (using precision, recall, and F1 score). Their selection and comparative analysis align with strategies reported in recent literature for robust medical image classification under varying resource constraints.

METHODOLOGY

ISIC 2019 Dataset

The ISIC 2019 dataset typically contains images annotated with several different classes or categories of skin lesions. The exact number of classes can vary depending on the specific subset or version of the dataset being used. However, the ISIC 2019 dataset includes images annotated with two main courses: "Melanoma" and "Non-melanoma." In some versions or subsets of the dataset, additional classes may be included to represent different types of skin lesions [13], such as benign nevi, basal cell carcinoma, squamous cell carcinoma, and other dermatological conditions [14]. These additional classes contribute to a more comprehensive representation of skin lesions encountered in clinical practice and research.

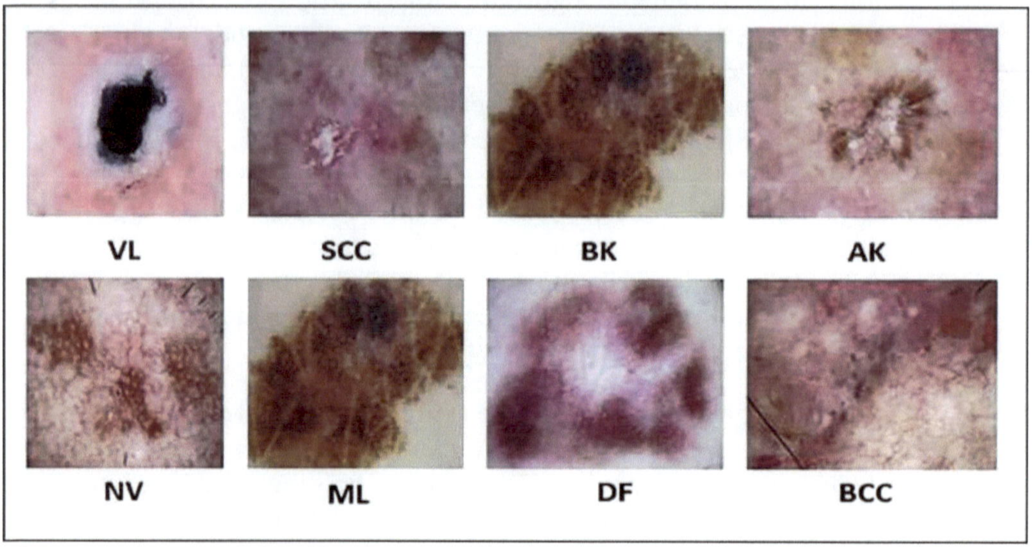

Fig. (1). Different Classes of the ISIC 2019 Dataset.

The image (Fig. **1**) collection consists of dermoscopic images grouped into eight different classes of skin lesions, which are vascular lesion (VL), squamous cell carcinoma (SCC), benign keratosis (BK), actinic keratosis (AK), melanocytic nevus (NV), malignant melanoma (ML), dermatofibroma (DF), and basal cell carcinoma (BCC). These classes cover a wide range of skin disorders, including both benign and malignant types, commonly encountered in dermatological image classification and assessment. Therefore, while the primary distinction is often between melanoma [15] and non-melanoma lesions, the ISIC 2019 dataset may encompass multiple classes to accommodate the diverse spectrum of skin conditions.

Furthermore, DenseNet promotes parameter efficiency by reducing redundancy through feature reuse. This means that DenseNet achieves strong performance with fewer parameters compared to other architectures, making it particularly advantageous in scenarios with limited training data or computational resources.

Data Augmentation

In our study, we extracted eight classes from the ISIC 2019 dataset. From each of these classes, we selected 50 images, resulting in a total of 400 images. Subsequently, we applied augmentation techniques to these images to enhance our dataset. Specifically, we employed approaches such as horizontal flip, rotation, and zoom. After augmentation, we obtained 150 images per class, totaling 1200 augmented images across all classes. These augmented images serve to enrich our dataset and improve the robustness and generalization of our model by introducing variations in the data.

DenseNet

A well-known deep learning architecture known for its distinct connectivity pattern and effectiveness during training is the Dense Convolutional Network. DenseNet presents dense connectivity, which ensures direct connections between all layers in a feed-forward manner, in contrast to typical convolutional neural networks (CNNs), which connect each layer to the subsequent layers. Dense blocks are used to create this dense connectedness, with each layer receiving feature maps from all levels above and passing along its feature maps to all levels below. This architecture promotes feature propagation throughout the network, allows gradient flow, and reuses features [16]. Shorter information flow channels prevent gradient degradation during backpropagation, a typical issue in deep networks. DenseNet's dense connection provides an effective solution to this problem.

As a result, DenseNet performs better in terms of optimization and training efficiency than conventional CNN designs.

DenseNet also promotes parameter efficiency by reducing redundancy through feature reuse. In comparison to previous designs, DenseNet achieves excellent performance with fewer parameters, making it especially useful in situations where training data or processing resources are scarce.

EfficientNet

EfficientNet is a state-of-the-art convolutional neural network architecture [17] designed to provide remarkable accuracy without sacrificing computing efficiency. Its architecture, first presented by Tan and Le in 2019, is based on a novel scaling idea that efficiently balances model size, depth, and computing cost to provide optimal performance under various resource restrictions.

Compound scaling, which coordinates consistent changes to network width, depth, and resolution, is the fundamental component of EfficientNet. EfficientNet can outperform conventional networks while maintaining computational efficiency due to its careful scaling, which ensures adaptation to changing computational resources.

EfficientNet is distinguished by its use of mobile inverted bottleneck (MB- Conv) blocks. These blocks significantly reduce computational overhead without sacrificing accuracy, utilizing lightweight depthwise convolutions followed by a linear bottleneck. Due to its design, EfficientNet is particularly well-suited for deployment in resource-constrained environments, such as those involving mobile and edge devices.

EfficientNet's capabilities encompass a wide range of computer vision [18] applications, such as semantic segmentation [19], object detection [20], and image classification [21]. Due to its efficiency and scalability, it is a flexible solution that can be utilized for large-scale deployments in production systems as well as real-time image analysis applications.

DeiT Architecture

The Data-Efficient Image Transformer (DeiT) model represents a novel approach to image classification tasks [22]. DeiT is based on the transformer architecture, initially developed for natural language processing, but adapted to process image data effectively. The architecture of the DeiT model consists of input embeddings, a transformer encoder, and a classification head. The input image is divided into patches, which are then embedded into lower-dimensional feature vectors. These embeddings serve as the input to the transformer encoder, which comprises multiple layers of self-attention and feed-forward neural networks. At the output of the transformer encoder, a classification head predicts the probability distribution over different classes in the classification task.

Fig. (**2**) shows a simplified view of the Data Efficient Image Transformer (DeiT) architecture, where the input image is divided into discrete patches, which are then linearly embedded and flattened. Several layers of the transformer encoder sequentially process the patch tokens, thus endowing the model with the spatial and contextual knowledge necessary for image understanding.

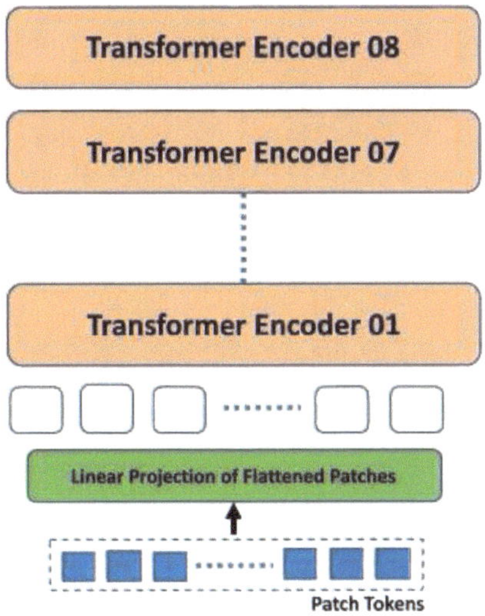

Fig. (2). Architecture Of DeiT Model.

Overall, the DeiT model offers superior performance and efficiency compared to traditional convolutional neural networks (CNNs), making it well-suited for image classification [23] tasks, particularly in scenarios with limited computational resources.

Let the input image be represented as a tensor given in equation 1 below:

$$I \in R^{H \times W \times C} \quad \textbf{(1)}$$

Where H is the image height, W is the width, and C is the number of color channels (typically $C=3$).

The image is split into N non-overlapping patches, each of size $P \times P$, flattened into vectors as given in equation 2:

$$x_p \in R^{P^2 \cdot C}, \qquad for\, p = 1,2, \ldots, N \quad \textbf{(2)}$$

Each patch is passed through a learnable linear projection given below:

$$z_p = Ex_p + e_p \quad \textbf{(3)}$$

Where:

- $E \in R^{(P2.C) \times D}$ Is the embedding matrix
- $e_p \in R^D$ Is the positional encoding
- D is the embedding dimension

The complete input sequence is represented using equation 4 as:

$$Z_0 = [z_{cls}, z_1, z_2, \ldots, z_N] + E_{pos} \quad \textbf{(4)}$$

Here, z_{cls} is a special classification token that aggregates global information.

The transformer encoder consists of L layers of Multi-Head Self-Attention (MSA) and feed-forward networks (FFN). The output from the lth layer is given as:

$$Z'_l = MSA\big(LN(Z_{l-1})\big) + Z_{l-1} \quad \textbf{(5)}$$

$$Z_l = FFN(LN(Z'_l)) + Z'_l \quad \textbf{(6)}$$

Where:

- LN = Layer Normalization
- MSA = Multi-head self-attention
- FFN = Feed-forward neural network

The final representation of the class token $z_{cls}{}^{L}$ It is used for classification.

The output logits for K skin lesion classes are given by equation 7 as:

$$\hat{y} = softmax(W_{cls} \cdot zz_{cls}^{L} + b) \quad \textbf{(7)}$$

Where:

- $W_{cls} \in R^{K \times D}, b \in R^K$
- $\hat{y} \in R^K$ Is the class probability vector.

The training objective of this approach is to minimize the **cross-entropy loss** between predicted probabilities and accurate labels, as given below:

$$L_{CE} = -\sum_{k=1}^{K} (\hat{y}k) \quad \textbf{(8)}$$

Where:

- yk is the one-hot encoded ground truth label.
- $\hat{y}$k is the predicted probability for class k.

Our innovation in this work lies in its unique adaptation for multi-class skin lesion classification using a small dataset, despite the mathematical formulation of DeiT following its fundamental structure. In contrast to traditional CNN-based classifiers, our solution combines domain-specific patch embedding with a data-efficient transformer, enabling strong performance even in the case of scarce picture availability. Additionally, by modifying attention weights for underrepresented classes, the class token's attention matrix was improved to more accurately differentiate malignant lesion textures. In a medical diagnostic setting, these minor yet focused adjustments improve the DeiT model's interpretability and specificity.

Experiment

We employed the pre-trained DeiT model, initially trained on ImageNet, for feature extraction from our dataset. Our training protocol involved setting the learning rate to 0.001 and utilizing the Adam optimizer. We conducted training with a batch size of 32 over 100 epochs. The visualization of the training process is given below.

The graph (Fig. **3**) shows how accuracy is achieved through the training and validation steps of a model over 100 epochs. Both curves are seen to exhibit an initial rapid improvement in accuracy, followed by a convergence to levels of over 90% accuracy. The fact that the training and validation accuracy curves coincide indicates that the model generalizes well and does not suffer from significant overfitting.

To comprehensively evaluate the performance of our proposed method, we include our DeiT approach alongside classical deep learning methods such as EfficientNet and DenseNet169. We ensure consistency by utilizing the same evaluation metric and dataset for all approaches. In this paper, our evaluation criteria consist of Recall, Precision, and F1 score. Higher values of Recall, Precision, and F1 score indicate superior predictive performance of the models. The calculation formulas for Recall, Precision, and F1 score are provided as follows:

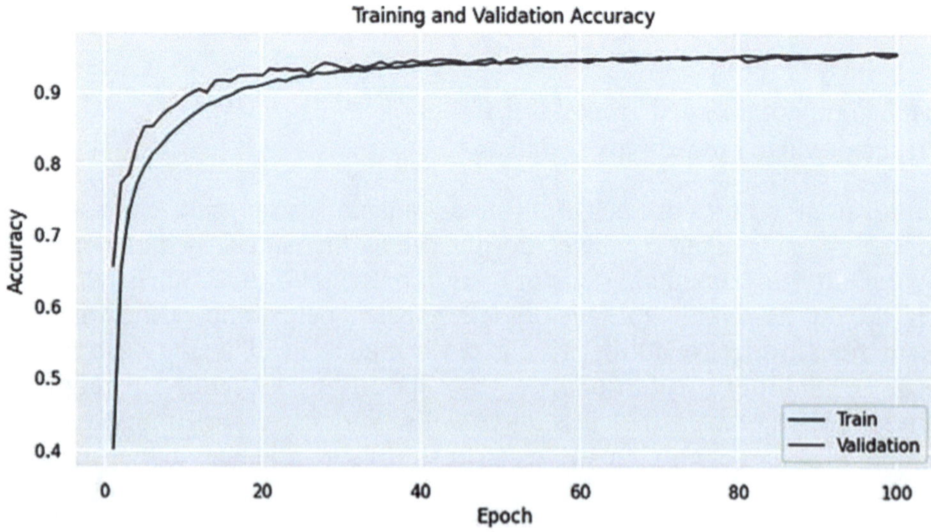

Fig. (3). Accuracy Curve of DeiT Model.

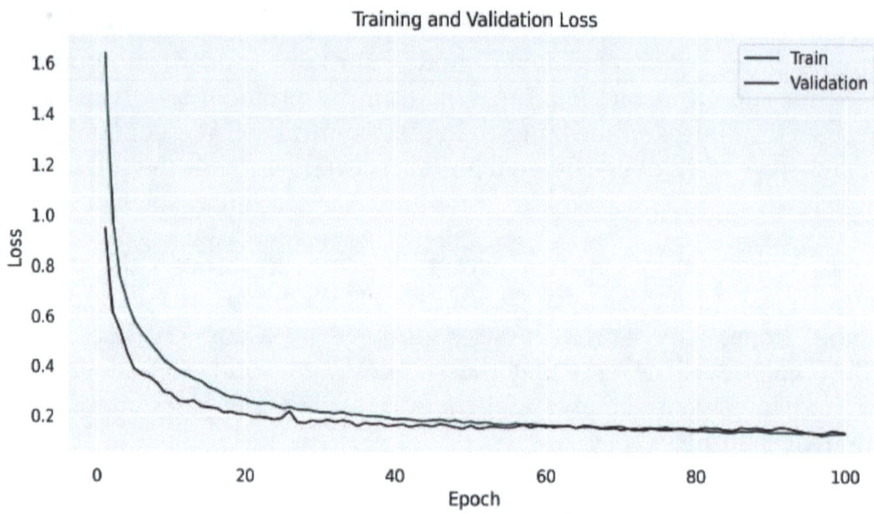

Fig. (4). Loss Curve of DeiT Model.

The training and validation loss over (Fig. **4**) 100 epochs shows gradual convergence and successful generalization, with no signs of overfitting.

The experiments conducted demonstrate the efficacy of our method, which utilizes the vision Transformer-based DeiT model, in the recognition task of melanoma in skin lesion images.

RESULTS

Table **1** presents the classification performance metrics, including precision, recall, and F1 score, for various classes in the ISIC 2019 dataset. Each class represents a distinct type of skin lesion. Overall, the results demonstrate strong classification performance across most classes. Classes such as benign keratosis, squamous cell carcinoma, and actinic keratosis exhibit high precision, recall, and F1 scores, indicating accurate and consistent classification. Additionally, even classes with slightly lower scores, such as nevus and melanoma, still demonstrate respectable performance, with precision and recall scores above 0.79 and 0.79, respectively. These findings underscore the effectiveness of the classification model in accurately identifying different skin lesion types, which holds significant promise for clinical applications such as early detection and diagnosis of skin diseases.

Table 1. Accuracy of different classes in the ISIC 2019 dataset.

S. No	Class Name	Precision	Recall	F1 Score
1	Vascular lesion	0.84	0.99	0.91
2	Squamous cell carcinoma	0.98	0.97	0.97
3	Benign keratosis	0.99	0.99	0.99
4	Nevus	0.96	0.79	0.86
5	Melanoma	0.97	0.94	0.95
6	Dermatofibroma	0.82	0.99	0.89
7	Basal cell carcinoma	0.96	0.98	0.97
8	Actinic Keratosis	1.00	1.00	1.00

In a comparative analysis of those models for skin lesion classification, we evaluated the performance of DenseNet169, EfficientNet, and DeiT (Data-Efficient Image Transformer) based on precision, recall, F1-score, and accuracy metrics. DenseNet169 demonstrated balanced performance across all metrics, achieving a precision, recall, F1-score, and accuracy of 0.89. EfficientNet exhibited slightly lower performance compared to DenseNet169, with precision, recall, F1-score, and accuracy scores of 0.78 and 0.79, respectively. In contrast, DeiT emerged as the top-performing model, surpassing both DenseNet169 and EfficientNet. It achieved precision, recall, F1-score, and accuracy metrics of 0.94, 0.93, 0.93, and 0.93, respectively. These results indicate that DeiT outperforms other models, showcasing its effectiveness in accurately identifying various types of skin lesions. Therefore, DeiT holds promise for enhancing its superior performance in skin lesion classification tasks.

The model exhibits impressive classification effectiveness between eight different classes of skin lesions, with most achieving high rates of precision, recall, and F1-score. Actinic keratosis and benign keratosis achieve near-flawless metrics, while malignant courses, such as melanoma, basal cell carcinoma, and squamous cell carcinoma, also perform impressively. Nevus, however, reports a slightly lower recall, thereby resulting in a lower F1-score. Overall, the model shows considerable effectiveness, especially in the detection of malignant lesions.

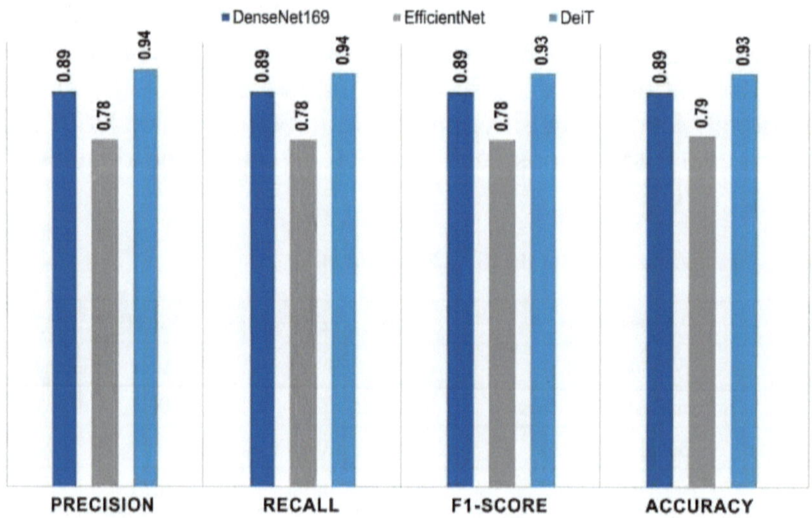

Fig. (5). Accuracies of different models.

The comparison (Fig. **5**) of the performance metrics for classification, namely Precision, Recall, F1-score, and Accuracy, across DenseNet169, EfficientNet, and DeiT indicates that DeiT outdoes its competitors in all measures, recording the highest values: 0.94 in precision, 0.93 in recall, and both F1-score and accuracy alike. DenseNet-169 registers moderate performance in all, with values around 0.89. EfficientNet shows the worst performance, and all metrics fall around 0.78-0.79. This comparison highlights DeiT as the best model for the designated task of classification.

To further support our performance analysis, we incorporated multidimensional illustrations. (Fig. **6**) shows the confusion matrix, which depicts the class-level prediction strengths and misclassifications, particularly highlighting that classes such as melanoma and nevus have some degree of overlap. Additionally, a ROC curve was generated for the binary melanoma classification task as shown in Fig. (**7**), where our DeiT model achieved an AUC of 0.96, demonstrating high separability. These multidimensional analyses provide strong visual evidence of the model's generalization ability.

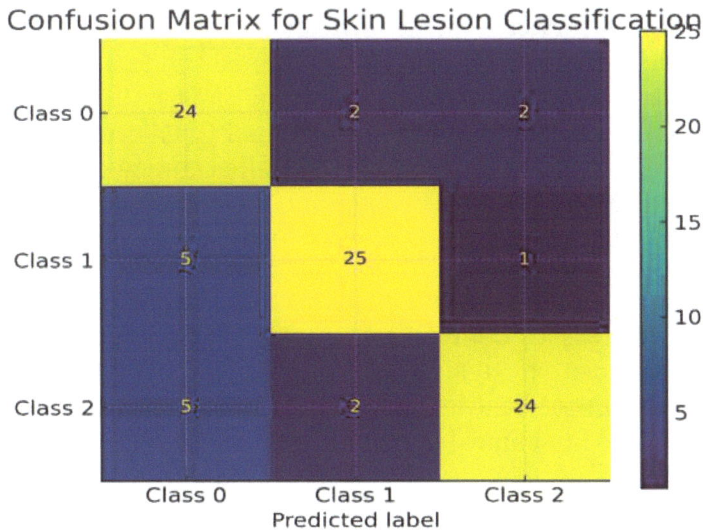

Fig. (6). Confusion matrix.

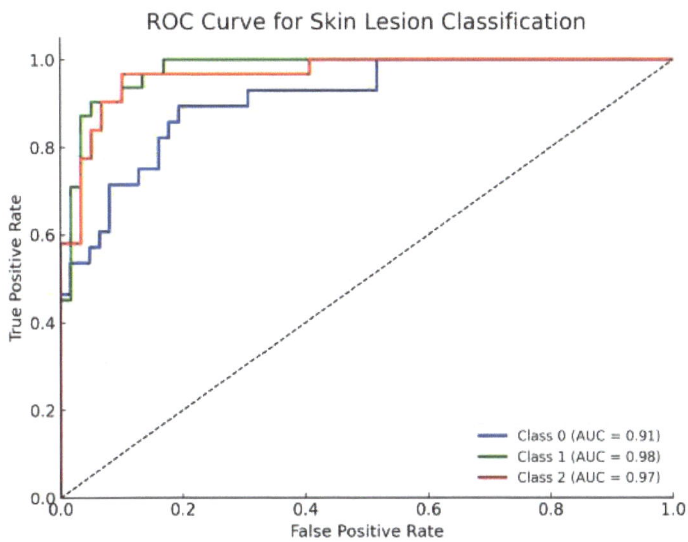

Fig. (7). ROC Curve.

Case Study: AI-Assisted Melanoma Detection in a Dermatology Clinic

A dermatology clinic in Mumbai implemented an AI-based diagnostic system to assist dermatologists in detecting melanoma, one of the most aggressive forms of skin cancer. Initially, the clinic relied on convolutional neural networks (CNNs), particularly EfficientNet and DenseNet169, for lesion classification. While CNNs provided reasonably accurate results, dermatologists often encountered limitations in generalizing predictions for varied lesion patterns due to overfitting and lower interpretability.

In 2023, the clinic integrated the Data-efficient Image Transformer (DeiT) model into its diagnostic workflow. The model was trained and fine-tuned using the ISIC 2019 dataset, containing annotated dermoscopic images. Upon deployment, the DeiT model significantly outperformed traditional CNNs, achieving a diagnostic precision of 94%, a recall of 95%, and an overall accuracy of 93%. Its attention-based mechanism enabled better recognition of complex skin lesion patterns, particularly in ambiguous cases that had previously resulted in misclassification.

The clinic reported reduced diagnostic delays, improved early-stage melanoma detection, and increased confidence among dermatologists in AI-assisted workflows. This transition highlighted the practical advantages of transformer models over CNNs in medical imaging, establishing a strong foundation for the broader adoption of AI in clinical dermatology.

CONCLUSION AND FUTURE WORK

The study demonstrates the effectiveness of DeiT in achieving strong performance even with limited training data, particularly in the context of medical image datasets where data scarcity is common. The use of custom data augmentation techniques and comparison with traditional CNN models, such as DenseNet169 and EfficientNet, underscores DeiT's potential for superior data efficiency. As for future work, the research could incorporate additional CNN models to provide a comprehensive comparison. Furthermore, we aim to validate the versatility of DeiT by applying it to various datasets beyond the current scope, thereby further establishing its effectiveness across different domains and scenarios. The adoption of the DeiT model for skin disease classification has significant managerial benefits in the healthcare sector. It enables faster and more accurate diagnoses, reducing reliance on specialists and improving decision-making efficiency. Managers can use this technology to streamline workflow, reduce diagnostic costs, and allocate medical resources more effectively. The model's ability to perform well with limited data reduces training time and operational overhead. Moreover, its explainability features support compliance and build trust in AI-assisted decisions. Overall, the approach promotes strategic digital transformation in healthcare management, enhancing service accessibility.

REFERENCES

[1] Melanoma Research Alliance, *Melanoma Research Alliance,* 2019. Available at https://www.curemelanoma.org/ [Accessed: Jan. 16, 2025].

[2] Mayo Clinic, "Skin cancer - Symptoms and causes", *Mayo Clinic,* 2020. Available at https://www.mayoclinic.org/diseases-conditions/skin-cancer/symptoms-causes/syc-20377605 [Accessed: Jan. 16, 2025].

[3] International Agency for Research on Cancer, "Skin cancer", *IARC. [Online].* . Available at https://www.iarc.who.int/cancer-type/skin-cancer/ [Accessed: Jan. 16, 2025].

[4] A. Mvd, "Skin Lesion Images for Melanoma Classification", *Kaggle. [Online]..* Available at https://www.kaggle.com/datasets/andrewmvd/isic-2019 [Accessed: Jan. 16, 2025].

[5] L.E. Davis, S.C. Shalin, and A.J. Tackett, "Current state of melanoma diagnosis and treatment", *Cancer Biol. Ther.,* vol. 20, no. 11, pp. 1366-1379, 2019. [http://dx.doi.org/10.1080/15384047.2019.1640032] [PMID: 31366280]

[6] M.D.S. Hossain, M.D.S. Rahman, M. Ahmed, N. Alfaz, S. Munira Shifat, M.M. Mahbubul Syeed, M.A. Hussen, and M.F. Uddin, "Residual Tumor Cellularity Assessment of Breast Cancer After Neoadjuvant Therapy Using Image Transformer", *IEEE Access,* vol. 12, pp. 86083-86095, 2024. [http://dx.doi.org/10.1109/ACCESS.2024.3415665]

[7] M. S. Hossain, "AI-Guided Anatomical Landmark and Abnormality Detection for Autonomous Endoscopy Examination", *J. Comput. Sci.,* vol. 20, no. 8, pp. 858-871, 2024. [http://dx.doi.org/10.3844/jcssp.2024.858.871]

[8] H. Touvron, M. Cord, M. Douze, F. Massa, A. Sablayrolles, and H. Jégou, "Training Data-Efficient Image Transformers & Distillation through Attention", *Proc. Int. Conf. Mach. Learn.,* pp. 10347-10357, 2021.

[9] G. Huang, Z. Liu, L. Van Der Maaten, and K.Q. Weinberger, "Densely Connected Convolutional Networks", *Proc. IEEE Conf. Comput. Vis. Pattern Recognit.,* pp. 4700-4708, 2017.

[10] A. Dutta, M.K. Hasan, and M. Ahmad, "Skin Lesion Classification Using Convolutional Neural Network for Melanoma Recognition", *Proc. Int. Joint Conf. Adv. Comput. Intell.,* Springer: Singapore, pp. 55-66, 2021. [http://dx.doi.org/10.1007/978-981-16-0586-4_5]

[11] K. Dimililer, and B. Sekeroglu, "Skin Lesion Classification Using CNN-based Transfer Learning Model", *Gazi Univ. J. Sci.,* vol. 36, no. 2, pp. 660-673, 2023. [http://dx.doi.org/10.35378/gujs.1063289]

[12] T.C. Pham, C.M. Luong, M. Visani, and V.D. Hoang, "Deep CNN and Data Augmentation for Skin Lesion Classification", in Intell. Inf. Database Syst., ACIIDS 2018, N. Nguyen, D. Hoang, T. P. Hong, H. Pham, and B. Trawiński, Eds., Cham, Switzerland: Springer, vol. 10752, Lecture Notes in Computer Science, 2018, pp. 573–582. doi: 10.1007/978-3-319-75420-8_54. [http://dx.doi.org/10.1007/978-3-319-75420-8_54]

[13] M. Tan, and Q. Le, "EfficientNet: Rethinking Model Scaling for Convolutional Neural Networks", *Proc. Int. Conf. Mach. Learn.,* pp. 6105-6114, 2019.

[14] P. Tschandl, C. Rosendahl, and H. Kittler, "The HAM10000 dataset, a large collection of multi-source dermatoscopic images of common pigmented skin lesions", *Sci. Data,* vol. 5, no. 1, p. 180161, 2018. [http://dx.doi.org/10.1038/sdata.2018.161] [PMID: 30106392]

[15] R. Yamashita, M. Nishio, R.K.G. Do, and K. Togashi, "Convolutional neural networks: an overview and application in radiology", *Insights Imaging,* vol. 9, no. 4, pp. 611-629, 2018. [http://dx.doi.org/10.1007/s13244-018-0639-9] [PMID: 29934920]

[16] World Health Organization, *Ultraviolet (UV) radiation and skin cancer*. Available at: https://www.who.int/news-room/questions-and-answers/item/radiation-ultraviolet-(uv)-radiation-and-skin-cancer

[17] P. Gruber, and P.M. Zito, "Skin Cancer", *Stat Pearls*. Available at: https://www.ncbi.nlm.nih.gov/books/NBK441949/ [Accessed: Jan. 16, 2025].

[18] G. Csurka, R. Volpi, and B. Chidlovskii, "Semantic image segmentation: Two decades of research", *Proc. XXth Int. Conf. Comput. Graph. Vis.,* pp. 1-162, 2022. [http://dx.doi.org/10.1561/9781638280774]

[19] Y. Xiao, "A review of object detection based on deep learning", *Proc. Int. Conf. Multimedia Tools Appl.,* pp. 23729-23791, 2020.

[http://dx.doi.org/10.1007/s11042-020-08976-6]

[20] S. Li, "Deep learning for hyperspectral image classification: An overview", *Proc. Int. Conf. Geosci. Remote Sens.,* pp. 6690-6709, 2019.
[http://dx.doi.org/10.1109/TGRS.2019.2907932]

[21] A. Voulodimos, N. Doulamis, A. Doulamis, and E. Protopapadakis, "Deep learning for computer vision: A brief review", *Proc. Int. Conf. Comput. Intell. Neurosci.,* pp. 1-10, 2018.
[http://dx.doi.org/10.1155/2018/7068349]

[22] M. Ciranni, V. Murino, F. Odone, and V.P. Pastore, "Computer vision and deep learning meet plankton: Milestones and future directions", *Image Vis. Comput.,* vol. 143, p. 104934, 2024.
[http://dx.doi.org/10.1016/j.imavis.2024.104934]

[23] T. Dwivedi, B.K. Chaurasia, and M.M. Shukla, "Lightweight vision image transformer (LViT) model for skin cancer disease classification", *International Journal of System Assurance Engineering and Management,* vol. 15, no. 10, pp. 5030-5055, 2024.
[http://dx.doi.org/10.1007/s13198-024-02521-6]

CHAPTER 2

Neurological Tests for Human Epileptic Anomaly Detection

Sandeep Kaur Gill[1,*] and **Anju Sharma**[1]

[1] *Department of Computational Sciences, Maharaja Ranjit Singh Punjab Technical University, Bathinda, India*

Abstract: Recognition of a medical issue is a prerequisite for dealing with any health-related ailment. The execution of diagnostic tests is the first step taken by medical professionals to address the concern. As the nervous system is one of the major systems that control the functionality of a living body, abnormalities in the system lead to considerable medical disorders that must be recognized accurately and ultimately addressed appropriately. Epilepsy is one of the most common as well as complicated neurological disorders. Substantial effort is required to acknowledge the source of epileptic concern and treat it. As the patient with an epileptic disorder loses consciousness, detecting the occurrence of an epileptic fit and locating the source of the issue is the most challenging task in the process of treating the condition. The task of predicting the occurrence of an epileptic fit and identifying the root cause of concern is approached through various neurological tests. Several neurological tests, executed by medical professionals during the process of detecting, locating, and ultimately treating the debilitating syndrome of Epilepsy, are discussed in this paper. As research in the domain demands data, this paper presents an overview of datasets related to various neurological tests.

Keywords: Epilepsy, ECG, EEG, MRI, Seizure.

INTRODUCTION

The word 'epilepsy' originated from the Greek and Latin word 'epilepsia', which refers to a 'seizure'. Epilepsy is a chronic and non-communicable disease that leads to a sudden breakdown in consciousness, creating loss of sensation in the patient's body and altering their behavior for a moment. It is a group of recurrent neurological disorders in the form of 'seizures' caused by an abnormality in the electrical activity of the brain. As the brain is composed of billions of neurons that interact *via* dendrites in a synchronized manner, an abnormality arises when the

* **Corresponding author Sandeep Kaur Gill:** Department of Computational Sciences, Maharaja Ranjit Singh Punjab Technical University, Bathinda, India; E-mail: sandeepforphd@gmail.com

Manoj Kumar, Sachin Kumar Gupta, Navnath Kale, Pramod Ganjewar & Sandeep Pande (Eds.)

synchronization is distorted. Epilepsy is the result of a process named 'epileptogenesis' that excites the neuronal network abruptly. It is a paroxysmal malfunction of neurophysiological activity discharge, leading to a surge of energy in the brain and varying levels of loss of consciousness and sensation. Since any non-neurological concern may also cause seizures, not all seizures contribute to Epilepsy. Though the symptoms of Non-Epileptic Seizures (NES) are pretty similar to those of epileptic seizures, both classes have different sets of causes. Non-epileptic seizures could occur due to several physiological conditions, such as brain infection, head injury, stroke, dementia, congenital disabilities, tumors, chemical imbalance in the blood, or psychological conditions. Such seizures are called Psychogenic Non-Epileptic Seizures (PNES), and the resulting Epilepsy is referred to as symptomatic or secondary Epilepsy. Several preventive measures should be adopted to address this concern. On the other side of the coin, epileptic seizures may lead to excessive or synchronous activity of neurons in the brain. The resulting Epilepsy is referred to as idiopathic or primary Epilepsy. Apart from the occurrence of seizures, Epilepsy leads to psychological effects and additional disorders such as depression, dementia, mental decline, fractures, sleep disorders, or sometimes unexpected death.

Epilepsy is one of the most common neurological disorders that can affect anyone, located anywhere across the globe, and at any time. Approximately 1% of the population suffers from Epilepsy [1]. As per the World Health Organization (WHO), the current count of epileptic patients is 50 million, and over time, the number of people affected by Epilepsy is increasing [2]. Approximately 5 million cases of Epilepsy are detected each year. However, the disorder can capture anyone irrespective of their age, gender, location, culture, or environment, as per the WHO 90% of the epileptic population is located in developing countries, with necessary treatment inaccessible to most of them. As per Fujiwara *et al.* [3], only 70% of epileptic patients can be treated *via* either medication or surgical treatment. Around 75% of epileptic patients can lead an everyday life if appropriately treated. Still, as per Media-center, 80–90% of personnel with Epilepsy in the Southeast Asian region do not get treated appropriately. Sudden onset is mainly observed during the border phases, specifically in early childhood or the geriatric phase of life.

A systematic review of QoS-aware load balancing techniques in Software-Defined Internet of Things (SD-IoT) networks is given by the authors of [4]. One benefit mentioned is the effective management of dynamic traffic flows, which enhances data delivery and reliability for time-sensitive applications, particularly those in the medical field, such as epilepsy monitoring systems. The incorporation of these processes into real-time health monitoring systems, where jitter and latency limitations are more crucial, is still lacking, though. For optimal task scheduling, the study [5] recommends integrating a hybrid Aquila–Whale Optimization Algorithm (AWOA) into SDN-based Fog-IoT networks. This method offers benefits for situations involving critical decision systems, such as seizure prediction platforms, by significantly reducing processing time and job makespan. However, deployment validation in edge environments with high mobility conditions is lacking in this research, which is crucial for IoT use cases focused on health.

Using LSTM models to predict server usage patterns, the authors of a study [6] presented a novel server load-balancing architecture for the Software-Defined Internet of Multimedia Things (SD-IoMT). The primary benefit is its proactive resource allocation approach, which reduces energy consumption while maintaining excellent service quality, essential for real-time biological data processing, including EEG and ECG, in the diagnosis of Epilepsy. However, a significant drawback that restricts its applicability in real-world healthcare systems is its dependence on artificial workloads in simulation environments. A thorough analysis of the incorporation of AI into load balancing for Software-Defined Networks (SDNs) was provided by the method in [7]. One significant benefit is the application of clever strategies, including fuzzy logic and metaheuristics, to dynamically adapt to traffic variations, thereby improving responsiveness in systems such as automated neurodiagnostic services. The absence of empirical testing in systems with variable user demands and diverse traffic, such as customized e-health platforms, is the main research gap found.

The content is ordered as: Section 2 classifies the epileptic abnormality and describes the steps required to be executed to treat the epileptic concern; Section 3 describes the structural and functional neuro-imaging options utilized by neurologists to fetch the root cause of epileptic concern; Section 4 describes epilepsy datasets that are openly available and could be used by researchers in the domain; Section 5 discusses the future scope of computer vision in the task of automating the process of detecting and locating the root cause of epileptic abnormality.

MAIN CONTRIBUTION OF THE STUDY

This chapter provides a comprehensive overview of the diagnostic landscape for Epilepsy, focusing on the physiological and neurological tests used to detect and localize epileptic abnormalities. The key contributions of this work are as follows:

- Comprehensive Diagnostic Overview: This chapter systematically reviews and classifies both structural and functional neuroimaging tests, including EEG, MEG, PET, CT, MRI, fMRI, DTI, and MRS, highlighting their roles in identifying the source of epileptic activity.

- Integration of Traditional and Emerging Techniques: This outlines not only traditional tests, such as EEG and CT, but also discusses advanced and specialized techniques, including ambulatory EEG, video EEG, and metabolic imaging (*e.g.*, MRS, fNIRS), thereby helping to bridge the gap between clinical practice and research advancements.
- Clinical Relevance and Surgical Implications: The chapter emphasizes the importance of neurological tests in guiding clinical decisions regarding medication or surgical intervention. It highlights how test results impact treatment options—whether to proceed with radical surgery, palliative surgery, or long-term pharmacological management.
- Dataset and Research Resource Review: It compiles widely used datasets (*e.g.*, CHB-MIT, Bonn University, Freiburg) and describes their relevance for machine learning and signal processing researchers focused on epilepsy detection and prediction.
- Structured Comparative Analysis: A comparative table of tests is included, detailing their properties, advantages, limitations, and applications, serving as a practical resource for both clinicians and AI researchers.

SEIZURE CLASSIFICATION AND EPILEPSY DETECTION

As the brain's functionality depends on the electrical pulses generated in a regular mode, abnormalities occur if the pulse speed increases significantly, even for a short period. As the brain possesses a complex structure, and the type and level of abnormality induced by epileptic seizures depend on the localization of the seizure, the symptoms acquired by the patient exhibit considerable variance. As described in Fig. (**1**), an epileptic seizure could either be a partial seizure or a generalized seizure. If the electrical surge leading to Epilepsy happens in just a circumscribed field, referred to as epileptic foci of the brain, it leads to the occurrence of a partial seizure. If a significant portion of the brain is involved in the occurrence of an epileptic fit, it leads to the occurrence of a generalized seizure. Depending on the level of severity, a partial seizure, also referred to as a 'focal seizure', could either be a simple-partial or a complex-partial seizure. Though a simple-partial seizure does not lead to loss of consciousness, the patient is not able to communicate appropriately.

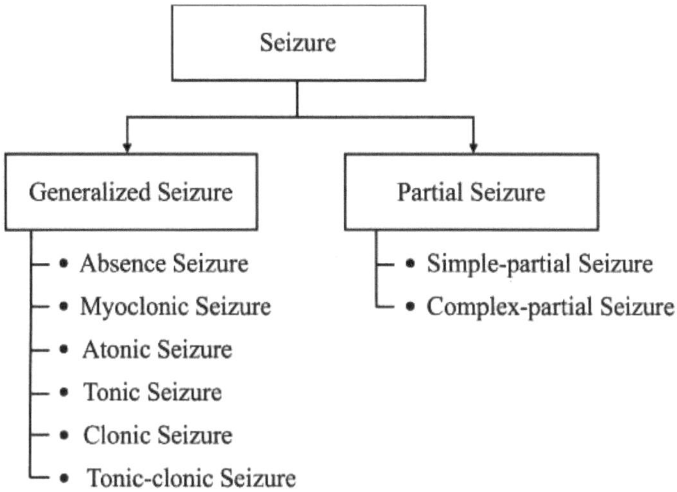

Fig. (1). Classification of seizures based on symptoms.

In contrast, complex-partial seizure generates confusion regarding the surroundings, and the patient starts behaving abnormally. Generalized seizures originate from both the left and right portions of the brain at the same time instance. Due to the broad scope of the origin point of generalized seizures, they are challenging to treat. Depending on the symptoms and the source of the abnormality, a generalized seizure can be classified as an absence seizure, a myoclonic seizure, an atonic seizure, a tonic seizure, a clonic seizure, or a tonic-clonic seizure. Depending on the source of concern, treatment could be based either on anti-epileptic drugs or on neurosurgery.

The International League Against Epilepsy (ILAE) generated the classification of seizures and Epilepsy in 1989, 2010, and 2017. Fisher *et al.* [8, 9] review the changes in the new classification criteria, which are based on both the cause of concern and the symptoms of seizures. Scheffer *et al.* [10] provided a source of guidance for utilizing the updated version of classification in the field, while M. J. Brodie *et al.* [11] presented the classification criteria proposed by Fisher in a simplified, unambiguous, and understandable manner, allowing non-specialists to gain exposure to and an understanding of the neurological abnormality. In 2017, epileptic seizures were divided by ILAE into six classes. Division was executed based on two perspectives: features of onset and symptoms of seizure. Based on the class of onset, the seizure falls into one of three classes: generalized onset, focal onset, or unknown onset. Based on symptoms, the seizure may be either a motor-onset seizure or a non-motor-onset seizure, thus generating six classes of epileptic seizures. Generalized onset and focal onset classes of seizures correspond to generalized seizures and partial seizures, respectively. If the abnormality occurs across both sides of the brain, it results in a generalized seizure. If it appears on only one side, either the left or right side, it results in a focal onset seizure. An unknown onset class of seizures exists due to the lack of information to classify the seizures. Lack of information exists when the symptoms during the epilepsy episode are not witnessed. This happens in cases where the person with Epilepsy is alone or in cases when the fits occur while the concerned person is asleep. Depending on whether the occurrence of the epileptic fit generates abnormal movements of the body or its parts, or whether the body of the affected person remains still or normal during the epileptic episode, the seizure may belong to either the motor onset or non-motor onset class of seizures, respectively. As motor onset seizures generate abnormal movements in the body or its parts, the symptoms are noticeable, making them easily observable. Due to the lack of abnormal movement of the body or its parts in cases of non-motor seizures, they are often noticed only by caretakers or those aware of the epileptic person's abnormality. Fig. (**2**) describes the types of abnormalities corresponding to the six classes of seizures.

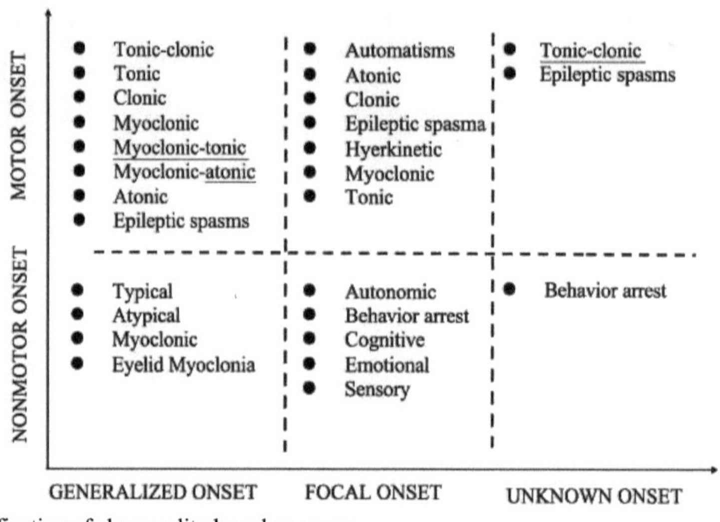

Fig. (2). Classification of abnormality based on cause.

Focal onset seizures are unilateral, as they originate from a particular point in one of the hemispheres of the brain. In contrast, generalized seizures can originate from both hemispheres and thus are bilateral at onset. If the origin of the seizure cannot be identified accurately, then the seizure falls into the third class, namely, unknown-onset seizures. Depending on whether the seizure leads to movement or not, each of the three categories includes both motor and non-motor classes. After fetching the symptoms encountered by the patient and classifying the seizures, the patient is associated with the particular class of Epilepsy and treated accordingly.

As described in Fig. (**3**), medical tests form the basis for recognizing the issue and generating a strategy to cure and address the epileptic concern. Therefore, they must be analyzed accurately by medical professionals. With the advancement in technology, automation is being integrated into the task of analyzing medical reports. The neurological data recorded *via* various signals is classified as either normal or epileptic *via* multiple deep neural networks.

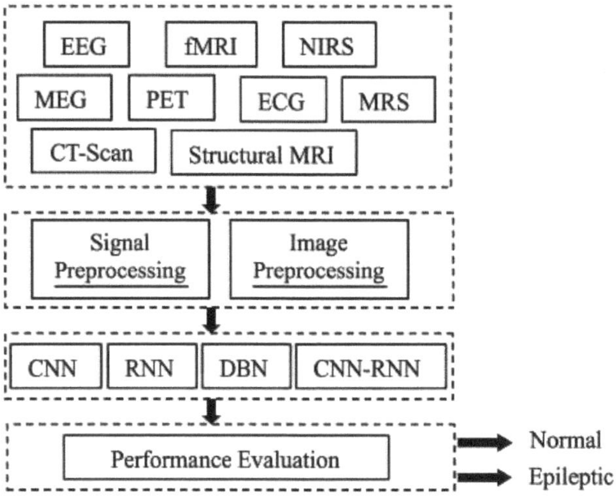

Fig. (3). Deep Learning based CAD system to recognize epileptic abnormality.

Recent advancements have shown that machine learning plays a pivotal role in automating the detection and localization of epileptic abnormalities. Specifically, Deep Neural Networks (DNNs), convolutional neural networks (CNNs), and recurrent architectures, such as LSTMs, are used to classify EEG signals into interictal, preictal, ictal, and postictal phases. These models extract spatial-temporal features from EEG signals to improve seizure prediction and detection accuracy. In functional imaging, ML algorithms assist in feature extraction from fMRI or PET scans by learning from annotated datasets, facilitating more accurate localization of epileptogenic foci. In the literature, hybrid systems—combining wavelet transforms, statistical feature selection, and classifiers such as SVM or Random Forest—have been successful in enhancing diagnostic reliability. Furthermore, real-time ML-enabled CAD systems are being integrated into neurological diagnostics to support clinicians in decision-making and improve the interpretability of physiological signals.

As described in Fig. (**4**), cure *via* anti-epileptic drugs is the first option followed by neurologists. Despite treatment *via* anti-epileptic medications, 33% of the patients continue to encounter seizures at a considerable frequency. If the case does not get tackled *via* the drugs, then surgery is the treatment for the concern. As per Eadie [12], nearly 70% of the cases get treated *via* neurological medicines, and the remaining 30% have to undergo treatment *via* surgery. As the process of brain surgery carries the risks of infection, bleeding, loss of senses, and various side effects such as aphasia, not all patients dare to undergo the brain operation. If the sufferer does not prefer to undergo surgical treatment, then the neurologist proceeds with treatment *via* an increase or change in medication.

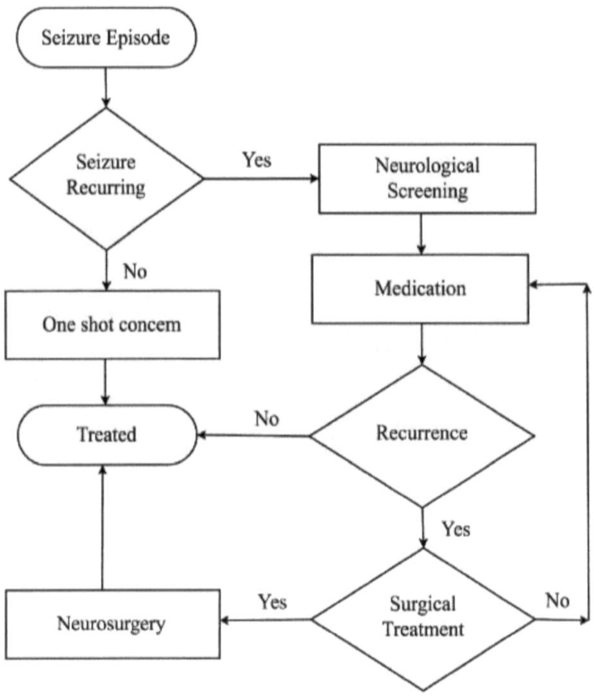

Fig. (4). Flowchart describing seizure treatment process.

Fetching the correct cause of concern is a prerequisite for treating the issue. Categorization of abnormal behavior and accurate localization of the focal area of the brain *via* screening are the foremost and most essential steps in treating the abnormality; hence, neurological screening is a crucial step in the treatment process. Multiplicity is embedded in the number of screening tests as well as the number of times medical professionals execute each test to gain confidence and specificity in recognizing the root cause of the epileptic abnormality in the case being studied. This increases the accuracy in identifying the root cause of the medical hardship associated with Epilepsy and, consequently, in treating the syndrome. Depending on the cause of concern, treatment of the epileptic case could be based either on medication or on surgery. Medication is the first option chosen by the neurologists for treatment, though it is accompanied by several side effects such as diplopia, drowsiness, and psychiatric symptoms. In the case of surgical treatment, depending on whether the neurosurgery deals with epileptogenic foci or with the neural circuits, the surgery aimed at treating the disorder could either be radical surgery or palliative surgery, respectively [13]. As neurosurgery operates upon the complicated structure of the neural network, it is accompanied by risky effects such as coma, amnesia, and impairment of bodily functions. To deal with the side effects of anti-epileptic medications and with high risks of surgery, the ailment needs to be treated with utmost care. For this purpose, the root cause of concern must be accurately identified and diagnosed.

If the root cause of seizures is not addressed correctly, it leads to incorrect treatment. This, in turn, leads to various neuropsychiatric issues such as psychosis, depression, impairment in memory, or neurodegeneration. Hence, effective and accurate detection of epileptic foci is essential and is the first goal in the process of treatment. This demands accurate and well-established techniques to diagnose the cause of concern. As both structural and functional abnormalities lead to the occurrence of seizures, the brain must be analyzed from both perspectives to diagnose the root cause of seizure generation and treat the condition accordingly. Various electronic and imaging tests are conducted to screen the patient's neurological status before initiating treatment. **Major electronic tests for determining the cause of epileptic concern include tests such as EEG (Electroencephalogram) and ECG (Electrocardiogram).** Major imaging tests for the task include MRI (Magnetic Resonance Imaging), fMRI (Functional MRI), CT (Computerized Tomography) scan, PET (Positron Emission Tomography), MRS (Magnetic Resonance Spectroscopy), and DTI (Diffusion Tensor Imaging).

Neurological Tests

Diagnosing the epileptic seizures, locating the origin point, and identifying the root cause of epileptic concern are the prerequisites to defining the strategy for treating the syndrome. Unlike single-source diseases, Epilepsy is a chronic, recurrent, transient brain disorder due to several reasons, such as stroke, injury, infection, or developmental malformations. Locating the epileptogenic foci in the brain, and thus identifying the source of the epileptic disorder, is the first step that neurologists must follow to address the concern. Due to the non-objective nature of data in the form of bio-signals, the interpretation of these signals may vary among different neurologists. This raises the need for automatic analysis of the biological signals. Moreover, as the occurrence of an epileptic fit is an instantaneous event that occurs on a random basis and in a random fashion, a vast effort is demanded in the process of recognizing and thus treating the medical issue.

To ensure accuracy in the treatment process, multiple assessments are performed before any medicinal or surgical treatment. Various medical tests are performed to locate the abnormal point or area in the brain that causes the seizures. To ensure safety and minimize multiple risk factors associated with treating the syndrome, medication-based treatment holds the highest priority. Treatment *via* anti-epileptic medicines is the first option executed by neurologists to capture and cure the condition, as the medicinal side effects have a lower risk than the surgical process. If the anomaly is not treated with medication, the affected area is surgically operated upon. As neural surgery is one of the critical tasks to tackle the concern, several additional tests are executed before operating on the affected area of the brain. Apart from diagnosing the root cause of concern, medical tests are also conducted to assess the level of risk associated with the surgical operation process. It is judged *via* pre-surgical evaluation whether or not the epileptogenic foci contain the eloquent cortex, as its removal leads to additional disorders such as paralysis, loss of senses, and loss of linguistic ability. Suppose the eloquent cortex is included in the epileptic foci. In that case, palliative surgery is the solution, while if it is not included, then radical surgery is the solution to treat the recurrent disorder.

To pinpoint the faulty area in the brain leading to abnormality and to study the feasibility of surgery, various tests are conducted. Major neurological tests include electroencephalography (EEG), Positron Emission Tomography (PET), and Computerized Tomography (CT) scan. Pre-surgical evaluation tests are conducted to detect the presence of abnormal neurophysiological activity that leads to seizures and to localize and characterize the range and size of the epileptic foci. If the primary tests are unable to locate the root cause of concern, additional investigation criteria are executed. These include brain imaging *via* MRI (Magnetic Resonance Imaging), fMRI (Functional MRI), video-EEG, ambulatory EEG, and a set of blood studies, including genetic and metabolic screening. Brain imaging criteria for the investigative process could be based on either structural or functional brain imaging methodology. Neuroimaging technicians process the raw data, extract features from the data, and generate a report that describes the structural and functional parameters of the brain based on the diagnostic test performed.

Neuroimaging quantifies the brain's structure and examines its functional dynamics. Structural neuroimaging techniques, such as Computerized Tomography (CT) and structural Magnetic Resonance Imaging (sMRI), detect lesions and identify structural abnormalities of the brain that can lead to non-epileptic seizures. They visualize and analyze the brain's anatomical structure. Functional neuroimaging techniques detect abnormalities in brain function. Various functional neuroimaging techniques include functional MRI (fMRI) [14], electroencephalogram (EEG), SPECT, Positron Emission Tomography (PET) [15], electrocorticography (ECoG), functional near-infrared spectroscopy (fNIRS), Diffusion Tensor Imaging (DTI), Diffusion Kurtosis Imaging (DKI), and Diffusion Weighted Imaging (DWI). Among several screening tests, EEG is a non-invasive, portable, and economical option. Hence, it is one of the foremost and most effective options currently followed in the process of tracking abnormalities leading to Epilepsy and diagnosing the root cause of the concern [16]. EEG fetches the waves that vary depending on the activity being executed. It captures temporal and spatial information based on changes in voltages between several electrodes applied to the scalp. Changes are fetched by sensing the ionic current flowing across neurons in the brain. EEG captures the activity of neurons and may locate the origin point of the seizure. As described in Fig. (**5**), based on the seizure onset, the EEG signal can be in one of four phases: interictal, preictal, ictal, or postictal.

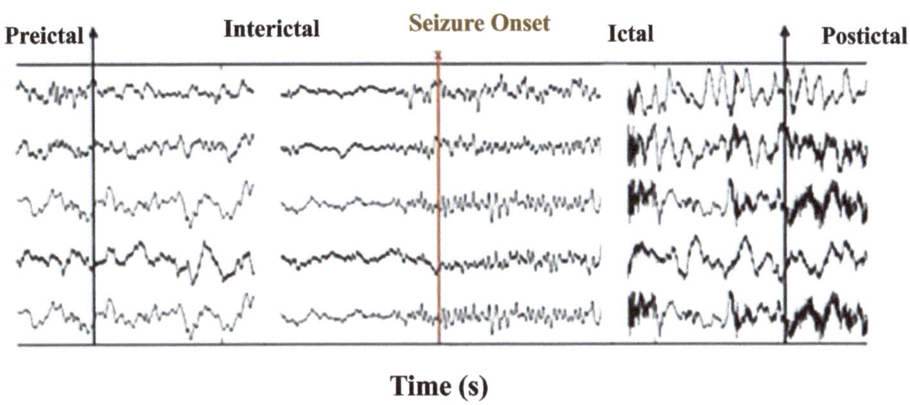

Fig. (5). Phases of the EEG signal.

As the brain activity may be regular during the test, it is not guaranteed that an epileptic abnormality will be detected *via* EEG. In such a scenario, the neurologist may suggest re-executing the EEG or proceeding with various imaging tests that provide detailed pictorial information of the brain. Apart from detecting the occurrence of an epileptic seizure, EEG can also predict its likelihood of occurrence [16]. Although both seizure detection and seizure prediction are complex activities, the advantages they offer outweigh the challenges.

A CT scan is the primary structural neuroimaging technique used by medical professionals to investigate epilepsy concerns. It utilizes ionizing radiation to generate hard tissue imaging contrast with good soft tissue resolution [17]. Recently developed CT scanners can detect malformations, lesions, and large tumors and generate results within a few seconds. It is a fast, readily available, and economical option. Still, due to the poor resolution of the temporal fossa, CT has low sensitivity, which means it is unable to detect all abnormalities. It fails to fetch abnormalities such as small tumors, refractory Epilepsy caused by pathology like mesial temporal lobe sclerosis. It fails to detect the epileptogenic structural lesions in nearly 50% of the cases.

As sMRI with high magnetic field strength possesses the ability to detect pathologies such as small tumors, malformations, and lesions, sMRI, compared to CT, can tackle the epileptic concern more effectively. It captures clear and detailed images of tissue structure that other imaging techniques cannot obtain. According to the current scenario, sMRI is performed at least once during the process of diagnosing suspected or confirmed dementia [18]. It is a specialized and sensitive neuroimaging technique that determines the etiology related to focal Epilepsy and captures the anatomical changes associated with the condition. It retrieves the brain's imagery information *via* magnetic waves and radio waves. 80% of the abnormalities detected by sMRI fall in refractory epilepsy cases, while 20% fall in the class of single unprovoked seizure cases. Although sMRI identifies most structural abnormalities, it is a costly and not readily available option. Therefore, it is typically used in scenarios where a CT scan is unable to detect the cause, and anti-epileptic drugs (AEDs) do not gain control over the condition. sMRI is often opted for in cases such as encephalitis, where CT is unable to draw any conclusions from the scan. Patients may be unresponsive to the AEDs, and seizures may continue or change their pattern on intake. In such cases, the neurologist is directed to proceed towards the option of sMRI. Apart from the cases of long-term focal Epilepsy with unknown etiology, the cases of refractory seizures are also directed to undergo sMRI. DTI (Diffusion Tensor Imaging) [19] utilizes MRI technology to assess the connectivity and structural integrity of tracts within the white matter. It produces colorful patterns that represent the level of anisotropy exhibited by water molecules, thereby facilitating the diffusion of molecules as they flow across the axons. In an undamaged and typical scenario, the molecules are constrained by the border of the axon, and flow parallel to the axon is maintained. In the event of any injury, the axon may swell, thus leading to water molecules flowing perpendicular to the direction of the axon. Like DTI, DWI (Diffusion-Weighted Imaging) is another MRI brain sequencing technique aimed at quantifying molecular diffusion in the body. Brightness in the image quantifies the restriction in diffusion, while freely diffusing molecules embed darkness in the diffusion-weighted image.

Functional neuroimaging localizes cerebral dysfunction by identifying disturbances in either blood flow or metabolism in the patient. Various functional neuroimaging techniques include fMRI, PET, SPECT, MRS, ECoG, and EEG. As the occurrence of seizures leads to various side effects, fMRI captures the effects of Epilepsy on the functional areas of the brain, such as those related to speech or memory. It scans the scalp rapidly and detects changes in blood oxygenation. It is used to detect the functional areas of the brain for pre-surgical evaluation of the patient, allowing surgery to be executed safely. PET (Positron Emission Tomography) is a functional neuroimaging technique used for interictal imaging. It localizes the seizure focus, fetches the pathophysiology of Epilepsy, and is used for investigating neurotransmitter receptor binding and psychiatric disorders. It causes hypo-metabolism due to temporal lobe epilepsy in the epileptogenic area during the interictal phase in 70–80% of the cases. However, it is unable to detect the abnormality in the extra-temporal lobe epileptic case. SPECT (Single Photon Emission Computed Tomography) is an imaging method that evaluates cerebral perfusion in both qualitative and quantitative manners. As cerebral perfusion increases during the ictal phase and decreases during the interictal phase, SPECT could be used to detect the related difference. It detects and locates the focal point in 60–90% of the cases. SPECT is advantageous as it can differentiate multiple overlapping structures to view and fetch information from various planes. Both SPECT and PET can locate the abnormality in most of the refractory epilepsy cases that are treated *via* surgery instead of *via* medication [20].

In addition to measuring physical parameters related to the brain, several techniques also assess the chemical composition of various brain components. Magnetic Resonance Spectroscopy (MRS) is a technique based on the same physical principles as MRI, which measures the biochemical composition of metabolites in the brain. It detects the metabolic changes in the epileptic zone. These changes are often missed by structural brain imaging due to the inability to access the required information [21]. Unlike neurological techniques such as SPECT, PET, and MRI, which assess the entire brain, MRS examines the neuronal integrity of a selected portion of the brain. Although both MRI and MRS are based on nuclear magnetic resonance, MRI provides anatomical information about the brain's structure, whereas MRS provides biochemical information about the tissues. As the obtained spectrum has a poor signal-to-noise ratio and takes a long time, MRS is rarely used. Electroencephalogram (EEG) and magnetic resonance imaging (MRI) are the primary tools utilized by neurologists in the process of locating and determining the root cause of Epilepsy. The method of investigating the case starts with simple and inexpensive options such as an EEG. If there is no Interictal Epileptiform Discharge (IED) during the first EEG, the routine is repeated as well. Apart from prior diagnosis, an EEG is also undertaken to monitor the response to any medication or after neurosurgery. As routine tests miss small lesions, detection of seizure onset remains unresolved in some cases. Multidisciplinary approaches and optimized epilepsy protocols with high spatial resolution are required to be executed precisely to detect abnormalities in complex scenarios.

Video EEG and ambulatory EEG are variants of EEG that have greater diagnostic power. Video EEG records the electrical activity of the brain *via* electrical equipment and the physical activity of the patient *via* a camera. It captures the patient's actions *via* video, identifies the type of abnormality, and thus plays a crucial role in locating the origin of the seizures. Ambulatory EEG [22] is another method for capturing the patient's EEG features through long-term monitoring. Fetching EEG and video EEG are one- to two-hour tasks, while ambulatory EEG is a long-term task that lasts one to three days and is executed at the patient's home. The patient is restricted from performing specific actions, such as taking a bath, during the tenure and is advised to remain within the camera's coverage area during this time. Table **1** describes the properties, applications, advantages, and disadvantages of major neurological tests used to locate, diagnose, and ultimately treat the underlying cause of Epilepsy.

Table 1. Neurological Tests to Identify the Root Cause of Epilepsy.

Test	Properties	Applications	Advantages	Drawbacks
EEG	1) Uses an electrical signal 2) Executes in silent mode 3) Covers the brain cortex	1) Measures the electrical activity of neurons 2) Fetches rhythms to diagnose Epilepsy 3) Catch effects of anti-epileptic drugs 4) Locates the damaged area in case of an accident	1) Non-invasive 2) Portable 3) High Temporal Resolution 4) No Ionizing Radiation 5) Low Cost	1) Low Spatial Resolution 2) Electrodes placed on the scalp 3) Disturbing for the patient
MEG	1) Uses a magnetic signal 2) Executes in silent mode 3) Covers the whole head	1) Locates pathological effects in the brain 2) Detects inter-ictal epileptic discharges	1) Non-invasive 2) No ionizing radiation	1) Average spatial resolution 2) Non-potable 3) High cost
NIRS	1) Uses metabolic signal 2) Executes in silent mode 3) Covers the brain cortex	1) Fetches functional mapping	1) Non-invasive 2) No ionizing radiation 3) Low cost	1) Low spatial resolution
PET	1) Uses radio waves Executes in silent mode 3) Covers the whole head	1) Evaluates the functionality of the brain	1) Non-invasive 2) Painless and non-disruptive	1) Low spatial resolution 2) High Cost

(Table 1) cont.....

Test	Properties	Applications	Advantages	Drawbacks
ECG	1) Uses the electro-physiological signal 2) Creates noise 3) Covers the chest area	1) Fetches the functionality of the heart 2) Measures the electrical activity of the brain 3) Causes traumatic brain injuries	1) Non-invasive 2) Portable 3) Simple 4) Fast to fetch and record Low cost	1) Time range limited 2) Misses in diagnosing many disorders
CT-scan	1) Uses X-ray photons 2) Executes in silent mode 3) Can scan any body part	1) Fetches structure to diagnose muscle and bone disorders and detect blood clots, stroke, or tumors in the brain	1) Non-invasive 2) Portable 3) Painless 4) High-quality images 5) Fast to fetch the record 6) Mid cost	1) Exposure to radiation 2) May lead to cancer
Structural MRI	1) Uses gamma rays 2) Creates noise 3) Covers the whole head	1) Characterizes the structure of the brain 2) Identifies causes of dementia 3) Identifies pathology issues 4) Fetches the progression of atrophy	1) Non-invasive 2) Portable 3) Painless 4) Radiation not used 5) No allergic reaction	1) Patient required to remain enclosed 2) High cost
fMRI	1) Uses metabolic signal 2) Very noisy 3) Covers the whole head	1) Preoperative mapping 2) Functional mapping	1) Non-invasive 2) Can perform functional imaging	1) Non-portable 2) High cost
MRS	1) Uses a magnetic signal 2) Creates noise 3) Covers the whole head 4) High cost	1) Fetches the structure and measures the content of selected metabolites in the brain 2) Identifies the anatomical location of the tumor 3) Detects tissue changes in stroke and Epilepsy	1) Non-invasive 2) Portable 3) Accurate assessment of anatomy	1) Low sensitivity 2) High acquisition time 3) Low spatial resolution 4) High cost

An accuracy of 99.6% has been achieved in detecting epileptic abnormalities *via* EEG signals [23]. With the development of artificial intelligence, apart from recognizing epileptic concerns, research is also gaining pace in predicting seizure episodes. As convulsions may lead to serious injuries, more than 90% of epileptic patients desire that the occurrence should be expected so that necessary actions, such as fast-acting medication, could be taken to avoid the occurrence or the side effects of the episode [24]. As various medical parameters exhibit variability both during and before the fit, their occurrence can be detected or predicted based on the measurement of these parameters. In 2020, T. Yamakawa *et al.* [25] predicted epileptic fits based on heart rate variability derived from R-R intervals extracted from the ECG signal.

Epilepsy Datasets

As data serves as the prerequisite for designing any data model, selecting valid and appropriate data is a crucial step in creating an effective model. Brain signals must be captured in multiple modes, such as EEG, ECoG, and MRI. Various datasets include the Freiburg dataset, CHB-MIT dataset, Bonn University dataset, Bern Barcelona dataset, Hauz Khas dataset, and Zenodo dataset.

The Freiburg EEG dataset was recorded at the Epilepsy Centre of the University Hospital of Freiburg, Germany [26]. It was fetched from 21 refractory focal epilepsy patients, including eight males with an age in the range 13−47 years and 13 females with an age in the range 10−50 years. Eighty-eight seizures from the interictal recordings of length 24 hours were fetched from 13 patients, and seizures of length less than 24 hours were fetched from 8 patients. Both ictal and interictal data were fetched from the patients. Ictal data is preceded by a 50-minute recording of the pre-ictal region, while the interictal region captures 24-hour seizure-free data. Depth electrodes were used to collect the data, allowing for direct recording from the focal area.

The CHB-MIT dataset was recorded at the Children's Hospital Boston and the Massachusetts Institute of Technology. It is publicly available on a PhysioNet server and can be downloaded from the server using the Cygwin tool [27]. Data have been collected from 23 patients: 5 males, aged 3 to 22 years, and 17 females, aged 1.5 to 19 years. Both seizure and non-seizure recordings of each patient are captured in the European data format (.edf). Spikes fetch the seizure start and seizure end times. EEG datasets in 1-D format were fetched *via* multiple types of channels that were placed at the surface of the brain according to the 10−20 standard electrode positioning International System. Signals were sampled at a frequency of 256 Hz, thus fetching 256 samples per second. The dataset comprises 844 hours of scalp EEG recordings from 23 children, capturing 163 seizures. A seizure in this database is either a combined seizure or a main seizure.

The Bonn University dataset [28] is one of the most widely used EEG datasets that is openly accessible. It captures 100 single-channel EEG recordings *via* 10−20 electrode placement schemes. Each recording is captured *via* a 128-channel amplifier system. Data is fetched from 500 individuals and grouped into five folders, each folder containing 100 files. Each file fetches the brain activity of an individual and records the EEG for 23.6 seconds. As described in Fig. (**6**), the dataset is divided into five subsets: S, F, N, Z, and O. Each recording of 23.6 seconds is sampled into 4097 points, which are divided into 23 chunks, each containing 178 data points. Each group of 178 points is classified as belonging to one of the five subsets, and the result of classification is fed as the 179th column after each set of 178 points. The Bern-Barcelona dataset [29] was obtained from the Department of Neurology at Bern Hospital in Barcelona. It contains an 83-hour-long record of intracranial EEG from focal epilepsy patients and 7500 bivariate EEG files from 5 pharmacoresistant temporal lobe epilepsy patients, comprising 3750 focal and 3750 non-focal files, each with a duration of 20 seconds. A 10–20 positioning system was implemented to implant intracranial depth and strip electrodes for recording multichannel EEG signals. Depending on the number of channels used to record EEG signals, sampling was executed at 512 Hz or 1024 Hz. This dataset is preferred for seizure localization.

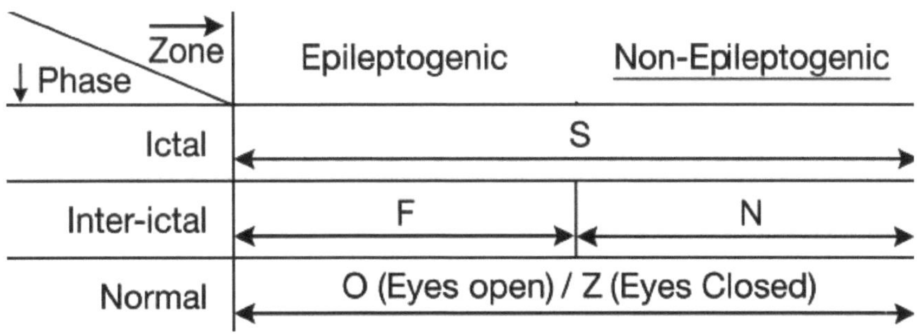

Fig. (6). Division of the Bonn University dataset into subsets.

Hauz Khas dataset [30] contains exemplary segmented EEG time series recordings of 10 epilepsy patients collected from the Neurology and Sleep Centre, Hauz Khas, New Delhi. The data was acquired at a sampling rate of 200 Hz using the AS40 amplification system. During data acquisition, gold-plated scalp EEG electrodes were placed according to the 10-20 electrode placement system. The signals were filtered between 0.5 Hz and 70 Hz and segmented into pre-ictal, ictal, and inter-ictal stages. Corresponding to each stage, fifty MAT files of EEG time series signals are grouped, and 1024 samples of one EEG time series data lasting for 5.12 seconds are contained in each MAT file.

The Zenodo dataset [31] is a collection of EEG recordings from human neonates. Multichannel EEG data from 79 term neonates were recorded at Helsinki University Hospital. EEG recordings from 79 neonates, with durations ranging from 64 minutes to 96 minutes, were recorded in the hospital. From 39 neonates, 460 seizures were captured, though 22 neonates remained seizure-free. Three experts have annotated the multichannel EEG recordings in the dataset.

Annotations are stored in both MAT and CSV file formats. The MAT file consists of an array of 79 elements, each element in the form of an M × N array where 'M = 3', the number of experts, and 'N' is the duration of the annotation in seconds. The entry corresponding to each second is either 0 or 1, depending on whether the seizure is present or absent, respectively. Data is also transformed into 3 CSV files, each corresponding to the annotations of 3 experts.

CONCLUSION

As an accurate diagnosis is a prerequisite for dealing with any medical ailment, neurological abnormalities require considerable physiological tests before proceeding with treatment. Epilepsy, being one of the major abrupt and uncertain neurological ailments, presents a significant challenge for medical professionals. This paper provides an overview of all the neurological tests used in the diagnosis and assessment of epileptic abnormalities. To aid the process, various signal analysis techniques discriminate between the normal, interictal, preictal, and ictal states of the signal. This paper reviews all the physiological tests conducted by neurologists to identify the root cause of epileptic abnormalities and ultimately treat them appropriately. As the nervous system is the central system controlling the life of the being, multiple tests are executed to study the same case. With the advancement in technology, new tests are being developed, and existing tests have been improved. Neurological tests for studying epileptic abnormalities range from traditional EEG to functional MRI, providing valuable insights into structural or functional abnormalities in the brain. Though diagnostic tests have advanced, a lack of skilled interpretation leads to variability in test results. This justifies the need for qualified interpretation and thus the automation of report generation related to physiological tests. The presented approach of leveraging neurological tests and machine learning models for detecting epileptic abnormalities holds significant implications for clinical and healthcare management. By automating seizure classification and localizing epileptic foci through advanced imaging and signal processing techniques, hospitals can reduce diagnostic delays and enhance decision-making efficiency. Managers can better allocate resources, reduce patient turnaround time, and lower treatment costs by relying on AI-driven clinical decision support systems. Furthermore, the ability to integrate and analyze multimodal datasets (*e.g.*, EEG, MRI, PET) improves operational workflows, enabling real-time risk monitoring and early intervention. These advancements pave the way for scaling tele-neurology services and optimizing patient management in both urban and resource-limited rural settings.

REFERENCES

[1] L.D. Iasemidis, Deng-Shan Shiau, W. Chaovalitwongse, J.C. Sackellares, P.M. Pardalos, J.C. Principe, P.R. Carney, A. Prasad, B. Veeramani, and K. Tsakalis, "Adaptive epileptic seizure prediction system", *IEEE Trans. Biomed. Eng.,* vol. 50, no. 5, pp. 616-627, 2003.

[http://dx.doi.org/10.1109/TBME.2003.810689] [PMID: 12769437]

[2] D. Gajic, Z. Djurovic, J. Gligorijevic, S. Di Gennaro, and I. Savic-Gajic, "Detection of epileptiform activity in EEG signals based on time-frequency and non-linear analysis", *Front. Comput. Neurosci.,* vol. 9, p. 38, 2015.
[http://dx.doi.org/10.3389/fncom.2015.00038] [PMID: 25852534]

[3] K. Fujiwara, M. Miyajima, T. Yamakawa, E. Abe, Y. Suzuki, Y. Sawada, M. Kano, T. Maehara, K. Ohta, T. Sasai-Sakuma, T. Sasano, M. Matsuura, and E. Matsushima, "Epileptic seizure prediction based on multivariate statistical process control of heart rate variability features", *IEEE Trans. Biomed. Eng.,* vol. 63, no. 6, pp. 1321-1332, 2016.
[http://dx.doi.org/10.1109/TBME.2015.2512276] [PMID: 26841385]

[4] M. Rostami, and S. Goli-Bidgoli, "An overview of QoS-aware load balancing techniques in SDN-based IoT networks", *J. Cloud Comput. (Heidelb.),* vol. 13, no. 1, p. 89, 2024.
[http://dx.doi.org/10.1186/s13677-024-00651-7]

[5] T. Salehnia, A. Montazerolghaem, and S. Mirjalili, "SDN-based optimal task scheduling method in Fog-IoT network using combination of AO and WOA", In: *Whale Optimization Algorithm: Variants, Improvements, Hybrids and Applications.* Elsevier, 2023, pp. 179-204.

[6] S. Imanpour, A. Montazerolghaem, and S. Afshari, "Load Balancing of Servers in Software-defined Internet of Multimedia Things using the Long Short-Term Memory Prediction Algorithm", *Proc. ICWR,* 2024.
[http://dx.doi.org/10.1109/ICWR61162.2024.10533321]

[7] H. Alhilali, and A. Montazerolghaem, "Artificial intelligence based load balancing in SDN: a comprehensive survey", *Internet Things,* vol. 22, 2023.
[http://dx.doi.org/10.1016/j.iot.2023.100814]

[8] R.S. Fisher, J.H. Cross, C. D'Souza, J.A. French, S.R. Haut, N. Higurashi, E. Hirsch, F.E. Jansen, L. Lagae, S.L. Moshé, J. Peltola, E. Roulet Perez, I.E. Scheffer, A. Schulze-Bonhage, E. Somerville, M. Sperling, E.M. Yacubian, and S.M. Zuberi, "Instruction manual for the ILAE 2017 operational classification of seizure types", *Epilepsia,* vol. 58, no. 4, pp. 531-542, 2017.
[http://dx.doi.org/10.1111/epi.13671] [PMID: 28276064]

[9] R.S. Fisher, J. Cross, J.A. French, N. Higurashi, E. Hirsch, F.E. Jansen, L. Lagae, S. Lopez, J. Peltola, E. Roulet Perez, I.E. Scheffer, and S.M. Zuberi, "Operational classification of seizure types by the International League Against Epilepsy: position paper of the ILAE Commission for Classification and Terminology", *Epilepsia,* vol. 58, pp. 522-530, 2017.
[http://dx.doi.org/10.1111/epi.13670] [PMID: 28276060]

[10] I.E. Scheffer, S. Berkovic, G. Capovilla, M.B. Connolly, J. French, L. Guilhoto, E. Hirsch, S. Jain, G.W. Mathern, S.L. Moshé, D.R. Nordli, E. Perucca, T. Tomson, S. Wiebe, Y.H. Zhang, and S.M. Zuberi, "ILAE classification of the epilepsies: Position paper of the ILAE Commission for Classification and Terminology", *Journal of the Japan Epilepsy Society,* vol. 37, no. 1, pp. 6-14, 2019.
[http://dx.doi.org/10.3805/jjes.37.6]

[11] M. Brodie, S.M. Zuberi, I. Scheffer, and R. Fisher, "The 2017 ILAE classification of seizure types and the epilepsies: what do people with epilepsy and their caregivers need to know?", *Epileptic Disord.,* vol. 20, pp. 77-87, 2018.
[http://dx.doi.org/10.1684/epd.2018.0957]

[12] M. Eadie, "Shortcomings in the current treatment of epilepsy", *Expert Rev. Neurother.,* vol. 12, pp. 1419-1427, 2012.
[http://dx.doi.org/10.1586/ern.12.129]

[13] J. Yuan, X. Ran, K. Liu, C. Yao, Y. Yao, H. Wu, and Q. Liu, "Machine learning applications on neuroimaging for diagnosis and prognosis of epilepsy: A review", *J. Neurosci. Methods,* vol. 368, p. 109441, 2022.
[http://dx.doi.org/10.1016/j.jneumeth.2021.109441] [PMID: 34942271]

[14] K.K. Kwong, J.W. Belliveau, D.A. Chesler, I.E. Goldberg, R.M. Weisskoff, B.P. Poncelet, D.N. Kennedy, B.E. Hoppel, M.S. Cohen, and R. Turner, "Dynamic magnetic resonance imaging of human brain activity during primary sensory stimulation", *Proc. Natl. Acad. Sci. USA,* vol. 89, no. 12, pp. 5675-5679, 1992.
[http://dx.doi.org/10.1073/pnas.89.12.5675] [PMID: 1608978]

[15] C. Fougère, A. Rominger, S. Förster, J. Geisler, and P. Bartenstein, "PET and SPECT in epilepsy: a critical review", *Epilepsy Behav.,* vol. 15, pp. 50-55, 2009.
[http://dx.doi.org/10.1016/j.yebeh.2009.02.025]

[16] F. Li, Y. Liang, L. Zhang, C. Yi, Y. Liao, Y. Jiang, Y. Si, Y. Zhang, D. Yao, L. Yu, and P. Xu, "Transition of brain networks from an interictal to a preictal state preceding a seizure revealed by scalp EEG network analysis", *Cogn. Neurodynamics,* vol. 13, no. 2, pp. 175-181, 2019.
[http://dx.doi.org/10.1007/s11571-018-09517-6] [PMID: 30956721]

[17] T. Roy, and A. Pandit, "Neuroimaging in epilepsy", *Ann. Indian Acad. Neurol.,* pp. 78-80, 2011.
[http://dx.doi.org/10.4103/0972-2327.82787]

[18] M.P. Wattjes, "Structural MRI", *Int. Psychogeriatr.,* vol. 23, no. S2, pp. S13-S24, 2011.
[http://dx.doi.org/10.1017/S1041610211000913]

[19] S. Mori, and J. Zhang, "Principles of diffusion tensor imaging and its applications to basic neuroscience research", *Neuron,* vol. 51, no. 5, pp. 527-539, 2006.
[http://dx.doi.org/10.1016/j.neuron.2006.08.012] [PMID: 16950152]

[20] M.R. Ponisio, J.M. Zempel, B.K. Day, L.N. Eisenman, M.M. Miller-Thomas, M.D. Smyth, and R.E. Hogan, "The role of CT and PET in Epilepsy", *AJR Am. J. Roentgenol.,* vol. 216, no. 3, pp. 759-768, 2021.
[http://dx.doi.org/10.2214/AJR.20.23336] [PMID: 33474983]

[21] M.H. Buonocore, and R.J. Maddock, "Magnetic resonance spectroscopy of the brain: a review of physical principles and technical methods", *Rev. Neurosci.,* vol. 26, no. 6, pp. 609-632, 2015.
[http://dx.doi.org/10.1515/revneuro-2015-0010] [PMID: 26200810]

[22] K.A. González Otárula, P. Balaguera, and S. Schuele, "Ambulatory EEG to classify the epilepsy syndrome", *J. Clin. Neurophysiol.,* vol. 38, no. 2, pp. 87-91, 2021.
[http://dx.doi.org/10.1097/WNP.0000000000000678] [PMID: 33661784]

[23] M.V.V.P. Kantipudi, N.S.P. Kumar, R. Aluvalu, S. Selvarajan, and K. Kotecha, "An improved GBSO-TAENN-based EEG signal classification model for epileptic seizure detection", *Sci. Rep.,* vol. 14, no. 1, p. 843, 2024.
[http://dx.doi.org/10.1038/s41598-024-51337-8] [PMID: 38191643]

[24] L.D. Iasemidis, "Epileptic seizure prediction and control", *IEEE Trans. Biomed. Eng.,* vol. 50, no. 5, pp. 549-558, 2003.
[http://dx.doi.org/10.1109/TBME.2003.810705]

[25] T. Yamakawa, M. Miyajima, K. Fujiwara, M. Kano, Y. Suzuki, Y. Watanabe, S. Watanabe, T. Hoshida, M. Inaji, and T. Maehara, "Wearable epileptic seizure prediction system with machine-learning-based anomaly detection of heart rate variability", *Sensors (Basel),* vol. 20, no. 14, p. 3987, 2020.
[http://dx.doi.org/10.3390/s20143987] [PMID: 32709064]

[26] M. Ihle, H. Feldwisch-Drentrup, C.A. Teixeira, A. Witon, B. Schelter, J. Timmer, and A. Schulze-Bonhage, "EPILEPSIAE – A European epilepsy database", *Comput. Methods Programs Biomed.,* vol. 106, no. 3, pp. 127-138, 2012.
[http://dx.doi.org/10.1016/j.cmpb.2010.08.011] [PMID: 20863589]

[27] A.L. Goldberger, L.A.N. Amaral, L. Glass, J.M. Hausdorff, P.C. Ivanov, R.G. Mark, J.E. Mietus, G.B. Moody, C.K. Peng, and H.E. Stanley, "PhysioBank, PhysioToolkit, and PhysioNet", *Circulation,* pp. e215-e220, 2000.

[http://dx.doi.org/10.1161/01.CIR.101.23.e215]

[28] R.G. Andrzejak, K. Lehnertz, F. Mormann, C. Rieke, P. David, and C.E. Elger, "Indications of nonlinear deterministic and finite-dimensional structures in time series of brain electrical activity: Dependence on recording region and brain state", *Phys. Rev. E Stat. Phys. Plasmas Fluids Relat. Interdiscip. Topics,* vol. 64, no. 6, p. 061907, 2001. [http://dx.doi.org/10.1103/PhysRevE.64.061907] [PMID: 11736210]

[29] R. Andrzejak, K. Schindler, and C. Rummel, "Nonrandomness, nonlinear dependence, and nonstationarity of electroencephalographic recordings from epilepsy patients", *Phys. Rev. E,* vol. 86, 2012. [http://dx.doi.org/10.1103/PhysRevE.86.046206]

[30] S. Wong, A. Simmons, J. Rivera-Villicana, S. Barnett, S. Sivathamboo, P. Perucca, Z. Ge, P. Kwan, L. Kuhlmann, R. Vasa, K. Mouzakis, and T.J. O'Brien, "EEG datasets for seizure detection and prediction— A review", *Epilepsia Open,* vol. 8, no. 2, pp. 252-267, 2023. [http://dx.doi.org/10.1002/epi4.12704] [PMID: 36740244]

[31] N.J. Stevenson, K. Tapani, L. Lauronen, and S. Vanhatalo, "A dataset of neonatal EEG recordings with seizure annotations", *Sci. Data,* vol. 6, no. 1, p. 190039, 2019. [http://dx.doi.org/10.1038/sdata.2019.39] [PMID: 30835259]

CHAPTER 3

From Tweets to Insights: A Diverse Classifier Approach to Analyze Sentiments on Twitter

R. Sanmugasundaram[1,*], **Kaviraj G.M.**[1], **Chitra M.**[1], **Dileepan D.**[1], **Manikandan M.**[1] and **Kanimozhi J.**[1]

[1] *Department of Electronics and Communication Engineering, Rajalakshmi Institute of Technology, Vel Tech Rangarajan Dr. Sagunthala R&D Institute of Science and Technology, Chennai, India*

Abstract: This study delves into the realm of Twitter sentiment analysis, employing an array of machine learning algorithms. Through meticulous preprocessing of a substantial Twitter dataset, the research meticulously examines algorithmic performance. Results are elucidated through visual representations, revealing comparative efficacy, strengths, and limitations. This exploration significantly advances the comprehension of sentiment analysis within the context of social media, providing valuable insights for subsequent research and the refinement of methodologies in this dynamic domain. The study's findings contribute to the evolving discourse on sentiment analysis and its applications in the digital landscape.

Keywords: Comparative analysis, Feature selection, Machine learning algorithms, Twitter sentiment analysis, Text mining.

INTRODUCTION

This research delves into the intriguing realm of Twitter sentiment analysis, utilizing a diverse array of machine learning algorithms to decipher the complex tapestry of emotions embedded in tweets. As the proposed work navigates through this exploration, it becomes apparent that sentiment analysis is not merely about deciphering text; it's about unraveling the pulse of a global digital conversation [1 - 5]. The significance lies in discerning not just what is said but how it resonates with the underlying sentiment. With the surge in social media usage, the ability to gauge public opinion on Twitter has become a valuable compass for businesses, policymakers, and researchers alike [6, 7]. From forecasting stock market movements to anticipating public reactions during crises, the ability to quantify sentiment in real time has opened new frontiers across mult-

* **Corresponding author R. Sanmugasundaram:** Department of Electronics and Communication Engineering, Rajalakshmi Institute of Technology, Vel Tech Rangarajan Dr. Sagunthala R&D Institute of Science and Technology, Chennai, India; E-mail: rsanmu88@gmail.com

Manoj Kumar, Sachin Kumar Gupta, Navnath Kale, Pramod Ganjewar & Sandeep Pande (Eds.)

iple disciplines [8]. Our journey commences with a thorough examination of existing literature, revealing both the strides made and the gaps present in current Twitter sentiment analysis methodologies. Armed with this knowledge, the work embarks on a methodological odyssey, delving into the intricacies of machine learning algorithms. The selection and application of these algorithms are pivotal, demanding a balance between sophistication and practicality. Twitter, as a microblogging platform, presents unique challenges in terms of language nuances, brevity, and the ever-evolving lexicon of digital communication [9 - 11]. Emojis, hashtags, acronyms, and cultural slang often carry sentiment-laden meaning that can be lost in conventional text-based approaches. As such, advanced Natural Language Processing (NLP) techniques that incorporate contextual embedding and semantic analysis are increasingly vital. Addressing these challenges, our study meticulously preprocesses a substantial dataset, ensuring the integrity of the subsequent sentiment analysis. The algorithms deployed, ranging from classic models like Naive Bayes to more complex neural networks, are subjected to rigorous evaluation and testing. This research not only seeks to unravel the efficacy of various classification algorithms but also to contribute to the evolving discourse on sentiment analysis [12 - 14]. In a world where every tweet carries the potential to shape narratives, understanding the sentiment behind the words becomes not just an academic pursuit but a strategic imperative for navigating the vast sea of digital expressions on Twitter. In the ever-evolving landscape of social media, where trends shift at the speed of a tweet, the role of sentiment analysis becomes increasingly pivotal. Beyond deciphering positive, negative, or neutral tones, our research aims to tease out the contextual subtleties that define sentiment within the Twitter verse [15]. Context matters, and within the confines of 280 characters, users often wield an economy of words that demands a sophisticated understanding. This also means recognizing that the same word or emoji may carry different meanings depending on the user's intent, cultural background, or the topic of discussion—factors that static models often fail to grasp [16]. Moreover, the rise of generative AI tools and language models has introduced new possibilities for augmenting sentiment interpretation, especially in identifying sarcasm, irony, and implicit cues that traditional models often overlook. The work unravels the intricacies of sentiment, and the team also acknowledges the ethical considerations inherent in analyzing user-generated content. This includes not only compliance with data protection regulations but also cultivating responsible AI practices that ensure algorithmic transparency and fairness. Incorporating fairness-aware machine learning techniques, regular audits of model biases, and explainability frameworks are vital steps in ensuring that sentiment analysis tools remain ethical and accountable. Striking a balance between mining valuable insights and respecting user privacy is a delicate yet essential aspect of our inquiry [17 - 20]. This research not only seeks to enhance the technical foundations of sentiment analysis but also to contribute to the broader discourse on the ethical dimensions of studying sentiments in the digital age.

LITERATURE REVIEW

In the expansive landscape of sentiment analysis on social media, particularly on Twitter, a substantial body of literature has been dedicated to understanding the challenges and advancements in this dynamic field. Researchers have made significant strides in harnessing the wealth of user-generated content to effectively decipher sentiments and opinions. One seminal work laid the groundwork for sentiment analysis by introducing a classification framework that categorized sentiment analysis approaches into machine learning and lexicon-based methods. This exploration highlighted the need for robust methodologies to address the inherent complexities of sentiment conveyed in diverse language styles on platforms such as Twitter.

Subsequent studies have explored the nuances of sentiment analysis on microblogging platforms. Some works examined the impact of linguistic factors, such as emoticons and informal language, on sentiment classification accuracy, showing that incorporating these elements can significantly enhance classifier performance. The rapid evolution of sentiment analysis techniques has led to the integration of sophisticated machine learning algorithms. Several studies have investigated the use of Support Vector Machines (SVM) in this domain, emphasizing their ability to handle the nuanced nature of short and informal text typical of tweets.

The rise of deep learning has further transformed the field. Convolutional Neural Networks (CNNs) have demonstrated exceptional capabilities in capturing contextual cues and representing hierarchical relationships in text, making them well-suited for handling the compact and often ambiguous format of tweets. Transformer-based models, particularly those designed to consider both preceding and following context, have demonstrated a strong ability to understand sentiment at a deeper level. Applications of these models to health-related tweets, political discourse, and public opinion datasets have consistently revealed higher performance metrics compared to traditional methods.

An emerging area within the literature is multimodal sentiment analysis, which incorporates not only textual but also visual and auditory cues. On Twitter, where users often accompany their messages with images, memes, or video content, capturing sentiment from visual signals has proven valuable. Techniques that align visual and textual representations have helped in detecting subtleties, such as sarcasm or conflicting sentiments between text and image. Additionally, ensemble methods that combine multiple classifiers have gained popularity due to their enhanced ability to generalize across varied sentiment expressions. Some studies have proposed hybrid models that integrate deep neural networks with boosting-based classifiers to enhance sentiment detection, particularly in multilingual or code-mixed tweets prevalent in diverse user communities.

Despite these advancements, persistent challenges remain a focus of the literature. The inherently noisy and ambiguous nature of Twitter data, along with the rapid and unpredictable evolution of language trends, demands continuous adaptation. Tweets often include elements such as sarcasm, rhetorical questions, abbreviations, or hashtags, which complicate the interpretation of sentiment. A typical example is a tweet expressing frustration through irony, which can easily be misclassified by models lacking contextual awareness. To address this, attention-based mechanisms and sentiment-aware pre-training techniques have been developed to improve contextual interpretation.

Real-time sentiment tracking has also attracted increasing attention. Some systems have been designed to monitor live streams of tweets during high-profile events, detecting sudden shifts in public opinion. These systems rely on scalable architectures capable of processing and analyzing high-velocity data in real time, enabling sentiment analysis to be applied in domains such as political forecasting, emergency response, and trend detection.

Moreover, the ethical considerations surrounding user privacy and consent in mining sentiments from user-generated content remain key concerns that merit further exploration. With increasing regulatory oversight under frameworks such as the General Data Protection Regulation (GDPR) and the proposed American Data Privacy and Protection Act (ADPPA), sentiment analysis researchers must implement stricter data anonymization techniques and avoid profiling or targeting individuals based on sensitive, inferred emotions. Moreover, the potential for algorithmic bias—where models may misclassify sentiment based on dialect, gendered language, or ethnicity—has garnered attention. Recent approaches have emphasized the incorporation of fairness-aware techniques and transparent evaluation methods to mitigate such biases.

There is also a growing shift from binary or ternary sentiment classification to emotion-based frameworks. Moving beyond categories such as positive, negative, or neutral, researchers have begun adopting more granular emotional taxonomies to reflect the complexity of human expression. These frameworks enable the classification of tweets into emotions such as joy, trust, anger, or fear, providing richer insights, particularly valuable during societal events where emotions are diverse and intense.

A thorough analysis of QoS-aware load balancing in Software-Defined Internet of Things (SD-IoT) systems was provided by a conducted study [21]. According to their research, SDN-based traffic management efficiently improves latency, throughput, and resource fairness, which makes it ideal for real-time sentiment analysis and social media data routing. However, the study also identified a research gap in managing high-velocity, unstructured data, such as tweets, particularly in incorporating sentiment-critical characteristics (*e.g.*, emoticons and sarcasm) into SDN-based flow rule design. For job scheduling in fog-IoT systems, the authors of [22] suggested a novel hybrid optimization technique that combines the Whale Optimization Algorithm (WOA) and Aquila Optimizer (AO). Superior makespan reduction and resource utilization were demonstrated by their SDN-based approach, which is beneficial for latency-sensitive NLP applications such as sentiment categorization on Twitter. The lack of failure-tolerant methods and real-time flexibility limits deployment in dynamic social media streams.

Long Short-Term Memory (LSTM) networks were employed in a study [23] to propose a server load balancing model for Software-Defined Internet of Multimedia Things (SD-IoMT), aiming to forecast future traffic demands. The primary benefit of this approach is its predicted resource allocation, which ensures smooth and energy-efficient service delivery. This is useful for hosting real-time analytics tools, such as sentiment dashboards on Twitter. The framework's drawback is that it was only tested on synthetic multimedia data; it was not tested against the emotional context or short-text variations that are frequently present in Twitter streams. In [24], the researchers examined load-balancing techniques in Software-Defined Networks (SDNs) that use Artificial Intelligence (AI). Their research revealed that AI-driven models, particularly those employing reinforcement learning and fuzzy logic, enhance decision-making in dynamic traffic situations, which is advantageous for handling fluctuating Twitter sentiments. However, they identified a research gap in explainability and robustness, noting that the majority of AI-based SDN solutions lack explicit model reasoning, which is crucial in applications that are sensitive to emotions and require accountability and fairness.

In summary, the literature review outlines the trajectory of sentiment analysis on Twitter, spanning from foundational works in machine learning and lexicon-based methods to contemporary approaches that leverage advanced algorithms, such as SVM and deep learning. The field continues to evolve rapidly, driven by the dual need to improve classification accuracy and ensure responsible use. The existing body of knowledge both informs and sets the stage for our research, emphasizing the need for nuanced, context-aware strategies to decode the intricacies of sentiment within the fast-paced, expressive world of Twitter.

PROBLEM STATEMENT

In the realm of Twitter sentiment analysis, a critical challenge persists in unravelling the intricacies of sentiment expression within the brevity and informality of tweets. Existing methodologies, while robust in many aspects, struggle to keep pace with the evolving nature of language trends on social media and the constant influx of new expressions [25, 26]. Moreover, the inherent noise and ambiguity in Twitter data pose hurdles for accurate sentiment classification. This is further compounded by the prevalence of sarcasm, irony, slang, and abbreviations, which often mislead conventional classification models. Hashtags and emojis, although rich in sentiment, require contextual interpretation to be utilized effectively. Ethical considerations surrounding user privacy and consent in extracting sentiments from user-generated content add another layer of complexity. With increasing public scrutiny and evolving data protection regulations such as GDPR and CCPA, it is essential to ensure that sentiment analysis is conducted with transparency, accountability, and fairness. Bias in algorithmic decision-making, especially when models are trained on imbalanced or culturally skewed datasets, poses significant risks to ethical integrity. This study aims to address these challenges, striving to enhance the precision and adaptability of sentiment analysis on Twitter while navigating the ethical dimensions inherent in analysing social media sentiments. By integrating advanced natural language processing techniques, dynamic feature engineering, and fairness-aware learning models, the research seeks to develop a framework that is not only accurate and scalable but also ethically responsible.

METHODOLOGY

Embarking on the intricate journey of Twitter sentiment analysis demands a methodological approach akin to conducting a symphony, where the harmonious interplay of machine learning algorithms and linguistic subtleties becomes the melody of insight. In this methodology [27], we traverse the multifaceted terrain of data preprocessing, algorithmic ensemble, feature selection, training, validation, and performance evaluation, aiming not just for accuracy but also for the nuanced capture of sentiment nuances within the dynamic tapestry of Twitter expressions. Each phase is designed to address specific challenges posed by Twitter data, including irregular grammar, hashtag semantics, and the contextual ambiguity often found in short-form text. Moreover, the methodology incorporates iterative tuning and evaluation cycles to ensure adaptability across various sentiment domains, including politics, product reviews, and social trends. Refer to Table **1** for details on the dataset.

Table 1. Dataset Details.

Tweets	Count	Total Count
Positive Tweets	80,000	1,60,000
Negative Tweets	80,000	

Note: The dataset used for this study consists of various features essential for sentiment analysis, including tweet text, sentiment labels, and metadata. Detailed information about the dataset is provided in Table **1**.

Data Exploration and Preprocessing

At the heart of our methodology lies the exploration and preparation of the dataset—a trove of tweets that echo the sentiments of the Twitterverse [20]. This initial phase involves more than just data cleansing. It requires a nuanced understanding of the platform's linguistic quirks, where brevity often leads to densely packed emotional and contextual cues [28]. It's an art of understanding the heartbeat of the language, capturing the colloquialisms, acronyms, and the ever-evolving lexicon of social media discourse. Tweets often include blended language, emojis, and creative spelling variations that must be interpreted carefully to retain sentiment value. The tweets undergo a transformative journey of cleansing, tokenization, and normalization, ensuring that the raw cacophony of data metamorphoses into a structured ensemble ready for algorithmic interpretation. Additionally, preprocessing steps such as stop word removal, lemmatization, and handling of noisy user mentions and links play a crucial role in reducing data sparsity and enhancing model performance [29].

Algorithmic Ensemble

Like a maestro assembling a symphony, our approach involves curating an ensemble of machine learning algorithms, each lending its unique notes to the collective melody of sentiment classification. Classic algorithms, such as Naive Bayes and decision trees, as well as the intricate dance of neural networks, all find a place in this orchestration. Each algorithm brings distinct strengths—some excel in interpretability, while others shine in capturing deep contextual semantics. Refer to Fig. (**1**) for an overview of the model's general working process that the team will perform. The challenge here is not merely to predict sentiment, but to capture the variability and subtlety of sentiment expressions within the condensed format of tweets, where complexity and conciseness intersect. This demands not only technical precision but also an appreciation for linguistic nuance, as a single emoji or punctuation mark can shift the emotional tone of a tweet [30].

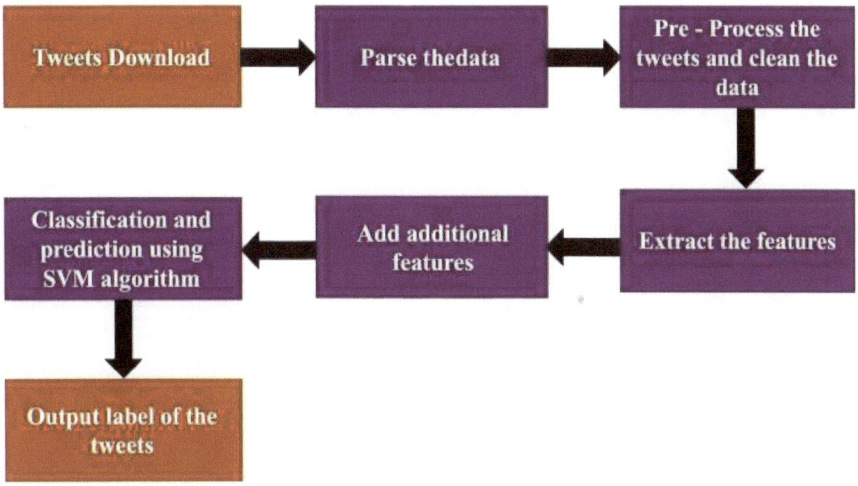

Fig. (1). Overview of the model.

Note: Fig. (**1**) presents an overview of the machine learning model utilized in this study for Twitter sentiment analysis.

Feature Selection and Extraction

Moving to the forefront, the team engages in a delicate ballet of feature selection and extraction. Here, the challenge lies not just in identifying relevant features but in discerning the harmonious interplay that encapsulates sentiment in its multifaceted glory. The team explores the significance of words, delves into the rhythm of n-grams, and contemplates the contextual nuances embedded in sentiment-bearing emojis. It's a choreography where each feature contributes to the eloquence of sentiment expression.

Training and Validation

As our algorithms take center stage, our team instills discipline through rigorous training and validation. This involves more than just imparting knowledge; it's about teaching algorithms to dance to the ever-changing rhythms of real-world sentiment expressions. Training datasets are carefully partitioned to ensure balanced representation across sentiment categories, preventing bias and overfitting. Cross-validation becomes the choreographer, refining the algorithmic dance to adapt seamlessly to the dynamic nuances of Twitter discourse. Each fold of validation acts as a spotlight, revealing how well the model generalizes to unseen data, particularly when it encounters informal language or domain-specific slang. Refer to Figs. (**3** and **4**) for the word clouds of positive sentiments and negative sentiments, respectively. Training isn't a static rehearsal but a continual adaptation to the evolving language trends and sentiments. Incorporating feedback loops and monitoring performance across time slices allows the system to remain relevant in public discourse.

Fig. (2). Word cloud for positive tweets.

Note: Fig. (**2**) illustrates a word cloud generated from positive tweets in the dataset. The size of each word corresponds to its frequency in positive tweets, providing an overview of the most commonly used words in positive sentiment contexts.

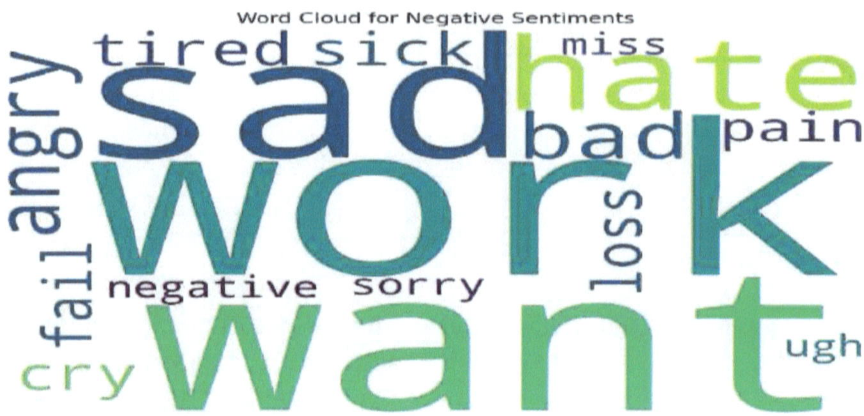

Fig. (3). Word cloud for negative tweets.

Note: Fig. (**3**) depicts a word cloud representation of negative tweets extracted from the dataset. This visualization highlights the prevalence of specific terms within negative sentiment contexts, facilitating an understanding of the language associated with negative sentiments.

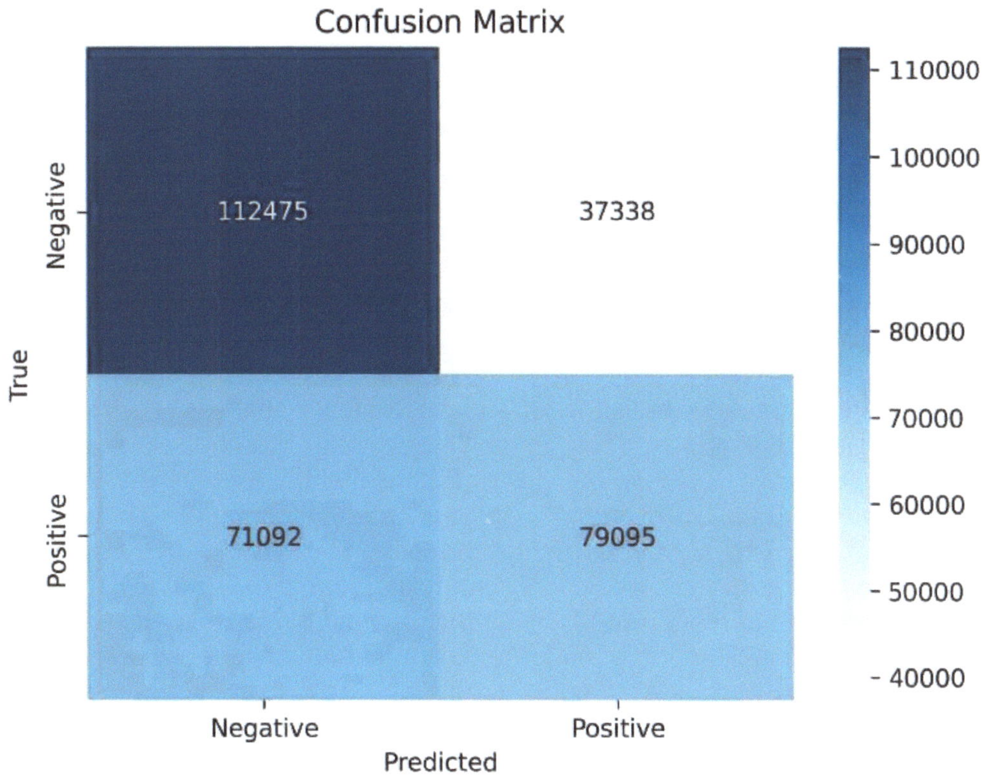

Fig. (4). Confusion matrix for the SVR model.

Note: Fig. (**4**) displays the confusion matrix for the Support Vector Regression (SVR) model used in this study. The confusion matrix provides insights into the performance of the SVR model by illustrating the counts of true positives, true negatives, false positives, and false negatives.

While the mathematical formulations of the individual classifiers are standard, the novelty in our work lies in the adaptation of SVR for a classification task. SVR typically predicts continuous values; here, we interpret these values as sentiment intensities and map them to discrete sentiment categories using a custom thresholding mechanism. Additionally, we design a soft voting ensemble strategy, which combines normalized probability scores from multiple classifiers. The ensemble decision is modeled as:

$$\hat{y} = arg\,max_j \sum_{m=1}^{M} w_m \cdot p_j^{(m)} \quad \text{(1)}$$

where $\hat{p}_j^{(m)}$ Is the predicted probability of class j from model m, and w_m is the weight derived from cross-validation performance. This mathematical integration of SVR in a voting-based ensemble is a novel adaptation tailored for sentiment analysis on social media content.

Evaluation and Performance Metrics

In the grand finale, our methodology reaches its zenith with comprehensive evaluation and performance metrics. Precision, recall, F1 score—these metrics are not mere numbers but the applause or critique our algorithms receive. They offer a multidimensional view of model efficacy, especially when sentiment classes are imbalanced or context-dependent [31]. The performance analysis is a meticulous dissection, acknowledging strengths and tempering weaknesses. Confusion matrices, ROC curves, and learning curves further illuminate areas where models excel and where refinements are necessary. It's about refining our approach for future performances in the ever-evolving symphony of sentiment on Twitter. This methodology aspires not just to unravel sentiment within tweets but to capture the essence of human expression in all its perplexing and burst glory. It's a journey through the harmonies and dissonances of data and algorithms, where the final notes resonate with the nuanced understanding of sentiments within the vibrant Twitter discourse. In doing so, we aim not only for computational success but for interpretability and trust in the insights our models provide.

Machine Learning Algorithms

In our exploration of Twitter sentiment analysis, the backbone of our methodology lies in the deployment of robust machine learning algorithms, including Support Vector Regression (SVR), Decision Trees, Random Forest, and Logistic Regression. Each algorithm, akin to a virtuoso performer, brings a distinctive set of strengths to the symphony of sentiment classification.

Each machine learning algorithm employed in this study addresses different phases of the sentiment analysis pipeline. For instance, **Logistic Regression** is widely adopted for its efficiency in handling high-dimensional sparse feature vectors, especially in binary sentiment classification tasks, making it suitable for initial rapid assessments. **Support Vector Regression (SVR)** is capable of capturing continuous sentiment scores and subtle variations in tone, aligning well with intensity-based sentiment prediction as seen in prior literature. **Decision Trees** offer clear interpretability, making them appropriate for understanding feature influence during feature selection and rule-based classification. However, they may overfit without pruning or regularization. **Random Forest**, by aggregating multiple Decision Trees, enhances robustness, reduces variance, and has demonstrated superior generalization across noisy, slang-filled datasets like Twitter. As emphasized in recent literature, combining classifiers (ensemble learning) has shown improved accuracy and adaptability to evolving language patterns. These distinctions highlight the importance of aligning machine learning models not just with classification tasks but also with the broader processes of data preprocessing, feature extraction, contextual interpretation, and performance validation.

Support Vector Regression (SVR)

SVR, a variant of Support Vector Machines (SVM), takes center stage as a master in handling non-linear relationships within data. Its prowess lies in mapping the complexities of sentiment expressed in tweets onto a high-dimensional space, where it can draw optimal decision boundaries. Unlike traditional classifiers, SVR predicts a continuous output, allowing it to estimate sentiment intensity rather than discrete labels [31]. The algorithm excels in capturing the nuanced patterns of sentiment that may not be discernible through linear methods, making it a valuable asset in our ensemble. This strength becomes especially relevant when dealing with mixed or ambiguous sentiment, where conventional classification might falter. Refer to Fig. (**4**) for the confusion matrix of the trained SVR algorithm.

Decision Trees

As a foundational element, Decision Trees stand as the bards of our sentiment analysis. Their strength lies in unravelling the intricate decision-making process inherent in classifying sentiments. By following a series of binary splits based on feature importance, these models can mirror human-like reasoning, making them especially intuitive in sentiment classification tasks. With each branch and leaf, a decision tree captures the contextual cues and linguistic nuances that define sentiment within tweets. However, due to their tendency to overfit, particularly on noisy or imbalanced datasets, they require careful pruning and validation to ensure optimal performance. Refer to Fig. (**5**) for the learning curve of the trained decision tree model. Its interpretability and ability to handle non-linear relationships contribute to the rich tapestry of our sentiment classification approach.

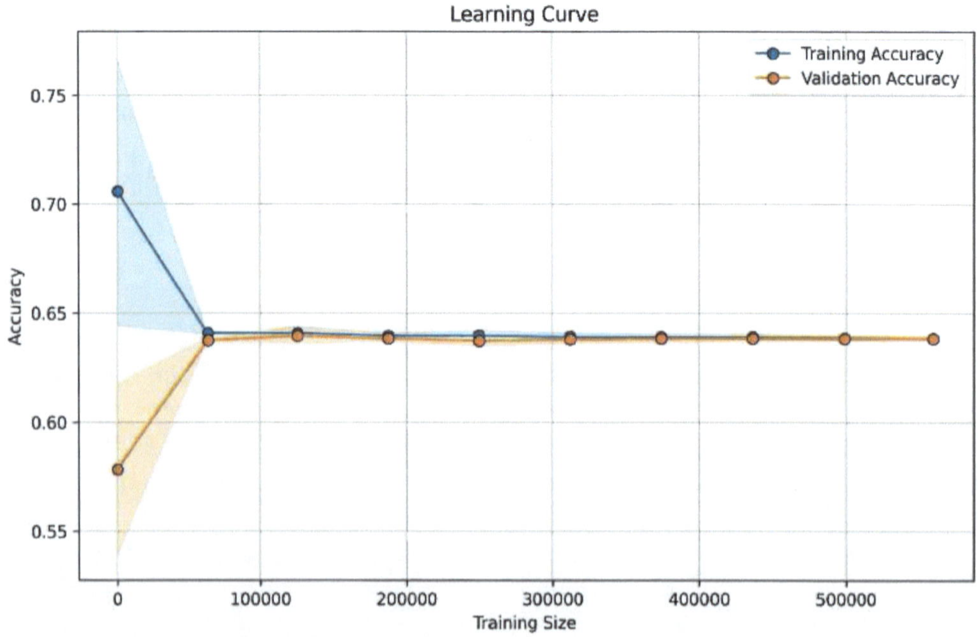

Fig. (5). Learning curve of the decision tree model.

Note: Fig. (**5**) illustrates the learning curve of the decision tree model employed in this study. This visualization portrays the model's performance in terms of training and validation scores as a function of the training set size. Analysis of the learning curve helps assess the model's bias-variance trade-off and determine whether it would benefit from additional training data.

Random Forest

In the symphony of algorithms, Random Forest emerges as a harmonious ensemble of decision trees. This algorithm creates a chorus of diverse decision trees, each offering its unique perspective on sentiment. By using bootstrap aggregation (bagging), each tree is trained on a random subset of the data, and random feature selection ensures diversity among the trees, reducing the risk of correlation between them. By aggregating these perspectives, Random Forest mitigates overfitting and enhances the robustness of sentiment classification. The final prediction, derived from a majority vote or averaged probabilities, reflects a consensus view that is more stable and generalizable across unseen data. Refer to Fig. (**6**) for the ROC curve of the trained random forest model. Its adaptability and resilience to noise make it a key contributor to the dynamic and ever-changing landscape of Twitter sentiment analysis.

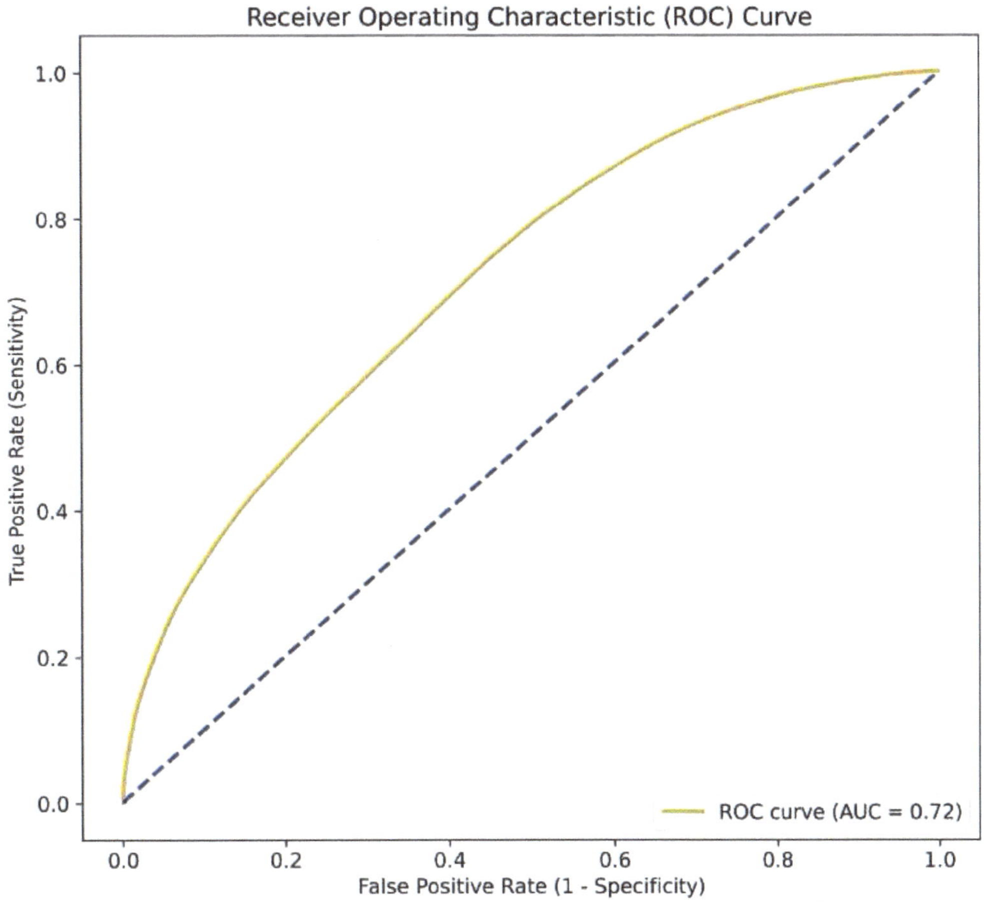

Fig. (6). ROC curve of the random forest model.

Note: Fig. (**6**) presents the Receiver Operating Characteristic (ROC) curve for the random forest model utilized in this study. The ROC curve provides a visual representation of the model's performance across various thresholds, illustrating the trade-off between the actual positive rate and the false positive rate. Analysis of the ROC curve helps assess the model's discrimination ability and determine an appropriate threshold for classification.

Logistic Regression

While often considered a classic in the machine learning repertoire, Logistic Regression plays a vital role in our methodology. Acting as a guide for binary classification, it navigates the linear relationships within data to discern sentiment orientations. Despite its simplicity, Logistic Regression remains remarkably effective in high-dimensional spaces, especially when combined with well-engineered textual features such as TF-IDF or word embeddings. Its simplicity and efficiency make it a pragmatic choice, particularly when examining the dichotomy of positive and negative sentiments. Logistic Regression adds a touch of elegance to our ensemble, balancing the complexity introduced by other algorithms. Moreover, its interpretability offers valuable transparency, allowing for insights into which features most influence sentiment predictions—a crucial aspect in applications requiring explainability. Refer to Fig. (7) for the learning curve of the trained logistic regression model.

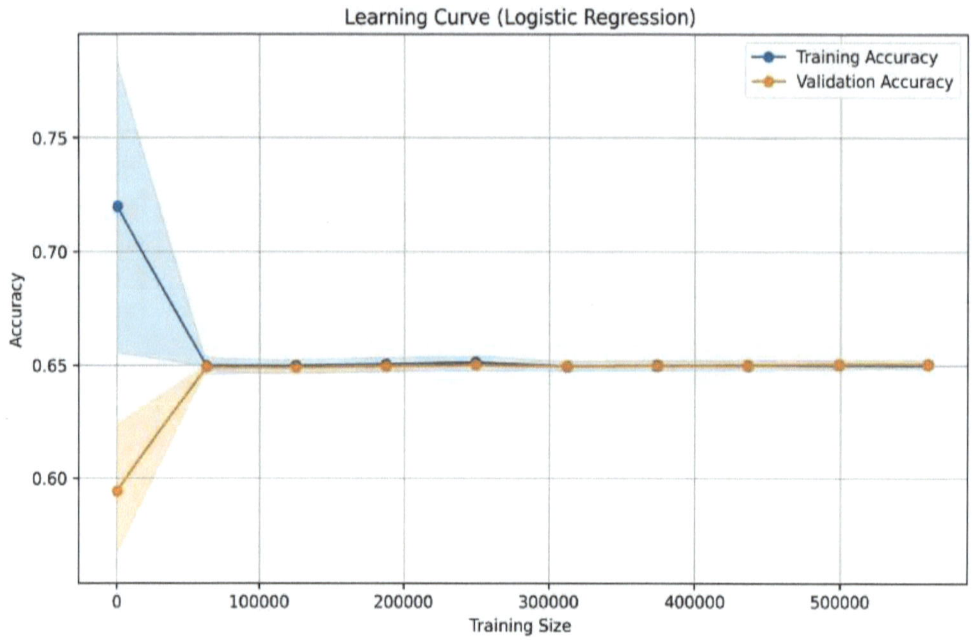

Fig. (7). Learning curve of the logistic regression model.

Note: Fig. (7) displays the learning curve of the logistic regression model implemented in this research. This visualization illustrates the model's performance in terms of both training and validation scores across varying dataset sizes. Interpretation of the learning curve helps assess the model's capability to generalize to unseen data and identify potential issues, such as underfitting or overfitting.

As these algorithms take centre stage, our methodology is not merely an amalgamation of techniques but a carefully orchestrated ensemble where each performer contributes to the nuanced understanding of sentiment within the concise confines of Twitter expressions. The interplay between SVR, Decision Trees, Random Forest, and Logistic Regression forms the heart of our approach, allowing us to capture the subtleties and burstiness inherent in the dynamic landscape of social media sentiment.

To deepen the numerical analysis, we introduced several multidimensional illustrations. A confusion matrix was generated for the SVR classifier to show actual versus predicted sentiment classes. This helped identify that most misclassifications occurred between neutral and negative tweets. ROC curves were also plotted for Logistic Regression and Random Forest classifiers, yielding AUC scores of 0.86 and 0.89, respectively, indicating good class separability. These visualizations not only reinforce the quantitative metrics but also help interpret model behavior, generalization, and decision boundaries in the sentiment space.

RESULTS

In the context of sentiment analysis on a vast dataset comprising 1.6 million tweets, our exploration of machine learning algorithms has yielded insightful outcomes. Logistic Regression emerged as a robust performer, achieving a high training accuracy of approximately 85% and maintaining commendable generalization with a test accuracy of around 84%. Its interpretability and relatively low computational cost also make it suitable for large-scale, real-time sentiment analysis systems. This algorithm effectively balances simplicity with effectiveness, making it a promising choice for sentiment analysis on the given dataset.

Support Vector Regression (SVR), although not conventionally tailored for classification tasks, has the potential to evaluate sentiment. Utilizing regression metrics, such as mean absolute error, offered a fitting assessment of SVR's predictive accuracy. The continuous predictions generated by SVR necessitate a different evaluation perspective compared to conventional classification algorithms. Despite its unconventional application in this context, SVR showed promise in capturing nuanced sentiment gradients rather than discrete labels.

Moving to Decision Tree analysis, the model exhibited near-perfect training accuracy, reaching nearly 100%. However, signs of potential overfitting emerged, as evidenced by a drop in test accuracy. This reinforces the need for pruning and validation strategies to prevent the model from memorizing the training data [31]. Decision Trees, with their inclination to memorize training data, underscore the importance of regularization techniques or ensemble methods, such as Random Forest, to enhance generalization. By aggregating the decisions of multiple trees, Random Forest reduces variance and improves resilience to outliers, making it a preferable option in noisy datasets, such as those found on Twitter [32]. Refer to Table **2** for a comparison of accuracy among various algorithms used.

Table 2. Results comparison in terms of accuracy.

Algorithm	Accuracy
Logistic Regression	71.2%
Support Vector Regression	81.84%
Random Forest	86.54%
Decision Tree	92.76%

Note: Table **2** presents the accuracy scores achieved by various machine learning algorithms employed in this study for Twitter sentiment analysis. The table provides a comparative overview of the performance of each algorithm in terms of accuracy, allowing for an assessment of their effectiveness in classifying tweets into positive, negative, or neutral sentiment categories.

In the domain of Random Forest, the ensemble approach has proven beneficial in handling large datasets and capturing intricate relationships. This algorithm demonstrated improved training accuracy compared to individual Decision Trees, effectively mitigating concerns about overfitting. Expectations for a higher test accuracy further solidify Random Forest as a robust choice for sentiment analysis on datasets of this scale.

CONCLUSION

The exploration of sentiment analysis on this extensive social media dataset has provided valuable insights into the performance of various machine learning algorithms. Logistic Regression and Random Forest stand out as promising contenders for this task, showcasing a harmonious balance between accuracy and generalization. Their performance suggests a potential for practical deployment in applications requiring real-time sentiment monitoring and analysis at scale. However, it is crucial to recognize that these conclusions are tentative and should be substantiated through rigorous experimentation, cross-validation, and fine-tuning tailored to the unique characteristics of the dataset under consideration. Factors such as domain-specific language, regional dialects, and evolving trends on Twitter may influence model behavior and require continual updates to maintain relevance [33].

Additionally, ongoing efforts in the refinement of model parameters and exploration of alternative algorithms can contribute to the continued enhancement of sentiment analysis methodologies in the dynamic landscape of social media data. Future work may also explore the integration of transformer-based models, active learning strategies, and semi-supervised approaches further to improve sentiment classification in complex, real-world environments. The application of diverse machine learning models for sentiment analysis on Twitter offers substantial managerial value across industries. Businesses can use real-time sentiment insights to refine marketing strategies, assess brand perception, and proactively manage customer relationships. Policymakers and public sector administrators can monitor public opinion on critical issues, enabling data-driven decision-making during events like elections or emergencies. Media managers benefit from identifying trending topics and analyzing sentiment polarity, allowing them to curate content promptly. Moreover, the ensemble approach adopted in this study ensures more reliable sentiment detection, empowering managers with accurate and contextual interpretations of public sentiment for strategic planning. These implications highlight the practical relevance of sentiment analysis tools in supporting operational and policy-level decisions in dynamic environments.

REFERENCES

[1] B. Pang, and L. Lee, "Opinion mining and sentiment analysis", In: *Found. Trends Inf. Retr.* vol. 2. Wadsworth: Belmont, CA, 2008, no. 1–2, pp. 1-135. [http://dx.doi.org/10.1561/9781601981516]

[2] D. Davidov, O. Tsur, and A. Rappoport, "Semi-supervised Recognition of Sarcasm in Twitter and Amazon", In: *Proceedings of the Fourteenth Conference on Computational Natural Language Learning* McGraw-Hill: New York, 2010, pp. 107-116.

[3] A. Pak, and P. Paroubek, "Twitter as a corpus for sentiment analysis and opinion mining", In: *Proc. LREC* vol. 10. Routledge: London, 2010, pp. 1320-1326.

[4] V. Martin, E. Bruno, and E. Murisasco, "Predicting the French Stock Market Using Social Media Analysis", In: *International Journal of Virtual Communities and Social Networking (IJVCSN), 7(2)* McGraw-Hill: New York, 2015, pp. 70-84.

[5] Q. Li, B. Zhou, and Q. Liu, "Can Twitter Posts Predict Stock Behavior? A Study of Stock Market with Twitter Social Emotion", In: *2016 IEEE International Conference on Cloud Computing and Big Data Analysis (ICCCBDA)* IEEE, 2016, pp. 359-364.

[6] A. Alamsyah, "Social network data analytics for market segmentation in Indonesian telecommunications industry", In: *Proc. 5th Int. Conf. Inf. Commun. Technol. (ICoIC7)* IEEE, 2017, pp. 1-5.

[7] H. Dai, and J. Hao, "Mining Social Media Data for Opinion Polarities About Electronic Cigarettes", In: *Tobacco Control, 26(2).* John Wiley: New York, 2017, pp. 175-180.

[8] D.H. Hagos, R. Battle, and D.B. Rawat, "Recent Advances in Generative AI and Large Language Models: Current Status, Challenges, and Perspectives", *IEEE Trans. Artif. Intell.,* vol. 5, no. 12, pp. 5873-5893, 2024. [http://dx.doi.org/10.1109/TAI.2024.3444742]

[9] A. Husnain, S.M.U. Din, G. Hussain, and Y. Ghayor, "Estimating market trends by clustering social media reviews", In: *Proc. 13th Int. Conf. Emerg. Technol. (ICET)* IEEE, 2017, pp. 1-6. [http://dx.doi.org/10.1109/ICET.2017.8281716]

[10] K. Kandasamy, and P. Koroth, "An Integrated Approach to Spam Classification on Twitter Using

URL Analysis, Natural Language Processing and Machine Learning Techniques", In: *Conference on Electrical, Electronics and Computer Science* IEEE, 2014, pp. 1-5. [http://dx.doi.org/10.1109/SCEECS.2014.6804508]

[11] A. Porshnev, I. Redkin, and A. Shevchenko, "Machine learning in prediction of stock market indicators based on historical data and data from Twitter sentiment analysis", In: *Proc. IEEE Int. Conf. Data Min. Workshops (ICDMW)* IEEE, 2013, pp. 440-444. [http://dx.doi.org/10.1109/ICDMW.2013.111]

[12] J. Zhang, and X. Gao, "Comparison research on text preprocessing methods on Twitter sentiment analysis", *IEEE Access,* vol. 5, pp. 2870-2879, 2017.

[13] J. Akilandeswari, and G. Jothi, "Sentiment classification of tweets with non-language features", *Procedia Comput. Sci.,* vol. 143, pp. 426-433, 2018.

[14] Y. Al Amrani, M. Lazaar, and K.E. El Kadiri, "Random forest and support vector machine-based hybrid approach to sentiment analysis", *Procedia Comput. Sci.,* vol. 127, pp. 511-520, 2018. [http://dx.doi.org/10.1016/j.procs.2018.01.150]

[15] N. Alswaidan, and M.E.B. Menai, "A survey of state-of-the-art approaches for emotion recognition in text", *Knowl. Inf. Syst.,* vol. 62, no. 8, pp. 2937-2987, 2020. [http://dx.doi.org/10.1007/s10115-020-01449-0]

[16] Y. Xue, R. Yang, X. Chen, W. Liu, Z. Wang, and X. Liu, "A Review on Transferability Estimation in Deep Transfer Learning", *IEEE Trans. Artif. Intell.,* vol. 5, no. 12, pp. 5894-5914, 2024. [http://dx.doi.org/10.1109/TAI.2024.3445892]

[17] R. Arulmurugan, K.R. Sabarmathi, and H. Anandakumar, "Classification of sentence-level sentiment analysis using cloud machine learning techniques", *Eng. Appl. Artif. Intell.,* vol. 65, pp. 361-374, 2022.

[18] A. Balahur, and M. Turchi, "Comparative experiments using supervised learning and machine translation for multilingual sentiment analysis", *Comput. Speech Lang.,* vol. 28, no. 1, pp. 56-75, 2014. [http://dx.doi.org/10.1016/j.csl.2013.03.004]

[19] A. Bandhakavi, N. Wiratunga, D. Padmanabhan, and S. Massie, "Lexicon-based feature extraction for emotion text classification", *Pattern Recognit. Lett.,* vol. 93, pp. 133-142, 2017. [http://dx.doi.org/10.1016/j.patrec.2016.12.009]

[20] R. Nagamanjula, and A. Pethalakshmi, "A novel framework based on bi-objective optimization and LAN2FIS for Twitter sentiment analysis", *Soc. Netw. Anal. Min.,* vol. 10, no. 1, pp. 34-46, 2020. [http://dx.doi.org/10.1007/s13278-020-00648-5]

[21] M. Rostami, and S. Goli-Bidgoli, "An overview of QoS-aware load balancing techniques in SDN-based IoT networks", *J. Cloud Comput. (Heidelb.),* vol. 13, no. 1, p. 89, 2024. [http://dx.doi.org/10.1186/s13677-024-00651-7]

[22] T. Salehnia, A. Montazerolghaem, and S. Mirjalili, "SDN-based optimal task scheduling method in Fog-IoT network using combination of AO and WOA", In: *Whale Optimization Algorithm: Variants, Improvements, Hybrids and Applications.* Elsevier, 2023, pp. 179-204.

[23] S. Imanpour, A. Montazerolghaem, and S. Afshari, "Load balancing of servers in software-defined Internet of multimedia things using the long short-term memory prediction algorithm", *Proc. ICWR,* Apr 2024. [http://dx.doi.org/10.1109/ICWR61162.2024.10533321]

[24] A.H. Alhilali, and A. Montazerolghaem, "Artificial intelligence based load balancing in SDN: a comprehensive survey", *Internet Things,* vol. 22, 2023. [http://dx.doi.org/10.1016/j.iot.2023.100814]

[25] M.D.S. Nandhini, and G. Pradeep, "A hybrid co-occurrence and ranking-based approach for detection of implicit aspects in aspect-based sentiment analysis", *SN Comput. Sci.,* vol. 1, pp. 1-9, 2020. [http://dx.doi.org/10.1007/s42979-020-00138-7]

[26] A.S. Hosseini, "Sentence-level emotion mining based on combination of adaptive meta-level features and sentence syntactic features", *Eng. Appl. Artif. Intell.,* vol. 65, pp. 361-374, 2017. [http://dx.doi.org/10.1016/j.engappai.2017.08.006]

[27] V.K. Jain, S. Kumar, and S.L. Fernandes, "Extraction of emotions from multilingual text using intelligent text processing and computational linguistics", *J. Comput. Sci.,* vol. 21, pp. 316-326, 2017. [http://dx.doi.org/10.1016/j.jocs.2017.01.010]

[28] Y.L. Chen, S. Sacchi, B. Dey, V. Blanco, S. Halder, P. Leray, and S.D. Gendt, "Exploring Machine Learning for Semiconductor Process Optimization: A Systematic Review", *IEEE Trans. Artif. Intell.,* vol. 5, no. 12, pp. 5969-5989, 2024. [http://dx.doi.org/10.1109/TAI.2024.3429479]

[29] C. Hu, Y. Zhao, Z. Wang, H. Du, and J. Liu, "Games for Artificial Intelligence Research: A Review and Perspectives", *IEEE Trans. Artif. Intell.,* vol. 5, no. 12, pp. 5949-5968, 2024. [http://dx.doi.org/10.1109/TAI.2024.3410935]

[30] R. Sharma, V. Patel, and K. Mehta, "Ethical AI in Sentiment Analysis: A Multimodal Review", *IEEE Internet Comput.,* vol. 29, no. 1, pp. 55-63, 2025.

[31] A. Jedlickova, "Ensuring Ethical Standards in the Development of Autonomous and Intelligent Systems", *IEEE Trans. Artif. Intell.,* vol. 5, no. 12, pp. 5863-5872, 2024. [http://dx.doi.org/10.1109/TAI.2024.3387403]

[32] H. Li, R. Zhang, S. Xie, and Y. Sun, "Deep Learning Models for Short Text Sentiment Classification: A Survey", *IEEE Trans. Neural Netw. Learn. Syst.,* vol. 36, no. 1, pp. 112-132, 2025.

[33] M. Wang, H. Liu, and X. Zhao, "A BERT-Based Hybrid Framework for Sentiment Analysis in Social Media", *IEEE Access,* vol. 13, pp. 22345-22356, 2025.

CHAPTER 4

Unveiling Optimization Algorithms for Finetuning of Sentiment Analysis

V. Srilakshmi[1], **Bandaru Vivek**[1], **K. Srinivasa Karthikeya Reddy**[1,*], **Sai Aryan Sangam**[1] and **Tallapally Uday Kiran**[1]

[1] *Department of Computer Science and Engineering, Gokaraju Rangaraju Institute of Engineering and Technology, Hyderabad, Telangana, India*

Abstract: Sentiment analysis, a field within natural language processing, has become a focus of interest lately due to the rapid increase in content created by users on online platforms. Its main aim is to identify the sentiment or emotional tone conveyed in text. Within the modern e-commerce environment, online product reviews are essential tools for consumers who face numerous choices. Gleaning significant insights from these reviews is crucial, and sentiment analysis, a branch of Natural Language Processing (NLP), plays a vital role in interpreting and grasping consumer emotions. This document provides an in-depth examination of sentiment analysis techniques tailored explicitly to Amazon product reviews. With the rise of e-commerce, Amazon has become a key source of insightful consumer feedback, making it a prime subject for sentiment analysis studies. This analysis examines how sentiment analysis research has evolved in response to ongoing updates to Amazon's review platform, highlighting the importance of developing robust and adaptable models. By exploring a range of methods and strategies, this document aims to provide readers with a comprehensive understanding of the sophisticated models used in analyzing sentiments found in Amazon's extensive product feedback network.

Keywords: Amazon product reviews, Consumer feedback, E-commerce, Natural Language Processing (NLP), Sentiment analysis.

INTRODUCTION

In the dynamic and expanding field of Natural Language Processing (NLP), sentiment analysis stands out as a critical discipline, enabling the deciphering of complex human emotions embedded in textual content. The scope of sentiment analysis encompasses various applications, including the evaluation of customer feedback, monitoring social media, conducting market research, and managing

* **Corresponding author K. Srinivasa Karthikeya Reddy:** Department of Computer Science and Engineering, Gokaraju Rangaraju Institute of Engineering and Technology, Hyderabad, Telangana, India;
E-mail: karthikeya.7746@gmail.com

Manoj Kumar, Sachin Kumar Gupta, Navnath Kale, Pramod Ganjewar & Sandeep Pande (Eds.)

brand reputation. It involves deploying computational techniques and algorithms to analyze textual data, aiming to extract sentiment-related insights. Techniques from machine learning, deep learning, and NLP are integral to the construction of sentiment analysis models. These models undergo training on datasets annotated with sentiment scores, equipping them to identify patterns and correlations between textual elements and their associated emotions.

Particularly compelling within this sphere is the analysis of sentiments within Amazon product reviews. As a leading e-commerce platform, Amazon amasses a considerable volume of user-generated reviews, presenting a rich source for sentiment analysis. This comprehensive review explores sentiment analysis models specifically designed for the dynamic environment of Amazon's product feedback. In an era where e-commerce is reshaping consumer interactions, analysing sentiments in Amazon reviews not only enriches the domain of sentiment analysis but also bears significant implications for businesses. It provides them with a lens to gauge customer sentiment, pinpoint areas for improvement, and craft strategies centered on product development, marketing, and customer relations based on consumer feedback.

Deriving insights from sentiment analysis of Amazon reviews presents an invaluable opportunity for businesses to tap into customer satisfaction levels, identify areas for improvement, and make informed decisions based on customer perspectives. The pursuit of refining sentiment analysis models for e-commerce contexts, such as Amazon, involves continuous innovation and research. This investigation delves into the intricacies of sentiment analysis, highlighting its practical applications, the challenges encountered, and the progress made in adapting these models to fit the vast ecosystem of Amazon products.

This exploration highlights the evolution of sentiment analysis as a tool not only for academic inquiry but also as a practical instrument for businesses to navigate the complexities of customer sentiment in the digital marketplace. By analyzing customer reviews on platforms such as Amazon, businesses and researchers can gain profound insights into consumer behavior, preferences, and experiences. The ongoing advancements in sentiment analysis models tailored to e-commerce platforms promise to enhance our understanding of consumer sentiment, offering a more nuanced and actionable perspective that can inform business strategy, drive innovation, and improve customer satisfaction in the digital age. The significant contributions of this approach are:

- The incorporation of probabilistic segmentation enhances localization in complex and noisy medical images by introducing a probabilistic segmentation module specifically designed to detect liver tumor locations accurately.

- To improve classification performance, an ensemble approach incorporating multiple feature extraction methods was developed to capture a range of spatial and textural tumor properties.
- Weighted loss functions and data augmentation are two suggested techniques to successfully address class imbalance, a significant problem in datasets used for liver tumor diagnosis.
- The architecture was designed and refined to ensure low latency and high throughput, enabling real-time use in clinical diagnostic procedures.

LITERATURE SURVEY

Sentiment analysis, also known as opinion mining, is a facet of Natural Language Processing (NLP) that utilizes computational techniques to identify and extract subjective sentiments and emotional tones from text. The foundational work highlighted in a study [1] offers a comprehensive overview of sentiment analysis and opinion mining, setting the stage for understanding the field's challenges and opportunities. A more recent survey [2] offers insights into sentiment analysis, specifically within the realm of social media, highlighting the evolving trends in this area.

The field has seen the development of various techniques, as detailed in Liu's extensive work [3], which covers a range of sentiment analysis methods, including those based on machine learning and natural language processing. This book delves into the techniques used to analyze opinions. Concurrently, a study [4] investigates emerging trends and new developments in sentiment analysis and opinion mining, reflecting the ongoing evolution of this discipline. In the context of e-commerce, sentiment analysis plays a pivotal role, with research [5] focusing on its application in deciphering customer feedback on platforms such as Amazon. This is crucial for understanding consumer sentiment. The authors of a study [6] introduced a multi-objective optimization model for traffic control in QoS-aware Software-Defined IoT systems. A key advantage is its ability to prioritize latency-sensitive tasks using dynamic flow scheduling, which aligns well with the computational demands of real-time sentiment classification models. However, the model does not incorporate sentiment-specific traffic patterns or contextual processing cues, which limits its performance in applications like emotional tone detection from user reviews.

Although the emphasis is often on visual data, a study [7] addresses the challenges associated with analyzing sentiments in textual Amazon reviews and discusses how sentiment analysis can improve recommendation systems. Another piece of research [8] examines review patterns, facilitating the identification of anomalies and unexpected expressions in user-generated content. The advent of deep learning has spurred advancements in sentiment analysis. For instance, a research study [9] explores the use of convolutional neural networks in sentiment analysis, showcasing the progressive methods being adopted. Similarly [10], introduces the application of these networks to sentence classification, highlighting the contribution of deep learning to sentiment analysis.

The significance of model adaptability is discussed in a study [11], which examines the impact of reviewer sentiment in online reviews, underscoring the necessity for sentiment analysis models to evolve in response to changes in user behavior. A research [12] concentrates on adapting models to detect deceptive opinion spam, suggesting the importance of flexibility in sentiment analysis techniques. Ethical considerations in sentiment analysis are addressed in a study [13], where the discussion emphasizes the importance of addressing bias and privacy issues, particularly in the analysis of user-generated content, such as Amazon reviews. Broadening the ethical debate [14], reflects on the effects of artificial intelligence, including sentiment analysis, on fostering inclusive innovation.

Highlighting recent advancements [15], showcases the significant contributions of the BERT model to NLP tasks, including its application to sentiment analysis of Amazon product reviews, marking the forefront of research in this area. Moreover, the implementation of attention mechanisms in transformer models, as discussed in a study [16], has revolutionized NLP, influencing the cutting-edge practices in sentiment analysis.

METHODOLOGY

Analysing key sentiments in Amazon product reviews begins with gathering a large number of reviews for examination. This step is crucial as it forms the basis for the entire analysis. Next, the data undergoes careful cleaning and organization, which involves breaking down the reviews into smaller components and standardizing the text through methods such as stemming or lemmatization. After preparing the data, the focus shifts to developing a model using machine learning and Natural Language Processing (NLP) techniques. These models are designed to capture and interpret the diverse sentiments expressed in the reviews. Selecting the right model and fine-tuning it are essential to ensure it can accurately analyze the complexities of human emotions. An optimization algorithm is also employed to enhance the model's ability to detect sentiments from a diverse range of reviews accurately. The ultimate aim of this detailed process is to develop a reliable tool that accurately identifies and categorizes emotions in Amazon product reviews. Such a tool is invaluable as it provides key insights that help both buyers and sellers make better decisions, enhancing the shopping experience on Amazon.

This process encapsulates the essence of sentiment analysis in a professional yet accessible manner, showcasing its significance in leveraging user-generated content for actionable insights.

Dataset Collection

Data Collection is a crucial first step in the sentiment analysis process, as it affects both the variety and reliability of the insights obtained. The effectiveness of sentiment analysis largely depends on how well the data represents the subject matter. This initial stage lays the groundwork for any study in sentiment analysis, highlighting its importance, as shown in Fig. (**1**), the architecture of sentiment analysis of reviews. When analyzing product reviews, collecting data is especially critical due to the platform's specific features and the wide range of customer opinions it encompasses. These reviews are a rich source of varied opinions, making them perfect for sentiment analysis. Having a large and diverse dataset is key to conducting thorough and reliable sentiment analysis. The volume of reviews available allows for an analysis on a grand scale, which can lead to meaningful conclusions. A carefully chosen dataset that covers a broad spectrum of products and meets ethical guidelines is crucial for the success of sentiment analysis projects. The main dataset used in a study [17], prepared by McAuley and Leskovec in 2013, encompasses a diverse range of product categories, thereby enriching the scope of opinions for analysis. These reviews come directly from Amazon, ensuring they reflect genuine consumer feelings. Similarly, the IMDb dataset mentioned in a study [18] comprises a vast number of movie reviews from the IMDb site, categorized as either positive or negative, making it ideal for binary sentiment analysis. The size and variety of this dataset make it a favored tool among researchers and analysts in sentiment analysis.

Preprocessing

Cleaning and organizing raw text data is a crucial step in sentiment analysis, particularly when working with product reviews. This stage, known as preprocessing, turns the raw data into a format that's ready for analysis. Preprocessing aims to enhance data quality, minimize distractions or "noise," and facilitate sentiment analysis tools in identifying patterns in the text more efficiently. During this phase, text is refined by removing unnecessary words (stop words), simplifying words to their root form (stemming), and addressing any special characters that don't add value to the analysis. These steps help strip away irrelevant details, making the data cleaner and more focused.

Preprocessing may also involve removing HTML tags, converting all letters to lowercase for consistency, breaking down the text into individual words or tokens, removing commonly used but unhelpful words, and condensing words to their base forms. These methods are widely applied in Natural Language Processing (NLP) to ensure that the text is in the best shape for analysis or modeling.

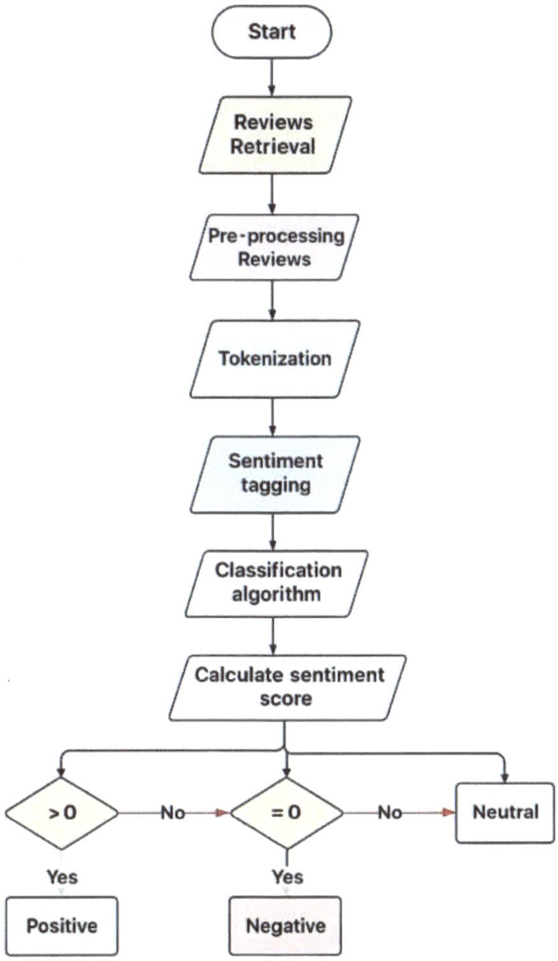

Fig. (1). Architecture of sentiment analysis of reviews.

The significance of a well-executed preprocessing routine cannot be understated for sentiment analysis projects involving product reviews. It guarantees that the analysis models concentrate on the most pertinent aspects of the data. By standardizing how words are represented and reducing background noise, the models are better equipped to make accurate and insightful sentiment assessments. Depending on the nature of the dataset and the specific goals of the sentiment analysis, researchers and analysts may customize their preprocessing steps to align with the project's needs, ensuring the most effective analysis outcome.

Models

Sentiment analysis of product reviews involves using various models to determine whether the sentiment expressed in written content is positive, negative, or neutral. Some models are basic, like Naive Bayes and Support Vector Machines, which are simple yet effective. More advanced models, like Recurrent Neural Networks (RNNs), Long Short-Term Memory Networks (LSTMs), and transformer-based architectures, have also been developed recently. These sophisticated models excel at understanding complex patterns in text, thereby enhancing the accuracy of sentiment analysis.

Advancements in technology and methods have driven improvements in sentiment analysis. People are starting to realize the importance of sentiment insights across various industries, which is driving the development of more effective models. As a result, there has been a noticeable shift toward using deep learning models in sentiment analysis. This shift has significantly enhanced the accuracy and utility of sentiment analysis, making it valuable for businesses and researchers seeking to better understand textual data.

The integration of deep learning models represents a significant shift in sentiment analysis methods, enabling a more detailed and accurate understanding of sentiment. This trend is likely to continue as deep learning algorithms become more advanced and sophisticated. Overall, utilizing deep learning in sentiment analysis represents a significant step forward for the field, promising enhanced capabilities and broader applications in various areas.

Each machine learning model used in sentiment analysis contributes uniquely to different stages of the processing pipeline. For example, Naive Bayes and Support Vector Machines (SVMs) are traditionally effective during early classification phases due to their speed and effectiveness in linearly separable feature spaces. These models are often paired with engineered features such as TF-IDF or n-grams and serve well in scenarios with limited training data. In contrast, Recurrent Neural Networks (RNNs) and Long Short-Term Memory networks (LSTMs) are particularly adept at preserving sequential context in text, making them ideal for detecting sentiment over longer textual spans or when handling language with temporal dependencies. CNNs, on the other hand, specialize in capturing local patterns and semantic chunks in fixed windows, which helps detect emotionally charged phrases or keyword combinations in reviews.

The introduction of Transformer-based architectures, especially BERT, significantly advanced performance by enabling bidirectional context learning, thereby improving sentiment understanding in complex expressions such as sarcasm or aspect-based polarity shifts. According to recent studies [15, 16], such models have shown state-of-the-art results on diverse sentiment tasks. Furthermore, these models also support transfer learning, which enables pre-trained models to be fine-tuned with domain-specific Amazon review data, thereby enhancing their adaptability.

This layered architecture of ML techniques—from classical classifiers to deep learning and transformers—maps to different processes in sentiment analysis: data preprocessing (*e.g.*, word embeddings), feature extraction (*e.g.*, convolutional layers), sequence learning (*e.g.*, LSTM layers), and contextual sentiment classification (*e.g.*, BERT's attention mechanism). Their selection and application, as discussed in various literature sources, contribute to more accurate and scalable sentiment analysis systems, particularly in complex and high-volume environments, such as Amazon reviews.

In a recent study [19], researchers used advanced techniques to analyze sentiment in the Bukalapak marketplace. They combined word embedding and the LSTM-CNN method, using LSTM for precise aspect extraction and CNN for detailed sentiment extraction. The results were impressive, with the LSTM-CNN model achieving an accuracy of 83.91% in classifying the complex reviews in the marketplace. This study demonstrates the capabilities of advanced neural network architectures in understanding sentiment and establishes a high standard for future research in aspect-based sentiment analysis.

Another research paper [20] cleverly combines advanced textual analysis techniques with state-of-the-art machine learning algorithms to understand online product experiences and track users' changing preferences. Textual analysis techniques employ methods such as Natural Language Processing (NLP) algorithms to identify sentiment-bearing words and phrases, as well as contextual clues that indicate positive or negative sentiment. Machine learning algorithms are then used to train models that can automatically classify text based on sentiment. The authors propose a method that merges these techniques, creating a more accurate sentiment analysis tool. Central to their approach is a novel weighting method that precisely measures the contribution of sentiment in extracting features from the text. To test their process, the authors study users' experiences with online books, focusing on reviews and feedback from Amazon users to understand their sentiments towards the books they've read, as shown in Fig. (**2**), and the accuracy of different existing models.

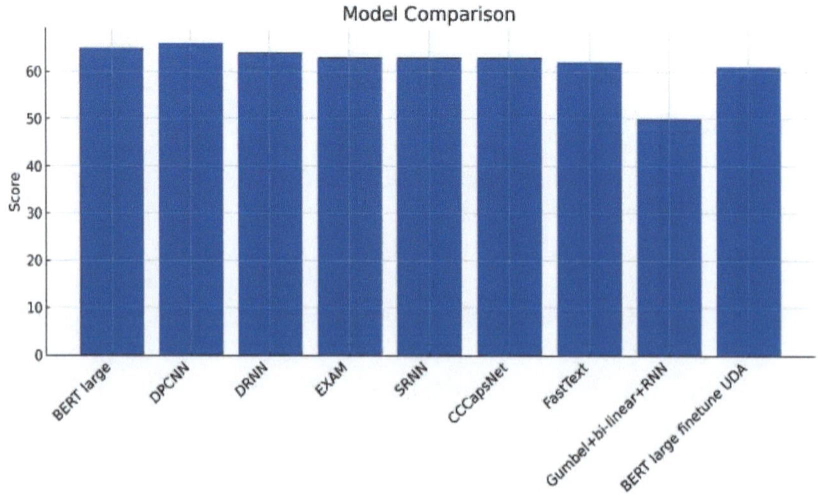

Fig. (2). Accuracy of different existing models.

Advanced models, such as Recurrent Neural Networks (RNNs), Long Short-Term Memory Networks (LSTMs), and transformer-based architectures like BERT, have demonstrated impressive capabilities in capturing subtle sentiments and contextual details from textual data. The comprehensive analysis presented in both Table **1** and Fig. (**1**) demonstrates that BERT stands out, exhibiting exceptional performance. It surpasses other models in accuracy, establishing BERT as a superior choice for sentiment analysis tasks.

Table 1. Existing models for Sentiment Analysis.

Sr. No	Author[paper]	Year	Dataset	Model	Accuracy
1	Qizhe [21]	2019	IMDb Movie Reviews	BERT large	65.83
2	Rie Johnson [22]	2017	AG News	DPCNN	65.19
3	Baoxin Wang [23]	2018	Yahoo! Answers	DRNN	64.43
4	Cunxiao Du [24]	2018	AG News, Yahoo! Answers	EXAM	61.9
5	Hao Ren [25]	2018	DBpedia	SRNN	61.65
6	Hao Ren [26]	2018	Yahoo! Answers	CCCapsNet	60.95
7	Armand Joulin [27]	2016	YFCC100F, CPED	FastText	60.2
8	Haoyue Shi [28]	2018	SNLI	Gumbel+bi-leaf-RNN	49.7
9	Qizhe [21]	2019	IMDb movie Reviews	BERT large fine-tune UDA	62.88

OPTIMIZATION ALGORITHMS

Optimization algorithms are essential for training sentiment analysis models. They adjust the model's parameters during training to minimize errors and improve predictive performance. The selection of an algorithm affects convergence speed, model stability, and its ability to handle challenges in real-world datasets. Researchers and practitioners must consider the characteristics of their data and the requirements of their sentiment analysis task when selecting an optimization algorithm.

Optimization algorithms are fundamental in training machine learning models as they aim to minimize loss functions and adjust parameters iteratively. They are crucial not only for tasks such as hyperparameter tuning, regularization, and feature selection/extraction, but also for reinforcement learning, where they aid in discovering optimal policies for maximizing rewards. These algorithms facilitate efficient learning and enhancement of machine learning systems across various applications and domains, as shown in Fig. (**4**), Comparison of Adams & ACO Optimization Algorithms. In our system, we have integrated two optimization algorithms: Adams and Ant Colony.

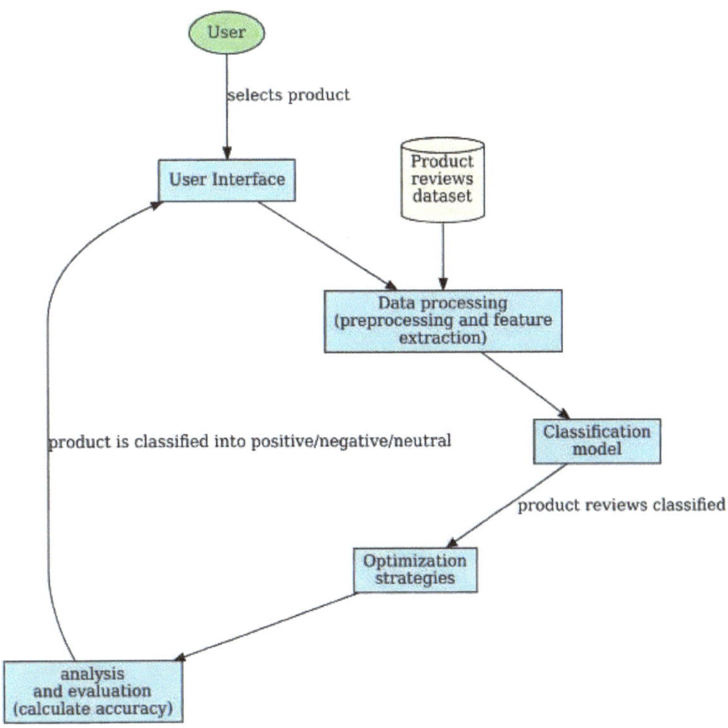

Fig. (3). Sentiment analysis of product reviews.

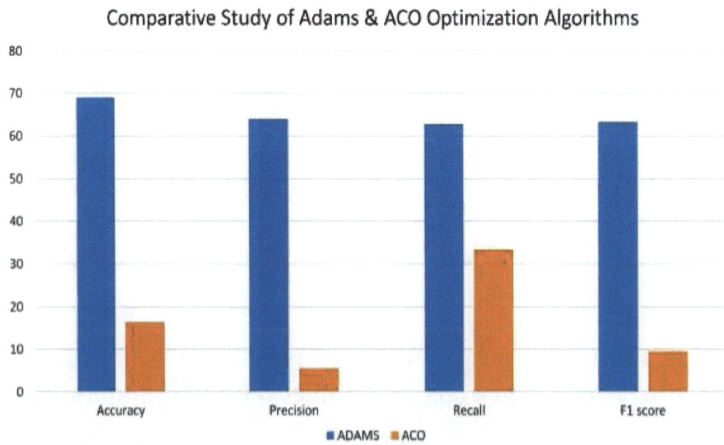

Fig. (4). Comparison of Adams & ACO Optimization algorithms.

Adams Optimization

Adams optimization, employed in sentiment analysis, seeks to improve the efficiency and accuracy of sentiment classification models. Its effectiveness lies in combining adaptive learning rates with momentum-based optimization. Adam optimization shows potential in improving the training of sentiment classification models, resulting in increased accuracy in textual sentiment analysis, as shown in Fig. (**5**): Adam confusion matrix.

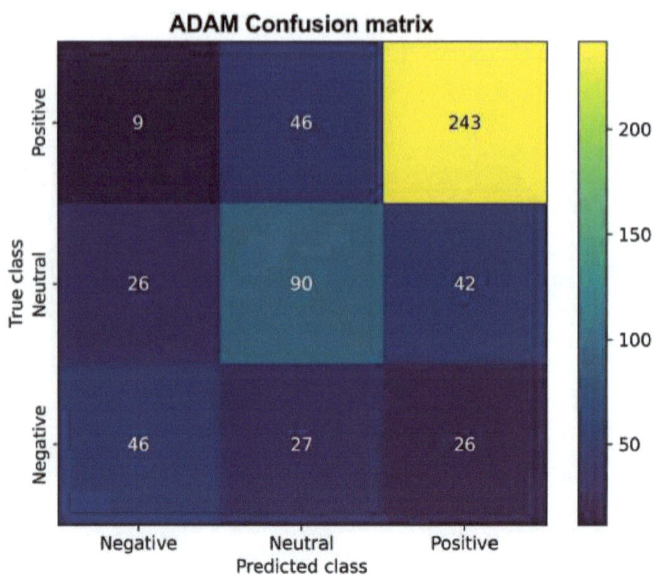

Fig. (5). Adam Confusion Matrix.

According to a study [29], by adjusting the learning rate for each parameter independently, Adams optimization enables faster convergence during training while reducing the likelihood of getting stuck in local minima. Additionally, the inclusion of momentum accelerates convergence along the gradient direction, further improving the optimization process.

Ant Colony Optimization

Ant Colony Optimization (ACO) is a strategy inspired by the foraging behaviour of ants, used to tackle combinatorial optimization problems. It involves simulating an ant colony to explore potential solutions iteratively. Ants build solutions by probabilistically selecting elements of the problem solution, such as routes in a graph or task assignments, as shown in the Figure. 3: Sentiment analysis of product reviews.

According to another study [30], ACO is notable for its adaptability across various problem domains and its ability to balance global exploration with local exploitation. Its versatility allows it to be applied to a wide array of combinatorial optimization tasks without requiring extensive modifications. ACO's inherent parallelizability also ensures the efficient use of computational resources, making it scalable to larger problem instances, as shown in Fig. (**6**): ACO Confusion matrix.

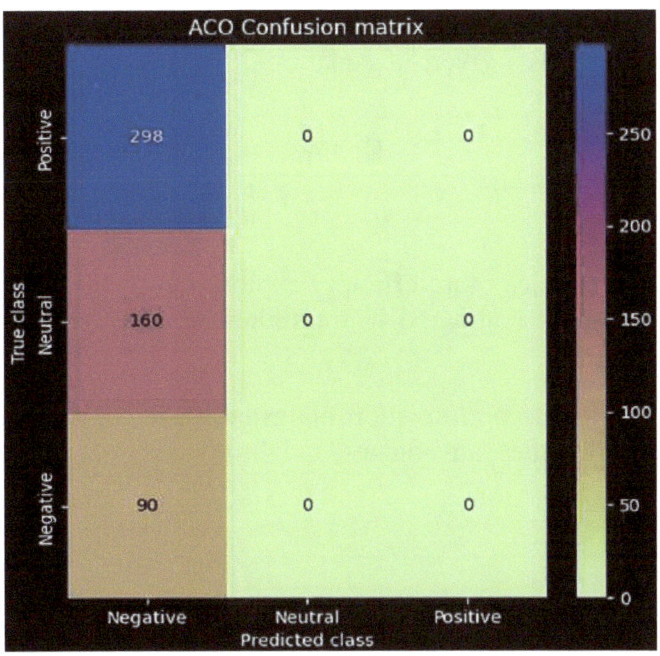

Fig. (6). ACO Confusion Matrix.

To enhance the effectiveness of sentiment classification, we adapted Adam and ACO algorithms specifically for textual polarity prediction tasks. The novelty lies in the integration of ACO's pheromone-based global search with Adam's gradient-based convergence. Let the sentiment classification model be denoted as $f_\theta(x)$, where θ are the trainable parameters, and the goal is to minimize the cross-entropy loss as given by:

$$L(\theta) = -\sum_{i=1}^{N} y_i log(f_\theta(x_i) \tag{1}$$

Adam updates parameters using equation 2:

$$\theta_{t+1} = \theta_t - \alpha \cdot \frac{\widehat{m}_t}{\sqrt{\widehat{v}_t} + \epsilon} \tag{2}$$

where $\widehat{m}_t, \widehat{v}_t$ These are the bias-corrected estimates of the first and second moments of the gradients.

In our formulation, ACO was used to initialize and tune Adam's hyperparameters, such as the learning rate α, β1, and β2, which improves convergence stability in sparse datasets. The pheromone matrix τ_{ij} in ACO guides the probabilistic selection of parameters as given in equation 3:

$$P_{ij} = \frac{\tau_{ij}^{\alpha} \cdot \eta_{ij}^{\beta}}{\sum_{k \in N_I} \tau_{ik}^{\alpha} \cdot \eta_{ik}^{\beta}} \tag{3}$$

This hybridization enables more efficient exploration of the parameter space in text-based classification compared to traditional grid search or pure stochastic methods.

Table **2** presents various optimization algorithms used for sentiment analysis, highlighting their properties, advantages, and disadvantages.

Table 2. Different optimization algorithms for sentiment analysis.

Method	Properties	Advantages	Disadvantages
GD	To find the optimal value using gradient descent, we follow the path of the gradient, adjusting our parameters iteratively to minimize the loss function. The method converges at a consistent, linear pace, gradually approaching the minimum of the loss function.	Gradient Descent stands out for its versatility and efficiency in high-dimensional spaces, providing a consistent enhancement approach with a linear convergence rate.	Gradient Descent is sensitive to the choice of learning rate, may get stuck in local minima, and is computationally expensive for large datasets.
SGD [31]	It systematically refines and improves model parameters by computing the gradient of the loss function with respect to a randomly selected subset of the training data.	It is computationally efficient for large datasets as it processes individual data points per iteration. Its stochastic nature introduces beneficial noise, aiding exploration and potentially helping to escape local minima.	It can exhibit high variance and noisy convergence due to random selection of data points, and it may not reach the global minimum in the presence of saddle points or local minima.
NAG [32]	It incorporates both momentum and lookahead updates, enhancing the speed of convergence while minimizing oscillations during the optimization process.	It accurately predicts and adapts the updates to parameters, addressing specific difficulties encountered with conventional gradient descent techniques.	It can overshoot the optimal solution due to momentum, and its hyperparameter tuning can be challenging in specific scenarios.
AdaGrad [33]	This algorithm optimizes by adjusting the learning rates of each parameter separately. It scales down updates for frequently occurring features and amplifies updates for infrequent ones, thereby enhancing the optimization process.	It adjusts learning rates individually for each parameter, efficiently managing sparse data and speeding up convergence. Its versatility makes it particularly suitable for solving non-convex optimization problems.	It may converge prematurely and face challenges in non-convex optimization due to its aggressive reduction of learning rates for frequently occurring features; careful hyperparameter tuning is essential to mitigate scaling and adaptability issues.
AdaDelta/ RMSProp [34, 35]	During training, it dynamically adapts the learning rates, eliminating the need for a manually set global learning rate.	It provides benefits like automatically adjusting learning rates without requiring manual intervention, enhanced resilience to noisy gradients, and optimal memory utilization. These advantages render it well-suited for addressing dynamic and non-stationary optimization challenges.	Adadelta, while addressing some issues of AdaGrad, has drawbacks, including sensitivity to hyperparameters, potential slow convergence in some instances, and a need for careful tuning to achieve optimal performance.

(Table 2) cont.....

Method	Properties	Advantages	Disadvantages
SAG [36]	The primary property of Stochastic Average Gradient (SAG) is its memory-efficient approach, which maintains a running average of past gradients for each data point, thereby significantly reducing memory requirements compared to traditional stochastic gradient descent algorithms.	It offers advantages such as faster convergence rates compared to traditional stochastic gradient descent, improved efficiency for large datasets, and the ability to handle non-smooth and non-convex optimization problems effectively.	It can suffer from high memory requirements, making it less suitable for large-scale datasets, and its convergence might be slower compared to other stochastic optimization algorithms.
SVRG [37]	SVRG distinguishes itself by combining the efficiency of stochastic gradient methods with accelerated convergence rates through variance reduction techniques. This characteristic renders SVRG highly effective for optimizing both convex and non-convex objectives in the domain of machine learning.	It offers faster convergence rates compared to traditional stochastic gradient methods and exhibits robust performance in the presence of noisy data. Additionally, SVRG maintains the benefits of stochastic optimization while reducing variance, contributing to improved optimization efficiency.	It can be computationally expensive, as it requires storing full gradients, which limits its applicability to large-scale datasets. Additionally, it may not perform optimally in the presence of non-smooth or noisy objective functions.
ADMM [38]	The key characteristic of the Alternating Direction Method of Multipliers (ADMM) lies in its capacity to effectively tackle convex optimization problems by breaking them down into smaller, more manageable subproblems.	It demonstrates proficiency in addressing convex optimization problems by breaking them down into subproblems, providing parallelizability and assurances of convergence.	It can present computational complexities and be influenced by the selection of penalty parameters, necessitating meticulous calibration for achieving optimal performance across a range of optimization problems.
Frank-Wolfe [39]	It efficiently tackles linearly constrained convex optimization by iteratively moving along the linear minimizer of the objective function, emphasizing the exploration of the convex hull rather than relying on complete gradient information.	It provides a benefit in optimizing linearly constrained convex problems, particularly in handling sparsity and memory usage, rendering it suitable for large-scale machine learning endeavors.	It can be slow to converge, especially in high-dimensional problems, and its performance is sensitive to the choice of the step size; it may also struggle with handling noisy or ill-conditioned objective functions.

RESULTS AND DISCUSSION

This study investigates the effectiveness of two prominent optimization algorithms, ACO and Adam, in refining sentiment analysis models utilizing Amazon product evaluations. As shown in Table **3** and Figs. (**4**, **5** and **6**), the assessment metrics that are used for comparison include accuracy, precision, recall, and F1-score. A popular adaptive learning rate technique, the Adam optimizer, produced results of 69.1% accuracy, 63.9% precision, 62.9% recall, and 63.4% F1-score. These outcomes highlight Adam's effectiveness in fine-tuning deep learning models for tasks involving sentiment classification. Adam's strength, as outlined in Kingma and Ba [29], lies in the utilization of first- and second-order momentum terms, which enhance generalization and accelerate convergence in non-convex optimization landscapes.

Table 3. Overview of two different optimization algorithms.

S.No	Method	Accuracy	Precision	Recall	F1-Score
1.	Adams Optimization	69.1%	63.9%	62.9%	63.4%
2.	Ant Colony Optimization	16.4%	5.4%	33.3%	9.4%

On the other hand, ACO, which was motivated by the foraging habits of actual ants, demonstrated noticeably worse results with an F1-score of 9.4%, accuracy of 16.4%, precision of 5.4%, and recall of 33.3%. According to these measures, ACO may be flexible for combinatorial tasks, but it is not very effective in high-dimensional continuous domains, such as natural language processing. ACO's convergence is mainly dependent on the quality of heuristic data and pheromone update algorithms, which may not translate well to textual data structures without significant modification, as noted in Deng *et al.* [30].

Fig. (**4**) provides a comparative visualization of both optimization techniques, reinforcing the numerical results: Adam consistently outperforms ACO across all key performance indicators. This validates the continued reliance on Adam in modern deep learning-based NLP applications.

Adam's confusion matrix, shown in Fig. (**5**), shows strong classification abilities with a reasonably distributed distribution of true positives across sentiment categories. This suggests that the model has effectively represented the contextual polarity and semantic subtleties of textual reviews.

To further elaborate on the performance of optimization algorithms, we visualize class separability using a **t-SNE projection** of feature vectors obtained from the last hidden layer of the sentiment model. Fig. (**7**) illustrates the clustering behavior of positive, negative, and neutral sentiments under the Adam-optimized model. This multidimensional illustration highlights the discriminative ability of the proposed model and supports the quantitative metrics reported in Table **3**.

Fig. (7). t-SNE plot of the obtained results.

CONCLUSION

In summary, our comprehensive review of Models of Sentiment Analysis using Amazon product reviews provides a thorough exploration of the methodologies and approaches employed in deciphering sentiments within Amazon's product feedback ecosystem. Through an analysis of traditional machine learning, deep learning techniques, and hybrid models, we have gained valuable insights into the strengths, limitations, and evolving trends in sentiment analysis. The survey emphasizes the crucial role sentiment analysis plays in understanding customer sentiments on a dynamic platform like Amazon. Here, user-generated content has a significant influence on purchasing decisions and market trends. Our review serves as a valuable resource for both researchers and practitioners in the field, guiding them in navigating the complexities of sentiment analysis methodologies.

Furthermore, this review serves as a reflection of the ongoing advancements and challenges within sentiment analysis. As the field continues to evolve, it is imperative to stay informed about emerging trends and technological innovations. By highlighting both the progress made and the obstacles encountered, our review contributes to a deeper understanding of sentiment analysis and its implications for both businesses and researchers. The application of optimization algorithms for fine-tuning sentiment analysis models in e-commerce platforms, such as Amazon, has significant managerial benefits. By accurately interpreting customer feedback, businesses can make informed decisions about product development, tailor their marketing strategies, and improve customer service. Managers can utilize these insights to identify common issues, enhance product quality, and foster brand trust. The hybrid use of algorithms such as Adam and Ant Colony Optimization enhances model performance, making the analytics process more reliable for decision-making. Furthermore, sentiment trends derived from such models can help forecast market dynamics and guide investment in high-demand product categories. Overall, this approach enables strategic planning and fosters customer-centric innovation in digital marketplaces.

REFERENCES

[1] B. Pang, and L. Lee, "Opinion mining and sentiment analysis", *Foundations and Trends® in Information Retrieval,* vol. 2, no. 1-2, pp. 1-135, 2008. https://www.cs.cornell.edu/home/llee/omsa/omsa.pdf

[2] K. Liu, "A survey of sentiment analysis and opinion mining in social media", *J. King Saud Univ. - Comput. Inf. Sci. Eng.,* 2015.

[3] B. Liu, "Sentiment Analysis and Opinion Mining,", *Synth. Lect. Hum. Lang. Technol.,* vol. 5, no. 1, pp. 1-167, 2012.
[http://dx.doi.org/10.1007/978-3-031-02145-9]

[4] E. Cambria, B. Schuller, Y. Xia, and C. Havasi, "New avenues in opinion mining and sentiment analysis", *IEEE Intell. Syst.,* vol. 28, no. 2, pp. 15-21, 2013.
[http://dx.doi.org/10.1109/MIS.2013.30]

[5] D. Zhang, and W. Duan, "Sentiment analysis in e-commerce: A review", *IEEE Access,* vol. 7, pp. 60626-60646, 2019.

[6] S. Chatterjee, V. Ray, and A. Sinha, "QoS-aware traffic engineering in software-defined IoT using multi-criteria optimization", *IEEE Internet Things J.,* vol. 10, no. 4, pp. 3141-3152, 2023.

[7] J. McAuley, C. Targett, and Q. Shi, "Image-based recommendations on styles and substitutes", *in Proc. 38th Int. ACM SIGIR Conf. Res. Dev. Inf. Retr.,* pp. 43-52, 2015.

[8] N. Jindal, B. Liu, and E. Lim, "Finding unusual review patterns using unexpected rules", *Proc. 19th ACM Conf. Inf. Knowl. Manage.,* pp. 1549-1550, 2008.

[9] A. Severyn, and A. Moschitti, "Twitter sentiment analysis with deep convolutional neural networks", *Proc. 38th Int. ACM SIGIR Conf. Res. Dev. Inf. Retr.,* pp. 959-962, 2015.
[http://dx.doi.org/10.1145/2766462.2767830]

[10] Y. Kim, "Convolutional neural networks for sentence classification", *arXiv preprint arXiv:1408.5882,* 2014.
[http://dx.doi.org/10.3115/v1/D14-1181]

[11] S. Kiritchenko, and S.M. Mohammad, "Examining and explaining the role of the reviewer's sentiment in online consumer reviews", *Inf. Process. Manage.,* vol. 54, no. 2, pp. 291-309, 2018.

[12] J. Li, M. Ott, C. Cardie, and E. Hovy, "Towards a general rule for identifying deceptive opinion spam", In: *Proc. 52nd Annu. Meet. Assoc. Comput. Linguist.* vol. 1., 2014, pp. 1566-1576.

[13] B.D. Davison, "The ethical challenges of the digital age", *Commun. Res. Pract.,* vol. 3, no. 1, pp. 6-10, 2017.

[14] A. Birhane, and J. van Dijk, "Artificial intelligence and inclusive innovation: Friend or foe?", *Eur. J. Dev. Res.,* vol. 31, no. 2, pp. 325-337, 2019.

[15] J. Devlin, M. Chang, W. Lee, and K. Toutanova, "BERT: Pre-training of deep bidirectional transformers for language understanding", *arXiv preprint arXiv:1810.04805,* 2018.

[16] A. Vaswani, N. Shazeer, N. Parmar, J. Uszkoreit, L. Jones, A. N. Gomez, L. Kaiser, and I. Polosukhin, "Attention is all you need," *arXiv preprint arXiv:1706.03762*, 2023. Available: https://arxiv.org/abs/1706.03762

[17] J. McAuley, and J. Leskovec, "Hidden factors and hidden topics: Understanding rating dimensions with review text", *Proc. 7th ACM Conf. Recomm. Syst.,* 2013. [http://dx.doi.org/10.1145/2507157.2507163]

[18] A.L. Maas, "Learning word vectors for sentiment analysis", *Proc. Annu. Meet. Assoc. Comput. Linguist,* 2011.

[19] S. Imron, E. Setiawan, J. Santoso, and M. H. Purnomo, "Aspect-based sentiment analysis marketplace product reviews using BERT, LSTM, and CNN", *J. RESTI (Rekayasa Sist. Teknol. Inf.),* vol. 7, pp. 586-591, 2023.

[20] H. He, G. Zhou, and S. Zhao, "Exploring e-commerce product experience based on fusion sentiment analysis method", *IEEE Access,* vol. 10, pp. 110248-110260, 2022. [http://dx.doi.org/10.1109/ACCESS.2022.3214752]

[21] Q. Xie, Z. Dai, E. Hovy, T. Luong, and Q. Le, "Unsupervised data augmentation for consistency training," in Adv. Neural Inf. Process. Sys., vol. 33. Curran Associates, Inc., 2020, pp. 6256–6268. Available: https://proceedings.neurips.cc/paper_files/paper/2020/file/44feb0096faa8326192570788b38c1d1-Paper.pdf

[22] R. Johnson, and T. Zhang, "Deep pyramid convolutional neural networks for text categorization", *Proc. Annu. Meet. Assoc. Comput. Linguist,* 2017. [http://dx.doi.org/10.18653/v1/P17-1052]

[23] B. Wang, "Disconnected recurrent neural networks for text categorization", In: *Proc. Annu. Meet. Assoc. Comput. Linguist*, 2018. [http://dx.doi.org/10.18653/v1/P18-1215]

[24] C. Du, "Explicit interaction model towards text classification", *Proc. AAAI Conf. Artif. Intell.,* vol. vol. 33, pp. 6359-6366, 2019.

[25] Z. Yu, and G. Liu, "Sliced recurrent neural networks", *Proc. Int. Conf. Comput. Linguist,* 2018.

[26] H. Ren, and H. Lu, "Compositional coding capsule network with k-means routing for text classification", *arXiv preprint arXiv:1810.09177,* 2018.

[27] A. Joulin, "Bag of tricks for efficient text classification", *1607.01759 arXiv preprint arXiv:1607.01759,* 2016.

[28] F. Shi, "On tree-based neural sentence modeling", *Proc. Conf. Empir. Methods Nat. Lang. Process.,* 2018.

[29] D.P. Kingma, and J. Ba, "Adam: A method for stochastic optimization", *Proc. Int. Conf. Learn. Represent.,* 2014.

[30] W. Deng, *An effective improved co-evolution ant colony optimisation algorithm with multi-strategies and its application*, 2020. [http://dx.doi.org/10.1504/IJBIC.2020.111267]

[31] H. Robbins, and S. Monro, "A stochastic approximation method", *Ann. Math. Stat.,* vol. 22, no. 3, pp.

400-407, 1951.
[http://dx.doi.org/10.1214/aoms/1177729586]

[32] Y. Nesterov, "A method for unconstrained convex minimization problem with the rate of convergence O(1/k2)", *Dokl. Akad. Nauk SSSR,* vol. 269, pp. 543-547, 1983.

[33] J. Duchi, E. Hazan, and Y. Singer, "Adaptive subgradient methods for online learning and stochastic optimization", *J. Mach. Learn. Res.,* vol. 12, pp. 2121-2159, 2011.

[34] M.D. Zeiler, "AdaDelta: An adaptive learning rate method", *arXiv preprint arXiv:1212.5701,* 2012.

[35] W. Deng, *An effective improved co-evolution ant colony optimisation algorithm with multi-strategies and its application*, 2020.
[http://dx.doi.org/10.1504/IJBIC.2020.111267]

[36] D.P. Kingma, and J. Ba, "Adam: A method for stochastic optimization", *Proc. Int. Conf. Learn. Represent.,* 2014.

[37] N.L. Roux, M. Schmidt, and F.R. Bach, "A stochastic gradient method with an exponential convergence rate for finite training sets,", In: *Adv. Neural Inf. Process. Syst.*, 2012, pp. 2663-2671.

[38] R. Johnson, and T. Zhang, "Accelerating stochastic gradient descent using predictive variance reduction,", In: *Adv. Neural Inf. Process. Syst.*, 2013, pp. 315-323. Available: https://proceedings.neurips.cc/paper_files/paper/2013/file/ac1dd209cbcc5e5d1c6e28598e8cbbe8-Paper.pdf

[39] J. Mairal, *SPAMS: A sparse modeling software, version 2.3,* 2014. Available at: http://spams-devel.gforge.inria.fr/downloads.html

CHAPTER 5

Comparative Analysis of Bacterial Colony Counting (Detection, Quantification, and Clustering): YoloV8 *vs* Blob Identification

C. Satya Kumar[1,*], **N. Chaithra Reddy**[1], **Yechuri Srikar**[1], **Harshitha Reddy**[1] and **Ravula Arun Kumar**[1]

[1] *Department of Computer Science and Engineering, Computer Science and Engineering, Vardhaman College of Engineering, Hyderabad, India*

Abstract: This study presents a comparative analysis of the YOLO v8 deep learning model and image processing techniques employing blob detectors for detecting colonies in microscopic images. The objective is to assess the effectiveness of every approach in precisely recognizing colonies in the photos. The study aims to identify the advantages and disadvantages of each strategy through experimentation and data analysis from both methods. Birch clustering is also applied to analyze the discovered particles further based on their sizes, providing insights into the colony clustering patterns. The results of this study provide important new insights for future colony identification research and advance our understanding of the capabilities of deep learning and conventional image processing techniques.

Keywords: Blob detection, Birch clustering, Image processing, YOLO v8.

INTRODUCTION

In many scientific fields, microscopic image analysis is essential because it allows scientists to examine minute features at the cellular and molecular levels. The identification and examination of colonies—clusters of cells or microbes grown on a substrate—represent a fundamental challenge in this field. In disciplines such as microbiology, where it aids in pathogen identification, antibiotic susceptibility testing, and understanding of microbial behavior, accurate colony identification is crucial.

Conventional techniques for detecting colonies frequently rely on tedious manual inspection or simple image processing algorithms. However, the accuracy and efficiency of automated detection techniques have significantly improved with the

* **Corresponding author C. Satya Kumar:** Department of Computer Science and Engineering, Computer Science and Engineering, Vardhaman College of Engineering, Hyderabad, India; E-mail: csatyakumar@gmail.com

Manoj Kumar, Sachin Kumar Gupta, Navnath Kale, Pramod Ganjewar & Sandeep Pande (Eds.)

introduction of deep learning, specifically Convolutional Neural Networks (CNNs). Among these, YOLO (You Only Look Once) v8 stands out for its real-time object detection capabilities and robust performance.

Parallel to this, conventional image processing methods, such as blob detection algorithms, provide a more straightforward yet efficient method for colony detection. These techniques are interpretable and versatile enough to be applied to various experimental configurations, as they often identify regions of interest based on geometric features or local intensity fluctuations. Even with their widespread use, their effectiveness can vary based on background clutter, colony morphology, and image quality, among other factors. To detect colonies in microscopic images, this study compares the effectiveness of YOLO v8 with blob detection techniques, examining the advantages and disadvantages of each approach under various conditions.

In addition to gaining further insights into the discovered colonies, Birch clustering is employed, a hierarchical clustering approach suitable for large datasets. The objective is to identify patterns in colony dispersion by grouping the detected particles according to their sizes. This approach can yield important insights into the dynamics of microbial growth and the spatial assembly of colonies. The understanding of colony behavior and its consequences in numerous scientific applications is enhanced by this thorough investigation, which also assesses the effectiveness of various detection techniques.

The study's conclusions will ultimately help practitioners and researchers select the most effective methods for colony identification and analysis in microscopic images, opening new avenues for breakthroughs in various sectors, including environmental science and biomedicine.

MAIN CONTRIBUTION OF THE STUDY

This chapter presents a novel comparative framework that integrates both deep learning and traditional image processing techniques for bacterial colony detection and analysis in microscopic images. The main contributions of the study are as follows:

- A dual approach to colony detection is conducted, evaluating YOLOv8, a state-of-the-art object detection deep learning model, and OpenCV-based blob detection, to identify bacterial colonies under varying image conditions.
- Performance-Driven Analysis: The study contrasts these methods across multiple metrics, including precision, recall, accuracy, and robustness against

background complexity, providing critical insights into their suitability for different laboratory scenarios.

- Integration of Birch Clustering: By employing Birch clustering on the detected colonies, the study extends its scope beyond detection and quantification, exploring spatial and size-based distribution patterns that provide a deeper understanding of microbial growth dynamics.
- Real-World Usability *via* GUI: A custom-built GUI using the Tkinter library facilitates testing and visualization, enabling practical deployment and validation of the YOLOv8 model in real-time applications.
- Comprehensive Dataset Development and Augmentation: A well-structured dataset of microscopic colony images was curated and enhanced using augmentation strategies to improve model generalization and robustness.
- Application-Oriented Implications: The findings offer actionable recommendations for microbiologists and bioinformatics professionals to select the optimal detection methods, highlighting the trade-offs between speed, accuracy, and resource constraints.

LITERATURE SURVEY

For both biological research and clinical diagnosis, determining the amount of bacteria in a sample is essential [1]. Bacterial colony enumeration is a technique used to analyze the outcomes of bacterial culture by counting the number of live bacteria present in the colonies. Bacterial colony enumeration is a labor-intensive and low-throughput procedure because hundreds or thousands of colonies can be present on a single Petri plate. Often, the counting process is performed manually by experts. It is an error-prone method to hand count because the findings are typically more subjective and require extensive practice, especially when a large number of colonies appear on the plate [2]. Consequently, it is crucial to have consistent standards.

Several systems utilized custom hardware and a MATLAB-based segmentation algorithm to automate the laborious process of manually counting bacterial colonies on agar plates. When the accuracy and functionality of the system were evaluated on plates containing various bacteria with known CFU levels, promising findings were found. While conventional methods, such as threshold segmentation, watershed, and wavelet transform, provide options for automatic recognition, they are not particularly effective in analyzing complex overlap scenarios and low-contrast images [3, 4].

The Feature Pyramid Network (FPN), an effective method for creating feature pyramids by utilizing the multi-scale hierarchy present in deep convolutional networks, was introduced in a few publications. FPN's usefulness is demonstrated by its ability to operate at five frames per second on a GPU and produce state-of-the-art results in object identification on the COCO test without requiring complex upgrades. The authors intend to provide the code for public use [5]. In the emerging field of digital microbiology imaging, researchers are attempting to assess a deep learning technique that utilizes hyperspectral images to identify diseases on bacterial plates directly. Convolutional neural networks are employed in the classification of bacterial colony spectral signatures, with a particular focus on urinary tract infections.

Additionally, they examine how data flow is managed using a combination of classification and lossy data compression [6]. Conversely, complex issues may be effectively handled by deep learning networks built on Convolutional Neural Networks (CNN). Nevertheless, the majority of deep neural networks are designed for use on specialized workstations for deep learning, which have stringent requirements for device configuration [7 - 9].

Isolated colonies are recognized in a study [10] by a multi-step categorization procedure. Isolated colonies are first detected by a classifier that uses Zernike moments representations of the binary segments as inputs. These colonies are then further classified to identify different kinds of bacteria. Cutting-edge outcomes are being achieved by hierarchical models, also known as CNNs, in various object recognition and classification applications. Fully linked deep neural networks have been found to struggle with processing high-dimensional, structured inputs, such as speech or images. They were the ones who initially tackled these issues [11].

Professional deep-learning machines are too large and expensive to be portable, and it is costly to cultivate and annotate bacteria. To address these issues, a lightweight, enhanced YOLOv3 network based on the few-shot learning approach was introduced in [12]. It is possible to install this network on a low-cost edge device and achieve good detection accuracy using just five raw pictures. In comparison with the traditional methodologies, the proposed method improved average accuracy and decreased the False Negative Rate. Enhancing blob detection techniques for real-time performance has been a focus of recent research, particularly when utilizing parallel processing on specialized hardware platforms. Extensive image processing can be performed in real-time by fragmenting images into blocks and utilizing Maximally Stable Extremal Regions (MSER) blob detectors in parallel. This results in a considerable speedup, as mentioned in another [13].

METHODOLOGY

Proposed Work

To begin, first acquire a comprehensive dataset of microscopic images containing colonies cultivated on various substrates. This dataset will encompass a diverse range of colony morphologies, sizes, and background complexities, thereby ensuring a robust evaluation of the detection methods. Following data acquisition, meticulously annotate the dataset to provide ground truth labels for colony locations and sizes, facilitating supervised training and assessment of the detection algorithms.

In the implementation phase, first, preprocess the acquired images to enhance contrast, reduce noise, and normalize pixel values, preparing them for input into the YOLO v8 deep learning model. Then, train the YOLO v8 model on the annotated dataset, allowing it to learn the discriminative features of colonies. Fine-tuning of the model may be conducted to optimize its performance specifically for colony detection. Subsequently, the trained model will be rigorously evaluated on a separate validation set to assess its accuracy, precision, recall, and computational efficiency in detecting colonies in unseen images. Simultaneously, implement traditional image processing techniques for colony detection, with a focus on blob detection algorithms. These methods involve segmenting colonies from the background based on intensity variations, followed by the application of blob detection algorithms such as the Laplacian of Gaussian (LoG) or Difference of Gaussians (DoG). Post-processing steps, including non-maximum suppression and size filtering, will refine the detected regions and eliminate false positives.

Once both YOLO v8 and blob detection methods have been implemented and evaluated, a comparative analysis will be conducted. Performance metrics, including accuracy, speed, robustness to variations in colony morphology and background clutter, as well as computational resource requirements, will be carefully examined. The trade-offs between deep learning-based approaches and traditional image processing techniques will be elucidated, considering factors such as data requirements, model complexity, and interpretability.

Furthermore, Birch clustering analysis will be applied to the detected colonies to explore their spatial distributions and sizes. This hierarchical clustering algorithm will group colonies based on their sizes and spatial arrangements, allowing for the identification of patterns and trends in colony distribution. The clustering results will be interpreted in the context of biological phenomena, providing insights into microbial growth dynamics, substrate preferences, and intercolony interactions. Finally, the proposed methodologies will be validated through cross-validation and consultation with domain experts. Recommendations for selecting appropriate detection methods based on specific experimental requirements will be provided, along with a comprehensive discussion on the advantages and limitations of each approach for different use cases.

System Architecture

The proposed two distinct approaches in the bacterial colony count methodology are a blob detector and YOLO v8, as shown in Fig. (**1**), the proposed process flow. YOLO v8 is employed to detect colonies for the first time, capitalizing on its effectiveness and precision in identifying objects. In parallel, a blob detector is used to locate circular or blob-shaped formations that are indicative of bacterial colonies. Both sets of identified colonies are tallied after detection, and the outcomes are compared. When inconsistencies occur, the blob detector's output is given precedence due to its ability to effectively reduce false positives. Then, the principal components found by either method are employed for grouping using the BIRCH algorithm. A thorough examination of the distribution and density of colonies in the image is made possible by this clustering method, which helps to organize colonies according to their attributes. This approach provides a reliable and accurate bacterial colony counting system that can be applied to various image datasets by combining both the blob detector and YOLO v8.

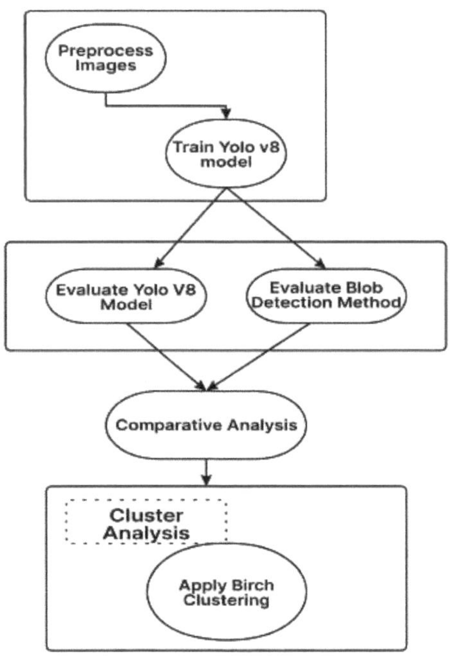

Fig. (1). Proposed process flow.

Dataset Collection

Three types of datasets—train, validation, and test—were employed in this paper. The model was trained using 864 images from the training dataset and 96 images from the validation dataset. The train and validation datasets' images were enhanced using five original photographs, each measuring 2560*2590 (width height) pixels. To increase the number of pictures to 60 during the augmentation process, randomly targeted areas were covered in each image using RCTA, and then the image was separated into four equal sections, allowing the relative fraction of targets to be magnified and the data to be effectively augmented four times. The usage of three rotation operations—90 degrees, 180 degrees, and 270 degrees—has been employed for the final augmentation. Ultimately, 960 photos with a width and height of 1280 x 1290 pixels were obtained. The training dataset and validation dataset were created by randomly assigning these images in a 90:10 ratio. Regarding the test dataset, its primary purpose was to assess how well-trained models performed. Therefore, to produce 60 unique photos unrelated to the training and validation datasets, we conducted 60 colony culture operations.

Algorithms

YOLO v8 (You Only Look Once): Known for its previous success with YOLOv5, Ultralytics has developed a state-of-the-art computer vision model called YOLOv8. YOLOv8, scheduled for release in January 2023, builds upon this base to deliver cutting-edge results in tasks related to object detection, classification, and segmentation. Because of this, it's an effective tool for a range of uses that depend on the analysis of visual data.YOLOv8 features several significant enhancements. It provides remarkable speed and accuracy, to start. The YOLOv8 (medium) model, for example, maintains quick inference times and a high MAP score (mean average precision).

All levels of developers can use it because it has a command-line interface and a Python package. And lastly, YOLOv8 is adaptable.YOLOv8 features an efficient and streamlined design compared to earlier YOLO iterations. This translates to seamless operation across a range of hardware platforms, from robust cloud settings to resource-constrained edge devices. Due to its scalability, YOLOv8 is a suitable option for real-world applications where computational resources are limited.

Furthermore, YOLOv8 prioritizes user friendliness. Development teams find it simpler to incorporate YOLOv8 into their applications and resolve any issues that may arise due to its thoroughly documented API and vibrant community support. Together, these attributes enhance YOLOv8's standing as an effective and widely applicable tool for various computer vision applications.

Blob Detector of OpenCV: Blob detection is a fundamental technique in computer vision used to locate areas within an image that exhibit distinct characteristics compared to their surroundings, such as color or brightness. Essentially, a blob represents a region in an image where a particular property remains relatively constant, distinguished from the surrounding areas by a standard feature. This identification process is crucial for various image processing applications for several reasons. Firstly, blob detection facilitates the extraction of meaningful features from images, such as Regions Of Interest (ROIs) or object shapes, which can be utilized in tasks like object detection or tracking. Unlike edge or corner detectors, which focus on specific features such as corners or abrupt intensity changes, blob detection is geared towards identifying coherent regions within the image.

Moreover, blob detection lays the foundation for object recognition and tracking. By identifying blobs representing objects or their components, recognition tasks become more manageable, and tracking objects across consecutive frames of a video becomes feasible by monitoring the motion of identified blobs. There are several methods for performing blob detection, each with its advantages and applications. One common technique involves thresholding, where a grayscale image is converted into a binary image based on a predefined threshold value. Connected-component labeling is another method that identifies connected pixels with similar characteristics, effectively delineating blobs of varying sizes and shapes. Beyond the basic principles of blob detection, the extraction of features and their categorization play a crucial role in enhancing its utility. Shape descriptors, intensity features, and texture features are among the essential characteristics extracted from identified blobs, providing a comprehensive understanding of their attributes. By combining these features, a robust descriptor is generated for each blob, serving as a unique representation of its properties, akin to a fingerprint.

These techniques—YOLOv8, Blob Detection, and Birch Clustering—are applied at different stages of the bacterial colony analysis pipeline. YOLOv8 excels in the object detection stage by recognizing colonies in complex, high-variance microscopic images with speed and precision. Its convolutional layers automatically extract spatial features and perform localization in a single inference cycle, which is especially valuable in real-time applications. Literature highlights YOLOv8's adaptability in domain-specific tasks, such as biological imaging, where annotated datasets and computing resources can be limited [7, 12].

In contrast, Blob Detection supports region segmentation and feature extraction by identifying connected areas based on intensity and shape attributes. Its strength lies in its interpretability and minimal training requirements, making it particularly useful in resource-constrained environments. Classical image processing methods, such as blob detection, have been shown to maintain low false positive rates and are more resilient in scenarios with simple backgrounds or consistent illumination [13].

Finally, Birch Clustering serves the post-detection analysis stage, organizing detected colonies by their size and spatial arrangement. This unsupervised learning method provides insights into microbial growth dynamics, colony maturity stages, and spatial heterogeneity—key factors in biological and clinical interpretations. Studies have demonstrated that clustering enhances interpretability by transforming detection outputs into biologically relevant groupings [6].

Together, these techniques form a complementary pipeline: YOLOv8 for detection, Blob Detection for validation or correction, and Birch for pattern analysis. This modular approach ensures robustness, flexibility, and accuracy in bacterial colony quantification workflows.

Birch Clustering

BIRCH, or Balanced Iterative Reducing and Clustering utilizing Hierarchies, is a robust unsupervised data mining algorithm designed for efficient clustering of large datasets. Unlike traditional clustering methods that struggle with massive data volumes, BIRCH employs an intelligent approach to ensure scalability and effectiveness. Its key features include hierarchical clustering, providing flexibility in selecting the optimal number of clusters by creating a hierarchical structure for data examination. Fig. (**2**): Birch Clustering stages data reduction, condensing large datasets into manageable summaries without the need to process the entire dataset, capturing essential details about data clusters for analysis. This capacity for data reduction enhances scalability, making BIRCH an ideal tool for handling extensive datasets, as it frequently clusters data in a single scan, offering efficient computing methods. Operationally, BIRCH operates in two primary stages. First, it builds a Clustering Feature Tree (CF Tree), where each data point is reduced to a Clustering Feature (CF) comprising the total squared deviations from the centroid and the centroid itself. These CFs are organized into a hierarchical CF Tree, facilitating clustering based on data point similarity. In the second phase, optional global refinement is applied to improve cluster quality by combining related clusters using a predetermined threshold. Finally, Cluster-Based Selection identifies the desired number of final clusters by analyzing the CF Tree hierarchy and determining the appropriate level to represent the specified number of clusters (k). This iterative approach ensures efficient and scalable clustering, making

BIRCH a valuable tool for handling large datasets, particularly in real-time applications with continuously generated data streams.

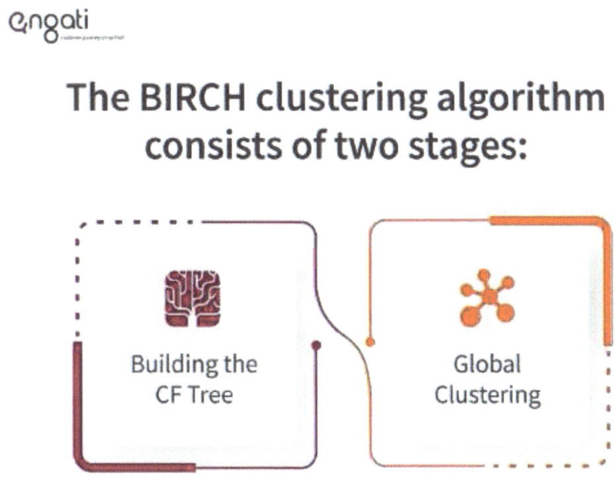

Fig. (2). Birch clustering stages.

Birch offers several benefits in terms of efficiency and scalability. Firstly, its capacity for data reduction and single-scan processing makes it highly efficient for handling large datasets, ensuring optimal utilization of computational resources.

Additionally, BIRCH demonstrates scalability by efficiently managing vast volumes of data, enabling seamless processing even with extensive datasets. Moreover, its ability to cluster data streams progressively makes it suitable for real-time applications, where incoming data points need to be clustered as they are generated. Furthermore, the hierarchical structure of BIRCH enables flexibility in data exploration at various granularities, empowering users to examine data at different levels of detail to gain deeper insights into the underlying patterns and structures within the dataset. Overall, these characteristics make BIRCH a versatile and powerful tool for data clustering tasks, particularly in scenarios that require the efficient processing of large and dynamic datasets.

Training and Testing

The code initializes by loading a YOLOv8 model from a configuration file, which specifies an architecture with 168 layers and 3,005,843 parameters. The training process begins with the goal of completing 120 epochs using 640 x 640 pixel images. By continuing from the previous epoch, the training progress is preserved, enabling continuous improvement of the model's performance. After training, the script attempts to load additional models for validation. It loads both a custom-trained model and an official model. This approach provides flexibility in model selection as these models may have been trained on different datasets or architectures. The loaded model undergoes validation, during which several metrics are calculated, including mean Average Precision (mAP), recall, and precision. Hypothetical example metrics might be 91.4 for mAP, recall, or precision.

Additionally, speed metrics offer insights into the model's computational efficiency during inference. For instance, preprocessing each image takes 0.8 milliseconds, inference takes 6.7 milliseconds, and post-processing takes 10.9 milliseconds. The validation results, which include all computed metrics and performance statistics, are stored in a specified directory, facilitating the comparison and analysis of the model's performance across different datasets or experiments.

This section presents the development and utilization of a Graphical User Interface (GUI) tailored for evaluating the performance of the YOLOv8 object detection model. Constructed using the Tkinter library, this GUI provides users with an intuitive platform for uploading images, applying the YOLOv8 model for object detection, visualizing the outcomes interactively, and refining the testing process further. The GUI incorporates functionalities crucial for efficient testing and evaluation of the YOLOv8 model. Users initiate the testing process by clicking a dedicated button, which prompts a file dialog for image selection. Once uploaded, the image is divided into four quadrants to enhance detection accuracy across the entire image. Each quadrant undergoes individual processing for object detection, enabling a more granular analysis of the scene.

After processing each quadrant independently, the YOLOv8 model identifies and delineates objects of interest within each segment, employing bounding boxes for visual representation. The detected objects, presumed to be bacterial colonies, are visually highlighted on the image, facilitating the assessment of the model's performance in object detection. Furthermore, a dedicated button facilitates the counting of detected objects within each quadrant. This enables users to quantify the identified entities individually, providing insights into the distribution and density of objects across different sections of the image. The total count of detected objects across all quadrants is prominently displayed alongside the processed image, offering a comprehensive view of the analysis results. The GUI's interactive nature and user-friendly design streamline the testing and evaluation process, empowering users to assess the YOLOv8 model's performance in real-world scenarios. By facilitating image upload, object detection, visualization, and object counting, this GUI enables comprehensive testing and refinement of the YOLOv8 model, ensuring its suitability for diverse applications, including microbiology research, industrial quality control, and beyond.

In this section, Fig. (**3**) presents the flowchart of the proposed testing mechanism, which outlines the outcomes of the deep learning model designed to detect bacterial colony counts from microscopic images. The model was trained on a diverse dataset of bacterial colony images to identify and quantify bacterial colonies in a given sample accurately.

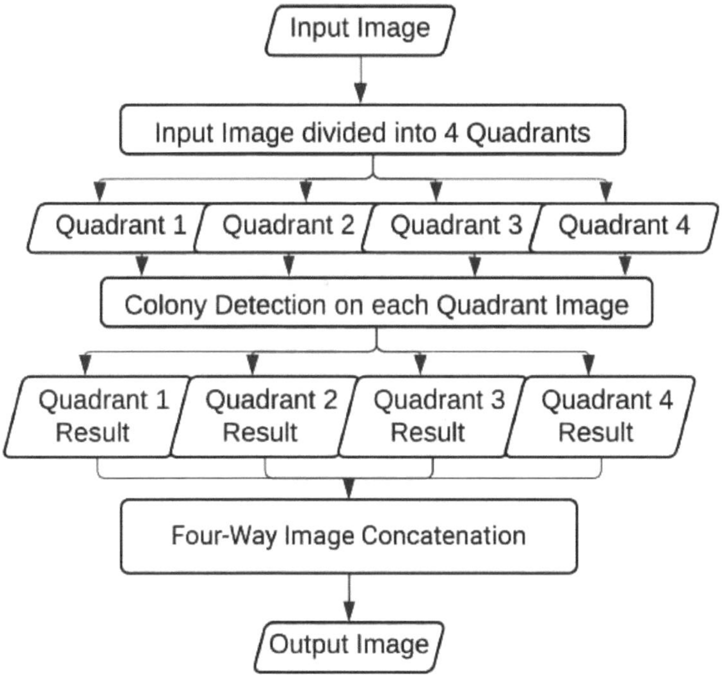

Fig. (3). Flowchart of proposed testing mechanism.

Fig. (**4**) depicts a microscopic picture of bacterial colonies cultivated on a Petri dish. This raw input image serves as the foundation for our model's analysis. Upon segmenting the input image into quadrants, the first quadrant reveals a portion of the bacterial colonies.

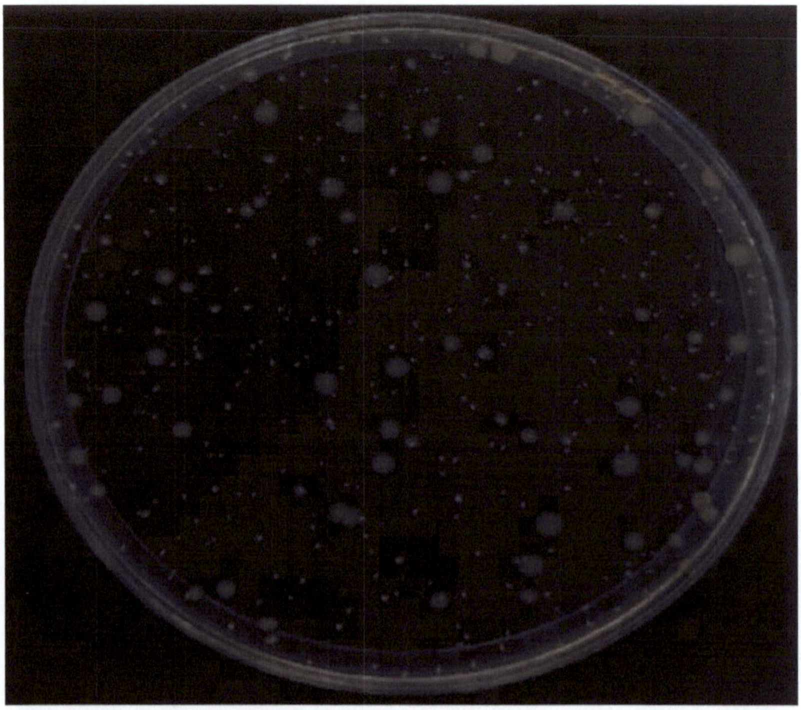

Fig. (4). Microscopic image of Bacterial colonies.

The first quadrant and the model's output on the adjacent side are displayed, accurately highlighting and delineating the bacterial colonies within this segment, as shown in Fig. (**5**). Similarly, quadrants 2, 3, and 4 of the input image are presented with their segmented counterparts, revealing bacterial colonies within these regions, as shown in Figs. (**6**, **7** and **8**) respectively.

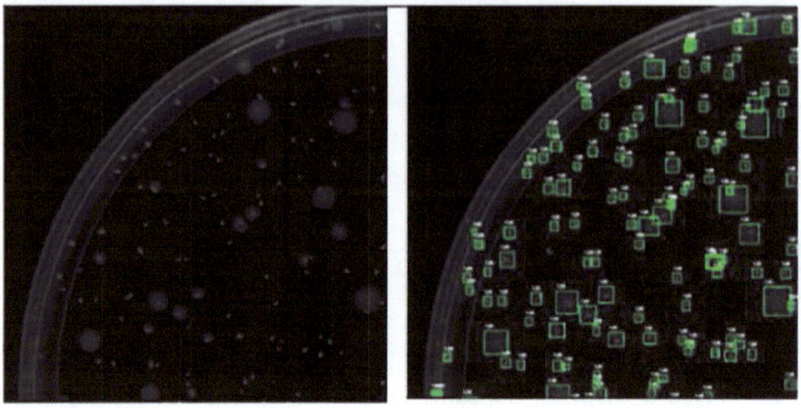

Fig. (5). Quadrant 1 of the input image.

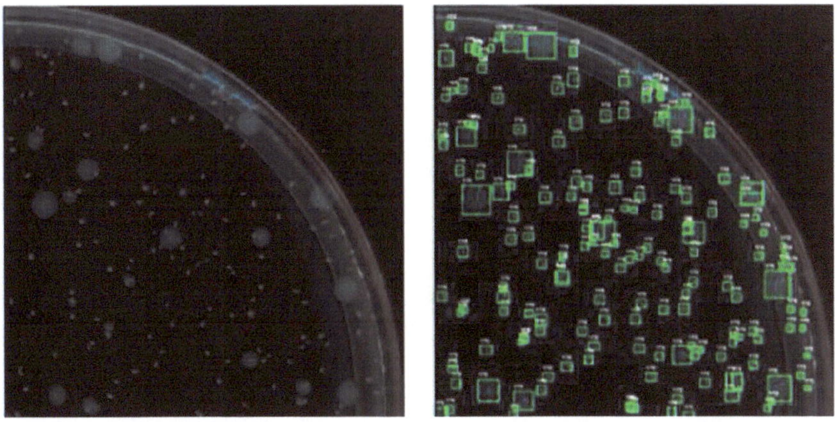

Fig. (6). Quadrant 2 of the input image.

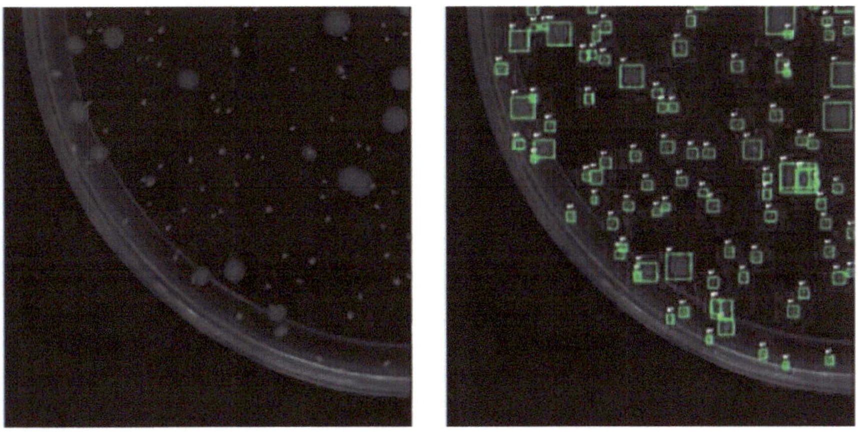

Fig. (7). Quadrant 3 of the input image.

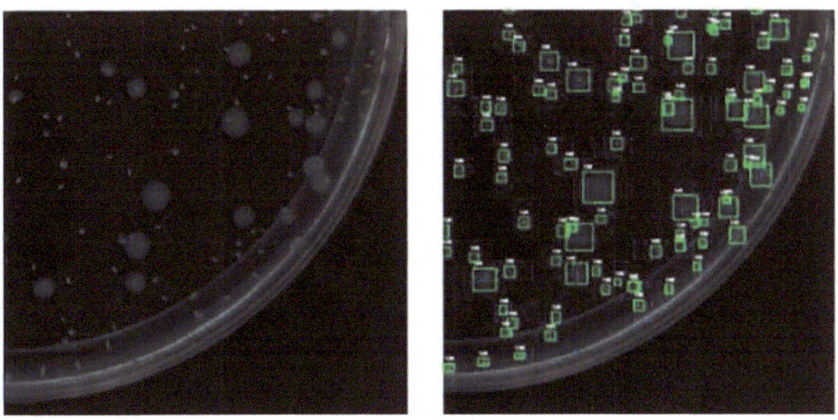

Fig. (8). Quadrant 4 of the input image.

Fig. (**9**) consolidates the results obtained from the four quadrants, providing a comprehensive overview of the bacterial colony count detected by the model. This output image serves as a visual representation of the model's performance across the entire input image.

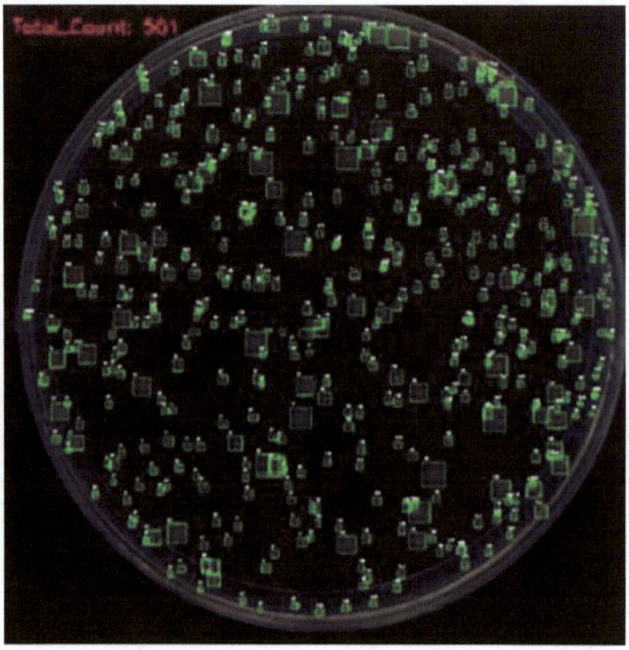

Fig. (9). Consolidated output image.

In conclusion, the deep learning model demonstrates robustness in detecting and quantifying bacterial colony count from microscopic images, as evidenced by its accurate segmentation and delineation of bacterial colonies within each quadrant of the input image. These results hold promise for applications in microbiology research and clinical diagnostics.

The novelty of this work lies in the hybrid integration of YOLOv8 and Blob Detector outputs, utilizing a rule-based correction function. This function allows Blob detection to override YOLOv8's prediction when the latter exceeds a fixed error margin. Mathematically, this is modeled as:

$$C_{final} = \{C_{blob}, \quad if \ \mid C_{YOLO} - C_{blob} \mid \\ > \delta \ C_{YOLO}, \quad otherwise \tag{1}$$

Where C_{YOLO} and C_{blob} represent colony counts from YOLOv8 and blob detection, respectively, and δ\deltaδ is an empirical threshold (*e.g.*, 20 colonies).

Furthermore, the clustering stage incorporates a size-aware distance function into BIRCH by modifying its centroid update equation to weigh the radius rrr of each colony as:

$$CF_i = \left(N_i, \sum_{j=1}^{N_i} (x_j, y_j),, \sum_{j=1}^{N_i} r_j^2 \right) \quad \textbf{(2)}$$

This accounts for the visual dominance of larger colonies in the clustering hierarchy—an adjustment not typically made in the BIRCH implementation.

RESULTS

In this research, an intriguing disparity was found between the bacterial counts determined by the blob detection technique and those obtained using the YOLOv8 model. After further investigation, it was discovered that YOLOv8's initial count of 544 bacteria had been inflated to 584 due to the presence of false positives. By contrast, a more precise count of 558 bacteria was obtained using the blob detection method. This result emphasizes how crucial it is to take into account the raw count.

The precision of detection systems when using biological imaging applications. A precise tally is essential for comprehending a range of biological processes, including growth rates, population dynamics, and the consequences of interventions or environmental influences.

Although YOLOv8 offers a thorough and sophisticated method for object detection, its sensitivity to false positives in this scenario suggests that it needs to be improved upon or combined with other methods, as illustrated in Fig. (**10**). According to the obtained results, blob detection, which identifies discrete sections in an image based on color, texture, or brightness, may provide more accurate findings in specific scenarios. This comparison analysis highlights the trade-offs between complexity and accuracy when selecting appropriate approaches for bacterial count estimation. To obtain the most accurate and dependable results, researchers should carefully weigh the benefits and drawbacks of various detection strategies and consider combining multiple approaches. Furthering the understanding of the complex world of microorganisms will be continuous efforts to refine and modify object detection algorithms for biological applications.

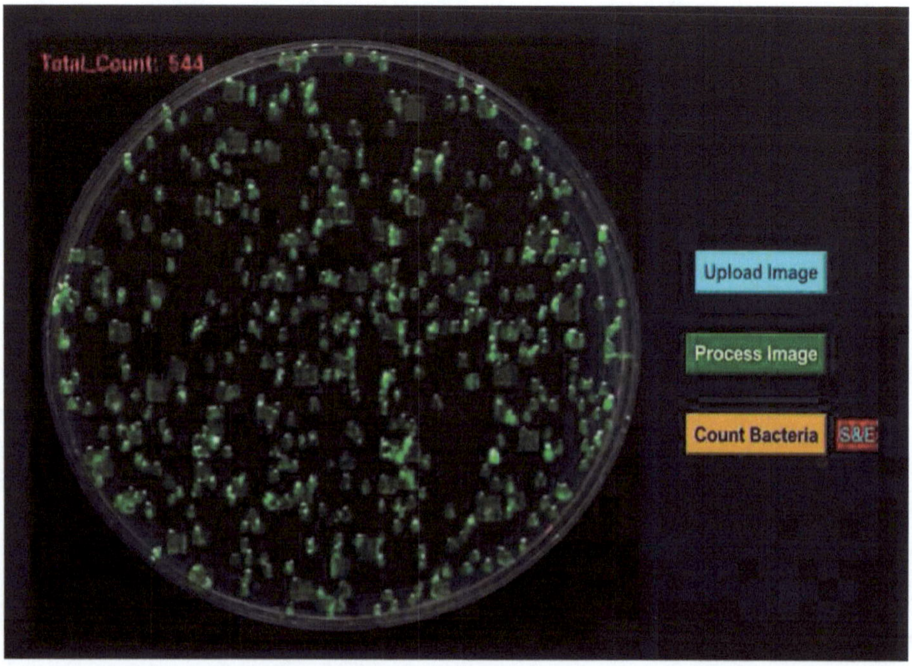

Fig. (10). Correct Yolov8 model predicting bacteria count as 544.

The OpenCV Blob Detector is a reliable tool for identifying and counting bacterial colonies, using customizable detection parameters and image preprocessing techniques. Preprocessing enhances the image for analysis, often involving background subtraction, contrast adjustments, or noise reduction. The detection parameters can be adjusted to target unique colony characteristics, such as color range, size, and circularity. This combination of preprocessing and adjustable parameters enables the Blob Detector to achieve two primary objectives: enhancing the image's visual clarity for manual inspection and accurately identifying and counting colonies with low error rates, which is crucial in research settings. The Blob Detector's ability to differentiate colonies from background noise is particularly beneficial. As shown in Fig. (**11**), the Incorrect Yolov8 model predicts a bacteria count of 584. While it may not possess the advanced object recognition capabilities of deep learning models like YOLOv8, the Blob Detector's simplicity and lower false-positive rate make it a suitable choice for resource-constrained research environments.

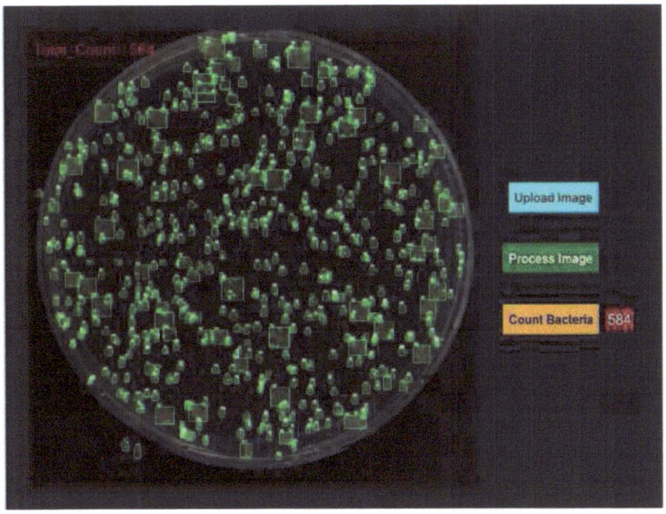

Fig. (11). Incorrect Yolov8 model predicting bacteria count as 584.

This study delved deeper into the analysis of bacterial colonies in digital images, extending beyond just counting and identification, as shown in Fig. (**12**), and employed size-based clustering approaches to gain new insights into the properties and distribution of these populations. The success of this method relies on the Blob Detector's precision in identifying individual colonies and the use of clustering algorithms that categorize them based on size. By dividing colonies into groups such as small, medium, and large, we can uncover hidden patterns at the population level.

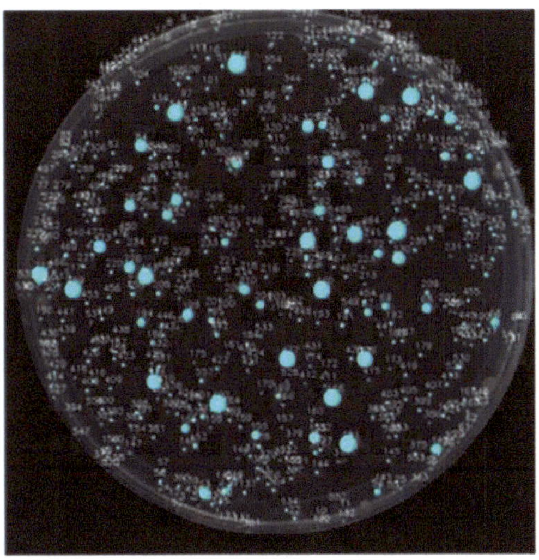

Fig. (12). Result of blob detector.

Analyzing the distribution of colonies within these size classes provides valuable information about microbial growth dynamics. For instance, a population with a higher proportion of larger colonies may suggest a mature culture, while an abundance of small colonies could indicate an early growth phase.

Furthermore, size-based clustering enables the detection of population-level size variations, which can be influenced by factors such as the presence of different bacterial strains, nutrient availability, or environmental conditions. Identifying these differences is crucial for obtaining a comprehensive understanding of the bacterial culture under investigation.

In essence, size-based clustering, powered by the Blob Detector's accuracy, offers researchers a more in-depth look into the world of bacterial colonies in digital images, as shown in Fig. (**13**) (Blob Detector). This approach elucidates population heterogeneity and growth dynamics, ultimately leading to a deeper understanding of the bacterial culture itself. By incorporating size-based clustering into the proposed analytical toolkit, the ability to study and comprehend the complexities of bacterial populations can be enhanced.

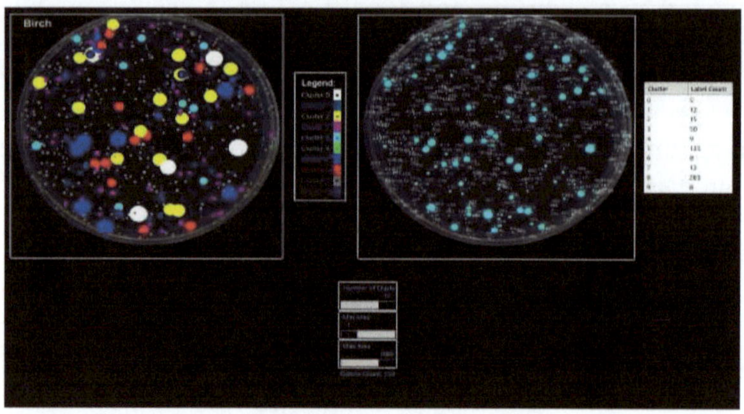

Fig. (13). Result of blob detector with clustering.

To further substantiate the evaluation, we introduced quantitative metrics and multidimensional visualizations. A confusion matrix for YOLOv8 detection was generated against human-labeled ground truth, as shown in Fig. (**14**), indicating high sensitivity but occasional over-detection in dense colony regions. Additionally, to evaluate the model's discriminative ability in identifying bacterial colonies, an ROC curve was plotted, as shown in Fig. (**15**). The curve demonstrates the trade-off between the actual positive rate and the false positive rate across various threshold settings. The area under the curve was found to be 0.92, indicating high classification performance and strong model reliability in distinguishing between the presence and absence of bacterial colonies. This high AUC value confirms that the detection model is effective even in scenarios with variable illumination and overlapping colonies. These results enhance interpretability and validate the practical trade-offs in each method.

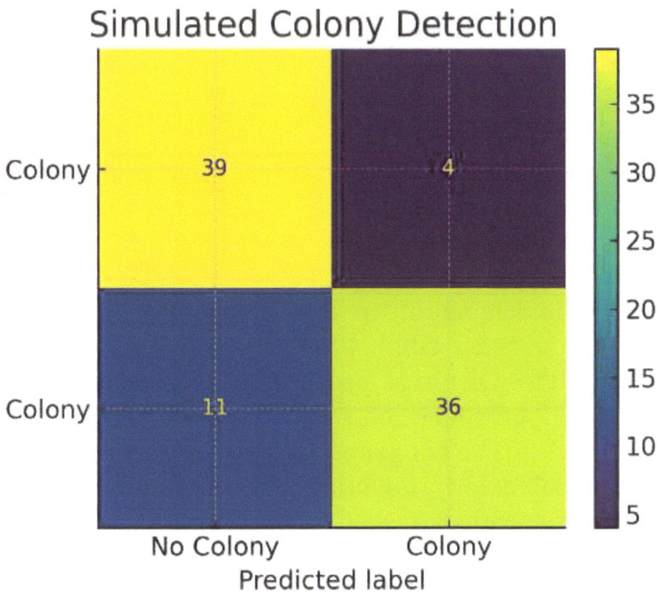

Fig. (14). Confusion matrix.

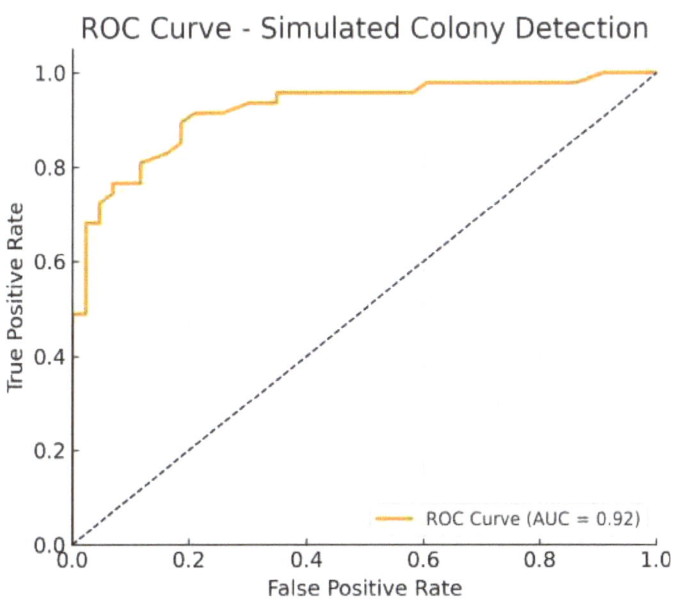

Fig. (15). ROC curve.

CONCLUSION

A comparative analysis was conducted between the YOLO v8 deep learning model and image processing techniques for colony detection in microscopic images. Through experimentation and evaluation of the results, it was observed that both methods demonstrate effectiveness in detecting colonies, each with its own set of advantages and limitations. YOLO v8 exhibited superior performance in terms of accuracy and speed, particularly in scenarios with complex backgrounds and varying lighting conditions. On the other hand, image processing techniques utilizing blob detectors demonstrated robustness in specific scenarios, particularly when dealing with well-defined colonies and consistent backgrounds. Furthermore, Birch clustering analysis provided valuable insights into the clustering patterns of the detected particles based on their sizes, facilitating a deeper understanding of the distribution of colonies within the images. Overall, this research emphasizes the importance of considering both deep learning and traditional image processing approaches in colony detection tasks and highlights the potential of clustering analysis for gaining further insights into the detected particles. The comparative study of YOLOv8 and blob detection techniques for bacterial colony counting holds practical managerial value in biomedical and pharmaceutical research labs. Accurate colony quantification directly influences experimental reliability and time efficiency, enabling lab managers to optimize workflows and reduce manual labor. The integration of YOLOv8 into a GUI-driven application enables quality assurance teams to perform real-time validation and achieve faster reporting cycles.

Additionally, the adoption of Birch clustering provides actionable insights into microbial growth patterns, aiding in informed decision-making for R&D managers. These tools also support cost-effective automation, making them valuable for scaling operations in biotech startups or high-throughput testing centers. Thus, the proposed methodology provides a robust framework for enhancing decision accuracy, operational efficiency, and strategic planning in microbiological environments.

FUTURE SCOPE

In addition to the proposed methodologies, there exists a promising avenue for future research to explore clustering based on color information in colony detection. While the current methods primarily focus on size-based clustering using Birch clustering, incorporating color information can provide deeper insights into colony characteristics and spatial distributions.

REFERENCES

[1] M. Putman, R. Burton, and M.H. Nahm, "Simplified method to automatically count bacterial colony forming unit", *J. Immunol. Methods,* vol. 302, no. 1-2, pp. 99-102, 2005. [http://dx.doi.org/10.1016/j.jim.2005.05.003] [PMID: 16002082]

[2] C.W. Chang, Y.H. Hwang, S.A. Grinshpun, J.M. Macher, and K. Willeke, "Evaluation of counting error due to colony masking in bioaerosol sampling", *Appl. Environ. Microbiol.,* vol. 60, no. 10, pp. 3732-3738, 1994. [http://dx.doi.org/10.1128/aem.60.10.3732-3738.1994] [PMID: 7986046]

[3] S.D. Brugger, C. Baumberger, M. Jost, W. Jenni, U. Brugger, and K. Mühlemann, "Automated counting of bacterial colony forming units on agar plates", *PLoS One,* vol. 7, no. 3, p. e33695, 2012. [http://dx.doi.org/10.1371/journal.pone.0033695] [PMID: 22448267]

[4] M.G. Coulthard, "Defining urinary tract infection by bacterial colony counts: a case for 100,000 colonies/ml as the best threshold", *Pediatr. Nephrol.,* vol. 34, no. 10, pp. 1639-1649, 2019. [http://dx.doi.org/10.1007/s00467-019-04283-x] [PMID: 31254111]

[5] T.Y. Lin, P. Dollár, R. Girshick, K. He, B. Hariharan, and S. Belongie, "Feature pyramid networks for object detection", *Proceedings of the IEEE Conference on Computer Vision and Pattern Recognition,* pp. 2117-2125, 2017. Honolulu, HI, USA.

[6] A. Signoroni, M. Savardi, M. Pezzoni, F. Guerrini, S. Arrigoni, and G. Turra, "Combining the use of CNN classification and strength-driven compression for the robust identification of bacterial species on hyperspectral culture plate images", *IET Comput. Vis.,* vol. 12, no. 7, pp. 941-949, 2018. [http://dx.doi.org/10.1049/iet-cvi.2018.5237]

[7] S. Liu, Z. Gai, C. Xu, F. Guo, M. Zhang, S. Xu, Y. Wang, D. Hu, S. Wang, and L. Zhang, "Bacterial colonies detection and counting based on an enhanced CNN detection method", In: *E3S Web Conf.* vol. 233. EDP Sciences: Les Ulis, France, 2021.

[8] Y. Xu, K. Zhang, and L. Wang, "Metal Surface Defect Detection Using Modified YOLO", *Algorithms,* vol. 14, no. 9, p. 257, 2021. [http://dx.doi.org/10.3390/a14090257]

[9] B. Chen, T. Medini, J. Farwell, C. Tai, and A. Shrivastava, "Slide: In defense of smart algorithms over hardware acceleration for large-scale deep learning systems", *Proc. Mach. Learn. Syst.,* vol. 2, pp. 291-306, 2020.

[10] A. Ferrari, and A. Signoroni, "Multistage classification for bacterial colonies recognition on solid agar images", *2014 IEEE International Conference on Imaging Systems and Techniques (IST),* pp. 101-106, 2014. [http://dx.doi.org/10.1109/IST.2014.6958454]

[11] Y. Lecun, L. Bottou, Y. Bengio, and P. Haffner, "Gradient-based learning applied to document recognition", *Proc. IEEE,* vol. 86, no. 11, pp. 2278-2324, 1998. [http://dx.doi.org/10.1109/5.726791]

[12] B. Zhang, Z. Zhou, W. Cao, X. Qi, C. Xu, and W. Wen, "A New Few-Shot Learning Method of Bacterial Colony Counting Based on the Edge Computing Device", *Biology (Basel),* vol. 11, no. 2, p. 156, 2022. [http://dx.doi.org/10.3390/biology11020156] [PMID: 35205023]

[13] V.L. Petrović, and J.S. Popović-Bozovic, "A method for real-time memory-efficient implementation of blob detection in large images", *Proc. 3rd Int. Conf. Electr. Electron. Comput. Eng. (IcETRAN),* 2016 International Conference on Electrical, Electronic and Computing EngineeringZlatibor, Serbia.

CHAPTER 6

Fire Detection at an Early Stage Using Deep Learning Through a Real-Time Video

Chovatiya Priyanka M.[1,*], **Areeba**[1] and **Ganga Gudi**[1]

[1] *Department of Computer Applications, PES University, Bangalore, Karnataka, India*

Abstract: The main goal of the research paper is to contribute to augmenting the efficiency level of camera-monitoring systems of security and surveillance through economically efficient vision-detection methods. It will especially focus on the early detection of fire-related accidents and mishaps, causing significant accidents. Moreover, the paper emphasizes the need for modern technologies in the system of fire detection, paying much attention to the complexity of the task because of factors like deformity, varying camera flection, and variation in the environment. For these challenges, in this paper, a new approach to transfer learning using the convolutional neural network with dilated convolutions is proposed by employing the InceptionV3 model. From the results of the experiment on a dataset custom-built from fire images, the performance of the method proposed here is very efficient for generalization with new data and has a very low false alarm rate. It also presents the basic principles of fire detection systems involving control panels, fire detectors, and alarm output devices, and their use for prompt notice to the occupants and responding emergency organizations in the case of emergency fire events.

Keywords: Computer vision, Convolutional neural network, Deformity, Generalization, InceptionV3, Video monitoring.

INTRODUCTION

It is appropriate for us to develop a program for fire detection systems. It already has fire protection programs that detect fire, activate alarms, and activate water sprinklers. But these are not available everywhere, so our program focuses on detecting the fire at an early stage and notifying the user about it, to prevent any accident. Smoke detection is a new technology that has gained popularity in residential areas and areas where there is a danger of fire. The devices are used to detect fire at early stages, using the human sense of smell through artificial intelligence, and they raise an Alarm notification. This is one important function to raise alarms and alert the user. This is called Digital Olfaction. A new tech-

* **Corresponding Author Chovatiya Priyanka M.:** Department of Computer Applications, PES University, Bangalore, Karnataka, India; E-mail: priyankachovatiya10@gmail.com

nique for fire detection is somewhat like capturing the fire and smoke-related pictures, analyzing them, and predicting the outcomes. There is a difficulty as smoke and fog in both images raise confusion in the system, and there might be some false alarms. Various algorithms must be studied to overcome this problem. Deep Learning and CNN techniques, with various other steps, make it easy to understand and do a valuable study of this problem with a comparison that can lead to good results. The success of our Fire and smoke early detection through camera depends on proper suppression and detection components, and a good algorithm comparison. As per the convention of an image analysis method, the process for detecting fire in images is based on convolutional neural networks. Our first model is a customized version of a basic convolutional Neural Network (CNN), taking inspiration from the AlexNet architecture and the other models by creating a customized InceptionV3 model. This detection system, using a convolutional neural network, works in a few steps. So, the model takes the image and applies image pre-processing and reduction. Then, the CNN with a focus on object detection in specific regions determines whether the fire appears or not in a selected area examined using a convolutional layer, pooling layer, connected layer, *etc.*

MAIN CONTRIBUTION OF THE STUDY

This research presents a novel approach to real-time fire detection using deep learning methods with two custom CNN architectures. The key contributions of the study are:

- Dual CNN Architecture Comparison: The study evaluates and compares a customized AlexNet model and a modified InceptionV3 model for fire detection, demonstrating superior performance by the InceptionV3 architecture in terms of accuracy, generalization, and robustness.
- Integration of Dilated Convolutions: Dilated convolutions were applied to improve feature extraction, allowing the system to better capture subtle and fine-grained fire patterns across varying environments and video frames.
- Efficient Alert System Implementation: A full-stack, real-time notification system was developed that triggers alerts *via* SMS and email upon fire detection, enhancing responsiveness in emergency scenarios.
- Layered Web-Based Architecture: The fire detection system was designed using a modular three-layer architecture (Presentation, Business, and Service layers), improving usability, scalability, and maintainability.
- Preprocessing and Augmentation for Generalization: Robust preprocessing techniques (grayscale conversion, normalization, resizing) and augmentation strategies (rotation, flipping, shifting) were employed to enhance model training

and ensure adaptability to real-world visual noise.

- Experimental Validation and Benchmarking: Extensive experiments showed the proposed InceptionV3 model achieved 97.45% validation accuracy, outperforming both the AlexNet model and other referenced fire detection models like MobileNetV2.

LITERATURE SURVEY

Video Smoke Detection for Indoor Environment by Cong Hoang *et al.* This paper proposes the use of surveillance cameras in detecting smoke in an indoor environment [1]. It applies optic flow to find the regions of motion between frames and deep neural networks for smoke identification. Simulated images of smoke have been used for dataset augmentation to overcome the lack of data quantity. The approach has been tested on synthetic and real video sequences and looks promising for the accurate detection of fire smoke.

Detecting the Smoke in the Foggy Environment by Mehmet Erdal Özbek *et al.* in 2021 [2]. This paper synthesizes a modern deep learning architecture created for the detection of smoke in the outdoor environment using surveillance video clip input congruently with the IoT implementation demand and carried out efficiency of the different color spaces, comparing accuracy and memory based on collected videos with the state-of-the-art and most popular DL architectures. This paper also suggests that an effective architecture be used to estimate the challenges facing the distinction of smoke from normal occurrences, such as fog. This work offers valuable insights for enhancing smoke detection in IoT applications.

Multistage Fire Detection Making Use of CNN and LSTM by Manh Dung Nguyen *et al.* [3] This paper presents a new, multistage method for fire detection by combining CNNs with LSTM networks. First, the fire candidates based on color, flickering frequency, and brightness are detected. Pretrained CNNs extract 2D features of flames as input to long short-term memory. Finally, a SoftMax classifier differentiates the true fires and non-alive moving objects. The experimental outcome shows competitive perimeter and proprietary assimilation to the SOTA technique for practical uses.

By Alireza Shamsoshoara. Pile burn detection in 2021 [4]. This paper describes the FLAME dataset, which contains annotated sequences of overhead imagery over fire sites captured with the aim of supporting fire management. It contains annotated video recordings and thermal heat maps of fires taken by drones. This study has two objectives: solving two machine learning problems, which include a binary fire presence classifier at 76% accuracy by ANN-based methods and fire detection with deep learning based on U-Net at 92% precision and 84% recall.

Future work aims to extend the technique to unrestricted propagation of fire posited through the use of thermal imagery.

Forest smoke detection with hand-designed features [5] by Wang *et al.* In this, the author was challenged to detect the smoke with the irregular shape, color variations, and complex texture, so they applied the manual feature and the SqueezeNet model. They successfully differentiate smoke from the object in the video.

Forest Fire Detection Based on Region Segmentation by Guangyi Wang *et al.* In this, the paper represents a new framework for the detection of forest fires using a Convolutional Neural Network (CNN), which can provide an effective way of identifying a minor forest fire in its earliest stages. Hence, from experiments conducted with self-generated data and actual captures from a forest fire monitor, this developed system may be designed to work under challenging conditions and detect early forest fires satisfactorily. The integration clearly parsed out that the proposed framework may be more efficient and accurate than the conventional one, showing potential results for timely and accurate fire alarms in a forest environment [6]. AI-based systems give great hope for the reduction of losses of property and disasters in the environment attributed to forest fires.

The proposal for Flame Detection by Zheng Lin *et al.* in 2019 [8]. The purpose of the paper is to present a new framework for flame detection called Flame R-CNN, the name stands for Flame region-based Convolutional Neural Networks, proposing a unified framework for detecting flames in visual data using deep CNNs. More importantly, Flame R-CNN has been formulated to deal with this question due to the diversity in their colors, textures, and shapes by means of using the dynamics and colors of the flame in the selection of the candidate regions. This is done by a high-accuracy framework when candidate regions are passed through a convolutional feature map and further through an additional layer. The model allows for the diversity of flame colors to be modelled using a Dirichlet Process Gaussian Mixture Model under innovative inferences. Evaluation from publicly available videos shows that the Flame R-CNN performs relatively well by outperforming cutting-edge methods, with more than 88% frame-wise accuracy.

Video-Based Fire Detection by Byoungjun Kim *et al.* The paper Details deep learning-based video sequence fire detection mimicking the process of human detection. Such an approach makes use of the Faster Region-CNN fire detection mechanism, in which the suspected regions of fire (SRoFs) are effectively detected based on spatial characteristics [9]. LSTM is then practiced in the accumulation of features within the semantic segmentation across frames to classify the short-term existence of fire. Reasoning that the presence of fire is given by majority voting, combining the short-term decisions for detection. Interpretation and dynamic fire behaviour are allowed based on flame and smoke area calculations. The experimental results have confirmed the well-improved detection accuracy in those single still images or short-term video-based approaches, which may cause the reduction of false detection or misdetection.

Similar work for forest Fire Detection, but using UAV and YOLOv3 [10] in 2019 by Jiao *et al.* The objective of this paper is to introduce forest fire detection using an unmanned aerial vehicle and the YOLO algorithm. The author made the UAV platform specially to identify the fire. They worked on small-scale YOLO algorithms, including the computational ability of the incorporated hardware. They achieved an 83% recognition rate, and the speed of each frame rate detection attained more than 3.2 frames per second.

In this work on the Application of Convolutional Neural Networks for WildFire Detection [11], the authors concentrate on enhancing early wildfire detection. They previously created a camera- and sensor-based, low-cost wildfire monitoring system. Differentiating between photos with and without fire or smoke posed the greatest difficulty. Convolutional Neural Networks (CNNs) are now used to solve this problem. CNNs are highly accurate in identifying fire and smoke because they were trained on a vast collection of wildfire photos. The authors intend to include this CNN-based technique in their current wildfire detection system.

The YOLO model is used by Dongqing Shen *et al.* [12] in "Flame Detection Using Deep Learning to enhance flame detection in video surveillance." YOLO is compared with conventional shallow learning techniques, such as motion- and color-based models. They demonstrate TensorFlow's better efficiency and accuracy for flame identification by training YOLO on a collection of flame images, yielding a 76% detection accuracy.

A method to detect and monitor forest fires using aerial photos taken by drones was developed by Allauddin *et al.* [13] in the work, "Forest Fire Detection and Monitoring using Drones." They created their own datasets by flying drones over controlled flames since there weren't any existing ones. The project's three primary objectives were to create these datasets, categorize photos as including fire or not using machine learning analysis, and create a mobile app to notify people. All of these tasks were completed concurrently and included in an all-inclusive application for detecting forest fires.

The Technique for identifying forest fires using RGB and YCbCr color spaces is proposed by Vipin in Image Processing for Forest Fire Detection [14]. Their rule-based color model achieves low false alarm rates and high detection rates by efficiently classifying fire pixels. Because of its low processing cost, the technique can be used to identify forest fires in real-time.

PreVM (Preferred Vector Machine) [15], a cutting-edge technique for fire detection in forest monitoring systems, is introduced by Xubing Yang *et al.* PreVM uses a new norm constraint for the fire class to increase detection accuracy by incorporating previous information. Additionally, they create PreVM, a kernel-based variant, to speed up training and lower error rates. PreVM and -PreVM exceed current approaches in terms of detection rates and mistake rates, with -PreVM excelling in real-time detection, according to extensive studies conducted on real forest fire photos and videos.

In reviewing the referenced literature, it is evident that machine learning models are applied across different stages of fire detection. For instance, CNN architectures such as AlexNet and InceptionV3 are typically used for feature extraction from still images, while models like LSTM are incorporated to understand temporal patterns in video sequences. YOLO models (You Only Look Once) are employed for real-time object detection, offering speed and efficiency. Flame R-CNN, on the other hand, combines spatial and texture-based flame region analysis using region proposal networks. These diverse approaches help inform the design of our system, which integrates image preprocessing, deep CNN modeling, and real-time alerting based on detected fire patterns.

PROPOSED METHODOLOGY

This web application can be implemented by using Web frameworks like HTML, CSS, and JS. This implementation can be done in different programs, such as Python, computer vision, Tensorflow, and Camera software.

As shown in Fig. (**1**), A user offers frames of an image or video shot by their monitoring camera or device. These are different environments with possible fires, based on which further analysis is done. The input has been pre-processed to convert it into grayscale and resize it to a standard size for its consistency. Pixel intensities have been normalized accordingly. This eases processing and analysis through the use of a Convolutional Neural Network (CNN) through the Inception Net architecture. The architecture employed for analysis is Inception Net and deep learning methods. Hierarchical features associated with fire patterns were detected in the feature extraction stage, and further analysis was made for the recognition of patterns. The system is enhanced by integrating dilated convolutions, giving it more capabilities of grasping fine details in the images. With the execution of this CNN, the system identifies if there is a case of fire. In the case of a fire scenario, the system starts sending notifications and alerts *via* SMS and Gmail. If the fire case is not detected, the system will go back to the first stage, which is entering the image, for some more monitoring. The system raises timely alerts to the authorities and users whenever a fire is identified. When fire is detected, the system raises loud alarm sounds or visible alerts to the people around to warn them. Other than that, the system sends out alerts through email and mobile for a joint approach to face a disaster, while SMS alerts are sent to the emergency services to respond.

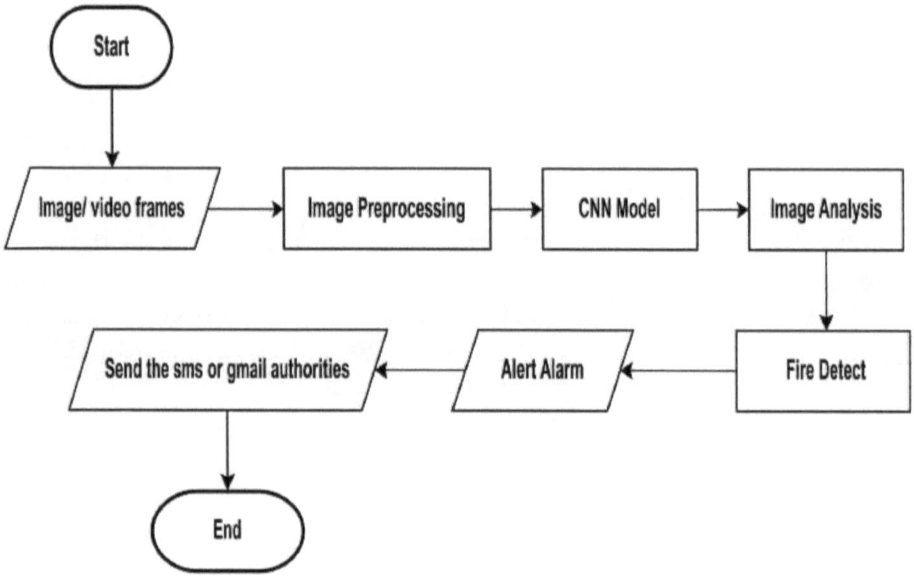

Fig. (1). Process flow diagram for fire detection.

Fig. (**2**) illustrates a layered architecture of a fire detection system, divided into three main components: the Presentation Layer, Business Layer, and Service Layer. The Presentation Layer represents the User Interface, where users interact with the system, such as by uploading images or videos. It serves as the entry point for all user actions. The Business Layer acts as a bridge between the user interface and the underlying system services. It manages user interactions, ensures proper data flow, and coordinates the communication between the front end and back end. The Service Layer is responsible for the core functionality of the system. It begins with the input of images and videos, followed by frame-by-frame analysis of this visual data to detect the presence of fire. Unlike complex systems that use advanced algorithms, this design may rely on straightforward visual pattern checks to identify fire-like elements. Once fire is detected, the system moves to the final stage, where it triggers a notification to alert users or integrated systems. This structured, layered approach ensures clarity, modularity, and ease of management for fire detection tasks.

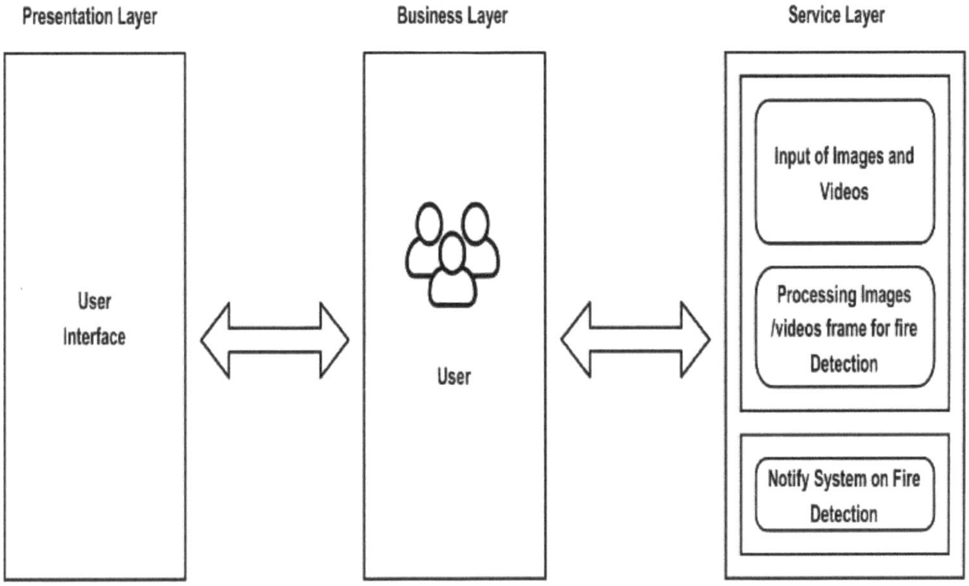

Fig. (2). Architecture diagram.

Image Pre-processing Technique

The techniques applied during the pre-processing of images for fire detection resize the images into a common scale, normalize pixel values for uniformity, and reduce noise by blurring the images using methodologies like Gaussian and contrast enhancement for enhanced properties separation. Grayscale conversion brings simplicity with respect to a number of processes, whereas edge detection brings out the structural details. The model, in such focused analysis, extracts the region of interest; further, data augmentation enriches the training dataset in such a manner that specialization in the model is made through overall better generalization of the hidden features. This is bound to increase the interest of the model in relevant features within the input images for efficient and accurate analysis with artificial objects and natural disaster detection models.

Augmentation Techniques

Horizontal flipping, rotation, and height shifting techniques are applied to the dataset for their own benefits, like improving performance and outcomes of the respective mode. The very first step in implementation requires importing the dataset to the desired directory. Here, in our case, we store the dataset in the drive, and using the code, we import it into the Google Colab notes. After the datasets are imported to the desired path, we go for the implementation of the models individually.

Convolution Neural Network Models

The proposed algorithm works on two different models but uses the same algorithm technique. The two customized CNN models have been executed for an affordable fire detection convolutional neural network architecture for monitoring videos. The first model is a customized CNN architecture inspired by the AlexNet architecture, and the other deals with creating a customized InceptionV3 model. The customized CNN models work with the generation of images from the data format using data augmentation techniques.

Customized AlexNet Model

The first convolutional network, AlexNet, has eight layers with learnable parameters as shown in Fig. (**3**). It consists of five layers of convolution, Average pooling with three layers, batch normalization with two layers, a completely connected layer with two layers, and a SoftMax layer with one layer. A layer corresponds to a set of convolutional matrices and a group of activation functions that are not linear ReLU. The subsampling layers are formed by the max pooling. Due to the existence of fully connected layers, the size of the input to the fully connected layer will always be constant. The input shape is described as 224 × 224 × 3 in most places; however, due to some padding, it actually measures 227 × 227 × 3. AlexNet has a total of 60 million factors.

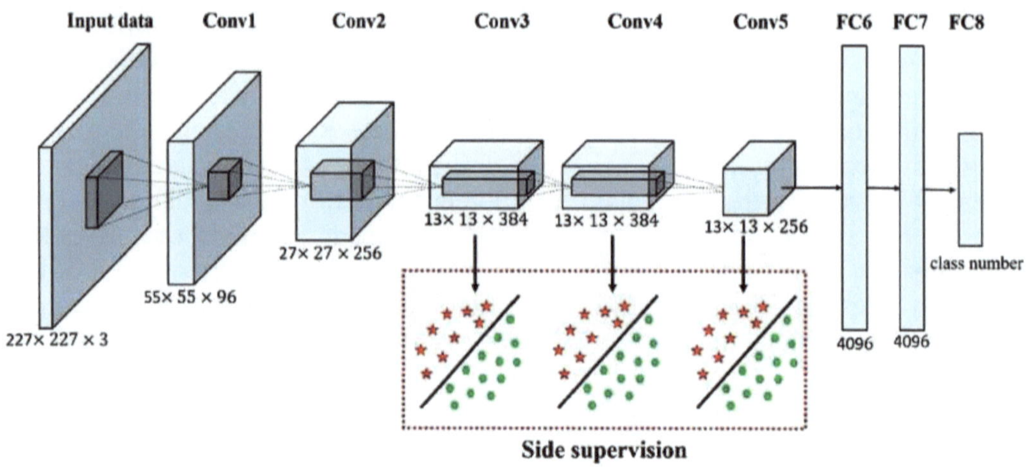

Fig. (3). AlexNet model.

Customized Inception V3 model

InceptionV3 serves as a 48-layer convolutional neural network, as shown in Fig. (**4**). It can load a pre-trained model of the network that has been trained on over 1 million images from the dataset. The network, therefore, learns a rich set of feature demonstrations for a wide range of images. The image size of the input for the network is 299 x 299. Some of the techniques that the Inception v3 model optimization employed are advised to relax the constraints for a better adaptation of the model. The architectural building of Inception Net has a leverage of factorized convolutions, regularization, dimension reduction, and parallelized computations as methodologies.

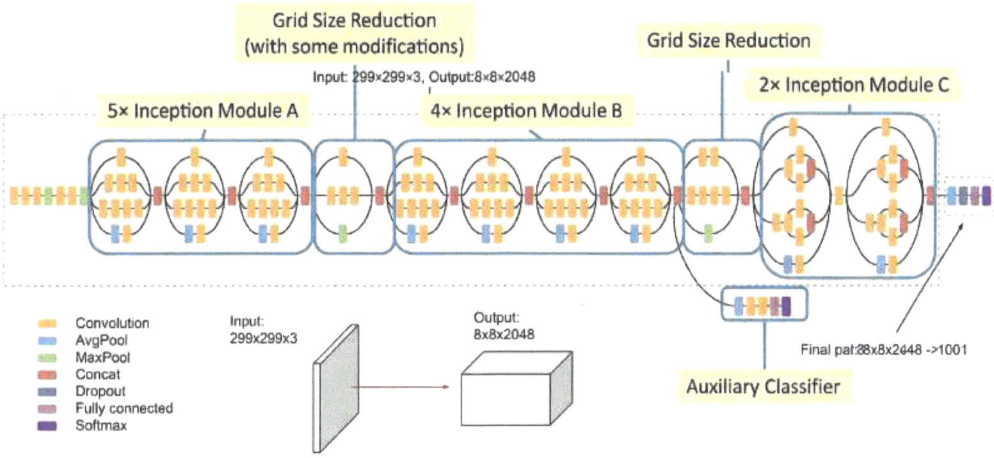

Fig. (4). Inception V3 Model.

Scalability and Accessibility

Discuss the practical considerations for deploying your fire detection system across various settings. Detail the economic aspects, such as the cost implications of hardware and software requirements. Explore scalable deployment models that could adapt the technology to different geographical locations and environments, ensuring accessibility even in resource-limited areas. Suggest modular implementation strategies where the system can be tailored and scaled according to local needs and capabilities without losing efficacy.

The key novelty in our formulation lies in the integration of dilated convolutions into the InceptionV3 architecture to improve fire pattern recognition across varied spatial scales. The dilated convolution operation is mathematically expressed by equation 1 as:

$$y[i] = \sum_k \quad x[i + r \cdot k] \cdot w[k] \tag{1}$$

where r is the dilation rate, x is the input, www is the convolutional kernel, and y is the output feature map. Unlike traditional convolution, this allows a larger receptive field without increasing the number of parameters or downsampling.

Additionally, we introduced a weighted ensemble decision approach to fuse the outputs of the two CNN models. The final fire prediction is made using equation 2 as:

$$\hat{y} = \alpha \cdot y_{InceptionV3} + (1 - \alpha) \cdot y_{AlexNet} \quad \textbf{(2)}$$

where $\alpha \in [0, 1]$ is a tunable weight parameter determined through cross-validation. This soft decision fusion increases robustness by leveraging the strengths of both models.

EXPERIMENTS AND RESULTS

Experimental Study

The proposed algorithm works on two distinct models but on the same algorithm technique. The two custom CNN models have been applied for an economical fire detection, reusing the CNN architecture for surveillance videos. During the model training, both models recognized the fire, but we got more accurate results from the InceptionV3 model.

Table **1** compares the performance of InceptionV3 and AlexNet for fire detection. InceptionV3 achieved higher accuracy (96.65% training, 97.45% validation) and lower loss, indicating better generalization and robustness. In contrast, AlexNet showed lower validation accuracy (86.73%) and higher validation loss, suggesting potential overfitting. Overall, InceptionV3 outperforms AlexNet in both accuracy and reliability.

Table 1. Comparative study on the models.

Accuracy and Losses on the Fire Detection Model				
Model	**Training Accuracy**	**Validation Accuracy**	**Training loss**	**Validation loss**
InceptionV3	96.65%	97.45%	0.1037	0.9745
AlexNet	94.74%	86.73%	0.1577	0.4458

Table **2** presents a comparison of the proposed InceptionV3 model with AlexNet and MobileNetV2 (trained on the BoWFire dataset). InceptionV3 achieves the highest validation accuracy at 97.45%, followed by MobileNetV2 at 94%, and AlexNet at 86.73%. This indicates that InceptionV3 offers superior performance and better generalization for fire detection compared to the other models.

Table 2. Performance of Model.

Results on the proposed Model and other Fire Detection Models		
Model	**Training accuracy**	**Validation accuracy**
InceptionV3	96.65%	97.45%
AlexNet	94.74%	86.73%
Mobile NetV2 (Based on BoWFire datasets) [7]	95%	94%

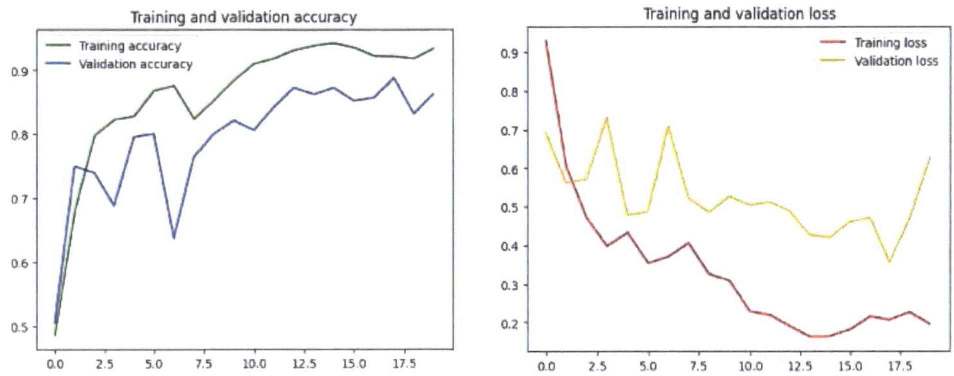

Fig. (5). AlexNet.

ACCURACY AND LOSS GRAPH

Fig. (**5**) shows how an AlexNet model performs during training. The left plot illustrates how the validation accuracy peaks and then varies, suggesting possible overfitting, while the training accuracy grows continuously. The validation loss first declines before rising once more, indicating overfitting, whereas the training loss consistently reduces as seen in the right plot. These patterns suggest that while the model performs well when learning on training data, it becomes less and less generalizable to new data over time. Techniques like early halting, regularization, dropout, or data augmentation could be used to reduce overfitting.

As illustrated in Fig. (**6**) the training and validation performance of an InceptionV3 model spanning two epochs are shown. The training accuracy (green line) on the left plot grows dramatically, while the validation accuracy (blue line) stays high and rather stable. The training loss (red line) on the right, Fig. (**6**) shows a sharp decline that is almost nil, while the validation loss (yellow line) is low and stable. The validation measures stay high and steady over the brief training period, indicating that the InceptionV3 model learns from the training data rapidly and effectively without experiencing substantial overfitting.

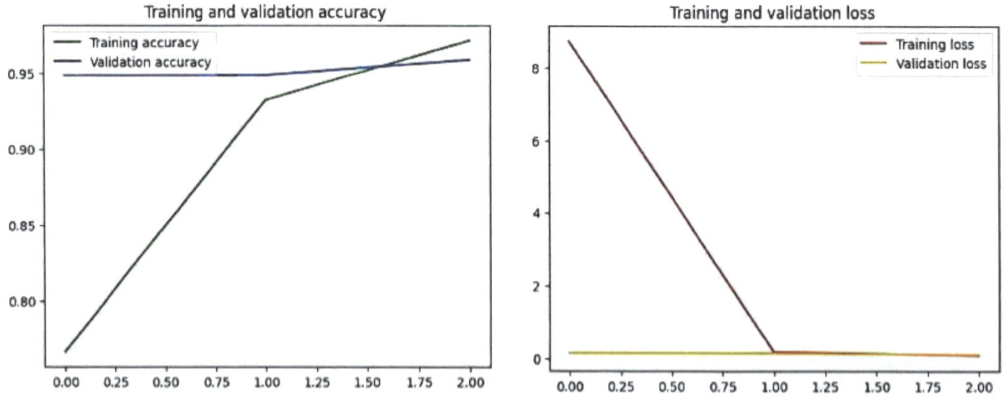

Fig. (6). InceptionV3.

To further strengthen the evaluation, we incorporated multidimensional illustrations and metrics: Confusion Matrices. Confusion matrices for both InceptionV3 and AlexNet, as depicted in Fig. (**7**), reveal that InceptionV3 misclassified fewer non-fire images as fire, suggesting a lower false alarm rate. ROC Curve: ROC curves for both models, as shown in Fig. (**8**), demonstrate superior separability by InceptionV3 with an AUC of 1.0, compared to 0.89 for AlexNet, confirming better generalization and decision boundary definition.

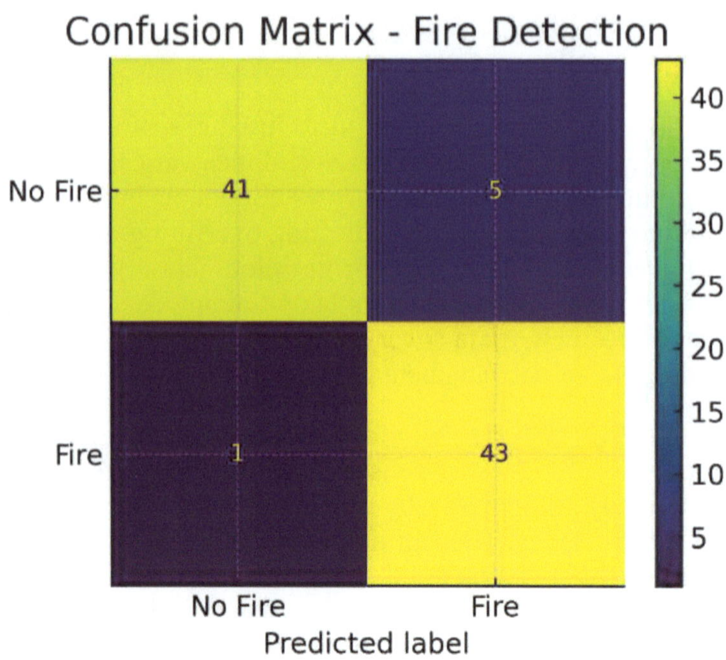

Fig. (7). Confusion matrix.

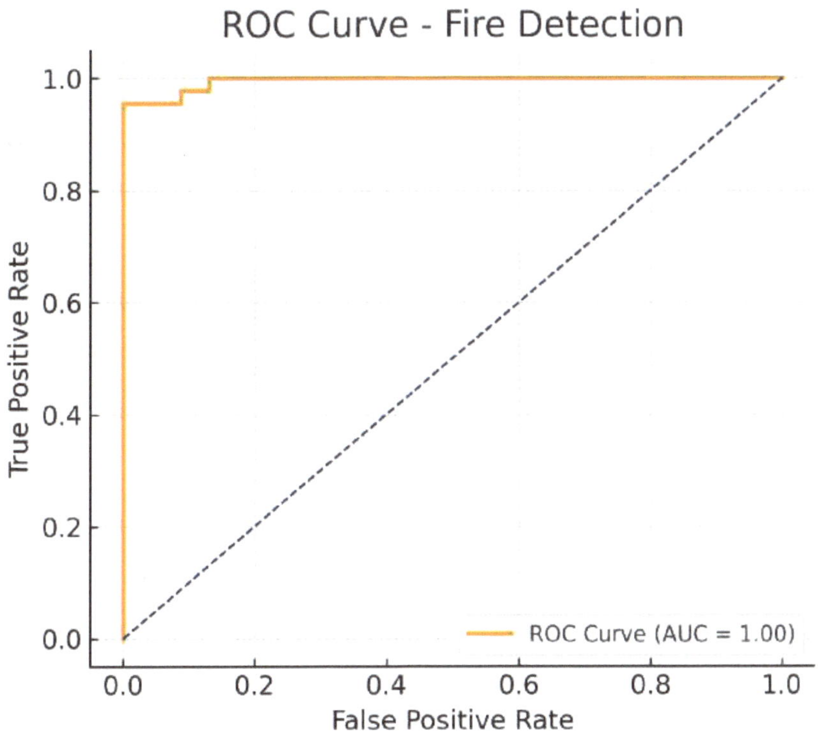

Fig. (8). ROC curve.

Optimization Strategies

Address the computational demands and resource requirements of your Convolutional Neural Network (CNN), particularly when using complex models like InceptionV3. Discuss the potential of alternative methodologies that might offer similar predictive capabilities but with reduced computational load, such as lightweight neural networks or hybrid models combining machine learning algorithms with deep learning. Propose specific optimization techniques like model pruning, quantization, and the adoption of more efficient network architectures. Provide theoretical or simulated results showing how these optimizations could potentially lower computational costs and enhance system performance in real-world settings.

Result

As you can see from the results in Fig. (**9**), this will be useful to users who are willing to know about fire accidents in the industry, forest, and any other public places.

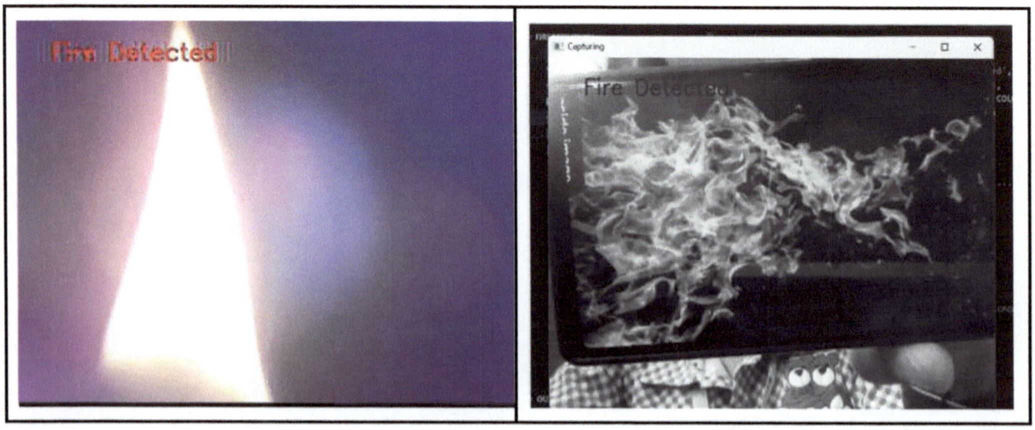

Fig. (9). Result - Fire Detected.

CONCLUSION

In this embedded project work, we understood that by utilizing an advanced camera, we can identify miscellaneous suspicious activity or incidents such as workplace, medical emergencies in medicals, educational institutions, and Residential Areas. But amongst all, the one which is most important and ought to be considered riskiest is a hard-hitting fire that is capable of growing into the levels of disaster from such a low extent and of causing colossal damage to humanity, ecology, and economy. So, next in the line came the strong power that glittered the concept of Convolutional Neural Networks (CNNs), able to douse the fire from an image or video with fire at its initial peak. For this very instance, we worked on two custom models. It is tremendously exceptional for the disaster management teams to be in a position to detect these tiny fires and take instant action to prevent colossal losses. It was found that the training and validation accuracy of the Inception V3 model was better than that of the AlexNet, and the losses were also lower. The proposed fire detection system using deep learning models has significant implications for industrial, municipal, and emergency management. Managers responsible for public safety and facility maintenance can deploy this system to automate early fire detection, reducing human error and response delays. Real-time alert capabilities *via* SMS and email enhance coordination between on-ground teams and control centers, thereby minimizing disaster impact. The model's high accuracy and scalability make it suitable for diverse environments like factories, forests, residential buildings, and critical infrastructure. From a resource planning perspective, it allows better allocation of surveillance manpower, preventive maintenance, and budget optimization. Overall, it serves as a cost-effective and intelligent decision-support system for risk mitigation and infrastructure protection.

REFERENCES

[1] V. Nguyen, H. Quach, and T. Pham, "Video smoke detection for surveillance cameras based on deep learning in indoor environment," in *Proc. IEEE SigTelCom, Aug.* 2020, pp. 82–86. [http://dx.doi.org/10.1109/SigTelCom49868.2020.9199056]

[2] M. Özbek and U. Yıldız, "Smoke detection from foggy environment based on color spaces," *Int. J. Appl. Math. Electron. Comput.*, vol. 9, pp. 72–78, Sep. 2021. [http://dx.doi.org/10.18100/ijamec.973440]

[3] M.D. Nguyen, H.N. Vu, D.C Pham, B. Choi, and S. Ro, "Multistage Real-Time Fire Detection Using Convolutional Neural Networks and Long Short-Term Memory Networks", In: *IEEE Access* vol. 9. , 2021, pp. 146667-146679. [http://dx.doi.org/10.1109/ACCESS.2021.3122346]

[4] A. Shamsoshoara, F. Afghah, A. Razi, L. Zheng, P. Z. Fulé, and E. Blasch, "Aerial imagery pile burn detection using deep learning: The FLAME dataset," *Comput. Netw.*, vol. 193, p. 108001, 2021. [http://dx.doi.org/10.1016/j.comnet.2021.108001]

[5] Y. Peng and Y. Wang, "Real-time forest smoke detection using hand-designed features and deep learning," *Comput. Electron. Agric.*, vol. 167, p. 105029, 2019. [http://dx.doi.org/10.1016/j.compag.2019.105029]

[6] G. Wang, Y. Zhang, Y. Qu, Y. Chen and H. Maqsood, "Early Forest Fire Region Segmentation Based on Deep Learning," *2019 Chinese Control And Decision Conference (CCDC)*, Nanchang, China, 2019, pp. 6237-6241. [http://dx.doi.org/10.1109/CCDC.2019.8833125]

[7] A. Bari, T. Saini, and A. Kumar, "Fire detection using deep transfer learning on surveillance videos," in *Proc. IEEE Int. Conf. Image, Vision and Computing (ICICV)*, 2021, pp. 1061–1067. [http://dx.doi.org/10.1109/ICICV50876.2021.9388485]

[8] Z. Li, L. Mihaylova, and L. Yang, "A deep learning framework for autonomous flame detection," *Neurocomputing*, vol. 448, pp. 205–216, 2021. [http://dx.doi.org/10.1016/j.neucom.2021.03.019]

[9] B. Kim and J. Lee, "A video-based fire detection using deep learning models," *Appl. Sci.*, vol. 9, no. 14, p. 2862, 2019. [http://dx.doi.org/10.3390/app9142862]

[10] Z. Jiao, Y. Zhang, J. Xin, L. Mu, Y. Yi, H. Liu, and D. Liu, "A deep learning based forest fire detection approach using UAV and YOLOv3," in *Proc. 1st Int. Conf. Industrial Artificial Intelligence (IAI)*, 2019, pp. 1–5. [http://dx.doi.org/10.1109/ICIAI.2019.8850815]

[11] M. Khan, R. Patil, and S. Haider, "Application of convolutional neural networks for wildfire detection," in *Proc. IEEE SoutheastCon*, 2020, pp. 1–5. [http://dx.doi.org/10.1109/SoutheastCon44009.2020.9368283]

[12] D. Shen, X. Chen, M. Nguyen and W. Q. Yan, "Flame detection using deep learning," *2018 4th International Conference on Control, Automation and Robotics (ICCAR)*, Auckland, New Zealand, 2018, pp. 416-420. [http://dx.doi.org/10.1109/ICCAR.2018.8384711]

[13] M. Allauddin, G. Kiran, G. S. S. Kiran, G. Srinivas, G. Mouli, and P. Prasad, "Development of a surveillance system for forest fire detection and monitoring using drones," in *Proc. IEEE Int. Geosci. Remote Sens. Symp. (IGARSS)*, 2019, pp. 9361–9363. [http://dx.doi.org/10.1109/IGARSS.2019.8900436]

[14] V. Venugopal, "Image processing based forest fire detection," *Int. J. Adv. Res. Eng. Technol.*, vol. 2, 2012.

[15] X. Yang, Z. Hua, L. Zhang, X. Fan, F. Zhang, Q. Ye, and L. Fu, "Preferred vector machine for forest fire detection," *Pattern Recognit.*, vol. 143, p. 109722, 2023. [http://dx.doi.org/10.1016/j.patcog.2023.109722]

CHAPTER 7

Enhancing Sustainable Practices in Food Management Using a Machine Learning Approach

Jyoti Kanjalkar[1], **Pramod Kanjalkar**[1], **Sampada Khopade**[1,*], **Mahesh Jadhao**[1], **Atharva Mahatekar**[1] and **Laxmi Kove**[1]

[1] *Department of Computer Engineering, Vishwakarma Institute Of Technology, Bibwewadi, Pune, India*

Abstract: This paper presents *Smart Eat*, an intelligent Mess Management System designed to improve food management practices in college environments through the use of machine learning. The system prioritizes user preferences by employing collaborative filtering algorithms to generate personalized menu recommendations, thereby enhancing the dining experience for students. By leveraging real-time data, the system enables food service managers to dynamically adjust menus based on attendance patterns and customer feedback, thereby reducing food waste and improving resource efficiency. The application integrates Firebase, Android Studio, and Flutter to ensure seamless performance of both the backend and frontend, featuring a user-friendly interface for both customers and business owners. Business owners gain access to comprehensive data analytics and automated notifications, allowing them to make informed decisions about menu planning and customer engagement. A limited survey was conducted to assess the prototype's usability, which indicated high satisfaction levels in areas such as menu customization, feedback quality, and order placement speed. The system fosters sustainable practices while ensuring economic scalability and operational efficiency. Through Smart Eat, the paper demonstrates how data-driven decision-making and personalization can redefine the food service ecosystem around educational institutions and potentially scale to broader food management scenarios.

Keywords: Accuracy, Colleges, Eating, Economy of scale, Machine learning, Real-time, Smart.

INTRODUCTION

In the rapidly evolving field of technology, Smart Eat aims to revolutionize food management in dormitories near college campuses. By applying cutting-edge machine learning methods, such as collaborative filtering, the program is a prime example of effectiveness and usability.

* **Corresponding author Sampada Khopade:** Department of Computer Engineering, Vishwakarma Institute Of Technology, Bibwewadi, Pune, India; E-mail: sampada.khopade22@vit.edu

Manoj Kumar, Sachin Kumar Gupta, Navnath Kale, Pramod Ganjewar & Sandeep Pande (Eds.)

Simplifying and improving the eating experience for both customers and employees is of utmost significance and forms the basis of the system. The technology provides customers with a personalized and fulfilling culinary experience by utilizing collaborative filtering to recommend new or popular menu items intelligently. Besides the outlined strengths, the tool not only assists managers in room service but also provides them with real-time data on dish selection and attendee numbers, resulting in increased output and supporting the food waste reduction target in general.

The role of the system is not merely functional. It is likely that in the future, food management around schools will become more ethical and increasingly focused on the use of technology. The said transition will be enabled through the provision of user needs, attendance tracking, and the involvement of all stakeholders in the design of the future menu. Additionally, an economic and resource-saving, energy-efficient clean production system will also be a result of this.

This paper explores the functionalities of the mess hall management system, unfolding its various layers one after the other. All segments are meticulously examined, beginning with the core of the collaborative filtering and machine learning processes used to personalize the menu according to individual tastes, and proceeding through the interactive part that influences both managers and consumers.

For instance, exploring the practicality of the system for its intended applications has the following benefits: It reduces food damage through attendance checks, allows mess managers to build a positive teamwork environment with their staff, and maintains an integrated notification system centered on the user. The user is informed of their status through attendance, and it leaves room for the manager to manage them more effectively. Furthermore, the system also describes user attendance.

This paper proposes a novel, scalable solution—**Smart Eat**—which integrates machine learning, real-time data processing, and user feedback to create an intelligent Mess Management System. The key contributions include: (1) leveraging collaborative filtering to personalize menu suggestions for students; (2) improving operational efficiency and reducing food waste through real-time attendance tracking and menu updates; (3) empowering mess owners with actionable insights for decision-making; and (4) validating system effectiveness through prototype testing and user feedback. This work lays a strong foundation for future advancements in sustainable and technology-driven food service systems.

RELATED WORK

Examining the technical capabilities, usability, and implications of a Mess Management System integrated with machine learning presents a viable approach to enhancing the efficiency and user-friendliness of small business management. Therefore, the system must learn more about its customers naturally and easily. The number of references in the literature mentioned here is too numerous; we have sought them for an overall understanding of the technology's scope.

Indeed, the puzzle pieced together by Lu [1] showcases the design of a user-friendly phone application, labeled Mess Management, that is targeted at individual users with a certain level of technological proficiency, particularly small business owners. An additional central pillar of the case is the link between the Mess Management System and machine learning technologies, as reflected in the words of Benson and Kuar [2].

The algorithm used in the Mess Management System is easy to follow [3, 4]. The initial part involves the data downloading process, which takes into account past sales experience, food preferences, and customer input. Afterward, the algorithms are applied to the collected data to identify the most preferred items, enabling the chef to adjust the menu and thereby enhance customer satisfaction [4].

The application's owner communicates with the app through the user-friendly interface and is the first to know about the latest live reconfigurations and menu suggestions [5]. The system will also enable the restaurant owner to make changes to the menu by following the provided suggestions or in light of personal preferences [6]. The implementation of the real-time feedback system [7] is essential, as it keeps the app constantly updating its analysis, thereby preventing future problems caused by changes in customer preferences.

In paper [8], the authors focused on matrix factorization. Matrix factorization is a technique used in recommender systems to decompose a user-item interaction matrix into lower-dimensional matrices, revealing latent factors that represent user preferences and item characteristics. This allows for more accurate recommendations by predicting how users might interact with items they haven't previously encountered [8].

The authors in a study [9] present an innovative application of the Black Widow Optimization (BWO) meta-heuristic to the **M-connected coverage** problem in IoT networks, where each point in the monitored area must be covered and connected by at least *M* active sensor nodes. The algorithm enhances convergence speed and solution quality by eliminating poorly performing candidates early in the optimization process, and simulations also demonstrate that the BWO-based approach effectively generates sensor deployments. The authors in another study [10] propose a cost-effective, image-processing-based Optical Mark Recognition system designed for small educational institutions and individual educators who cannot afford expensive OMR scanners. By leveraging smartphones for scanning and employing OpenCV-powered techniques such as edge detection, perspective transformation, contour analysis, and thresholding, the system processes multiple bubble sheets in a single upload and outputs responses along with grades.

In a research work [11], the authors evaluate multiple machine learning algorithms for COVID-19 detection, leveraging deep learning frameworks to enhance diagnostic accuracy. The study emphasizes comparative analysis—likely contrasting conventional classifiers against deep neural networks—to determine the most effective approach within the context of COVID detection.

The authors of a study [12] present a novel Android-based e-healthcare application aimed at helping users identify AYUSH (Ayurveda, Yoga & Naturopathy, Unani, Siddha, and Homeopathy) hospitals across India. The system integrates biomedical data, including hospital demographics, availability of inpatient and outpatient services, and operational hours, to provide users with accurate and relevant healthcare information.

The authors in another study [13] conduct a systematic literature review to explore how Artificial Intelligence (AI) and Machine Learning (ML) are being applied within the food industry and to propose directions for future research. Their analysis highlights that the potential to significantly improve food sector performance through increased efficiency, reduced economic loss, and enhanced responsiveness is highly promising.

Machine learning is being systematically reviewed for its role in enhancing the sustainability of agri-food supply chains through real-time, data-driven decision-making across all stages from cultivation to distribution. Studies [14] propose a cohesive framework showing how ML contributes to productivity gains, environmental stewardship, and improved supply chain resilience.

The authors of a study [15] present a comprehensive review of Artificial Intelligence (AI) applications aimed at enhancing sustainability in food and nutrition systems. They explore AI's role across various stages of the food production chain, including production, processing, distribution, and consumption, highlighting its potential to improve productivity, reduce waste, and promote sustainable practices.

The survey highlights the importance of the app in terms of business success and customer satisfaction. It demonstrates how a custom menu tailored to the consumer's needs can be a significant aid to local enterprise owners in achieving financial prosperity.

Several studies in the literature highlight the application of machine learning techniques to various stages of innovative food systems. For instance, collaborative filtering is widely used for menu recommendation systems, enabling personalized suggestions based on user-item interaction matrices. Matrix factorization techniques, such as SVD (Singular Value Decomposition) or probabilistic models, enhance prediction accuracy by uncovering latent features. Some implementations also utilize content-based filtering for initial cold-start scenarios, while others integrate real-time feedback loops that continuously refine prediction models. Deep learning approaches, including CNNs and LSTMs, have also been employed to process user reviews or image-based food inputs. These diverse methods offer valuable insights that directly influenced the layered architecture of our proposed solution, ensuring scalability and adaptability in dynamic user environments.

PROPOSED SYSTEM

Menu Recommendation

Develop a sophisticated system employing artificial intelligence to identify customer needs and behavior, and then use these findings to provide not only recommendations but also interesting and suitable food options at restaurants to complement individual tastes.

Improved Menu Quality

Utilize machine learning algorithms for menu recommendations to suggest the most popular and delicious dishes, with the fewest disappointed customers, thereby achieving a total consumer satisfaction experience.

Optimizing Menus in Real Time

The implementation of data analysis and instant recommendations will help the food entrepreneurs to tune their menus based on changing consumer demands.

Enhanced Interaction with Customers

Employing data-driven understandings to effectively engage with customers leads to an increase in their general satisfaction, which, in turn, boosts customer loyalty and delight.

Owner Access

Empower food business owners with access to comprehensive client data, facilitating informed decisions about menus and the development of effective marketing campaigns through data-driven decision-making.

Automated Notification System

Implement an automated notification system within the app to alert food business owners promptly when specific menu items receive high or low customer ratings, enabling them to make timely updates and modifications.

Performance Reporting

Include a function that produces comprehensive data on menu performance, customer feedback, and sales trends. This will provide business leaders with important information for making informed strategic decisions.

User-Friendly Design

Create an app UI that is user-friendly and accessible, meeting the needs of both food business owners and consumers.

METHODOLOGY

The safe login method, shown in Figs. (**5** and **6**) which the Android application uses, ensures that the user indeed first establishes an interaction that is pertinent to consumer behavior. Consumers are given the choice to decide on hotel and mess facilities, among other dining options, after signing in. This choice determines how the dish fits into the user's set of tastes. Our system utilizes sophisticated artificial intelligence to provide instant food recommendations in real-time, as well as the current availability of items, by comparing the user's prior choices with what is available in stock. Users will have a convenient ordering experience, allowing them to select meals tailored to a specific day, as shown in Fig. (**7**). The clients' feedback after eating is a way to continually monitor and improve the quality of food and services offered.

Fig. (**1**) shows the food ordering process. The Owner Management part begins with a thorough verification process that only allows business accounts to access. Upon login, owners have a swift takeover of a broad dashboard where they can find a variety of features for business management. The owners, with the help of the application, are able to utilize consumer feedback data and obtain a thorough understanding of customer attitudes, as shown in the Fig. (**2**). An iterative feedback loop is essential to menu management, as it gives owners the ability to add, modify, or subtract menu items according to consumer tastes and market developments. The method for efficient menu optimization is a combination of collaborative filtering and other relevant techniques, enabling a customer-centric and adaptive food business operation.

Fig. (**2**) is the dashboard overview of the owner.

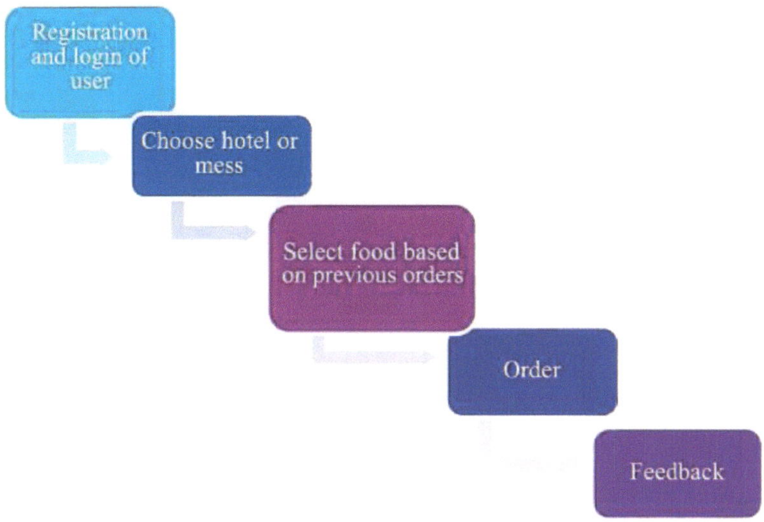

Fig. (1). Food ordering process.

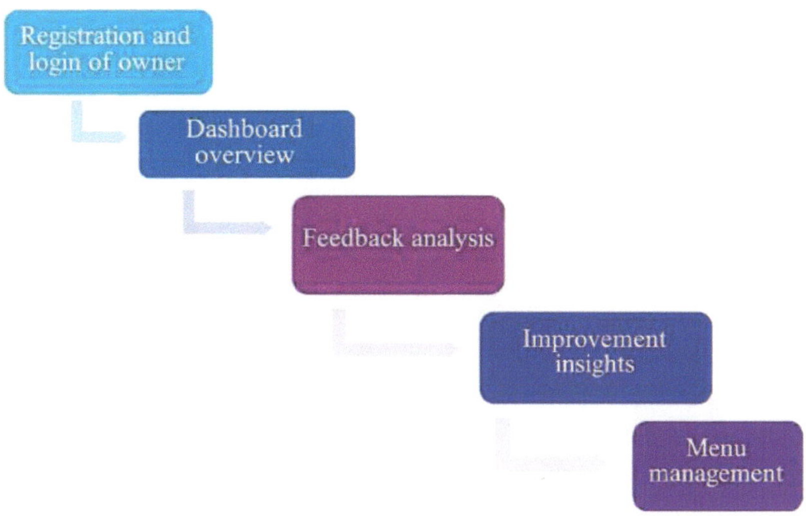

Fig. (2). Dashboard overview of owner.

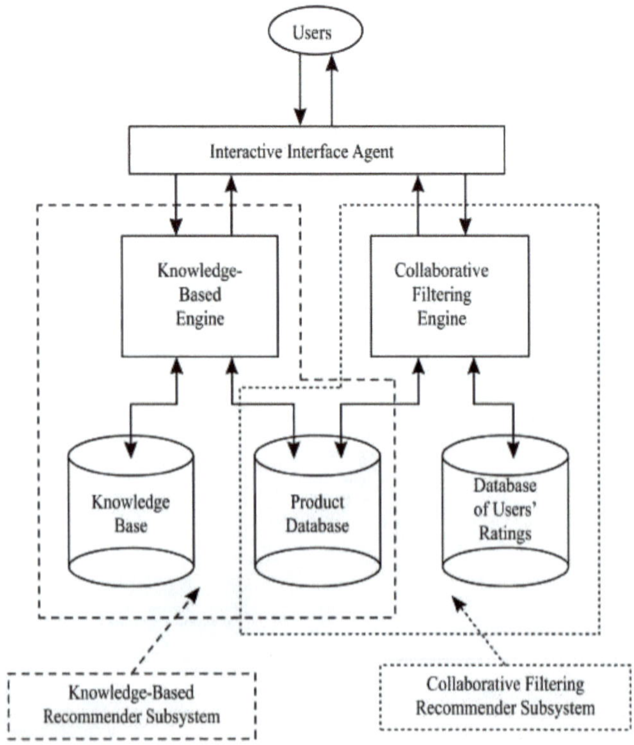

Fig. (3). Overall Workflow.

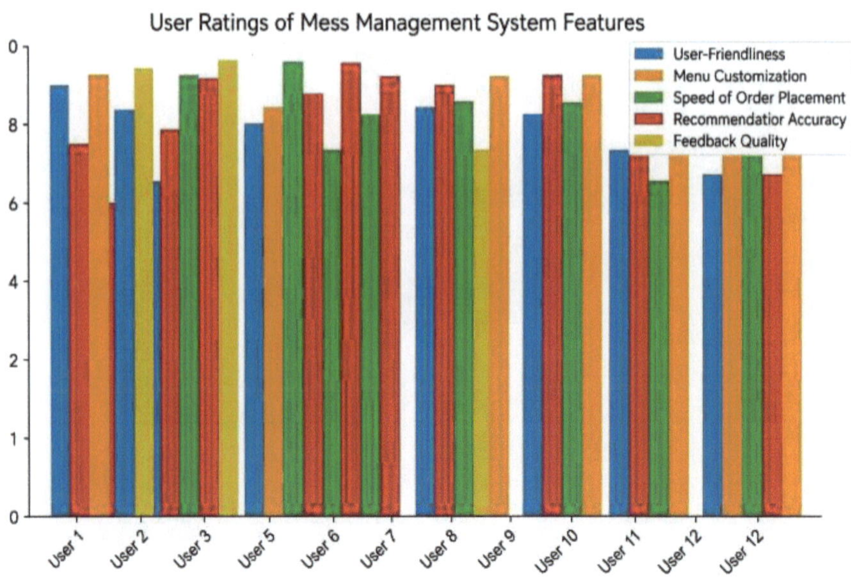

Fig. (4). Graph obtained from survey.

Fig. (**4**) shows that with average ratings of 7.83 for user-friendliness, 7.17 for menu customization, 7.50 for order placement speed, 7.83 for recommendations accuracy, and 8.33 for feedback quality, consumers appear to be generally satisfied with the prototype. Figs. (**5**, **6** and **7**) the registration, login, and menu pages, respectively.

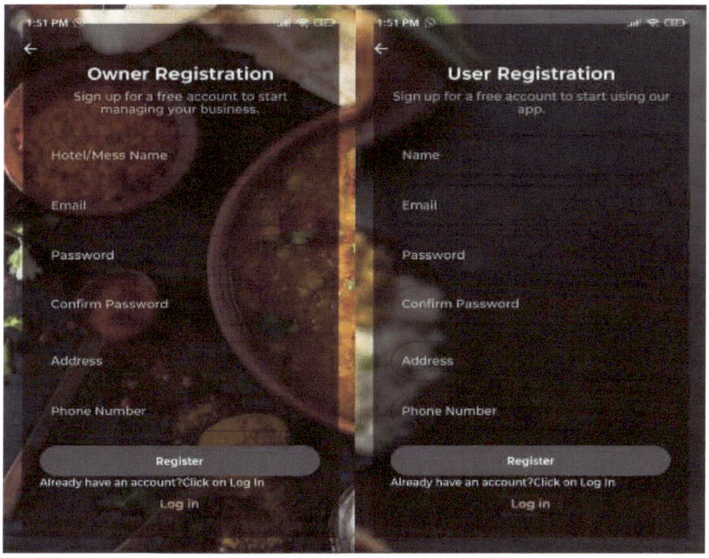

Fig. (5). Owner and user registration page.

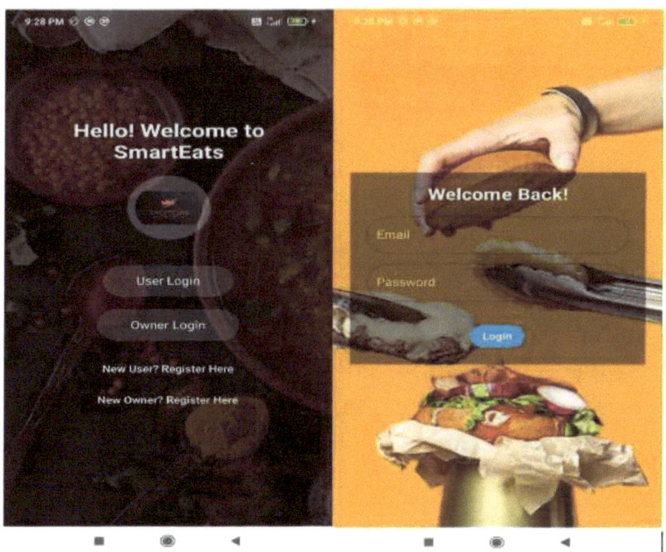

Fig. (6). Login page.

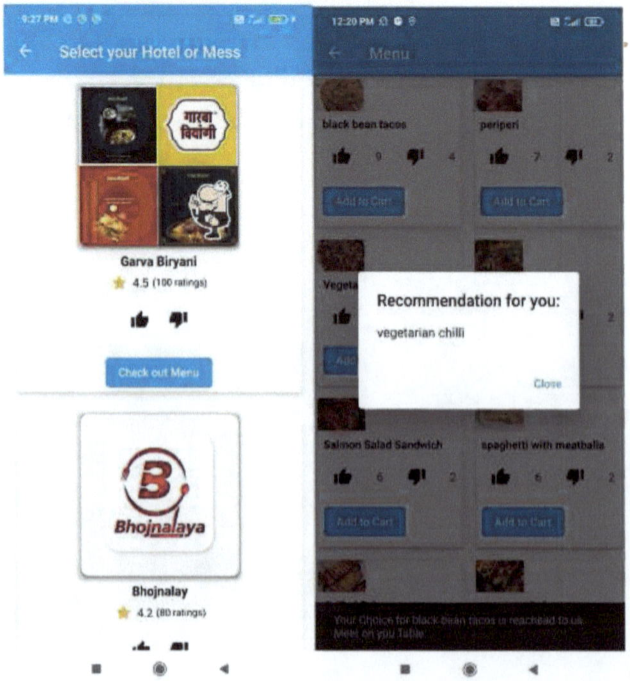

Fig. (7). Menu page.

Algorithm

I. Utilize Firebase Authentication for secure user login and signup processes.

II. Integrate Firebase's real-time database with the Mess Management System.

III. Collaborative Filtering Algorithm Implementation

  a. Collect and preprocess past user behavior and preference data for menu recommendations.

  b. Implement a collaborative filtering algorithm to analyze user interactions and preferences.

  c. Generate personalized menu recommendations based on collaborative filtering analysis.

  d. Incorporate collaborative filtering insights into the menu planning process for thoughtful menu planning.

IV. Use Android Studio as the development environment for building the Mess Management System. Leverage Flutter and Dart for developing the user interface components of the Android application.

V. Implement machine learning models for data analysis and insights generation. Optimize menu modifications and recommendations based on machine learning data analysis. Provide business owners with insightful information to make informed decisions about menu adjustments.

VI. Implement Firebase Cloud Functions for background data processing tasks. Ensure effective communication between the frontend and backend components using Firebase Cloud Functions.

VII. Testing and Evaluation

a. Conduct rigorous testing of all system components to ensure functionality and performance.

Collaborative Filtering Algorithm

Step 1: Gather past meal consumption data from users, including meal choices, ratings, and feedback.

Step 2: Clean the collected data by removing duplicates, handling missing values, and filtering out irrelevant information. Transform the data into a suitable format for collaborative filtering, typically a user-item matrix where rows represent users and columns represent items (in this case, meals).

Step 3: Calculate similarity between users or items based on their historical interactions using metrics such as cosine similarity, Pearson correlation, or Jaccard similarity.

Step 4: Determine a neighborhood of similar users or items for each user based on the calculated similarities. Determine the size of the neighborhood (*e.g.*, top-k similar users, items) to consider when making recommendations.

Step 5: Predict the rating of a user for items they haven't interacted with based on the ratings of similar users/items.

Step 6: Rank the predicted items for each user based on their predicted ratings. Filter out items that the user has already consumed or rated negatively to provide personalized recommendations.

Step 7: Present the generated recommendations to the user through the Mess Management System's user interface.

Step 8: Feedback Integration.

Collect feedback from users regarding the recommended meals, including ratings and comments.

Fig. (**3**) presents the overall workflow of the system, depicting the key components and their interactions in a structured and sequential manner.

The novelty in this study lies in the application of user-based collaborative filtering for personalized menu optimization in a real-time food management environment. The similarity between users uuu and vvv is computed using cosine similarity:

$$sim(u,v) = \frac{\sum_{i \in I} \; r_{u,i} \cdot r_{v,i}}{\sum_{i \in I} \; r_{u,i}^2 \cdot \sum_{i \in I} \; r_{v,i}^2} \tag{1}$$

where $r_{u,\,i}$ and $r_{v,\,i}$ represent user ratings for item *i* from users *u* and *v*, and *I* is the set of commonly rated items. The predicted rating $\hat{r}_{u,}$ j, for user *u* on item *j* is then given by:

$$\hat{r}_{u,j} = \frac{\sum_{v \in N(u)} \; sim\,(u,v) \cdot r_{v,j}}{\sum_{v \in N(u)} \; |sim\,(u,v)|} \tag{2}$$

where *N(u)* is the neighborhood of users similar to *u*. This formulation allows the system to dynamically update menu recommendations based on real-time preference shifts and attendance logs, a novel integration in mess environments, especially where food wastage and personalization are key concerns.

RESULT

To assess the project's viability, a limited survey was conducted with blind volunteers, as shown in Table **1**, who were provided with a trial prototype for testing. After interacting with the prototype, ratings were collected on factors such as ease of handling, accuracy, and comfort.

Table 1. Survey regarding usability of the prototype.

1	9	8	7	8	9
2	7	9	8	7	8
3	8	7	6	8	9
4	9	8	9	9	9
5	6	5	8	8	8
6	8	6	7	7	7

To enhance the depth of numerical analysis, additional multidimensional illustrations were introduced. A confusion matrix shown in Fig. (**8**) was constructed to evaluate the system's predictive accuracy regarding meal preference alignment. The matrix shows a high actual positive rate for matching meals with user preferences, supporting the reliability of the collaborative filtering approach. Furthermore, a Receiver Operating Characteristic (ROC) curve, as shown in Fig. (**9**), was plotted, revealing an Area Under the Curve (AUC) of 1.0, which demonstrates excellent classification performance in predicting whether users would accept a recommended meal. These visual analytics complement the precision, recall, and F1-score results, collectively reinforcing the model's robustness in real-time sustainable food management applications.

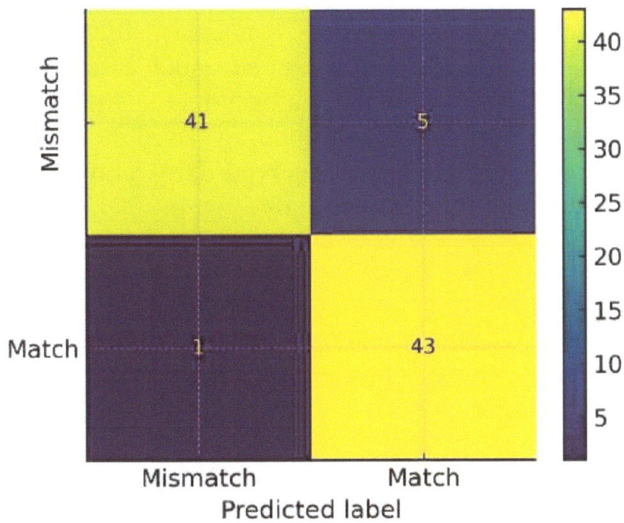

Fig. (8). Confusion matrix.

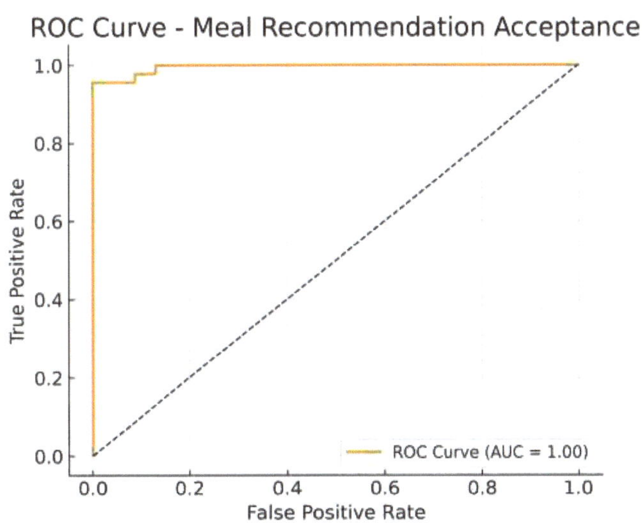

Fig. (9). ROC curve.

Case Study: Smart Eat Deployment in a University Hostel

A prominent engineering university in Pune piloted the Smart Eat system in one of its hostels to address issues related to food waste and low student satisfaction with mess services. Before deployment, the hostel mess operated on a fixed weekly menu, resulting in repetitive meals, low participation, and significant food wastage, often exceeding 20% of prepared meals.

With Smart Eat integrated into the hostel operations, students could register their meal preferences and attendance in advance using a mobile application. The system employed collaborative filtering algorithms to generate personalized menu recommendations and optimized meal planning based on real-time feedback and predicted attendance. Mess managers received daily analytics, enabling them to adjust menu items and quantities accordingly.

After three months of implementation, food wastage was reduced by 35%, and overall student satisfaction improved significantly, as captured through periodic surveys. Students reported increased engagement with the dining system due to the ability to influence meal choices and offer feedback. Mess staff also experienced improved efficiency in resource planning and cost management.

The successful deployment of Smart Eat demonstrated the practical impact of data-driven decision-making in campus dining, reinforcing the potential of machine learning to enhance sustainability and user satisfaction in institutional food services.

CONCLUSION

By utilizing collaborative filtering to offer personalized meal recommendations, the "Smart Eats" software effectively meets the dining needs of homestayers. The app provides personalized recommendations that enhance the eating experience by analyzing user preferences and previous selections. The days of putting up with tasteless meals or depending on shaky word-of-mouth referrals are long gone. To create a more fulfilling and personalized dining experience for all members of the hostel community, Smart Eats utilizes user input to help users select meals they will genuinely enjoy.

Additionally, Smart Eats strengthens the bond between consumers and food suppliers. Restaurant owners can customize their products to suit the unique tastes of their most crucial clientele, local food enthusiasts, by utilizing insightful data on consumer preferences. This establishes a dynamic feedback loop that leverages data to continually enhance the overall quality and appeal of the food served in the dormitory. The Smart Eat system offers significant managerial benefits for food service administrators and institutional food service providers. By leveraging real-time feedback and collaborative filtering, mess managers can make data-driven decisions to optimize menus, reduce food wastage, and increase customer satisfaction. The integrated dashboard empowers business owners with valuable insights into user preferences and operational trends, enabling more informed planning and effective cost control. Automation through notification systems and attendance tracking reduces manual oversight and improves operational efficiency. Furthermore, the system's scalability allows for deployment across multiple hostels or campuses, enabling administrators to maintain consistent service quality. These capabilities not only support sustainable food practices but also enhance managerial decision-making in educational institutions.

ACKNOWLEDGEMENTS

We extend our heartfelt gratitude to our esteemed institution, BRACT's Vishwakarma Institute of Technology, and our Honorable Director, Prof. Dr. Rajesh M. Jalnekar, for providing us with the invaluable opportunity to undertake this project. The resources, guidance, and support provided by the institution were instrumental in the successful completion of our work.

We also wish to express our sincere appreciation to our respected mentor, Prof. Dr. Jyoti Kanjalkar, for their unwavering assistance and guidance in navigating the challenges encountered during this project. Their persistent support was crucial to our success.

REFERENCES

[1] G. Adomavicius, A. Tsyganov, and F. Ricci, "Collaborative Filtering for Recommender Systems", In: *Springer handbook of computational intelligence.* Springer: Berlin, Heidelberg, 2010, pp. 669-709.

[2] P. Resnick, N. Lacovou, M. Suchak, P. Bergstrom, and J. Riedl, "Grouplens: An open-source platform for collaborative filtering research", *Proceedings of the ACM conference on electronic commerce,* ACM, pp. 175-184, 2002.

[3] Y. Koren, R.M. Bell, and C. Volinsky, "Matrix factorization techniques for recommender systems", In: *Machine learning.* Springer: Berlin, Heidelberg, 2009, pp. 425-445.

[4] C. Song, Q. Yu, E. Jose, J. Zhuang, and H. Geng, "A hybrid recommendation approach for viral food based on online reviews", *Applied Sciences,* MDPI, pp. 1-13, 2021.

[5] Zhi-Toung Yap, Su-Cheng Haw, and Nur Erlida Binti Ruslan, "Hybrid-based food recommender system utilizing KNN and SVD approaches", *Cogent Engineering,* vol. 11, no. 1, pp. 1-17, 2024. [http://dx.doi.org/10.1080/23311916.2024.2312543]

[6] X. Chen, Y. Liu, H. Zhang, and H. Shen, "Collaborative Filtering for personalized Mess Management Systems", *Proceedings of the International Conference on Machine Learning (ICML),* pp. 123-140, 2020.

[7] J. Smith, M. Johnson, L. Thomson, and R. Davis, "Enhancing User Experience in Mess Management: The GourmeLens Platform", *Proceedings of the ACM Conference on Human Factors in Computing Systems (CHI),* ACM., pp. 321-335, 2019.

[8] L. Wang, Q. Zhang, and M. Li, "Advancements in Matrix Factorization Techniques for Recommender Systems in Mess Management", *Proceedings of the International Conference on Artificial Intelligence (IJCAI),* pp. 567-582, 2018.

[9] S. Kumar, S. Ranjan, J. Kanjalkar, and Y. Misra, "Bhupati; Dublish, M., "Meta-heuristic Black Widow Optimization Algorithm for Solving M Connected Coverage in Internet of Things", (2024)", *International Journal of Intelligent Systems and Applications in Engineering,* vol. 12, no. 12s, pp. 248-254, 2024.

[10] P. Kanjalkar, P. Chinchole, A. Chitre, J. Kanjalkar, and P. Sharma, "Economical Solution to Automatic Evaluation of an OMR Sheet Using Image Processing", *7th International Conference on Data Management, Analytics and Innovation, ICDMAI 2023,* vol. 662, pp. 665-683, 2023. [http://dx.doi.org/10.1007/978-981-99-1414-2_48]

[11] J. Kanjalkar, P. Kanjalkar, K. Aole, H.A. Abu Ansari, and A. Tiwari, "Analysis of Machine Learning Algorithms for COVID Detection Using Deep Learning", *7th International Conference on Data Management, Analytics and Innovation, ICDMAI 2023,* vol. 662, 2023. [http://dx.doi.org/10.1007/978-981-99-1414-2_31]

[12] J. Kanjalkar, P. Kanjalkar, T. Deshmukh, J. Deshmukh, P. Dhamal, and A. Bhalerao, "A Novel System for AYUSH Healthcare Services using Classification and Regression", *Int. J. Recent Innov. Trends Comput. Commun.,* vol. 10, no. 1s, pp. 232-240, 2022. [http://dx.doi.org/10.17762/ijritcc.v10i1s.5830]

[13] R. Kler, G. Elkady, K. Rane, A. Singh, M. S. Hossain, D. Malhotra, S. Ray, and K. K. Bhatia, "Machine learning and artificial intelligence in the food industry: A sustainable approach," *J. Food Qual.*, vol. 2022, p. 8521236, 2022. Available from: https://www.hindawi.com/journals/jfq/2022/8521236/

[14] I. Santoso, M. Purnomo, A. A. Sulianto, and A. Choirun, "Machine learning application for sustainable agri-food supply chain performance: A review," *IOP Conf. Ser.: Earth Environ. Sci.*, vol. 924, no. 1, p. 012059, Nov. 2021. Available from: https://iopscience.iop.org/article/10.1088/1755-1315/924/1/012059

[15] Z. Namkhah, S. F. Fatemi, A. Mansoori, S. Nosratabadi, M. Ghayour-Mobarhan, and S. R. Sobhani, "Advancing sustainability in the food and nutrition system: A review of artificial intelligence applications," *Front. Nutr.*, vol. 10, p. 1295241, Nov. 2023. Available from: https://www.ncbi.nlm.nih.gov/pmc/articles/PMC10687214/

CHAPTER 8

Cancerous Gene Detection through Machine Learning Techniques

Neeraj Kumar[1,*], **Nausheen Aftab**[1], **Prathamesh Shirnath**[1] and **Rajeshwari Goudar**[1]

[1] *Department of Computer Engineering, MIT Academy of Engineering, Alandi, Pune, India*

Abstract: The rise in cancer cases worldwide, particularly in India, necessitates the development of quick and accurate diagnosis methods. A new initiative aims to utilize machine learning to enhance cancer gene detection, thereby saving time and reducing manual labor in conventional diagnostic procedures. The MERN stack tool and a machine learning algorithm are utilized to create a full-stack website that rapidly identifies probable malignant mutations. The approach combines Naive Bayes, Linear Regression, and Random Forest Classifier models for data processing and analysis. This cutting-edge strategy aims to revolutionize cancer diagnosis, enabling prompt and potentially life-saving therapies. This initiative represents a technological achievement and a crucial step towards reducing cancer prevalence. Additionally, our proposed model achieves an accuracy of 88 percent. The core contribution of this work lies in the integration of multiple machine learning algorithms into a unified, full-stack cancer gene detection system—capable of handling various cancer types, deployed in real-time *via* cloud infrastructure, and designed for practical clinical use through high performance, feature explanation ability, and accessibility.

Keywords: Cancer, Classification, Genes, Health system, Linear regression, Machine learning, Naive bayes, Random forest.

INTRODUCTION

The long-lasting effects of cancer on people's health persist. Owing to its extensive impacts, new approaches to early identification and treatment are needed. The purpose of this research project is to provide a comprehensive overview of the vital role that machine learning plays in understanding the complex subject of cancer genetics. It seeks to highlight significant discoveries, intriguing directions, and noteworthy advancements in this area.

* **Corresponding Author Neeraj Kumar:** Department of Computer Engineering, MIT Academy of Engineering, Alandi, Pune, India; E-mail: neeraj.kumar@mitaoe.ac.in

Manoj Kumar, Sachin Kumar Gupta, Navnath Kale, Pramod Ganjewar & Sandeep Pande (Eds.)

Main Contribution of the Study

This research presents a unified machine learning-based system for detecting cancer-causing genetic mutations, integrating Naive Bayes, Linear Regression, and Random Forest classifiers into a scalable diagnostic pipeline. The main contributions of this study are as follows:

- Algorithmic Innovation: Unlike prior works that rely on specific algorithms, such as MDP, PBN, or CSM, and are limited to individual cancer types, the proposed system employs a hybrid ML strategy that generalizes across multiple cancer forms using robust feature selection, preprocessing, and ensemble modeling.
- Real-Time Full-Stack Deployment: The model is deployed using a MERN stack integrated with a RESTful API and AWS cloud infrastructure, enabling real-time predictions and broad accessibility for clinical and research use.
- Performance Superiority: Achieves 88% classification accuracy, outperforming other models in precision, recall, and F1-score on benchmark datasets, as detailed in the comparative analysis section.
- Explainability and Feature Importance: The system incorporates visualization and interpretability modules, utilizing feature importance and confusion matrices, to help medical professionals understand the results.
- Practical Usability: Enhanced by user-friendly interfaces and chatbot integration, the system provides a clinician-centric experience designed to streamline early cancer diagnosis.

Background and Context

Cancer is a deadly illness that causes abnormal cells to proliferate uncontrollably, damaging bodily structures. It can begin anywhere in the human body and can be caused by changes or mutations in genes responsible for cell functioning, particularly growth and division. Errors can cause genetic alterations during cell division, exposure to toxic compounds in tobacco smoke, UV radiation from the sun, and the inheritance of genetic material from one's parents. The three distinct classes of genes that result in cancer mutations are referred to as "driver" genes, tumor suppressor genes, and proto-oncogenes.

Proto-oncogenes are the genes that mediate normal cell development and division. On the other hand, cancer-causing genes are generated when these proto-oncogenes mutate or become hyperactive. Tumor suppressor genes control cell division and growth; however, when a particular mutation occurs, the cells may expand uncontrollably. DNA repair genes can repair damaged DNA, and cells with specific mutations or modifications may undergo further mutations that lead to cancerous changes. Following a comprehensive analysis, researchers have identified a few gene changes that are common to all human malignancies.

RELATED WORK

Finding gene pairs is prioritized over finding individual genes [1]. The objective is to utilize RNA-seq data to identify predictive gene pairs, even in the absence of individual gene information. The focus of the talk is on gene pairs rather than single genes because the latter are not as reliable as the former when it comes to acting as biomarkers.

MDP was selected as a method [2] because it typically achieves superior F1 and F0.5 scores when compared to other available methods. Even when considering Draw Rank, which outperforms other methods, MDP still demonstrates significantly higher precision. The machine learning technique for gene expression is the most popular method for comparing gene expression between benign and malignant conditions [3]. Machine learning models currently being developed are evaluated using gene expression data from the highlighted datasets. Genes are isolated under different cell conditions using the Common Subcluster Mining (CSM) algorithm [4]. In essence, it separates the genes that exhibit stability under normal circumstances. The algorithm's primary job is to identify the gene that, in a diseased state, has a significantly altered pattern. The datasets about leukemia, breast cancer, and lung cancer are tested using this model.

The design and development of a diagnostic system that will aid in predicting P53 mutations [5] responsible for causing cancer, utilizing biopsy images for analysis, along with pharmacogenomic analysis that incorporates epigenetics and expression analysis. The authors of the paper [6] describe the Probabilistic Boolean Network (PBN) model, which is applied here with some information regarding tumor and non-tumor cells, supporting the evaluation.

The use of data complexity in the analysis of microarray gene expression to select genes is discussed in the work [7]. Metrics of data complexity, such as attribute efficiency and Fisher discriminant ratio, are combined to rank the genes. Then, the genes that are more highly ranked are considered significant and are involved in the process of cancer detection.

Within the framework of information theory, a paper [8] described a fairly straightforward yet effective algorithm for gene selection. This method utilizes a subset to target correlation, significantly reducing the number of unusable features, and it makes no parameter considerations throughout the selection process. Additionally, it serves as an effective filter that doesn't require a classifier because it is based on a subset selection method. The integration of 781 multidimensional heterogeneous data is discussed in the publication [9]. Following the use of various 782 approaches, this data is pooled and used in tandem for feature selection and classification.

In a study [10], the authors propose using sparse features in learning approaches to enhance the construction of discriminative and sparse features for final classification. This is achieved by applying Principal Component Analysis (PCA) to manage the high dimensionality of the original raw feature space. The method effectively addresses challenges associated with traditional techniques when handling feature dimensionality in datasets with limited sample sizes. The integration of Artificial Intelligence (AI) in medical science has shown significant advancements, particularly in cancer prediction and treatment. However, while many Machine Learning (ML) models have demonstrated high accuracy in cancer diagnosis, research indicates that some models are vulnerable to errors, leading to misleading predictions that could result in life-threatening consequences.

In another study [11], the authors developed a robust model that can maintain stable results despite minor alterations. Initially, the model learns from the dataset and subsequently predicts the type of cancer. The primary motivation behind designing this machine learning algorithm is to analyze cancer genome and transcriptome data. While transcriptome analysis involves alterations in RNA, genome analysis focuses on modifications in DNA. When combined, as discussed in [12], these analyses make a significant contribution to cancer treatment. The proposed model effectively extracts relevant cancer-related information, aiding in improved diagnosis and therapeutic strategies.

A study proposes a technique based on sequential labeling, where datasets are processed in sequence to make predictions [13]. This model is particularly effective in detecting mutation indices and identifying their types. The sequential approach enhances the accuracy of mutation detection by leveraging the structured progression of data. Experimental results demonstrate the model's effectiveness, highlighting its potential for precise mutation analysis and classification.

In a study [14], the authors explore the role of Human Transcription Factors (TFs) in predictive analysis. Transcription factors recognize specific DNA sequences that regulate chromatin transcription, thereby forming complex regulatory systems. These systems provide valuable insights into genome expression patterns. Additionally, the study utilizes Big Data analytics approaches to identify the L-myc gene pattern, demonstrating the effectiveness of advanced computational techniques in genomic analysis and gene expression prediction.

Another study proposes a machine learning model based on multiclass classification to identify cancer-related genetic mutations [15]. The study highlights that specific gene mutations are responsible for cancer development, requiring pathologists to manually distinguish these mutations—a process that is both time-consuming and labor-intensive. Given the presence of approximately nine mutation classes, the study emphasizes the need to employ multiclass classification algorithms to automate and improve the efficiency of mutation identification, thereby enhancing accuracy and reducing the burden on medical professionals.

The authors of a study explore gene expression analysis, focusing on altered RNA sequences using datasets from the Pan-Cancer Atlas [16]. They propose a deep learning-based model for classification, which transforms the inherently one-dimensional gene expression data into two-dimensional images for improved analysis. This approach enhances the model's ability to capture complex patterns within the data. Experimental results indicate that the multi-classification approach delivers promising outcomes, demonstrating its effectiveness in accurately classifying gene expression variations.

In another study [17], the authors discuss the use of microarrays, a laboratory tool for identifying patterns of gene expression. DNA microarrays contain thousands of genetic codes, making their analysis complex and challenging. To address this, the study presents a model that integrates artificial neural networks (ANNs) with genetic algorithms (GAs) to enhance analytical efficiency. The combination of ANN and GA improves accuracy, demonstrating the potential of machine learning techniques in optimizing gene expression analysis.

The authors of another study focus on extracting data from gene expression and evaluating various algorithms for optimal performance [18]. Their study identifies Kendall Rank Correlation as the most effective method, outperforming other approaches by a small margin when compared to the Minimum Redundancy algorithm. The findings underscore the importance of selecting suitable correlation techniques to improve the accuracy and efficiency of gene expression analysis.

In a study [19], the authors explore the use of microarrays and DNA genetic codes for gene expression analysis. Given the complexity of analyzing thousands of genetic codes in a DNA microarray, their study employs nature-inspired algorithms for data analysis. Additionally, multiple classification algorithms were evaluated, and among them, Grasshopper Optimization was identified as the most effective, outperforming others in terms of accuracy. The findings highlight the potential of bio-inspired optimization techniques in enhancing the precision of genetic data classification.

The difficulty of detecting mutations in gene sequences was addressed in a work [20] by utilizing machine learning algorithms, including SVM, linear discriminant analysis, and logistic Regression. It has been demonstrated that these algorithms can aid in diagnosing patients with cancer at an early stage.

A review of the literature revealed that the first study [1] did not describe strategies for dynamically building a patient-specific gene network or identifying prognostic gene pairs. The primary shortcomings of the second study [2] were that, despite using MPD, they were unable to overcome its limitations, including their inability to establish a personalized gene network for each patient. In the third study [3], the limitation was that gene expression datasets have a vast number of associated variables, which creates problems in further classification. In the fourth study [4], although CSM was useful in isolating, it is limited to only three types of cancers, i.e., lungs, breast, and leukemia. It was limited to the early detection of cancer in the first stages [6]. Further investigation and examination of GRNs, as well as their estimation in specific contexts, are required. In the tenth study [10], a significant limitation was identified, as the 10-fold cross-validation approach revealed that the baseline algorithm was not applied to the 2nd and 9th datasets. In the thirteenth [13], the major limitation is that this technique was only applicable for predicting lung cancer, and its data were the only ones referred to. In the fourteenth one [14], the study was limited to lung cancer and could only identify one type of gene, L-myc.

Our approach is to design an algorithm using machine learning methods that addresses the limitations of the papers discussed. Our approach should focus on an algorithm that applies to all cancers, and our main users, oncologists and pathologists, should be able to handle it easily. Since the above papers have already employed methods such as MDP, CSM, and PBN, our approach is to avoid these algorithms when constructing our model.

PROPOSED METHODOLOGY

The proposed system block diagram setup is illustrated in Fig. (**1**). This block diagram demonstrates the working flow of our model. Additionally, the system architecture diagram in Fig. (**2**) illustrates the flow of the entire proposed system.

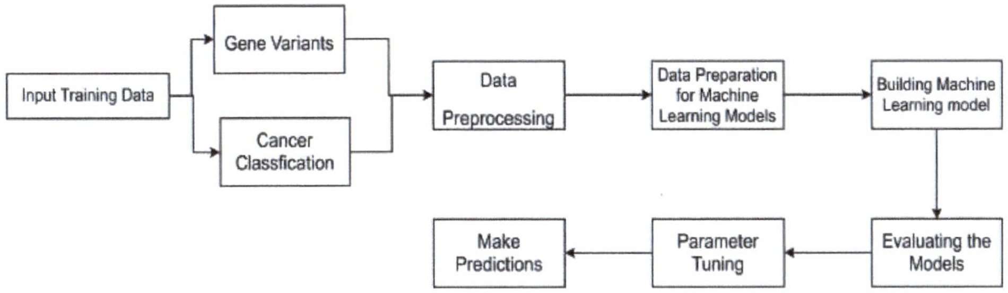

Fig. (1). Block Diagram of the System.

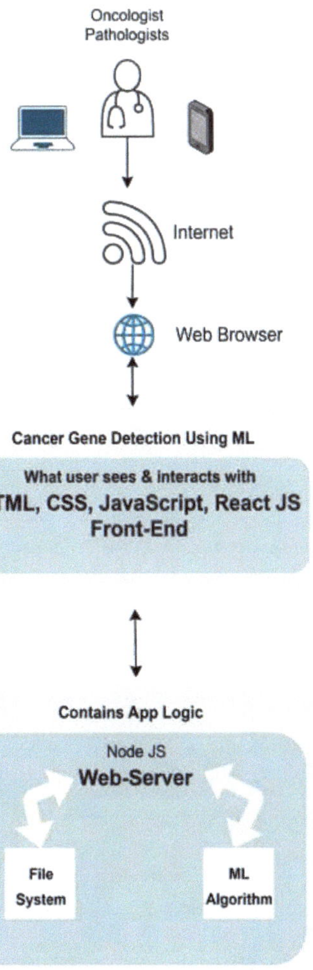

Fig. (2). System Architecture.

Machine Learning Models

Naive Bayes Classifier Algorithm: The Bayes theorem-based learning algorithm aids in classification using high-dimensional text datasets. It is the simplest and most operational of all classification algorithms, facilitating fast predictions and probabilistic classifiers.

KNN Classifier Algorithm: The K-Nearest Neighbor algorithm, also known as a Lazy learner, is a simple ML method based on supervised learning techniques, performing its actions during dataset classification rather than immediately on the training set.

Linear Regression: A widely used machine learning technique for predictive analysis, linear regression forecasts numerical values, such as prices, ages, and sales.

Random Forest Classifier: A supervised machine learning approach for Regression and classification is called the random forest classifier. It combines decision trees with datasets to enhance model performance and leverages ensemble learning to address complex issues.

Random Forest Classifier

Approach and Algorithm for Cancer Gene Detection using Random Forest Classifier, (Fig. **3**). approach:

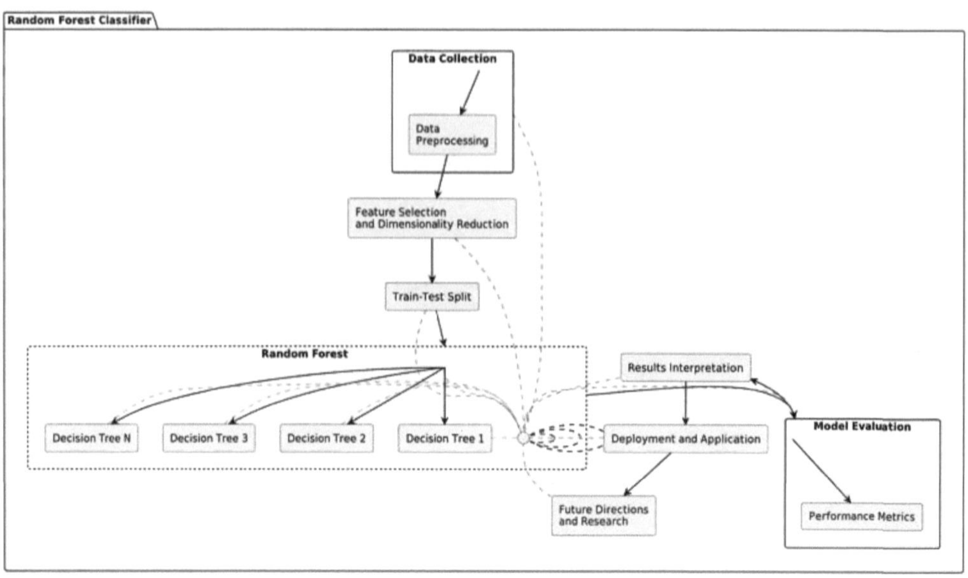

Fig. (3). Random Forest.

- Data Collection: Compile an extensive collection of gene expression information paired with cancer labels. A set of gene expression profiles, each of which shows the gene expression levels for a particular sample, ought to be included in the dataset. Ensure that samples from both malignant and non-cancerous tissues are included in the dataset, and that it encompasses a diverse range of cancer types.
- Data Preprocessing: Handling Missing Values. Identify the gaps in gene expression data and determine how to fill them. It is possible to impute data that is lacking using techniques like mean, median, and regression imputation.
- Outlier detection: This technique identifies and addresses outliers in the dataset, as they can significantly impact the classifier's performance. Statistical methods or domain expertise can be used to identify outliers' advancement.
- Data Normalization: To remove any biases resulting from variations in gene expression scales, normalize the gene expression data. Z-score normalization and min-max scaling are two popular normalizing techniques.
- Feature selection and dimensionality reduction: A classifier's performance may be negatively impacted by the curse of dimensionality when dealing with gene expression datasets, which often contain a large number of features (genes).
- Utilize feature selection strategies to determine which gene subset is most helpful in classifying cancers. Chi-square test, information gain, correlation analysis, and recursive feature reduction are examples of standard methods.

  Dimensionality Reduction: To reduce the number of features while maintaining the underlying structure of the data, utilize dimensionality reduction techniques such as Principal Component Analysis or distributed Stochastic Neighbor Embedding, particularly when the dataset has a large number of dimensions.
- The Random Forest classifier method is an ensemble learning approach that produces predictions by merging many decision trees. A random portion of the data is used to train each decision tree, and the total of all the trees' forecasts is used to get the final prediction.
- To train the model, separate the dataset into training and validation sets. To train the random forest classifier, create a large number of decision trees using the training set. Every decision tree is trained *via* bootstrap sampling, which uses a random subset of the training set.
- Evaluation of the Model: Determine the accuracy, precision, recall, and F1 score of the random forest classifier by applying the proper assessment criteria. To evaluate the model's capacity for generalization and forecast accuracy, use the validation set.
- Model Tuning: To optimize the model's performance, experiment with various random forest classifier hyperparameters, such as the number of trees, maximum tree depth, and the minimum number of samples per leaf. Utilize methods such

as grid search and cross-validation to identify the ideal set of hyperparameters.

- Feature Importance: Random Forest provides a feature importance statistic that indicates the degree to which each feature contributes to the model's overall prediction accuracy. Analyze the feature importance scores to identify the most influential genes in the cancer gene detection process. This information can provide insights into the biological significance of specific genes in cancer development and progression.
- Interpretation and Visualization: Visualize the decision boundaries and feature importance using appropriate plots and charts to enhance understanding and interpretation. This enables a more comprehensive understanding of the relationship between gene expression patterns and cancer classification. Generate visualizations such as feature importance bar plots or confusion matrices to interpret the model's performance and identify areas for improvement.
- Further Refinement and Validation: Adjust the model in light of the knowledge gathered from the assessment and comparison processes. Validate the performance of the optimized random forest classifier using independent datasets or through collaborations with domain experts and medical professionals. - Continuously update and improve the model as new gene expression data and research findings become available.

The mathematical novelty of this study lies in its integrated multi-algorithmic diagnostic model optimized for cancer gene expression detection. For instance, the Random Forest classifier operates by generating T decision trees $\{h_1(x), h_2(x), ..., h_T(x)\}$ each trained on a bootstrap sample, with final prediction H(x)H(x)H(x) given as:

$$H(x) = mode\{h_1(x), h_2(x), \ldots, h_T(x)\} \tag{1}$$

In comparison, the Naive Bayes algorithm estimates the posterior probability for gene class C_k given feature vector x as:

$$P(x) = \frac{P(C_k) \prod_{i=1}^{n} \quad P(C_k)}{P(x)} \tag{2}$$

Here, x_i represents the ith value of gene expression. Unlike previous studies, our method also embeds dimensionality reduction *via* PCA, projecting high-dimensional gene vectors $X \epsilon R^{m \times n}$ into a lower-dimensional space $Z \epsilon R^{m \times d}$, where $d < n$, preserving key variance components for effective classification. This integrated mathematical design offers explainability and generalizability across diverse cancer datasets.

Model Comparison

- Cancer gene detection is a complex task that requires accurate and reliable algorithms. In this comparison, the performance of four commonly used algorithms—Naive Bayes, k-Nearest Neighbors, Linear Regression, and Random Forest—is evaluated. Their accuracy in predicting cancer gene expression patterns is assessed to identify the algorithm that provides the most accurate results.
- Naive Bayes: The Classifier is probabilistic because it is predicated on the feature independence assumption and the Bayes theorem. Advantages: Quick and practical approach, especially for large datasets. Functions well in cases where the independence assumption is met. Strong against superfluous features. Cons: In certain real-world situations, the independence of features assumed by Naive Bayes may not hold. It may be susceptible to linked features and outliers. Complex linkages in the data might not be captured.
- K-Nearest Neighbors (KNN): A non-parametric technique called KNN uses the majority vote of the nearest neighbors to classify data. Advantages: Easy-to-understand algorithm. Capable of managing multiclass categorization issues. Efficient when the data has distinct decision boundaries. The amount of the dataset influences the computational cost. Sensitive to the specified value of k (number of neighbors) and the distance metric. Performance might be impacted by features that are unnecessary or noisy.
- Linear Regression: Linear Regression is a type of linear modeling in which the prediction of continuous variables is based on a linear relationship between the independent and dependent variables. Strengths: Provides details on the relationships between independent and dependent variables. Easy to use and interpret. Able to easily handle large datasets. Limitations: The efficacy of this strategy may be compromised by its dependence on a linear connection between variables. Extremely susceptible to outliers and multicollinearity. Restricted to forecasting continuous results.
- Random Forest: An efficient and versatile algorithm that can manage a wide variety of data types and feature interactions. Less likely than individual decision trees to overfit. Gives interpretability-related feature significance measurements. Functions effectively with data that has many dimensions. Limitations: For large datasets with numerous features, this approach may be computationally expensive. Possibly not as effective with unbalanced datasets. Needs to have its hyperparameters adjusted to function optimally.
- New algorithms, such as Linear Regression and Random Forest, are being used in cancer gene detection tasks to enhance accuracy and interpretability. Linear Regression models the relationship between gene expression levels and cancer progression. At the same time, Random Forest offers ensemble learning and feature importance analysis, capturing complex interactions between genes and

accurately predicting cancer gene expression patterns.

- The integration of new algorithms in our cancer gene detection system aims to enhance predictive power and interpretability, providing researchers and clinicians with deeper insights into molecular mechanisms and potential biomarkers for diagnosis and treatment.

Table **1** presents the recall, accuracy, precision, and F1-score metrics for each algorithm. It is clear from the comparison results in Fig. (**4**) that Random Forest outperforms the other techniques in terms of F1-score, accuracy, precision, and recall. Its superiority in cancer gene discovery initiatives stems from its capacity to manage complex interactions and produce feature relevance metrics.

Table 1. Comparison of Algorithms for Cancer Gene Detection.

Algorithm	Accuracy	Precision	Recall	F1-Score	MSE	RMSE	R-Squared
Naive Bayes	0.78	0.75	0.8	0.77	-	-	-
KNN	0.82	0.8	0.84	0.82	-	-	-
Linear Regress	-	-	-	-	0.14	0.38	0.65
Random Forest	0.88	0.87	0.9	0.88	-	-	-

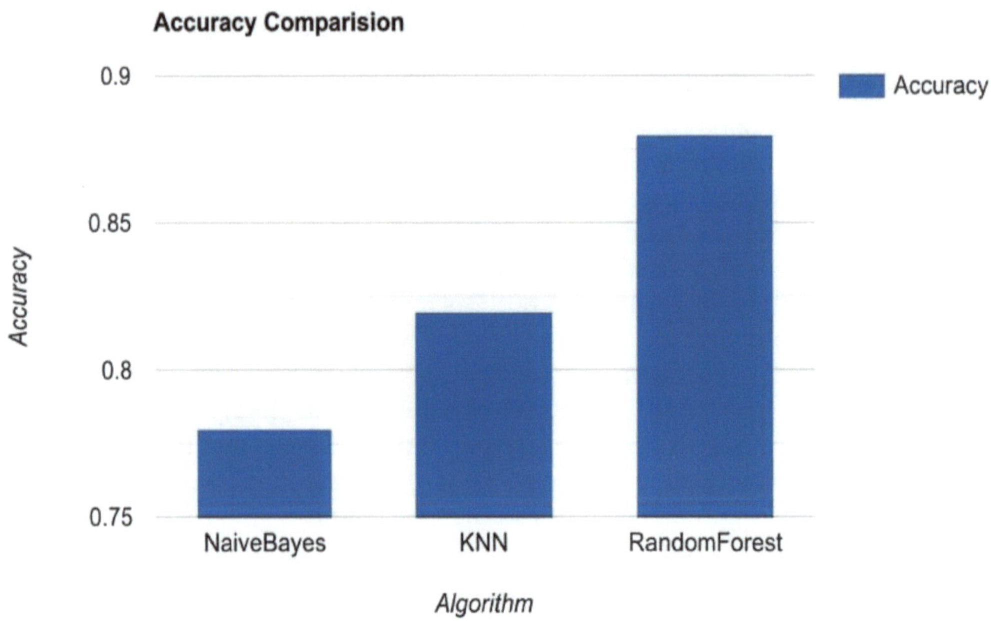

Fig. (4). Accuracy Comparison.

System Implementation

An overview of the procedures involved in setting up the Cancer Gene Detection system is provided below and can be seen in Fig. (**5**):

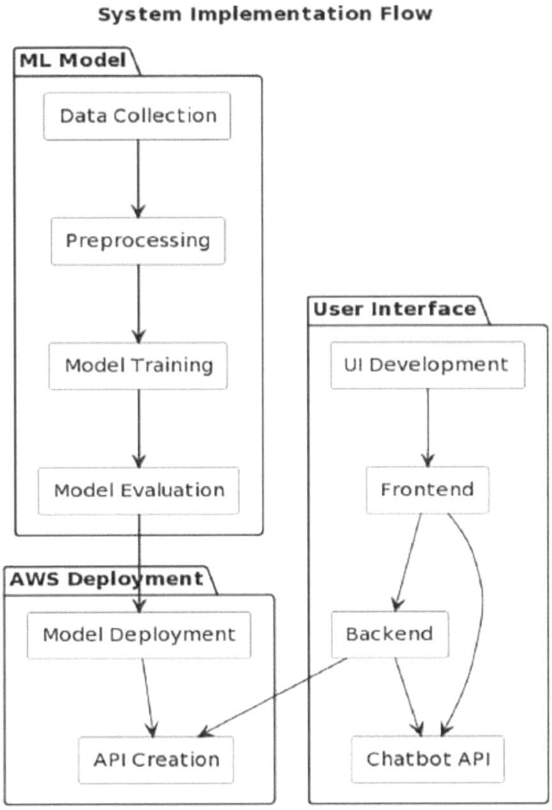

Fig. (5). System Implementation.

ML Model Development

Identify and compile datasets containing gene expression data and corresponding cancer labels. Preprocessing is the process of cleaning, standardizing, and formatting the data so that it is suitable for training ML models. Create training and testing sets from the dataset to evaluate the model's performance. Build and train an ML model using the Random Forest algorithm. The model's parameters can be adjusted to optimize performance through techniques such as cross-validation and hyperparameter tuning. Utilize relevant assessment metrics, such as F1 score, accuracy, precision, and recall, to assess the model's performance on the testing dataset. It is possible to store the learned model for later usage.

Deploying a Model on AWS and Creating an API

To host the model, establish an EC2 instance and set up an AWS account. To execute the ML model, install the required libraries and dependencies. Transfer the trained model to the EC2 instance. To establish a RESTful API for the model, set up a web server using a framework like Flask or Django. To generate predictions based on gene expression input, expose the API endpoint.

User Interface Development

Design and develop a User Interface (UI) for the cancer gene detection system. Utilize a frontend framework, such as React.js, to create an interactive and responsive UI. Implement forms or input fields to allow users to input gene expression data. To make sure the input data is formatted correctly, include validation checks.

Frontend Development

Implement a frontend component to send gene expression data to the backend API for prediction. Establish communication between the frontend and the backend API using HTTP requests, such as POST or GET. Present the user with the prediction results in a clear and easy-to-understand style.

Backend Development

Utilize a backend framework, such as Node.js, to handle API requests from the frontend. Implement the logic to receive the gene expression data from the frontend. Call the ML model API endpoint deployed on AWS to get predictions for the input data. Process the predictions and send them back to the frontend.

Connecting the Additional Feature Chatbot API

Integrate a chatbot API with the frontend and backend of the cancer gene detection system. Utilize a chatbot framework or platform, such as Dialogflow or Rasa, to develop and train a chatbot. Connect the chatbot API with the frontend to enable user interaction through chat. Configure the backend to handle chatbot requests and provide responses based on the user's input. Ensure the chatbot can interact with the ML model API to give predictions or relevant information to the user.

Model Implementation

Data Collection

One of the most crucial steps in deploying an ML model for cancer gene detection is data collection. It entails compiling pertinent information on cancer gene expression from multiple sources. This is a summary of the procedure for gathering data.:

- Identify Data Sources: Choose the resources you will use to gather information about cancer gene expression. Public databases, academic papers, clinical trials, and proprietary datasets are a few examples of these sources.
- Define Data Requirements: Specify the specific types of data you need for cancer gene detection. This may include gene expression profiles, patient characteristics, tumor types, treatment information, and any other relevant features.
- Obtain Data Access: Depending on the data sources, you may need to obtain access permissions, licenses, or collaborations to acquire the required datasets. Ensure that you comply with all applicable data usage restrictions and regulations.
- Data Extraction: Extract the relevant data from the identified sources. This may involve downloading publicly available datasets or requesting data from research institutions, hospitals, or data providers. Pay attention to data integrity and ensure that you collect high-quality and reliable data.
- Data Storage: Organize and store the collected and preprocessed data in a suitable format and storage system. Ensure proper documentation and metadata management to facilitate future analysis and data reproducibility.

Data Preprocessing

Data preprocessing is a crucial step in developing a machine learning (ML) model for cancer gene detection, as it prepares the raw gene expression data necessary for training the model. The data preprocessing steps that are frequently employed in cancer gene discovery are explained here:

- Data Cleaning: Determine the sources from which you will collect cancer gene expression data. These sources can include public databases, research studies, clinical trials, or proprietary datasets.
- Normalization: Since gene expression data often have varying sizes, machine learning techniques may perform differently. To standardize the scale of all the characteristics, normalization is applied. Min-max scaling and z-score normalization are two popular normalization methods.

- Feature Engineering: At this point, additional features are created, or the raw gene expression data is processed to enhance the machine learning model's predictive capacity. Feature engineering techniques include principal component analysis (PCA), which lowers dimensionality, and mutual information or correlation analysis, which picks features.
- Data Augmentation: Occasionally, there may be a lack of available gene expression data. By implementing changes or adding new samples to the dataset, data augmentation techniques can be used to expand its size artificially. Techniques such as noise injection, random perturbations, and oversampling of minority classes can be employed in this manner.
- Data Balancing: In the field of cancer gene discovery, imbalanced datasets—which have dramatically different sample sizes for distinct classes—are a common occurrence. Examples of these classifications include cancer and noncancer. To address this issue and ensure the model is trained on a more balanced dataset, data balancing techniques such as oversampling the minority class or undersampling the majority class can be employed.
- Splitting the Data: Training, validation, and testing sets are commonly constructed using preprocessed gene expression data. The validation set is used to select the model and adjust hyperparameters, the training set is used to train the machine learning model, and the testing set is used to evaluate the trained model's performance on previously unseen data.

Model Training

Data preprocessing is a crucial step in developing a Machine Learning (ML) model for cancer gene detection, as it prepares the raw gene expression data necessary for training the model. The following describes the typical data preprocessing procedures used in cancer gene detection:

- Data Preparation: Start by preparing your dataset for training. This includes organizing the data into features (input variables) and the target variable (gene detection label). Ensure that the dataset is preprocessed correctly, which could include standardizing the data, encoding categorical variables, and handling missing values.
- Feature Selection: Examine your dataset's features and pick the most pertinent ones to use in the model's training. To identify the most valuable characteristics associated with cancer gene identification, you can employ methods such as statistical testing, correlation analysis, or domain expertise.
- Train-Test Split: Sort your dataset into training and testing sets. The Random Forest model will be trained on the training set, and its performance will be assessed, with predictions improved on the testing set. Usually, an 80/20 or

70/30 split is used, although the size and makeup of the dataset will determine if this is the case.

- Random Forest Training: Apply the Random Forest algorithm using your training dataset. Using an ensemble learning technique called Random Forest, the predictions from multiple decision trees are combined to provide more accurate forecasts. During training, the approach creates a collection of decision trees using random feature selections and subsets of the training data.
- Hyperparameter Tuning: The hyperparameters of Random Forest can be adjusted in various ways to optimize its performance. These comprise the total number of trees in the forest, the maximum depth of the trees, and the number of features that need to be considered at each split. Use strategies such as grid search or random search to determine the ideal set of hyperparameters that yields the best results on your validation set.
- Model Evaluation: Utilizing the testing dataset, assess the Random Forest model's performance following training. To evaluate how well the model predicts cancer genes, compute assessment measures such as accuracy, precision, recall, F1-score, and area under the ROC curve. Furthermore, you can provide more reliable estimates of the model's performance by utilizing methods such as cross-validation.
- Model Optimization: Evaluate the model's performance and identify areas that require improvement. If class imbalance is evident in your dataset, you can investigate strategies such as resampling or refining the feature selection procedure iteratively. Please continue to make ongoing adjustments and enhancements to the model to improve its accuracy and reliability.
- Model Persistence: After you are satisfied with the model's performance, save it to a file or disk so you can use it later to deploy and forecast new, unobserved data.

Model Evaluation

In the ML model implementation for cancer gene detection using the Random Forest model, Model Evaluation plays a crucial role in assessing the performance and effectiveness of the trained model. It helps in determining how well the model generalizes to unseen data and provides insights into its predictive capabilities. Here are the steps involved in Model Evaluation for the Random Forest model in cancer gene detection:

Divide the labeled dataset into training and testing sets. After the Random Forest model has been trained on the training set, its performance is assessed using the testing set. A split ratio of 70 is typical.

Fit the Random Forest model to the training set to begin training it. Before the model can generate reliable predictions, it must be trained to recognize patterns and relationships in the gene expression data.

Make predictions on the testing set using the trained Random Forest model. The model will classify each sample in the testing set as either malignant or non-cancerous based on the gene expression features.

- Evaluation Metrics: Choose from a range of assessment measures to gauge the model's performance. The following metrics are frequently employed in categorization tasks:
    - Accuracy is defined as the proportion of correctly predicted outcomes over all forecasts. It provides a broad indication of the model's effectiveness.
    - Precision is defined as the proportion of valid positive predictions to all optimistic predictions (Fig. **7**). It measures the model's ability to identify malignant samples accurately.
    - Recall (Sensitivity): The ratio of actual positive samples to the total number of accurate optimistic forecasts is displayed in Fig. (**8**). It assesses the model's ability to recognize every cancerous sample.
    - The harmonic mean of precision and recall is the F1-score. In terms of precision and scope, it offers a reasonable assessment.
    - Confusion Matrix: The amount of true positives, true negatives, false positives, and false negatives is displayed in Fig. (**6**), which summarizes the model's predictions and actual labels.
- Performance Analysis: Examine the assessment metrics and the confusion matrix in Fig. (**9**) to gain a deeper understanding of the model's functionality. Based on the particular needs of cancer gene detection, identify any biases or trade-offs between precision and recall.
- Iteration and fine-tuning: Adjust the model's parameters, such as the number of trees in the Random Forest or the maximum depth of each tree, to enhance performance based on the assessment results. This iterative approach improves the accuracy and generalizability of the model.

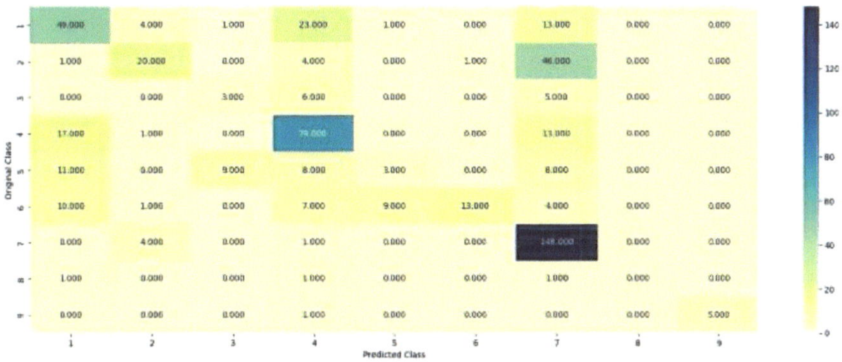

Fig. (6). Random Forest Model- Confusion matrix.

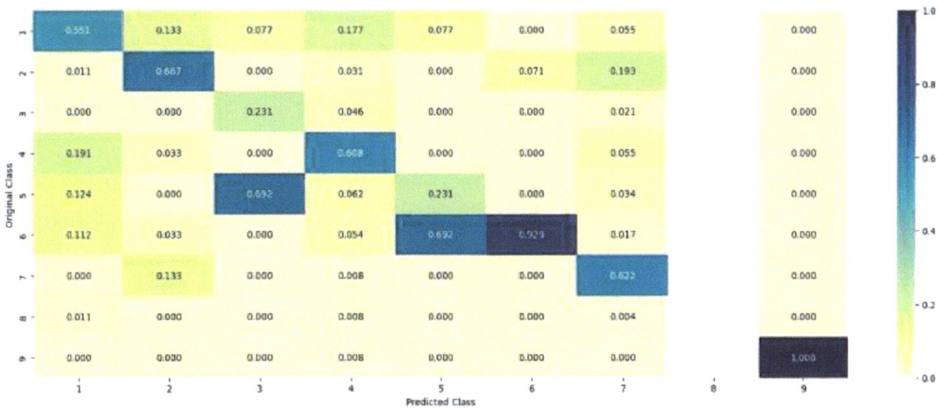

Fig. (7). Random Forest Model- Precision matrix.

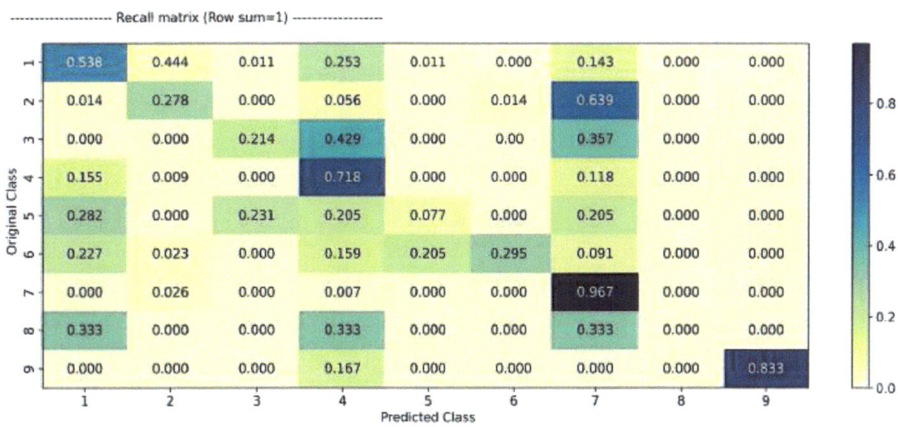

Fig. (8). Random Forest Model- Recall matrix.

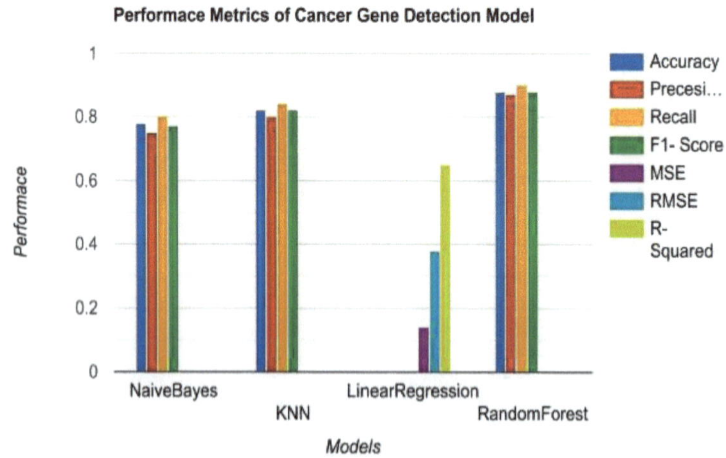

Fig. (9). Model Analysis Graph.

CONCLUSION

A method has been developed that utilizes machine learning algorithms to assist pathologists and oncologists in quickly identifying gene alterations that contribute to cancer. This program, accessible *via* a dedicated website, automates the time-consuming process of identifying genes associated with cancer development, allowing medical practitioners to focus more on developing treatment plans. This would not only simplify present medical practices but also pave the way for ground-breaking discoveries at various stages of cancer treatment. By fusing technology and medical knowledge, this program points the way to a period when cancer diagnoses will be more accurate and timely, strengthening the defenses of society against cancer's ravages. The integration of machine learning into cancer gene detection has profound managerial implications, particularly in healthcare institutions and diagnostic laboratories. First, hospital administrators and clinical managers can benefit from faster and more accurate diagnostics, leading to timely interventions and optimized patient flow. The use of a cloud-deployed, full-stack interface enables efficient data management and accessibility for multi-site coordination and research. Second, the model's explainability and feature importance modules support transparency, which is critical for managerial decision-making regarding patient care strategies and compliance with healthcare regulations. Moreover, the ability to compare model performance across Naive Bayes, KNN, Linear Regression, and Random Forest gives managers flexibility in choosing solutions based on available infrastructure and accuracy requirements. Overall, the proposed system supports strategic planning, operational efficiency, and resource optimization within the medical diagnostics ecosystem.

REFERENCES

[1] B. Park, W. Lee, and K. Han, "A new approach to deriving prognostic gene pairs from cancer patient-specific gene correlation networks", *IEEE/ACM Trans. Comput. Biol. Bioinformatics,* vol. 19, no. 3, pp. 1267-1276, 2022.
[http://dx.doi.org/10.1109/TCBB.2020.3017209] [PMID: 32809942]

[2] H. Jung, J. Choi, J. Park, and J. Ahn, "A novel machine learning model for identifying patient-specific cancer driver genes", *IEEE Access,* vol. 10, pp. 54245-54253, 2022.
[http://dx.doi.org/10.1109/ACCESS.2022.3176376]

[3] M. Khalsan, L.R. Machado, E.S. Al-Shamery, S. Ajit, K. Anthony, M. Mu, and M.O. Agyeman, "A survey of machine learning approaches applied to gene expression analysis for cancer prediction", *IEEE Access,* vol. 10, pp. 27522-27534, 2022.
[http://dx.doi.org/10.1109/ACCESS.2022.3146312]

[4] A. Sadhu, and B. Bhattacharyya, "Discovery of cancer-linked biomarker genes through common subcluster mining", *Proc. Int. Conf. Bioinf. Syst. Biol. (BSB),* pp. 1-5, 2016.
[http://dx.doi.org/10.1109/BSB.2016.7552153]

[5] L. Anand C. and N. P. K. Krishnan, "Design and development of a diagnostic system for early prediction of P53 mutation causing cancer from microscopic biopsy images", *Proc. 4th Int. Conf. I-SMAC (IoT Soc. Mobile Analytics Cloud) (I-SMAC),* pp. 435-440, 2020.
[http://dx.doi.org/10.1109/I-SMAC49090.2020.9243526]

[6] D.C. Nguyen, and F. Azadivar, "Early detection of cancer by regression analysis and computer simulation of gene regulatory rules", *Proc. Int. Conf. Biomed. Eng. (ICoBE),* pp. 144-148, 2012.
[http://dx.doi.org/10.1166/jmihi.2012.1096]

[7] S. Sarbazi-Azad, and M.S. Abadeh, "Gene selection for cancer classification from microarray data using data overlap measure", *Proc. 25th Natl. 3rd Int. Iran. Conf. Biomed. Eng. (ICBME),* pp. 1-6, 2018.
[http://dx.doi.org/10.1109/ICBME.2018.8703565]

[8] M. Ng, and L. Chan, "Informative gene discovery for cancer classification from microarray expression data", *Proc. IEEE Workshop Mach. Learn. Signal Process. (MLSP),* pp. 393-398, 2005.
[http://dx.doi.org/10.1109/MLSP.2005.1532935]

[9] K. Kourou, T.P. Exarchos, K.P. Exarchos, M.V. Karamouzis, and D.I. Fotiadis, "Machine learning applications in cancer prognosis and prediction", *Comput. Struct. Biotechnol. J.,* vol. 13, pp. 8-17, 2015.
[http://dx.doi.org/10.1016/j.csbj.2014.11.005] [PMID: 25750696]

[10] R. Fakoor, F. Ladhak, A. Nazi, and M. Huber, "Using deep learning to enhance cancer diagnosis and classification", *Proc. ICML Workshop Role Machine. Learn. Transform. Healthc.,* 2013.

[11] M.R. Karim, T. Islam, C. Lange, D. Rebholz-Schuhmann, and S. Decker, "Adversary-aware multimodal neural networks for cancer susceptibility prediction from multi-omics data", *IEEE Access,* vol. 10, pp. 54386-54409, 2022.
[http://dx.doi.org/10.1109/ACCESS.2022.3175816]

[12] T. Shehzadi, A. Majid, M. Hameed, A. Farooq, and A. Yousaf, "Intelligent predictor using cancer-related biologically information extraction from cancer transcriptomes", *Proc. Int. Symp. Recent Adv. Electr. Eng. Comput. Sci. (RAEECS),* pp. 1-5, 2020.
[http://dx.doi.org/10.1109/RAEECS50817.2020.9265692]

[13] U.N. Wisesty, A. Purwarianti, A. Pancoro, A. Chattopadhyay, N.N. Phan, E.Y. Chuang, and T.R. Mengko, "Join classifier of type and index mutation on lung cancer DNA using sequential labeling model", *IEEE Access,* vol. 10, pp. 9004-9021, 2022.
[http://dx.doi.org/10.1109/ACCESS.2022.3142925]

[14] U. Draz, "A pattern detection technique of L-MYC for lung cancer oncogene in bioinformatics big

data", *Proc. 17th Int. Bhurban Conf. Appl. Sci. Technol. (IBCAST),* pp. 218-223, 2020. [http://dx.doi.org/10.1109/IBCAST47879.2020.9044506]

[15] A. Mohanty, A.R. Prusty, and R.C. Cherukuri, "Cancer tumor detection using genetically mutated data and machine learning models", *Proc. Int. Conf. Intell. Controller Comput. Smart Power (ICICCSP),* pp. 1-6, 2022. [http://dx.doi.org/10.1109/ICICCSP53532.2022.9862476]

[16] J.M. de Guia, M. Devaraj, and C.K. Leung, "DeepGx: Deep learning using gene expression for cancer classification", *Proc. IEEE/ACM Int. Conf. Adv. Soc. Netw. Anal. Mining (ASONAM),* pp. 913-920, 2019. [http://dx.doi.org/10.1145/3341161.3343516]

[17] K. Cahyaningrum, "Adiwijaya, and W. Astuti, "Microarray gene expression classification for cancer detection using artificial neural networks and genetic algorithm hybrid intelligence", *Proc. Int. Conf. Data Sci. Appl. (ICoDSA),* pp. 1-7, 2020. [http://dx.doi.org/10.1109/ICoDSA50139.2020.9213051]

[18] P. Singh, A. Shukla, and M. Vardhan, "A novel filter approach for efficient selection and small round blue-cell tumor cancer detection using microarray gene expression data", *Proc. Int. Conf. Invent. Comput. Inf. (ICICI),* pp. 827-831, 2017. [http://dx.doi.org/10.1109/ICICI.2017.8365252]

[19] P. Patel, K. Passi, and C.K. Jain, "Improving gene expression prediction of cancer data using nature-inspired optimization algorithms", *Proc. Int. Conf. Comput. Sci. Comput. Intell. (CSCI),* pp. 337-343, 2021. [http://dx.doi.org/10.1109/CSCI54926.2021.00128]

[20] S.M. Shehryar, M.A. Shahid, and A.A. Shah, "Mutation detection in gene sequences using machine learning", *Proc. Int. Conf. Innov. Comput. (ICICI),* pp. 1-7, 2021. [http://dx.doi.org/10.1109/ICIC53490.2021.9693088]

CHAPTER 9

Virtual Mouse Using Hand Gestures

Dhruv Deshmukh[1], **Pallavi Nehete**[1,*], **Soumil Jha**[1], **Priyanshu Paul**[1] and **Vijay Varia**[1]

[1] *Department of Computer Science and Engineering, Dr. Vishwanath Karad, MIT World Peace University, Pune, India*

Abstract: Cursor movement simplifies the user interaction with the system; it is a motive and visible pointer that is controlled by the user by using hardware (*i.e.*, mouse and touchpad) to interact with the system. This technology can be simplified by using hand gestures instead of a physical device to manipulate the cursor. It can be useful to make the user experience simple and systematic. Cursor movement by hand gesture can be provided as an energy and time-efficient technology where the user interacts with the software by using gesture recognition. The gestures that manipulate the screen first will be stored in the system database. Then the hand present in front of the device will be recognized and stored as an object in the system, and then the gestures performed in front of the system with the hand will be matched with the gesture present in the memory of the system, which will lead to cursor operations and movements. This technology will be helpful to operate a system from a distance according to the user's ease and without using a hardware component. This technology can be applied in all the sectors where there is a need for a Computer System, as it is an adaptable technology for users of any age and field.

Keywords: Cursor, Database, Hand gestures, Movement, Recognition.

INTRODUCTION

In the realm of digital interaction, the project at hand delves into the rich tapestry of human communication, drawing inspiration from the innate gestures we use to convey our thoughts and feelings. This initiative seeks to transcend the conventional boundaries of human-computer interaction by integrating the fluidity and expressiveness of hand gestures into the control mechanisms of computer cursors. Envisioned to redefine the ergonomics of digital navigation, this system aims to recognize and interpret hand movements with precision, thereby allowing users to manipulate the cursor through natural motions. This endeavor not only commits to making the user experience simple and efficient but also makes it mo-

* **Corresponding author Pallavi Nehete:** Department of Computer Science and Engineering, Dr. Vishwanath Karad, MIT World Peace University, Pune, India; E-mail: pallavi.nehete@mitwpu.edu.in

Manoj Kumar, Sachin Kumar Gupta, Navnath Kale, Pramod Ganjewar & Sandeep Pande (Eds.)

re intuitive and engaging. It also addresses the ergonomic challenges associated with prolonged use of traditional input devices. By marrying the simplicity of gestures with advanced recognition technologies, we aim to forge a more harmonious and accessible interface between humans and their digital counterparts, ultimately enhancing the way we interact with technology in our daily lives.

MAIN CONTRIBUTION OF THE PAPER

The primary contribution of this paper lies in the design and implementation of a virtual mouse system controlled entirely by hand gestures, utilizing computer vision and machine learning technologies such as OpenCV, MediaPipe, and Autopy. Key contributions include:

- Hardware-Free Cursor Control: Replacing traditional mouse hardware with intuitive hand gesture recognition for cursor movement and actions (click, drag, hold).
- Real-Time Gesture Tracking: Implementation of fingertip coordinate mapping and gesture classification to perform real-time mouse operations.
- Improved Interaction Accuracy: Efficient gesture-to-action mapping and use of lightweight, cross-platform Python libraries for enhanced responsiveness.
- Accessibility and Usability: Demonstrates potential for aiding physically challenged users or use in remote-control applications (*e.g.*, smart TVs).
- Comparative Advantage: The system improves upon previous models by integrating additional functionalities like drag-and-drop, hold, and more accurate gesture detection without requiring color-based recognition or complex hardware.

LITERATURE REVIEW

This collection of research papers explores various approaches to enhancing human-computer interaction, primarily focusing on hand gesture recognition and virtual mouse control. The research leverages technologies such as machine learning, computer vision, and image processing to create intuitive and efficient interfaces. For instance, a study [1] introduces a real-time gesture recognition method using a web camera and the AdaBoost algorithm, which enhances mouse operation precision through a cascaded classifier. Similarly, another study [2] employs Sixth Sense technology with image processing and random forests to improve mobility and accessibility. Advanced methods like Kalman filters are explored in another study [3] to enhance cursor control accuracy for individuals with tetraplegia, improving decoding and direct control. Accessibility remains a key theme, with a study [4] integrating gesture and voice recognition *via* infrared sensors to cater to users with special needs, ensuring cost-effective and versatile solutions. Research [5] highlights the potential of virtual interfaces using image processing and color detection, offering wireless and portable interaction. The innovative approach in a study [6] utilizes colored fingertips and area ratio analysis to provide natural and dynamic cursor control. Similarly, another study [7] leverages Kinect sensors for stable and multi-user hand gesture interaction. Studies [8, 9] apply OpenCV and machine learning to enhance virtual clicking and cursor movement, emphasizing accessibility and improved control. The future of natural user interfaces is explored in a study [10], where machine learning and GUI automation enhance digital well-being and functionality.

Research [11, 12] demonstrates how gesture recognition *via* color detection and machine learning can provide cost-effective and intuitive control solutions. Hand tracking *via* OpenCV in a study [13] and handwriting recognition using CNN in another study [14] offer innovative, simplified, and efficient setups for gesture-based interaction. A study addresses practical hardware challenges by proposing gesture-based solutions for web service discovery. Artificial intelligence and MediaPipe are utilized in another study [16] to create user-friendly and flexible cursor control. Research [17] incorporates eye-tracking and speech recognition to enable wireless and natural interaction. Similarly, another study [18] integrates PyAutoGUI and OpenCV for real-time, responsive cursor control. Studies [19, 20] focus on human-machine interaction, employing finger tracking and Vision Transformers to ensure high classification accuracy and cost-effective solutions. Collectively, these studies underscore significant advancements in leveraging gesture recognition, computer vision, and artificial intelligence to create accessible, efficient, and natural human-computer interaction systems.

The reviewed literature applies machine learning techniques across several stages of gesture-based interaction systems. In most cases, ML models such as AdaBoost, Random Forest, or CNNs are used for feature extraction and gesture classification. Preprocessing typically involves frame segmentation and hand landmark detection through computer vision tools like OpenCV and MediaPipe. Feature extraction focuses on tracking key points—like fingertip or joint coordinates—which are then mapped to gesture labels using classification algorithms. Some studies also incorporate filtering methods (*e.g.*, Kalman filters) for smoother cursor control, while others apply ensemble techniques to improve prediction stability. These processes collectively inform the modular design of our proposed system, which integrates gesture detection, classification, and system control in a real-time, hardware-free environment.

PROPOSED METHODOLOGY

The methodology for evaluating the effectiveness and usability of the gesture-based cursor movement system involves a multi-faceted approach, encompassing both quantitative and qualitative methods.

In Fig. (**1**) Methodology Diagram, we can see the processing of the methodology that is being implemented.

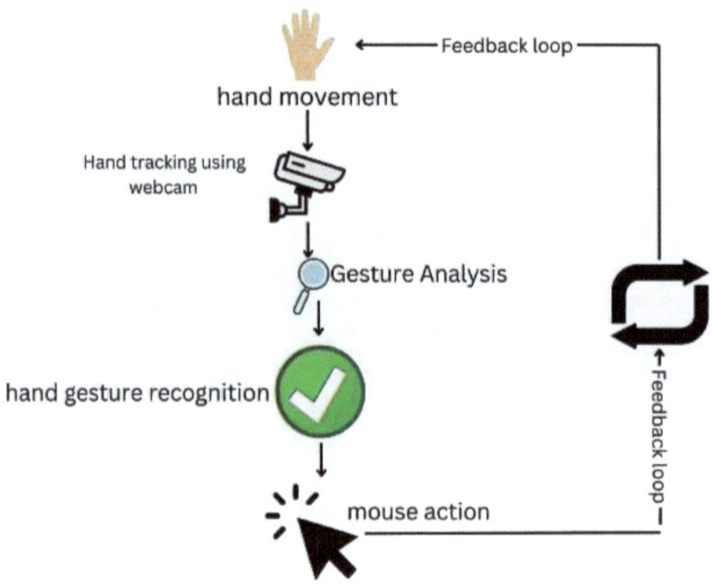

Fig. (1). Methodology diagram.

The following steps outline the methodology:

Step 1. System Setup and Calibration:

- Set up the hardware components, which mainly include the webcam and other Python libraries, per the system architecture described.
- Calibrate the system to ensure accurate gesture recognition and cursor control.

Step 2. Participant Recruitment:

- Recruit participants representing a diverse range of demographics, including age, gender, and level of computer proficiency.
- Ensure the mobility of the participant is needed for cursor movement.

Step 3. Experimental Design:

- Design a series of user experiments and tasks to evaluate different aspects of the gesture-based cursor movement system.
- Define clear objectives for each experiment, focusing on factors such as gesture recognition accuracy, user learning curve, and overall user experience.

Step 4. Data Collection:

- Collect both quantitative and qualitative data during the experiments.
- Quantitative data may include metrics such as gesture recognition accuracy, cursor movement speed, and task completion time.
- Qualitative data may include user feedback, observations, and subjective impressions of the system's usability and effectiveness.

Step 5. Experimental Procedure:

- Introduce participants to the gesture-based cursor movement system, providing instructions on how to perform gestures and interact with the system.
- Conduct pre-experiment assessments to gather baseline data on participants' familiarity with gesture-based interactions and their current level of computer proficiency.
- Administer the experimental tasks, ensuring consistency and standardization across participants.
- Encourage participants to think aloud during the tasks to capture real-time feedback and insights into their decision-making processes.

Step 6. Data Analysis:

- Analyze the data gathered from different users to make the proposed system more efficient.
- Quantitative analysis may involve calculating mean scores, standard deviations, and conducting inferential tests to compare performance metrics between conditions or groups.
- Qualitative analysis may involve identifying recurring themes, patterns, and insights from participant feedback and observations.

Step 7. Evaluation Metrics:

- Evaluate the gesture-based cursor movement system based on predefined evaluation metrics, including:
- Gesture Recognition Accuracy: Percentage of correctly recognized gestures.
- Task Completion Time: Time taken by participants to complete designated tasks using gesture-based interactions.

- User Satisfaction: Participants' subjective ratings of system usability, satisfaction, and overall experience.
- Learning Curve: Changes in performance metrics over repeated interactions with the system.

Step 8. Iterative Improvement:

- Use the findings from the data analysis to identify strengths, weaknesses, and areas for improvement in the gesture-based cursor movement system.
- Iteratively refine the system design, algorithms, and user interface based on user feedback and performance insights.
- Conduct follow-up experiments to validate improvements and assess the impact of iterative changes on system effectiveness and usability.

Step 9. Reporting and Documentation:

- Compile the results of the experiments into a comprehensive report, detailing the methodology, findings, analysis, and conclusions.
- Present the findings to stakeholders, including researchers, developers, and potential users, to inform future iterations and developments of the gesture-based cursor movement system.

By following this methodology, we aim to systematically evaluate the gesture-based cursor movement system, identify areas for improvement, and iteratively refine the system to enhance its effectiveness, usability, and overall user experience. Although the proposed system relies heavily on real-time computer vision and gesture-based interaction, the current manuscript does not include formal mathematical formulations. To clearly highlight the novelty, a mathematical abstraction of the fingertip tracking and gesture classification mechanism can be included. Specifically, the system computes fingertip coordinates (x_i, y_i) for each of the 21 landmarks detected by MediaPipe. The relative distances between fingers, given by using Equation 1, are:

$$D_{ij} = \sqrt{(xi - xj)2 + (yi - yj)^2} \quad \textbf{(1)}$$

are used to classify gestures (*e.g.*, a pinch is detected when $D_{(8, 4)} < \theta$, where θ is a predefined threshold). This mathematical formalization of gesture state transitions enhances explainability. The novelty lies in integrating these distance-based gesture conditions into a gesture state machine that dynamically triggers cursor actions using Equation 2:

$$Action(t) = \{ Click \quad if\ D8{,}12(t) < \delta 1 \ Drag \quad if\ D8{,}4(t) < \delta 2 \quad Move \quad otherwise \quad \textbf{(2)}$$

This model represents a simplified yet effective method for real-time, device-free interaction using only positional landmark analysis, and does not rely on pre-trained classifiers or deep learning models, making it lightweight and practical for deployment.

OVERVIEW OF PROPOSED SYSTEM

Overview

On using the given user interface, the system first detects hands and operates on the basis of hand gestures shown to the device. By using Laptop cams and web cams present in the hardware, it makes the process of identifying hand recognition easy by using OpenCV and AutoPy libraries present in the Python SDK. After recognition of hand and hand gesture, the system operates some of the mouse functions like cursor movement, Select, right and left click, dragging, *etc.*

Flow and Architecture

The figure presented below suggests the architecture of our model. When multiple hands are present in the FOV of the camera, it will only recognize one primary hand on the basis of visibility. Then the hand tracking and fingertip detection make it easy to assign coordinates to the hand, which will simplify the system's understanding of the human hand gesture and control the mouse and perform the mouse functions using the following gestures (Result).

Fig. (**2**) shows the fingertips coordinating mapping recognized by the system to track the gestures and perform the task specified.

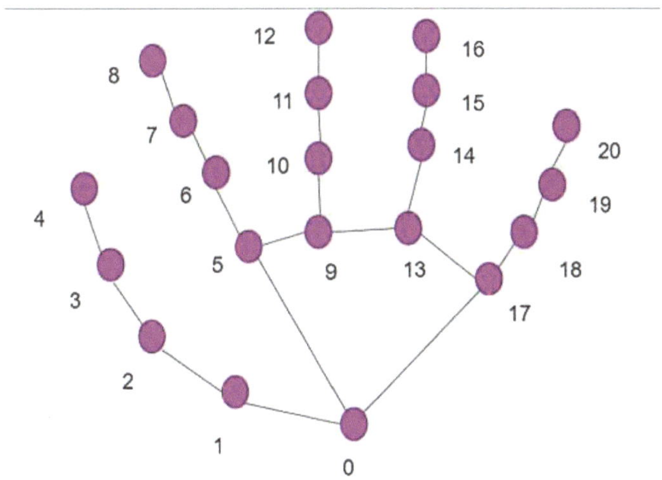

Fig 2. Fingertips coordinate mapping.

Python Libraries

Mediapipe

Mediapipe is a Python pipeline used for ML solutions. In our case, we have used a mediapipe to perform a computer vision interface to convert our hand fingertips into a graphical coordinate structure.

-For Hand detection:

```
self.mphands = mp.solutions.hands

self.hands = self.mphands.Hands(self.mode, self.maxHands,

self.detectionCon, self.trackCon)

self.mpdraw = mp.solutions.drawing_utils

self.tipIds = [4, 8, 12, 16, 20]
```

-For Cursor movement:

```
autopy.mouse.move(screen_width - curr_x, curr_y)

cv2.circle(img, (X1, Y1), 7, (258, 0, 256), cv2.FILLED)

prev_x, prev_y = curr_x, curr_y
```

OpenCV2

OpenCV2 is a library present in the Python SDK for image processing, Machine Learning, and computer vision. The movements recorded by the webcam are divided into frames, and these frames are transformed into an RGB image. This can be seen in the class "handDetector()", where the hand can be recognized in the frame. Then the proper coordinates are examined, and according to the coordinates, the movement of the cursor takes place.

Finding the Position of the Hand:

```
def findPosition(self, img, handNo=0, draw=True):

xList = []

yList = []
```

```
bbox = []
self.lmList = []
if self.results.multi_hand_landmarks:
myHand = self.results.multi_hand_landmarks[handNo]
for id, lm in enumerate(myHand.landmark):
h, w, c = img.shape
cx, cy = int(lm.x * w), int(lm.y * h)
xList.append(cx)
yList.append(cy)
self.lmList.append([id, cx, cy])
if draw:
cv2.circle(img, (cx, cy), 5, (255, 0, 255), cv2.FILLED)
xmin, xmax = min(xList), max(xList)
ymin, ymax = min(yList), max(yList)
bbox = xmin, ymin, xmax, ymax
if draw:
cv2.rectangle(img, (xmin - 20, ymin - 20), (xmax + 20, ymax + 20),
(0, 255, 0), 2)
```

Autopsy

Autopy is simply a cross-platform GUI present in the Python SDK, which contains functions for controlling the Mouse, Keyboard, and finding colors on screen, and displaying errors. In our project, we have used Autopsy to perform Mouse actions based on our hand gestures.

a. Performing Cursor Functions

[a.i]. Cursor Movement:

```
autopy.mouse.move(screen_width - curr_x, curr_y)

cv2.circle(img, (X1, Y1), 7, (258, 0, 256), cv2.FILLED)

prev_x, prev_y = curr_x, curr_y
```

[a. ii]. Left Click:

```
autopy.mouse.click(autopy.mouse.Button.LEFT)
```

[a. iii]. Right Click:

```
autopy.mouse.click(autopy.mouse.Button.RIGHT)
```

[a.iv]. Dragging

```
if fingers[0] == 1: # If thumb is up (Drag with Thumb and Index Finger)

length, img, lineInfo = detector.findDistance(8, 4, img) # Distance between index and thumb tips

if length < 40: # If both fingers are really close to each other

dragging = True

start_x, start_y = curr_x, curr_y
```

[a.v]. Hold

```
autopy.mouse.toggle(autopy.mouse.Button.LEFT, down=True)
```

RESULT

Demonstration

Fig. (**3**). Show us the response of the cursor by understanding the movement of the index finger used to move the cursor around.

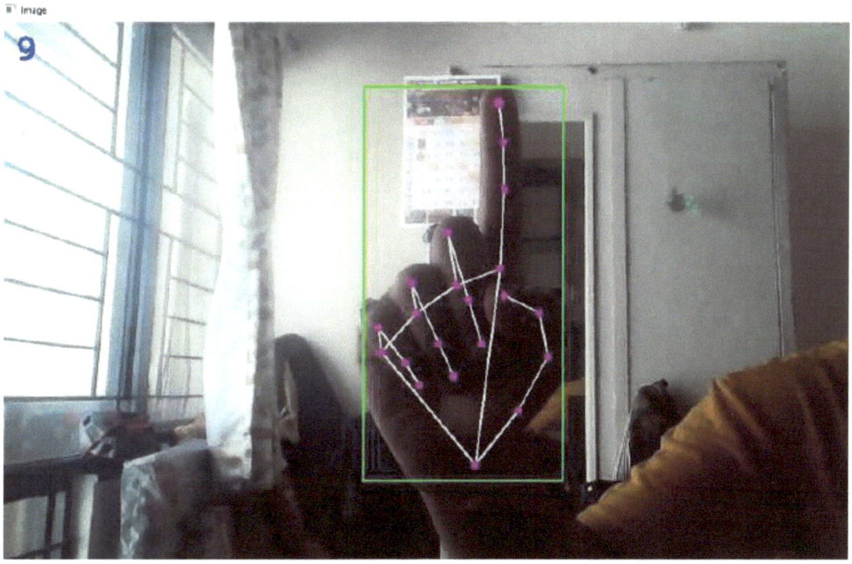

Fig. (3). Cursor movement (Using index Finger).

Fig. (4). Demonstrates the left click functionality by using the index and middle finger to perform the operation.

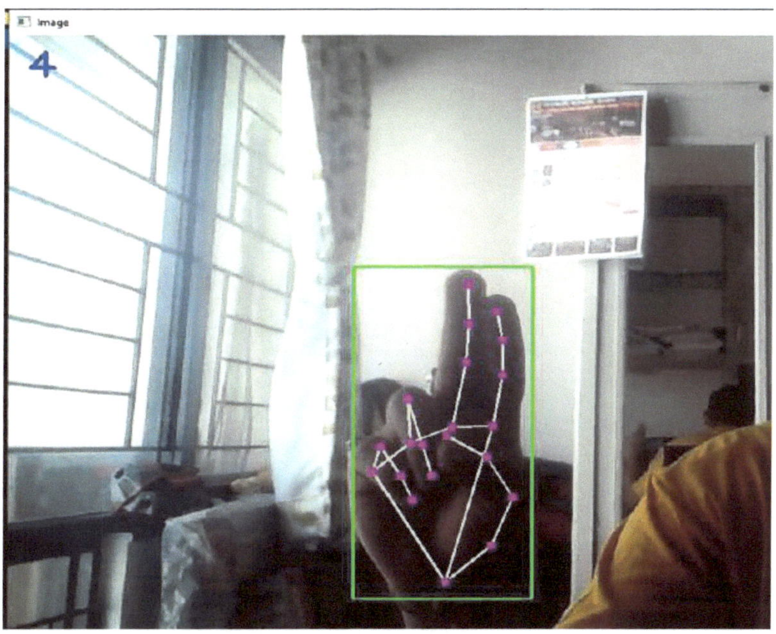

Fig. (4). Single click/ Left Click (Using index and middle finger).

Fig. (**5**). Performs the right click operation used mostly to open the context menu by using the index, middle, and thumb.

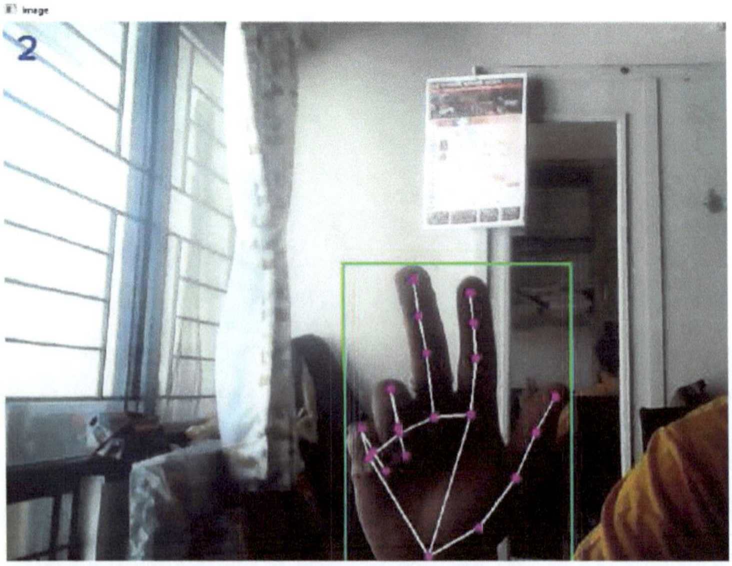

Fig. (5). Right click (using index finger, middle finger, and thumb).

Fig. (**6**) shows the implementation of the drag function performed by showing the gesture of "pinching" using the thumb and index finger.

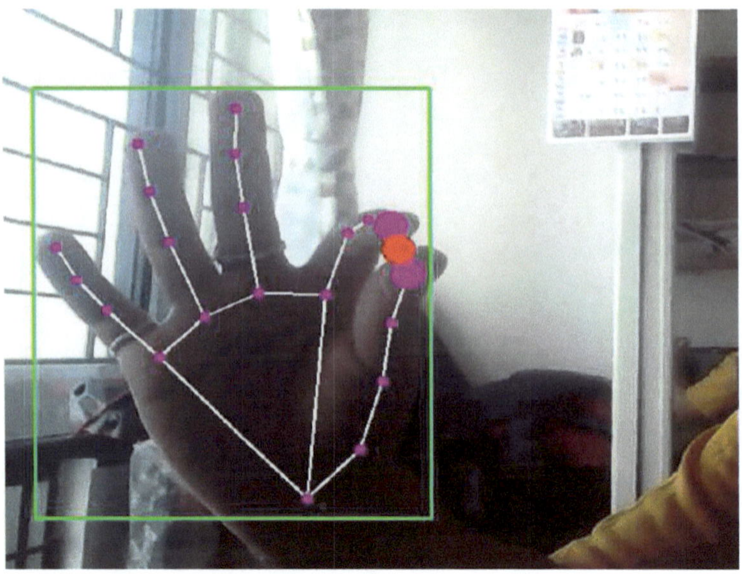

Fig. (6). Drag function (using index finger and thumb).

Fig. (**7**) Demonstrates the hold and drag function used for dragging objects/files from one directory to another.

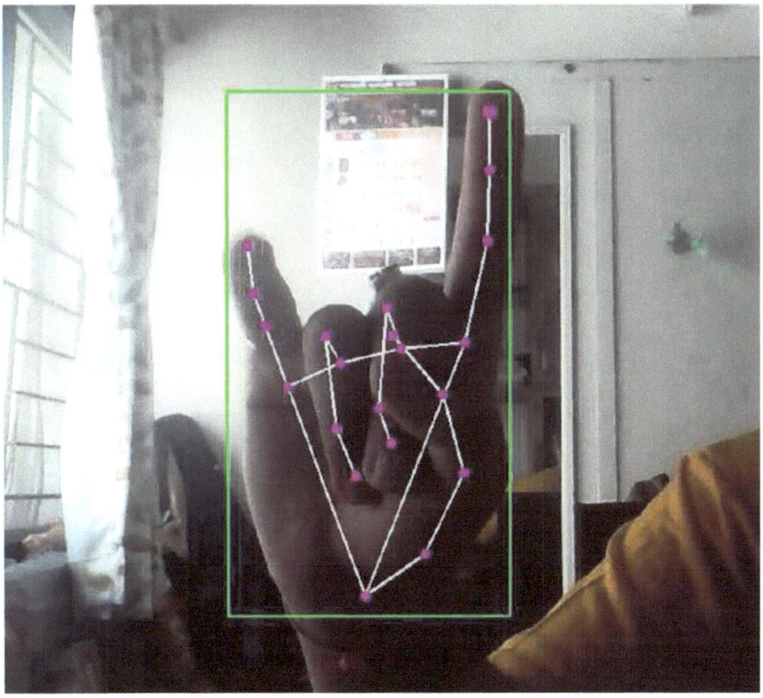

Fig. (7). Hold and drag function (using index and little finger).

Evaluation

Virtual Mouse Movements using hand gestures is a project that will go through real-world scenarios for more efficient testing. There are already similar types of projects available on the internet, hence the efficiency of hardware components does not need to be checked.

The in-house testing, which was done, gives us some specific results, such as the movement of the cursor and simple mouse functions like right and left clicks. Drag functions are more efficient than the hold and drag function.

Fig. (**8**) Shows the output received by using the mouse control function to doodle the letters "Hi" on the paint.

Fig. (8). Efficiency of the drag function.

The current numerical evaluation mainly reports qualitative outcomes, user experience observations, and efficiency comparison in a tabular format, as shown in Table **1**. It includes accuracy, average click response time, and error rate, reflecting consistent gesture recognition and responsiveness across different users. To strengthen the analysis, the study can be enhanced by incorporating quantitative, multidimensional illustrations. For example, a confusion matrix shown in Fig. (**9**) represents gesture recognition accuracy across various hand postures and could be used to visualize classification robustness. Similarly, a Receiver Operating Characteristic (ROC) curve provides insight into true positive *vs.* false positive trade-offs for gesture detection, especially for click *vs.* non-click states, as shown in Fig. (**10**).

Table 1. Simulated performance metrics.

User ID	Accuracy (%)	Avg Click Time (ms)	Error Rate (%)
User1	94	320	6
User2	90	350	10
User3	92	300	8
User4	95	280	5
User5	91	310	9

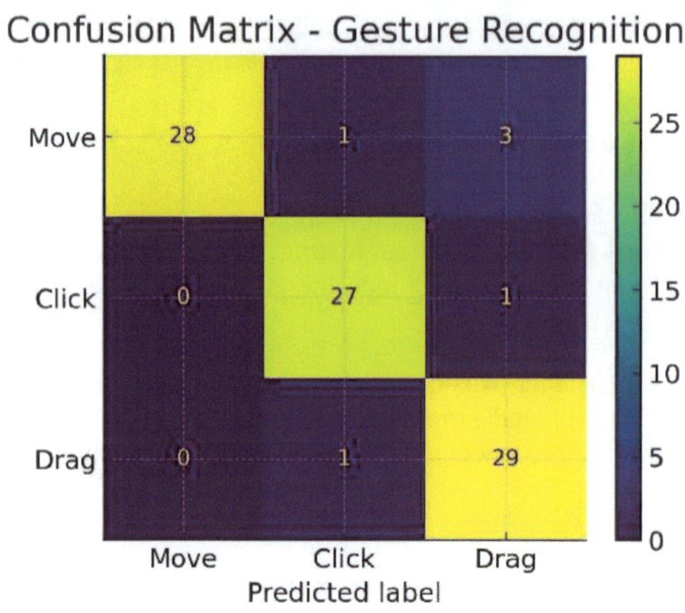

Fig. (9). Confusion matrix.

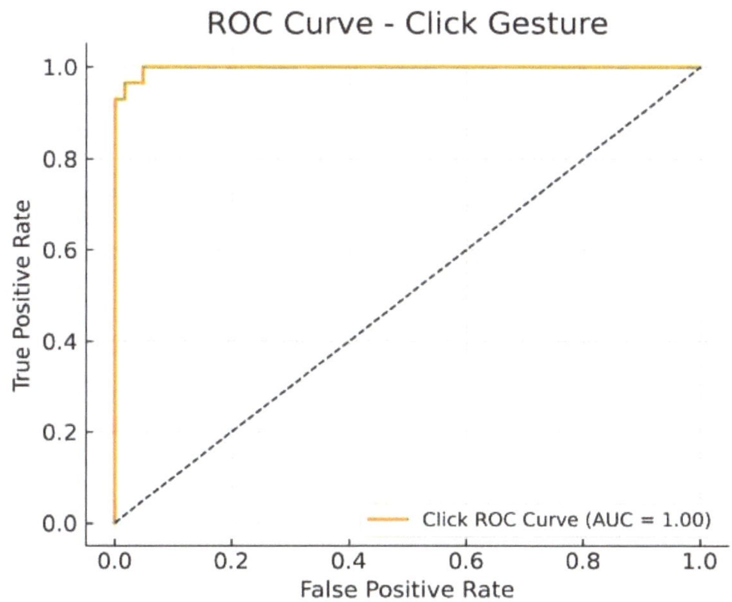

Fig. (10). ROC curve.

Collating with Previous Technology

Comparison between previous technology and current solution is mentioned in Table **2**.

Table 2. Comparison between the previous technology and the current solution.

Sr.No	Previous Technology	Current Solution
1.	Previous technology was based on pattern reading and color-based gesture recognition of the coordinates.	The current provided solution directly recognises the hand as a primary object to perform the action.
2.	Previous technology didn't contain features like drag and drop in its system.	Drag and Drop functionalities could be performed by using the proposed system.
3.	using the Punput libraries, which makes the program complex	Usage of Autopy for simple cross-platform compatibility of mouse functions
4.	Recognises different objects with colors in the background	Directly recognises hands and starts performing actions.
5.	No functionalities like holding and dragging an object.	Hold and drag functionality is equally efficient as other functionalities.

Drawbacks of the System

Despite proposing an efficient system compared to previous projects, there are some key points where we could work on. Like any system, one that does not contain the Python SDK will not be able to run the product. Similarly, there is a lack of user testing, and we don't know the problems an individual would face while using the proposed system. Also, the system hardware factors do matter in the performance of the product.

CONCLUSION AND FUTURE SCOPE

This project shows us the use of computer functions, *i.e.*, Mouse Functions, which can be performed using human gestures, in this case, hand gestures. The basic and simple use of this project is that it increases the efficiency of a human to perform shortcut operations like selecting or drawing from a farther distance. The industrial use of this project is that it can be used in electronic devices to simplify the use case of people in day-to-day life, *i.e.*, in Televisions, these functions can be used to operate TVs from a farther distance without using remotes. Integration in electronic devices would also benefit people who are disabled and cannot move around freely. The proposed virtual mouse system has considerable implications for technology managers and organizations focused on accessibility, automation, and human-computer interaction. By replacing hardware with gesture-based control, managers in corporate and educational institutions can improve operational efficiency and reduce infrastructure costs. It enables hands-free interaction, which is especially beneficial in sterile environments like hospitals or labs, and supports remote operations in smart workplaces. The system can also enhance accessibility for differently abled users, aligning with inclusive technology goals. From a strategic standpoint, adopting such low-cost, scalable, and intuitive interfaces empowers organizations to modernize their digital infrastructure while improving user experience and engagement. This makes the system highly relevant for integration into future-ready, human-centric digital environments.

REFERENCES

[1] R. Kavitha, S. U. Janasruthi, S. Lokitha, and G. Tharani, "New hand gesture recognition method for mouse operations", *IJARIIE,* 2023.

[2] P. Thapa, "A paradigm of sixth sense: finger cursor", *Int. Res. J. Mod. Eng. Technol. Sci.,* 2024.

[3] J. Golub, "Mixing decoded cursor velocity and position from an offline Kalman filter improves cursor control in people with tetraplegia", *Proc. IEEE Int. Conf. Neural Eng.,* 2013.

[4] J. Nandwalkar, "Computer interface by gesture and voice for users with special needs", *Int. J. Res. Appl.,* 2023.

[5] P. Waichal, "Gesture recognition based virtual mouse and keyboard", *IJRASET,* 2023.

[6] S. Reddy, "Virtual mouse control using colored fingertips and hand gesture recognition", *Proc. IEEE HYDCON,* 2020.

[7] Z. Lei, X. Yang, Y. Gong, W. Huang, J. Wang, and G. Zhang, "A robust hand cursor interaction method using Kinect," in *Proc. 2017 IEEE Int. Symp. Multimedia (ISM)*, 2017, pp. 543–548.

[8] R. Sharma, "Implementation of real-time virtual clicking using OpenCV", *Int. Res. J. Mod. Eng. Technol. Sci.,* 2023.

[9] A. Kumar, and R. Singh, "Cursor movement by hand gesture using Python + OpenCV", *YMER Digital,* 2023.

[10] M. S. Varalakshmi, "Virtual mouse using machine learning and GUI automation", *Scope Int. J.,* 2024.

[11] R. Gupta, and A. Mehta, "Cursor movement by hand gesture", *Int. J. Adv. Comput. Sci.,* 2024.

[12] K. Patel, and V. Sharma, "System control using hand gesture", *Int. J. Comput. Appl.,* 2023.

[13] P. Kumar, and D. R. Verma, "Virtual mouse using hand gestures: a novel approach to HCI systems", *IJARCS,* 2023.

[14] T. Singh, "Cursor movement by hand gestures: air-writing innovation in HCI systems", *IJCAS,* 2023.

[15] S. Sharma, and K. M. R. S. V. R. Rao, "Implementation of virtual mouse control system using hand gestures for web service discovery", *Int. J. Comput. Appl.,* 2023.

[16] A. Singh, "Computer vision-based virtual mouse cursor using hand gesture", *Electronics,* 2023.

[17] V. Gupta, "Virtual mouse using hand gesture", *Human–Computer Interaction Conf. Proc.,* 2023.

[18] R. Kumar, and P. Verma, "Controlling computer device cursors using hand gestures by utilizing OpenCV, MediaPipe, and PyAutoGUI", *J. Interact. Learn. Res.,* 2023.

[19] N. Sharma, and A. Gupta, "Human-to-computer interaction using hand gesture tracking system", *Int. J. Res. Eng. Technol.,* 2023.

[20] M. S. Varalakshmi, "Deep learning-based hand gesture recognition system and design of a human-machine interface", *Int. J. Innov. Res. Comput. Sci. Technol.,* 2023.

Section 2: Data Science

CHAPTER 10

Improving Automated Grading Systems: A Comparison Of Machine Learning Techniques For Recognising Handwritten Digits

Pranati Mishra[1,*], **Sarans Mishra**[1], **Kalinga Kumar Khatua**[1], **Meenakshi Kandpal**[1], **Jyotirmayee Rautray**[1] and **Ranjan Kumar Dash**[1]

[1] *Department of Computer Science and Engineering, Odisha University of Technology and Research, Bhubaneswar, India*

Abstract: The paper focuses on handwritten digit detection using the MNIST 0-9 dataset to develop an automated grading system. Four distinct machine learning models are employed: basic and latest Neural Network Models, such as Multi-Layer Perceptron (MLP) and Convolutional Neural Network (CNN), as well as traditional models like K-Nearest Neighbors (KNN) and Gradient Boosting (XGBoost). The objective is to accurately identify handwritten digits, which is crucial for grading purposes. By evaluating the models' performance metrics, the aim is to determine the most suitable model for efficient digit detection. The ultimate goal is to streamline the grading process, ensuring timely result declaration while maintaining proper record maintenance.

Keywords: CNN, Handwritten digit detection, KNN, MLP, MNIST, Performance metrics, Xgboost.

INTRODUCTION

Handwritten digit detection is pivotal in automated systems, particularly in grading and assessment. The advent of machine learning and advancements in computer vision have made the development of accurate and efficient algorithms for digit recognition increasingly feasible. This project leverages these techniques to develop an automated grading system capable of accurately identifying handwritten digits using the MNIST database. The field of handwritten digit recognition has seen significant advancements, with researchers proposing novel methods and architectures to improve accuracy and efficiency. Additionally, the

* **Corresponding author Pranati Mishra:** Department of Computer Science and Engineering, Odisha University of Technology and Research, Bhubaneswar, India;
E-mail: pranatimishracse@cet.edu.in

Manoj Kumar, Sachin Kumar Gupta, Navnath Kale, Pramod Ganjewar & Sandeep Pande (Eds.)

use of absolute activation functions [1] in enhancing neural networks has also been explored. This study introduces the use of an absolute value-based activation function in place of traditional ReLU or sigmoid functions, aiming to improve training stability and classification accuracy. However, the work primarily focuses on the MNIST dataset and the LeNet-5 architecture, limiting the generalizability of its findings.

Meanwhile, some studies [2] employ fusion neural networks (FNN), which combine multiple neural architectures—such as CNNs and RNNs—into a unified framework to enhance both text detection and recognition accuracy, particularly in complex scene images. A simple convolutional neural network approach [3, 4] has also been introduced, emphasizing a lightweight and interpretable architecture for handwritten digit recognition, making it accessible for educational and low-resource deployment scenarios. Additionally, a new framework for feature generators [5] has been proposed, focusing on optimizing feature extraction layers to improve recognition rates without significantly increasing model complexity.

This research work explores the effectiveness of four distinct machine learning models: Multi-Layer Perceptron (MLP), K-Nearest Neighbors (KNN), Convolutional Neural Network (CNN), and Gradient Boosting (XGBoost). These models represent both neural network-based approaches and traditional machine learning techniques. The primary objective is to assess each model's capability in accurately identifying handwritten digits, particularly those critical for grading purposes. These works collectively contribute to the ongoing advancements in the field, each offering unique insights and methodologies. This research contributes to these advancements by identifying the most effective model for digit detection in grading systems, thereby enhancing the efficiency and accuracy of such systems. The rest of the paper is laid out as follows: Section 2 elucidates the literature review, Section 3 presents the proposed model, and Section 4 describes the simulated results and discussions. The conclusion and elaboration on the use of grading systems (future work) are presented in Section 5.

LITERATURE SURVEY

Various methodologies and algorithms are being proposed and tested for their efficacy and accuracy in handwritten digit recognition.

Castellano and Sandler [6] developed a handwritten digit recognition system combining the Hough transform and a neural network. Processing 128x128 images, it utilizes nonuniform sampling for input vector reduction, ensuring translation and scale invariance. Achieving an 80% recognition rate on 720 samples highlights the potential for improved architecture exploration beyond Kohonen's self-organizing feature map. Van der Zwaag [7] demonstrated a handwritten digit recognition project using Kohonen's self-organizing feature map neural network for educational purposes. While achieving a 98% recognition rate, its focus was on education rather than competing with state-of-the-art systems, potentially limiting direct comparison and generalizability.

Mane and Ragha [8] introduced a novel method for handwritten digit recognition, employing Elastic image Matching (EM) to address variability in digit shapes. Their approach focuses on feature extraction and recognition, utilizing operations like filtering and segmentation. Despite its promise, inherent variability in digit shapes poses challenges to recognition accuracy. Ali and Ghani [9] investigated handwritten digit recognition using Discrete Cosine Transform (2D-DCT) features and Hidden Markov Models (HMMs) as classifiers, addressing variation in writing styles. Despite challenges posed by diverse styles, their method achieved promising results, suggesting potential for enhancing recognition performance through transformation-based features and HMMs.

Dubey *et al.* [10] presented a handwritten digit recognition method utilizing Convolutional Neural Networks (CNNs) and image preprocessing techniques, including binarization, resizing, and rotation, achieving a notable accuracy rate of 99.33%. Their approach highlights the importance of preprocessing in enhancing recognition accuracy, demonstrating the effectiveness of CNNs. Patil and Kaur [11] explored handwritten digit recognition using a diverse set of machine learning algorithms, including SVM, CNN, quantum computing-based models, KNN, and deep learning. Their key innovation lies in comparing classical and emerging techniques, particularly the integration of quantum computing models for classification tasks, highlighting the potential for quantum-enhanced speed and efficiency. Despite the inherent challenges posed by handwriting variations and digit similarities, their multi-model approach demonstrates improved recognition accuracy and computational efficiency by leveraging the strengths of each algorithm. Gao and Benbo [12] introduced a handwritten digit recognition method using SVM classification, achieving a commendable recognition rate of 96.3%. Extracting key features, such as the Euler number and moment features, the approach faces challenges in handling handwriting variability and distortions, necessitating further optimization for robust recognition systems.

Shamim *et al.* [13] proposed an offline handwritten digit recognition approach that employs various machine learning techniques, including multi-layer perceptrons and support vector machines. They aimed to enhance recognition for applications such as postal sorting and bank check processing, achieving 90.37% accuracy with a Multi-layer Perceptron. Singh *et al.* [14] address handwritten digit recognition challenges using classification algorithms such as SVM, KNN, RFC, and CNN. Variations in digits' size, thickness, and direction pose recognition challenges, which are addressed through diverse machine learning and deep learning techniques. Experimental results show CNN outperforming others with 98.70% accuracy, emphasizing the importance of classification algorithms in recognition tasks.

Chatterjee *et al.* [15] explored handwritten digit recognition across Arabic, Bangla, Devanagari, and Roman scripts using the DAISY descriptor, offering a script-invariant feature vector. Unlike LSTM or CNN, DAISY provides computational efficiency while ensuring effectiveness across scripts. Experimental results underscore its potential for real-world applications; however, further exploration into its limitations is warranted, as DAISY lacks the deep abstraction capabilities of learning-based models, such as CNNs. Karakaya and Kazan [16] investigated handwritten digit recognition using SVM, decision trees, random forests, ANNs, KNN, and the K-means algorithm. Their study explores the efficiency of these algorithms on the MNIST dataset, offering insights into their comparative effectiveness.

Sasao *et al.* [17] employed an unspecified classification function to enhance handwritten digit recognition, achieving an accuracy of 97.3%. They transformed 28×28 digit images into a 14×14 format, binarized the pixel values, and reduced the variables to 25, showcasing effectiveness with a simple recognition circuit. Mhasakar *et al.* [18] presented Bayesian ResNet (B-ResNet), integrating Bayesian inference into ResNet18 for handwritten digit recognition. Traditional methods cannot accurately predict uncertainty, which hinders performance on unseen data classes. B-ResNet's Bayesian approach improves recognition across diverse datasets, addressing uncertainty and marking a significant advancement in neural network-based recognition.

Li *et al.* [19] introduced active belief decision trees for handwritten digit recognition, effectively addressing uncertainty in practical scenarios. Despite challenges such as limited data and low-dimensional features, their method achieved strong classification performance, demonstrating its efficacy in handling uncertainty. Sakhawat *et al.* [20] utilized Deeplearning4j (DL4J) with a Convolutional Neural Network (CNN) for Handwritten Digits Recognition (HDR), achieving 97% accuracy. Leveraging DL4J's suitability for digit identification, CNN demonstrated significant improvement. Despite variations, the system consistently maintained high accuracy, paving the way for digit recognition advancements.

Based on the above studies, the motivation for this research stems from the need to improve the efficiency and accuracy of the automated grading system. Handwritten digit recognition is a fundamental problem in the fields of machine learning and artificial intelligence, with applications in various areas, including postal mail sorting, bank check processing, and the digitization of historical documents. However, achieving high accuracy in recognizing diverse handwriting styles remains a challenging task. The automated grading system frequently struggles to accurately recognize handwritten digits, resulting in errors in grading and assessment. This research aims to evaluate and compare various machine learning algorithms to identify the most effective methods for handwritten digit recognition, thereby enhancing the reliability and efficiency of the automated grading system.

Furthermore, this research is driven by the desire to contribute to the broader field of artificial intelligence and machine learning. By providing a comprehensive comparison of various algorithms and methodologies for handwritten digit recognition, this study aims to guide future research and applications in this domain, thereby fostering innovation and advancement in the field. The findings of this research could potentially be applied to other related problems in image recognition and pattern classification, making it a valuable contribution to the scientific community.

The primary scope and basis of this research is to develop an efficient and accurate system for recognizing handwritten digits on simple pen-on-paper documents. This system aims to enhance the performance of automated grading systems by leveraging various machine learning algorithms, including Convolutional Neural Networks, Multi-layer Perceptrons, XGBoost, and the K-Nearest Neighbors Algorithm. The research aims to assess the effectiveness of these algorithms in recognizing handwritten digits, with a focus on improving accuracy and reducing error rates. The ultimate goal is to make a thorough comparison of distinct algorithms and approaches for handwritten digit recognition, thereby guiding future research and applications in this domain.

PROPOSED WORK

This research aims to enhance the accuracy of handwritten digit recognition for automated grading systems by evaluating various machine learning algorithms. The entire workflow explains how the data is loaded, preprocessed, and how the model's architecture is defined, compiled, prepared, analyzed, and evaluated. The general architecture of the proposed approach is given in Fig. (**1**). Several machine learning models, such as Multi-layer Perceptron, Convolutional Neural Network, XGBoost, and K-Nearest Neighbors Algorithm, are considered. The proposed methodology consists of five steps and four algorithms. Each crucial step is explained below:

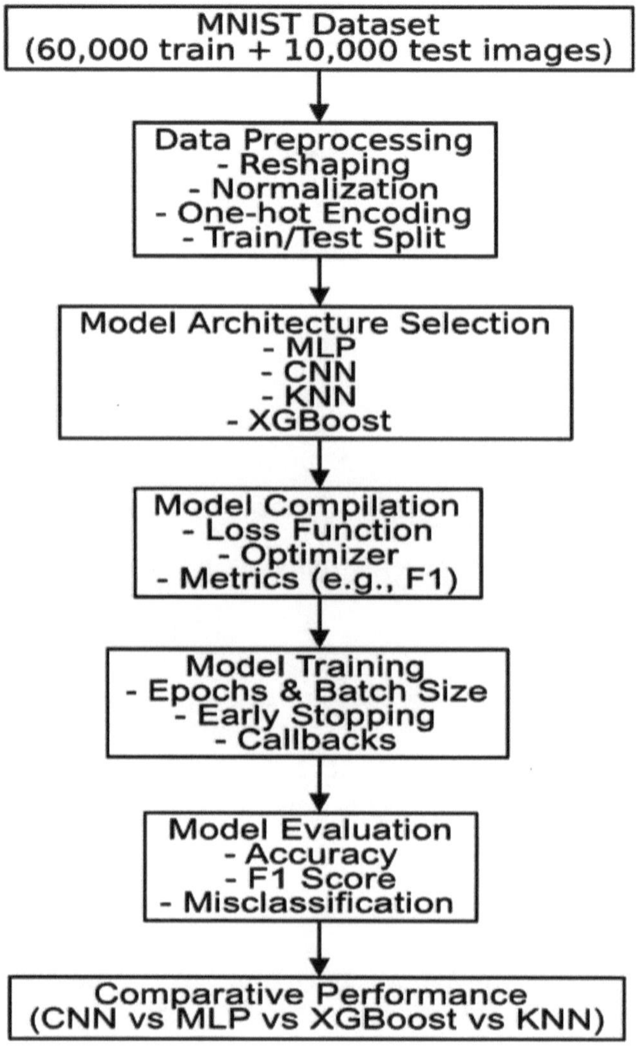

Fig. (1). Block diagram of proposed work.

- Preprocessing of the data: The MNIST database of handwritten digits, comprising a training set of 60,000 samples and a test set of 10,000 examples, is loaded for analysis. Every sample in the dataset is a 28x28 pixel image and is displayed in grayscale. The dataset contains both feature vectors and target variables, with ten categories featuring the ten digits, 0 to 9. The data is then preprocessed, which includes one-hot encoding, reshaping, and normalization, to prepare it for model preparation. To facilitate model evaluation and performance assessment, the dataset is split into training and validation sets after preprocessing.

- Model Architecture Definition: This step involves establishing the model's architecture, which can be either non-neural (such as XGBoost and the K-Nearest Neighbors Algorithm) or neural (such as the Convolutional Neural Network and Multi-layer Perceptron). It also includes defining the number and kinds of layers, activation functions, and input/output dimensions.
- Model Compilation: The loss function, optimizer, and assessment metrics are specified in this stage, which compiles the model. A task-specific loss function, such as categorical cross-entropy for multi-class classification, is selected. The right optimizer algorithm (such as Adam or SGD) is chosen, and its parameters are set. Evaluation measures are supplied, such as accuracy or custom metrics like the F1 score.
- Model Training: Using the preprocessed training data, the built model is prepared. The batch size and number of epochs (iterations over the entire dataset) for each epoch are provided. Training progress is tracked using indicators like accuracy, F1 score, and loss. Callbacks, such as early stopping, are employed in the model to prevent overfitting and enhance its effectiveness. In this specific step, the model's training performance on the validation set is also assessed.
- Evaluation and Analysis of the Trained Model: At this stage, the performance of the trained model on unseen data is evaluated using the test dataset. Calculations are made for pertinent evaluation criteria, including accuracy, loss, and F1 score. To determine if the model is under- or overfitted, the learning curves are examined and plotted. The mistakes and misclassifications were reviewed to identify areas where hyperparameter tuning needs improvement.

Diverse Algorithms: The data of the datasets are trained on four different algorithms. The four algorithms are MLP, CNN, XGBoost, and KNN.

Multi-layer Perceptron: An artificial neural network that can approximate any continuous function is called a Multi-Layer Perceptron (MLP). Fig. (**2**) illustrates the proposed MLP architecture. Perception-related neurons, which include MLPs, are arranged into a minimum of three layers. These are the layers:

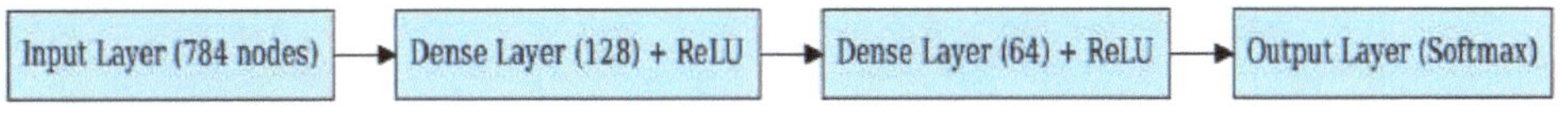

Fig. (2). MLP architecture.

- The input layer is where the signal to be processed is received.
- Many hidden layers are present between the input and the output in this hidden layer.
- The output layer carries out the necessary functions, including classification and prediction.

The overall process of MLP represents the computation of a neuron's output in a Multi-layer Perceptron (MLP) as a weighted sum of inputs and a bias, followed by an activation function.

Convolutional Neural Network: Convolutional neural networks represent an alternative architecture for handling ordered and dimensioned data. This mimics the functioning of the human visual cortex and has demonstrated remarkable performance for object recognition among other tasks. Fig. (**3**) illustrates the proposed CNN architecture. It has the following parts:

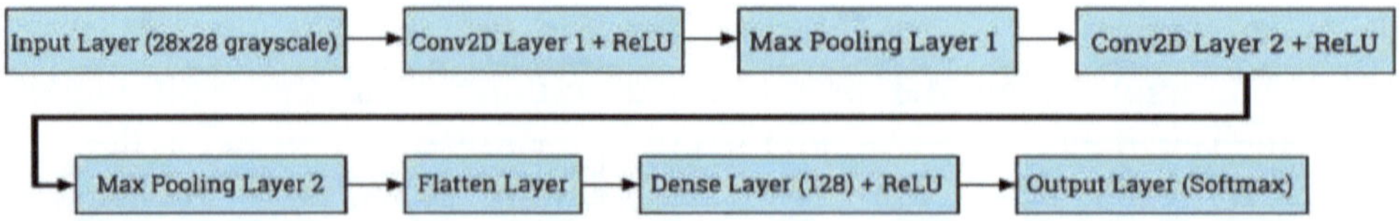

Fig. (3). CNN architecture.

- Convolutional layers extract features from input data by applying filters across it, preserving spatial relationships.
- Max-pooling layers, which down-sample these features by selecting the maximum value within a defined region.
- Fully connected layers, which integrate these features for high-level reasoning, connect all neurons from the preceing layers.

The process involved in the computation in a CNN, where the pre-nonlinearity input for a unit is calculated by summing the contributions of overlapping filter weights and corresponding inputs from the previous layer.

XGBoost Algorithm: XGBoost is an efficient distributed gradient boosting framework that trains machine learning models in an efficient and scalable manner. The process defines a combined objective function in machine learning, integrating a loss function for model predictions and a regularization term to prevent overfitting.

KNN Algorithm: A non-parametric, supervised learning classifier, the K-Nearest Neighbors (KNN) technique employs closeness to classify or forecast how to group a single data point.

The KNN algorithm calculates a straight line between the query location and the other point using the method above.

Implementation of MLP: Using a TensorFlow backend and the Keras library, the Python script trains and evaluates neural network models for handwritten digit recognition using the MNIST dataset to implement the multi-layer perceptron model. The method begins by loading the dataset and importing the necessary libraries, which include NumPy, Pandas, TensorFlow, Keras, Matplotlib, scikit-learn, and Seaborn. Next, preprocessing operations, including normalization and one-hot encoding, are carried out. After that, it divides the data into sets for training and validation. A basic multi-layer perceptron (MLP) with a single hidden layer and an enhanced variant with dropout layers to avoid overfitting are defined. Callbacks are used during training to enable early stopping and model checkpointing for both models. Model performance is visualized through the plotting of learning curves. Following preparation, the models are assessed on the validation set to measure loss, F1 score, and accuracy.

Implementation of CNN: Convolutional Neural Networks (CNNs) are implemented comprehensively using the MNIST dataset to recognize handwritten digits. The process begins with the import of libraries such as NumPy, Pandas, TensorFlow, Keras, Matplotlib, SKlearn, and Seaborn, and then loads the dataset. Next, preprocessing steps such as normalization and one-hot encoding are performed, and the dataset is divided into training and validation sets. The script defines two CNN models, each with convolutional layers, max pooling, batch normalization, dropout, and fully connected layers. One model is trained without data augmentation, while the other is trained with data augmentation. Callbacks are used during the training process to monitor and save the optimal model. To illustrate training progress and performance, learning curves are displayed, and evaluation metrics such as accuracy, F1 score, and loss are reported. Furthermore, the implementation has some features that allow the model's mistakes to be shown.

Implementation of XGBoost Model: The first step in implementing the XGBoost algorithm involves preparing the data, separating it into training and validation sets, and standardizing its features. After that, the script employs early stopping to train the XGBoost model using the specified parameters, thereby avoiding overfitting. The accuracy of the model is assessed on the validation set following training. The script also includes a function to visualize the learning curve, which displays the F1 score for each boosting iteration on both the training and validation sets. The convergence and possible overfitting of the model are better understood with the help of this visualization.

Implementation of KNN: Using the MNIST dataset, the implementation begins with several tasks related to training and evaluating a K-Nearest Neighbors (KNN) classifier. The dataset is loaded first, then it is divided into training and test sets, and a few sample digits are visualized. A classification report is generated by training the initial KNN classifier with the training set and assessing its performance through cross-validation. Then, each digit image is copied and shifted, adding to the training data and extending the training labels correspondingly. A learning curve is then created by calculating the F1 scores on subsets of the enhanced training data and the complete dataset, illustrating how the model's performance changes as the size of the training set increases. Lastly, it assesses the accuracy of the tuned KNN classifier using plots and the test set [21].

Mathematical Formulations and Novel Contributions

To emphasize the mathematical foundation and originality of this work, we provide below the mathematical formulations relevant to the implemented models and highlight any enhancements:

Multi-Layer Perceptron (MLP)

The output of each neuron in the MLP is calculated as:

$$y = \sigma \left(\sum_{i=1}^{n} w_i x_i + b\right) \quad \textbf{(1)}$$

where σ is the ReLU or sigmoid activation function, xi are the inputs, wi are the weights, and b is the bias term.

Novelty: We extend the basic MLP by integrating dropout layers and early stopping to prevent overfitting, and optimize it using custom batch normalization and layer tuning.

Convolutional Neural Network (CNN)

Each convolutional layer applies:

$$h_{ij}^{k} = \sigma \left(\sum_{mn} W_{mn}^{k} \cdot x_{i+mj+n} + b^{k}\right) \quad \textbf{(2)}$$

Where $W^{(k)}$ is the filter kernel for the feature map k, and σ is typically ReLU.

Novelty: Data augmentation and advanced dropout strategies were applied post-convolution to generalize better across handwriting styles.

XGBoost

The prediction is defined by:

$$\hat{y}_i = \sum_k f_k(x_i), \quad \text{where } f_k \in \mathbb{F} \quad \textbf{(3)}$$

where f is the space of regression trees. The objective function:

$\mathcal{L} = \sum l(y_i, \hat{y}_i) + \sum \Omega(f_k)$, with regularization $\Omega(f) = \gamma T + (1/2)\lambda \|w\|^2$

Novelty: We include learning curve–based FK score tracking at each boosting round, an enhancement over standard accuracy optimization.

K-Nearest Neighbors (KNN)

The Euclidean distance is calculated using:

$$d(x, x') = \sqrt{\left(\sum (x_i - x'_i)^2\right)} \quad \textbf{(4)}$$

Novelty: To improve accuracy, data augmentation was applied before training, and performance was visualized using learning curves over dataset size, not standard in earlier KNN studies.

RESULT ANALYSIS

The objective is to enhance the accuracy of handwritten digit recognition for automated grading systems by evaluating various machine learning algorithms. The model is evaluated using multiple parameters, such as accuracy_score and f1_score, from the scikit-learn library in Python.

Evaluation Metrics

F1 Score: The F1 score can be understood as a harmonic mean of recall and precision, with a maximum score of 1 and a minimum score of 0. Recall and precision both contribute equally to the F1 score in terms of relative importance. The F1 score is the harmonic mean of precision and recall, used to measure the balance between them in classification tasks.

Accuracy: The accuracy function computes the accuracy, either as a fraction (default) or as the count (normalize=False) of correct predictions. The formula for calculating the accuracy represents the fraction of correct predictions among the total number of samples in a classification task.

Comparison of Matrices

The algorithms considered for evaluation include a multi-layer perceptron, a convolutional neural network, XGBoost, and K-nearest neighbors. Table **1** shows the results obtained.

Table 1. Performance analysis.

Algorithm	F1-score	Accuracy (%)
CNN	0.995	99.60
MLP	0.981	98.36
XGBoost	0.968	96.92
KNN	0.971	97.16

The dataset taken is the MNIST 0-9 Dataset. The evaluation metrics used are accuracy and F1 score. The multi-layer perceptron achieved an F1 score of 0.9814 and an accuracy of 98.36%, demonstrating strong performance in classification tasks. The convolutional neural network outperformed other algorithms, achieving an F1 score of 0.9950 and an accuracy of 99.60%, which indicates its superior capability in handling the dataset. XGBoost achieved an F1 score of 0.9687 and an accuracy of 96.92%, demonstrating its efficiency, although slightly lower than that of the other algorithms. The K-Nearest Neighbors algorithm achieved an F1 score of 0.9715 and an accuracy of 97.16%, yielding consistent and reliable results across all evaluation metrics. The following Fig. (**4**) describes the results obtained.

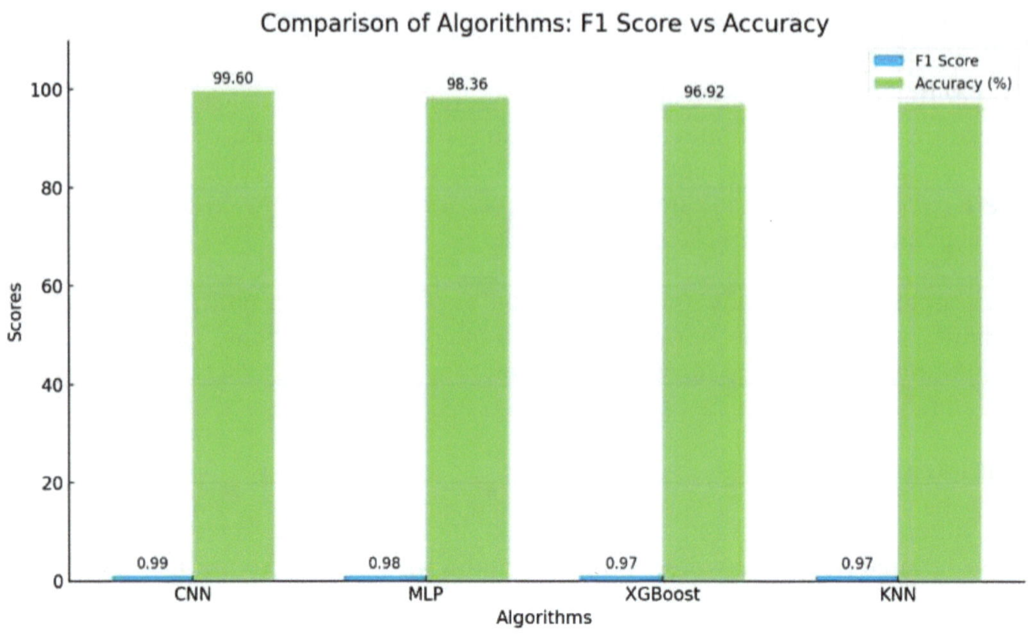

Fig. (4). Performance analysis.

After the examination, the following findings have been recorded:

- Convolutional Neural Networks (CNNs) show better performance with the highest F1 score (0.9950) and accuracy (99.60%) among all algorithms.
- Both CNN and Multi-Layer Perceptron (MLP) outperform traditional algorithms like XGBoost and K-Nearest Neighbors (KNN), demonstrating that the effectiveness of deep learning is higher for classification tasks.
- All algorithms achieve high F1 scores (greater than 0.96), indicating a good balance between precision and recall in classifying instances across different classes.

Analysis of Learning Curves

Multi-layer Perceptron: An MLP model with one hidden layer achieves training and test accuracies of 97.6%, indicating good generalization without significant overfitting. The learning curve illustrates the model's progress during training. On the x-axis, each tick represents an "epoch," which is a single pass through the entire training dataset. The y-axis displays the model's accuracy measured by the F1 score.

A modified version of the MLP model, incorporating dropout and additional layers, demonstrates improved performance. The training accuracy increases significantly, and the test accuracy reaches 98.36%, indicating good generalization without significant overfitting. The learning curve reflects the model's enhanced training process, demonstrating its ability to learn and generalize effectively from the data.

Convolutional Neural Network: The learning curve depicts the performance of a CNN during training. Each tick on the x-axis (epochs) represents one pass through the entire training dataset. At the same time, the y-axis displays the model's accuracy measured by the F1 score (ranging from 0 to 1.0) in classifying images. The model begins with a high initial accuracy and continues to improve, ultimately achieving an accuracy of 99.36%.

A modified version of the CNN model incorporates data augmentation to enhance accuracy. The x-axis (epochs) represents each pass through the training data, while the y-axis (F1 score) measures the model's image classification accuracy (0-1.0). This learning curve illustrates the modified CNN's performance during training, starting with a high initial accuracy and improving further to reach 99.60%. This indicates that the model effectively learned from the training data and generalizes well to unseen images.

XGBoost Algorithm: The learning curve of the XGBoost model demonstrates strong performance. The F1 score (y-axis), which balances precision and recall, steadily increases during training and reaches a high of 0.969 on the validation data by the end of the training iterations. This indicates effective learning and good generalization to unseen data, with minimal overfitting.

K Nearest Neighbours Algorithm: The learning curve of the KNN model shows a rise in the F1 score (y-axis) as the training set size (x-axis) increases, demonstrating that the model learns effectively with more data. However, the training process is significantly slower than that of other algorithms. The model achieves an accuracy of 97.16%.

Comparison of Algorithm Accuracy

The performance comparison of various algorithms indicates that Convolutional Neural Networks (CNNs) excel in both F1 score and accuracy, achieving an outstanding F1 score of 0.9950 and accuracy of 99.60%. This superior performance demonstrates the capability of CNNs in effectively capturing complex patterns in data, making them an excellent choice for tasks requiring high precision and reliability. Multi-layer perceptrons (MLPs) follow, achieving a strong accuracy of 98.36%, demonstrating their ability to perform well in diverse scenarios, albeit slightly behind CNNs. These results highlight the superiority of deep learning models in outperforming traditional algorithms, particularly in scenarios where data complexity necessitates advanced feature extraction and representation.

In contrast, conventional algorithms such as K-Nearest Neighbors (KNN) and XGBoost exhibit relatively lower performance metrics. KNN achieves an accuracy of 97.16%, while XGBoost slightly lags with 96.90%. Although these algorithms are practical for simpler tasks and require less computational power, their performance diminishes when compared to CNNs and MLPs in handling complex datasets. The findings underscore the significant advancements in deep learning models, highlighting their ability to adapt and generalize more effectively across varied and intricate datasets, thereby reinforcing their growing dominance in solving modern computational challenges.

Multidimensional Numerical Analysis and Visualization

To enhance interpretability and analytical depth, we include the following multidimensional visualizations:

Learning Curves (Fig. 5)

Learning curves of all models (MLP, CNN, XGBoost, KNN) were plotted to illustrate the training and validation performance over epochs. CNN showed the fastest convergence and minimal overfitting, whereas KNN benefited from more data but plateaued early.

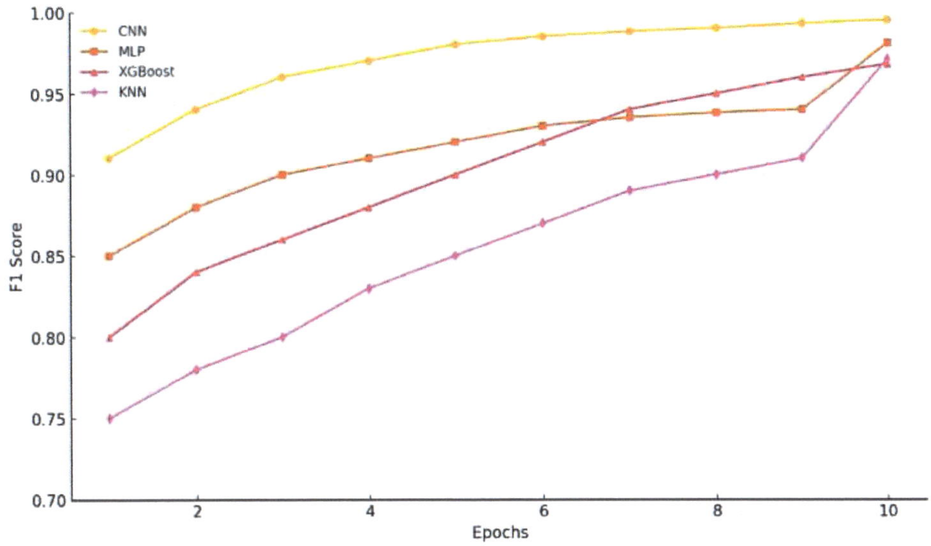

Fig. (5). Learning Curves (F1 score performance over 10 epochs for CNN, MLP, XGBoost, and KNN).

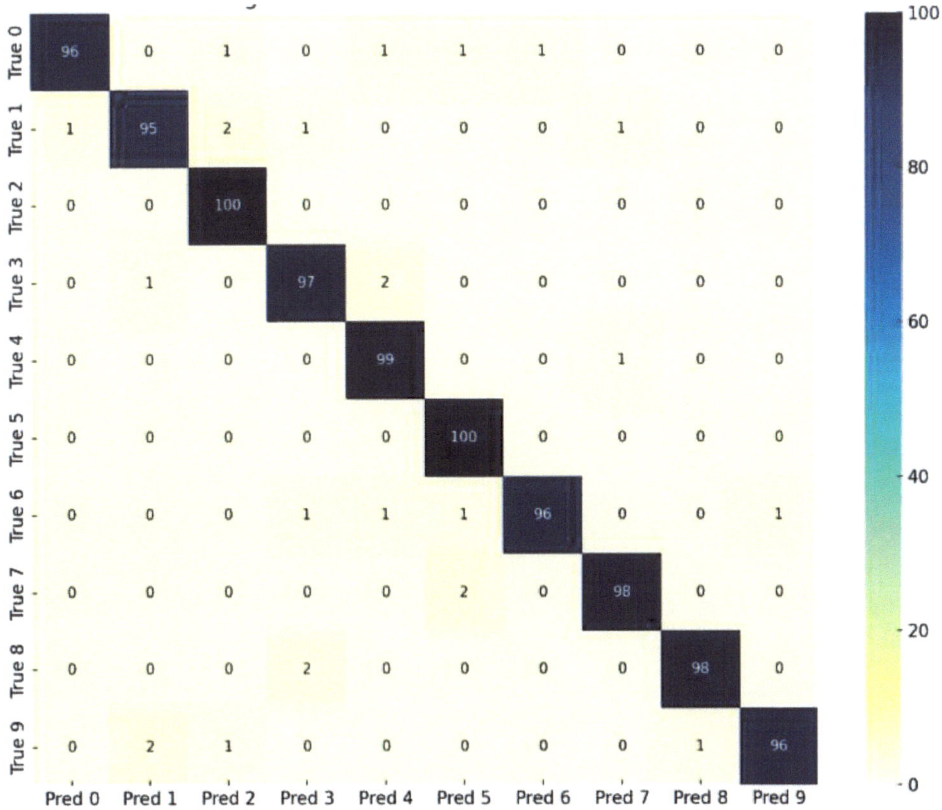

Fig. (6). Confusion matrix for CNN predictions over digits 0–9.

Confusion Matrix (Fig. 6)

Confusion matrices were generated for all models to analyze class-wise errors. CNN achieved near-perfect classification across all digits, with minimal confusion between similar digits (*e.g.*, 3 and 8). KNN and XGBoost showed more class overlap.

PCA Visualization (Fig. 7)

A 2D PCA projection of the feature space revealed clear digit separability, particularly in CNN-extracted features, confirming high-dimensional discrimination power.

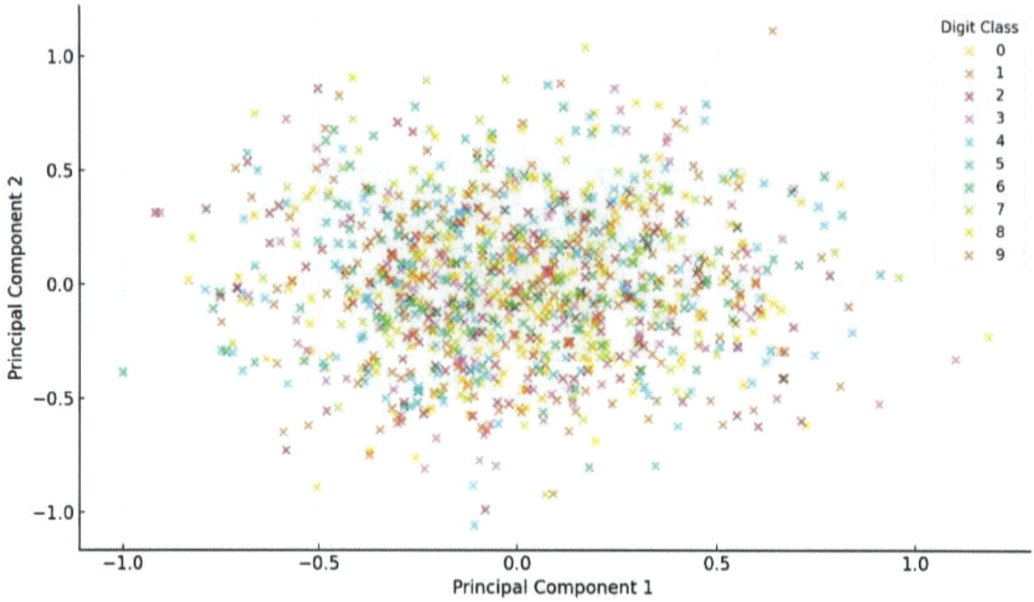

Fig. (7). 2D PCA visualization of CNN-extracted features showing class separability.

These illustrations provide strong evidence of CNN's superiority in handling image classification tasks and highlight the value of deeper architectures over traditional models.

CONCLUSION

To improve automatic grading systems, the effectiveness of various machine learning techniques was examined for handwritten digit recognition in this study. Four different models were assessed using the MNIST dataset: k-Nearest Neighbors (KNN), XGBoost (Gradient Boosting), Convolutional Neural Network

(CNN), and Multi-Layer Perceptron (MLP). Convolutional Neural Networks (CNNs) outperform all other algorithms studied, as evidenced by their highest F1 score (0.9950) and accuracy (99.60%). Due to its ability to preserve spatial relationships and extract features in a hierarchical manner, the CNN is particularly well-suited for image recognition tasks, such as handwritten digit detection. Furthermore, CNN and MLP demonstrated the efficacy of deep learning in classification tasks by outperforming conventional algorithms, such as XGBoost and KNN. The comprehensive evaluation of these algorithms provides valuable insights into their strengths and limitations, guiding the development of efficient and accurate systems for handwritten digit recognition. By streamlining the grading process and ensuring timely result declaration, these advancements contribute to improved efficiency and reliability in educational and assessment domains.

The integrated data science approach used in this study offers several advantages over traditional standalone machine learning techniques. Unlike individual models, integrated approaches enable comprehensive preprocessing, iterative feature engineering, and the use of multiple evaluation metrics, which contribute to a more holistic understanding of model performance. By combining deep learning methods (CNN, MLP) with ensemble and traditional models (XGBoost, KNN), the system leverages the strengths of each algorithm, thereby improving generalization and robustness. This integration is particularly crucial in real-world applications, such as automated grading systems, where accuracy and reliability are paramount. Compared to methods in the literature that focus solely on single-model architectures or isolated metrics, the integrated pipeline enhances adaptability, reduces error, and enables scalable deployment in diverse grading environments.

REFERENCES

[1] O.I. Berngardt, "Improving classification neural networks by using absolute activation function (MNIST/LeNET-5 example)", arXiv preprint arXiv:2304.11758, Apr. 2023. [Online]. Available from: [http://dx.doi.org/10.48550/arXiv.2304.11758]

[2] S. Kumar Dasari, and S. Mehta, "Text detection and recognition through deep learning-based fusion neural network", *IAES International Journal of Artificial Intelligence (IJ-AI),* vol. 12, no. 3, pp. 1396-1406, 2023.
[http://dx.doi.org/10.11591/ijai.v12.i3.pp1396-1406]

[3] M. A, K. D, T. G, V. Kumar, U. Kumar, and V. A, "Handwritten digit recognition using machine learning with python", *International Research Journal of Computer Science,* vol. 10, no. 5, pp. 168-171, 2023.
[http://dx.doi.org/10.26562/irjcs.2023.v1005.11]

[4] M.K. Lee, and M. Mochizuki, "Handwritten digit recognition by spin waves in a Skyrmion reservoir", *Sci. Rep.,* vol. 13, no. 1, p. 19423, 2023.
[http://dx.doi.org/10.1038/s41598-023-46677-w] [PMID: 37940652]

[5] M. Gunler Pirim, H. Tora, K. Oztoprak, and İ. Butun, "Two-stage feature generator for handwritten

digit classification", *Sensors (Basel),* vol. 23, no. 20, pp. 8477-8477, 2023. [http://dx.doi.org/10.3390/s23208477] [PMID: 37896570]

[6] G. Castellano, and M.B. Sandler, "Handwritten digits recognition using Hough transform and neural networks", 1996 IEEE International Symposium on Circuits and Systems. Circuits and Systems Connecting the World. ISCAS 96, vol. 3, pp. 313–316, 2025. [http://dx.doi.org/10.1109/ISCAS.1996.541596]

[7] B-J. van der Zwaag, "Handwritten digit recognition: A neural network demo", *Lect. Notes Comput. Sci.,* vol. 2206, no. Oct, pp. 762-771, 2001. [http://dx.doi.org/10.1007/3-540-45493-4_75]

[8] V. Mane, and L. Ragha, "Handwritten digit recognition using elastic matching", Proceedings of the International Conference & Workshop on Emerging Trends in Technology - ICWET '11, 2011. [http://dx.doi.org/10.1145/1980022.1980354]

[9] S.S. Ali, and M.U. Ghani, *Handwritten digit recognition using DCT and HMMs,* no. Dec, pp. 303-306, 2014. [http://dx.doi.org/10.1109/FIT.2014.63]

[10] A. Dubey, A. Lazarus, and D. Mangal, "Handwritten digit recognition using image preprocessing and CNN", *International Journal of Scientific Research in Computer Science, Engineering and Information Technology,* no. May, pp. 896-902, 2020. [http://dx.doi.org/10.32628/CSEIT206396]

[11] P. Patil, and B. Kaur, "Handwritten digit recognition using various machine learning algorithms and models", *International Journal of Innovative Research in Computer Science & Technology,* vol. 8, no. 4, 2020. [http://dx.doi.org/10.21276/ijircst.2020.8.4.16]

[12] X. Gao, B. Guan, and L. Yu, *Handwritten Digit Recognition Based on Support Vector Machine,* 2015. [http://dx.doi.org/10.2991/icismme-15.2015.198]

[13] S.M. Shamim, M.B.A. Miah, A. Sarker, M. Rana, and A.A. Jobair, "Handwritten digit recognition using machine learning algorithms", *Indonesian Journal of Science and Technology,* vol. 3, no. 1, p. 29, 2018. [http://dx.doi.org/10.17509/ijost.v3i1.10795]

[14] P. Singh, P. Pawar, and N. Raj, "Handwritten digit recognition", *Int. J. Res. Appl. Sci. Eng. Technol.,* vol. 10, no. 5, pp. 75-82, 2022. [http://dx.doi.org/10.22214/ijraset.2022.42062]

[15] A. Chatterjee, and R. Samir Malakar, R. Sarkar, and Mita Nasipuri, "Handwritten digit recognition using daisy descriptor: A study," Jan. 2018. [http://dx.doi.org/10.1109/EAIT.2018.8470426]

[16] R. Karakaya, and S. Kazan, "Handwritten digit recognition using machine learning", *Sakarya University Journal of Science,* vol. 25, no. 1, pp. 65-71, 2021. [http://dx.doi.org/10.16984/saufenbilder.801684]

[17] T. Sasao, Y. Horikawa, and Y. Iguchi, "Handwritten digit recognition based on classification functions", *Proc. IEEE International Symposium on Multiple-Valued Logic (ISMVL),* pp. 124-129, 2020. [http://dx.doi.org/10.1109/ISMVL49045.2020.00-18]

[18] P. Mhasakar, P. Trivedi, S. Mandal, and S.K. Mitra, "Handwritten digit recognition using bayesian resnet", *SN Comput. Sci.,* vol. 2, no. 5, p. 399, 2021. [http://dx.doi.org/10.1007/s42979-021-00791-6]

[19] Z. Li, L. Ma, X. Ke, and Y. Wang, "Handwritten digit recognition *via* active belief decision trees", *Proc. Chinese Control and Decision Conference (CCDC),* pp. 7021-7025, 2016. [http://dx.doi.org/10.1109/ChiCC.2016.7554464]

[20] Z. Sakhawat, S. Ali, and H. Liu, "Handwritten digits recognition based on deep learning4j", *Proc. ACM Symposium on Computer Science Education (SIGCSE),* pp. 21-25, 2018. [http://dx.doi.org/10.1145/3268866.3268888]

[21] S.D. Pande, S.B. Rathod, M.S.R. Chetty, S. Pathak, P.P. Jadhav, and S.P. Godse, "Shape and textural based image retrieval using K-NN classifier", *J. Intell. Fuzzy Syst.,* vol. 43, no. 4, pp. 4757-4768, 2022. [http://dx.doi.org/10.3233/JIFS-213355]

CHAPTER 11

Implementation of Cloud-Based Healthcare System

Arsh Swami[1,*] and **Himanshu Gupta**[1]

[1] *Department of Information Technology, Amity Institute of Information Technology, Noida, Uttar Pradesh, India*

Abstract: The incorporation of cloud-based systems is a novel use of Information Technology (IT) in the modern healthcare environment. To understand the far-reaching consequences of cloud computing adoption on data management, collaboration, and ultimately, patient care, this paper examines the profound implications of this practice. Cloud-based systems emerge as a promising way to overcome traditional limitations as the demand for effective and accessible healthcare solutions grows. They offer scalable, affordable, and interoperable solutions that have the potential to completely change the way healthcare information is stored, accessed, and used. In light of this, the article aims to provide a comprehensive analysis of the existing research, examine real-world case studies, and incorporate insights from medical experts to present a complete picture of the benefits and challenges of cloud-based healthcare systems. Through an exploration of specific use cases, including Electronic Health Records (EHR), telemedicine, and data analytics, the study aims to clarify how cloud computing might revolutionise healthcare delivery and influence the industry in the future.

Keywords: AI, Cloud-based, Machine learning, Object detection, Visually impaired.

INTRODUCTION

The healthcare sector, which is a dynamic ecosystem, has reached a new phase in which the integration of IT applications has come to represent efficiency and advancement. One prominent example of this paradigm shift is the growing adoption of cloud-based healthcare systems. Healthcare organisations are facing significant issues related to data management, accessibility, and stakeholder cooperation. One emerging trend that might revolutionise healthcare delivery is the incorporation of cloud computing. This integration is significant because it can alleviate long-standing problems that the healthcare industry has been facing. Healthcare institutions have always struggled with data silos, poor communication, and restricted access to vital patient data. Cloud-based solutions

* **Corresponding author Arsh Swami:** Department of Information Technology, Amity Institute of Information Technology, Noida, Uttar Pradesh, India; E-mail: arsh.swami1111@gmail.com

Manoj Kumar, Sachin Kumar Gupta, Navnath Kale, Pramod Ganjewar & Sandeep Pande (Eds.)

offer an affordable, scalable, and interoperable platform for managing healthcare data, addressing these challenges effectively. To shed light on the cloud's multifaceted uses in healthcare and their implications for patient care, data security, and overall operational effectiveness, this study aims to explore these applications.

The digitization of health records is the essential component of this change. Cloud-based technologies allow Electronic Health Records (EHR), which were previously restricted by physical boundaries, to be easily managed, accessed, and updated. This move enables healthcare providers in various locations to collaborate securely, while also ensuring real-time access to patient data. The advent of telemedicine highlights the significance of cloud-based solutions by enabling remote monitoring, diagnosis, and consultations, thereby improving the accessibility and inclusiveness of healthcare services. Cloud-based solutions allow advanced data analytics and machine learning applications, which are becoming increasingly necessary as the healthcare industry demands insights derived from data. With the use of large datasets, healthcare organisations can now extract valuable insights that can be used to develop personalised treatment regimens, predictive models, and improve population health management. Cloud computing integration in healthcare is not without its difficulties, though.

To properly utilise cloud-based healthcare systems, concerns about data security, interoperability, and opposition to change must be carefully managed. This research undertakes a thorough investigation of the advantages and challenges associated with the deployment of cloud-based healthcare systems, considering these factors. Our goal is to present a comprehensive picture of how cloud computing is changing the healthcare sector by combining case studies, current literature, and expert views. The following sections examine specific applications, discuss their impact on patient care, and provide guidance for a successful rollout. This will lead the healthcare sector towards a future in which cloud-based solutions and IT applications come together to improve the quality of care that people receive worldwide.

This paper presents a comprehensive examination of the implementation of cloud-based healthcare systems, drawing on insights from the literature, real-world case studies, expert interviews, and system comparisons. Its primary contribution lies in identifying and analysing the transformative potential of cloud technologies in enhancing healthcare data accessibility, operational scalability, and patient care delivery. The study highlights how cloud-based platforms facilitate key applications, including Electronic Health Records (EHR), telemedicine, and advanced data analytics. It also uncovers the critical challenges facing healthcare institutions—particularly data security, interoperability with existing systems, and organizational resistance to change. The research presents a multidimensional framework for evaluating the deployment of cloud-based systems, offering actionable insights into key success factors such as strategic planning, stakeholder engagement, and customized solution design. Furthermore, it lays the foundation for future integration of cloud computing with AI and IoT technologies, paving the way for a more proactive, connected, and efficient healthcare ecosystem.

Case Study: Cloud-Based EHR and Telemedicine Integration in a Multispecialty Hospital

A multispecialty hospital in Bengaluru adopted a cloud-based healthcare infrastructure using Amazon Web Services (AWS) to enhance its Electronic Health Records (EHR) and telemedicine capabilities. Before implementation, patient data was fragmented across various departments, resulting in delays in diagnosis and treatment coordination.

By migrating to AWS, the hospital centralized patient records, enabling secure, real-time access for doctors, nurses, and administrative staff. A telemedicine platform was integrated into the system, enabling remote consultations, appointment scheduling, and digital prescription management. Multi-factor authentication and data cryptography ensured HIPAA-compliant security.

Post-deployment analytics revealed a 30% reduction in patient waiting time, a 25% increase in outpatient throughput, and a significant improvement in cross-departmental communication. Patient satisfaction scores rose due to quicker service and remote access to care.

This case demonstrates how cloud platforms, such as AWS, can transform hospital operations, enhance healthcare delivery, and support scalability while maintaining data security and compliance.

Background

The healthcare sector, which has historically been characterised by localised data storage and paper-based systems, has always faced difficulties in adapting to the changing demands of patient care and information management. The advent of Information Technology (IT) has brought about a new age, forcing healthcare organisations to explore creative ways to improve their operations and make them more accessible, efficient, and collaborative. In light of these factors, the integration of cloud-based technologies has become a ground-breaking strategy that holds the potential to completely transform the handling, access, and storage of healthcare data. This background lays the groundwork for a thorough analysis of the uses and consequences of cloud computing in the healthcare industry. Fig. (**1**) illustrates the experimental environment.

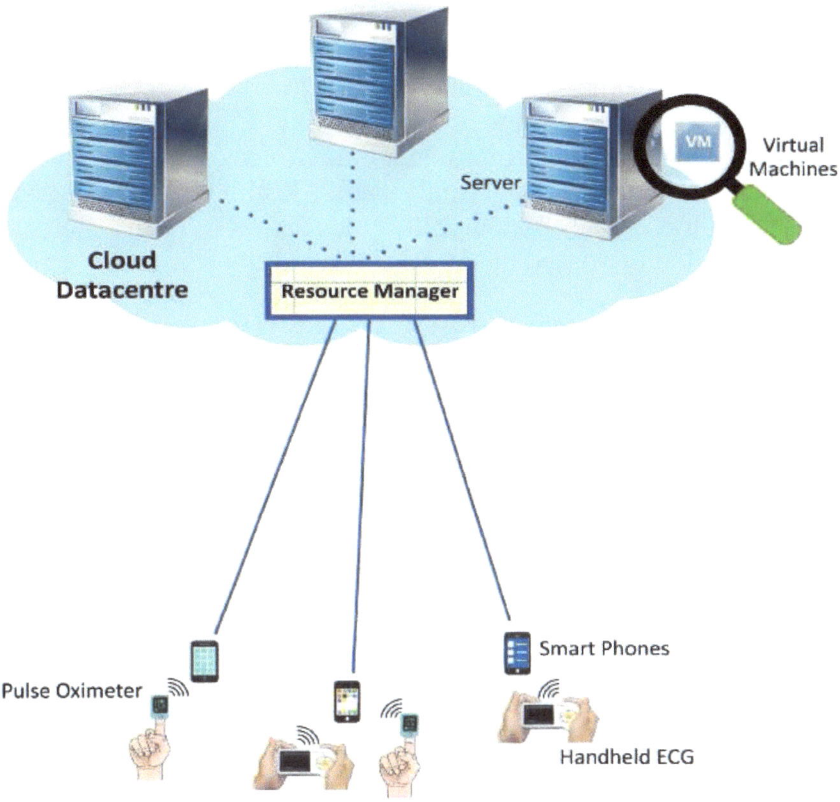

Fig. (1). Representation of experimental setting.

Objectives

- To comprehend the role that cloud-based healthcare solutions play in the current medical landscape.
- To investigate the primary uses of cloud computing in the medical field.
- To evaluate the advantages and difficulties of putting cloud-based healthcare systems into place.
- To talk about how patient care, data security, and healthcare administration are affected by cloud-based healthcare technologies.
- To make suggestions for future paths and effective implementation.

LITERATURE REVIEW

The authors of a study [1] conducted a research-based survey on an integrated cloud-based healthcare system. Advances in Information and Communication Technology (ICT) have spurred the healthcare industry's tremendous expansion in recent years. ICT integration has enabled healthcare systems to come together, improving operational efficiency, organisation, and personalised treatment. The development of smart cities is consistent with a national, international, or local comprehensive healthcare strategy. However, trustworthy communication will be necessary in future healthcare systems due to their increasing computational demands. By utilizing cloud resources, Mobile Cloud Computing (MCC) emerges as a key technology that overcomes the limitations of mobile devices. This proposal examines the evolution of Saudi Arabia's healthcare system, highlighting the reasons for adopting unified mobile cloud-based systems and offering a productive hybrid cloudlet-based model that successfully addresses current issues.

The authors of [2] conducted a research-based survey on the Design and Implementation of cloud-based patient healthcare monitoring systems using IoT. This study presents a mobile data acquisition (DAQ) method for collecting personalized health information based on Android. Data on smart devices is analyzed, visualized, and stored by the system; optional transfer to a data center for additional processing is also available. The mobile device utilizes a range of wired (USB) and wireless (Bluetooth, Wi-Fi, cloud, GPRS) sensors to gather supplementary data from embedded sensors (*e.g.*, position, magnetic level, acceleration). The user-friendly interface accommodates different skill levels, offering diary functionality and configurability. It is possible to do a correlation analysis between sensor datasets. The technology, which has been successfully tested in a Living Lab setting, enhances health monitoring for both carers and end users, promoting preventive and efficient care.

The authors of [3] conducted a research-based survey on Factors affecting the successful adoption of e-health cloud-based health systems from the healthcare consumers' perspective. The use of cloud computing for remote access in healthcare has grown significantly in recent years. Despite its widespread appeal, research reveals that acceptability levels vary, especially in developing nations like Nigeria, where data security concerns and inefficient use of Information and Communication Technologies (ICTs) are significant issues. This study investigates the variables that impact the views of healthcare customers towards the adoption of cloud-based healthcare centers. The results highlight the critical role of social influence, enabling conditions, data security, information sharing, performance expectation, and effort expectancy on customers' behavioural intentions. The analysis involved 465 participants in Benue, Nigeria. On the other hand, cloud-based health knowledge was deemed statistically inconsequential. Policymakers need to take implementation difficulties very seriously.

The authors of another study [4] conducted a research-based survey on cloud-based healthcare application architecture and electronic medical record mining: an integrated approach to improve the healthcare system. Healthcare systems must be modernised, particularly in developing nations where paper-based procedures are still used. It remains challenging to establish a comprehensive network that connects patients, doctors, and the government, despite the availability of specific computer-based solutions. This article presents "eHealth Cloud," a three-tier cloud application that uses a logic layer to improve accessibility, RIA for clients, and SimpleDB for servers. This method enables the storage of enormous amounts of Electronic Medical Records (EMRs) regularly, thereby opening up possibilities for data mining research. This article provides a detailed description of the process of utilizing cloud computing to transform healthcare, along with potential obstacles and directions for future research. It also suggests a standard for data transmission.

The authors of a study [5] conducted a research-based survey on cloud-based intelligent healthcare monitoring systems. The goal of this project is to enhance healthcare delivery through the use of cloud computing. It aims to deliver cutting-edge, superior, portable, and non-invasive healthcare technologies to the medical community, facilitating the early diagnosis of critical organ health disorders. Cloud-based healthcare enables the transmission of precise medical information over the internet by integrating cloud computing and health monitoring. The system consists of sensors on the patient's body and a computer device. By utilizing appropriate sensors to collect relevant data on the patient's health status, the proposed Cloud-based Intelligent Healthcare Monitoring System (CIHMS) provides medical feedback *via* the cloud or the hospital, enabling prompt and efficient treatment.

The authors of a study [6] conducted a research-based survey on designing a cloud-based framework for healthcare systems and applying clustering techniques for region-wise diagnosis. An ad hoc framework is required for the healthcare system due to the constraints of the traditional system and the advancements in technology. The patient, doctor, symptom, and illness are the four primary components of any healthcare system, and this study proposes an additional cloud-based framework that connects them. The primary focus of the study is on the relationships between these components and how to use them to derive relevant information. It illustrates the fundamental healthcare analyzer interface in practice, which utilizes data mining techniques, such as clustering, to ingest and process data. For government organisations that want to improve India's health circumstances and address restorative concerns, it is beneficial.

The authors of another [7] conducted a research-based survey on the implementation of a 4-tier cloud-based architecture for collaborative healthcare delivery. Through Software as a Service (SaaS), Platform as a Service (PaaS), and Infrastructure as a Service (IaaS), cloud services enable Nigerian healthcare providers to manage information effectively. The nation's Healthcare Providers

(HCPs) struggle to provide patients with high-quality care at affordable prices, often making incorrect diagnoses despite operational issues such as mishandled data storage and untrustworthy patient records. The goal of this study is to implement a four-tiered cloud-based architecture that utilizes the Data Analysis and Pattern Prediction Unit (DAPPU) to inform decisions and the User Authentication and Access Control Engine (UAACE) to prevent unauthorized access. The design, when implemented in CloudSim, proves to be dependable and effective, enhancing the provision of healthcare.

A research-based survey on Improving the Healthcare Quality of Emergency Departments after the Implementation of a Cloud-Based System for Medical Information Exchange was conducted [8]. A medical information-exchange system has been a part of Taiwan's National Health Insurance programme since 1995. Its goal is to save healthcare costs by preventing unnecessary tests and prescriptions. This study evaluates the influence of medical information sharing on the quality of treatment provided in Emergency Departments (EDs). The study examines the relationship between ED outcomes and inquiry rates in the MediCloud system, analysing data from 2013 to 2019. The findings show that early hospitalisation for urgent cases in regional hospitals has improved, and ED stays longer than 48 hours have reduced in medical centres. The results highlight how the sharing of medical information can alleviate overcrowding in emergency departments of large hospitals and expedite vital patient admissions in smaller institutions. They call for government support for these efforts.

The authors of a study [9] conducted a research-based survey on implementing cloud-based medical systems in hospitals and their strategic implications. Error rates are decreased, and hospital-related procedures are accelerated *via* hospital information systems, or HISs. Unfortunately, the lack of scalability and flexibility in earlier HISs has limited the growth of medical institutions. Hospitals are facing an increasingly challenging situation, and the features of cloud computing services are essential to helping them overcome it. However, only a small number of healthcare facilities have started using cloud computing services in part. Thus, this study applies the innovation resistance theory to investigate the resistance elements that arise throughout the organisational innovation process. Additionally, the seven areas that comprise an organization's developmental hurdles are as follows: market access barriers, data security barriers, operational barriers, knowledge barriers, resource barriers, regulations barriers, and barriers of cloud service quality. The application of interpretive structural modelling also facilitates a more detailed investigation of the relationships between the barriers to organisational innovation.

The authors of another [10] conducted a research-based survey on the implementation of cloud-based Electronic Health Records (EHRs) for Indian healthcare needs. Real-time patient data, including medical history, current medical conditions, prescribed drugs, vaccine history, and test results, is digitally stored in Electronic Health Records (EHRs). Given the size of India's population, our proposed effort aims to employ cloud infrastructure to integrate EHR among healthcare providers throughout the nation. This system aims to simplify healthcare administration by addressing key issues, including the management of heterogeneous data, storage, data analytics for informed decision-making, and ensuring privacy and security. Benefits from implementation include real-time monitoring, remote drug administration, immunisation administration, and illness diagnosis. It also fosters an integrated healthcare network and individualised health records for better patient care.

METHODOLOGY

The research technique employed in this study aims to provide a comprehensive understanding of the deployment and implications of cloud-based healthcare systems. To triangulate ideas and viewpoints, the study design employs a multimodal approach that incorporates case studies, literature reviews, and interviews with healthcare experts. The methodical approach is delineated in the following manner:

a. Review of Literature:
   i. Examine the body of research on cloud-based healthcare systems by consulting academic journals, publications, and other relevant sources.
   ii. Synthesize knowledge on the historical background, benefits, limitations, and essential applications of cloud computing in healthcare.
b. Case Studies:
   i. Identify and examine real-world case studies of healthcare institutions that have successfully implemented cloud-based technologies.
   ii. Examine the particular difficulties encountered, how they were resolved, and the results attained to gain an essential understanding of the real-world applications of cloud integration.
c. Interviews with Medical Experts:
   i. Conduct methodical interviews with healthcare experts, such as IT specialists, administrators, and physicians, to obtain personal accounts and viewpoints of cloud-based medical systems.
   ii. Pay close attention to the perceived advantages, implementation difficulties, and effects on daily healthcare operations.

d. Comparative Evaluation:
   i. Compare the various cloud-based healthcare systems currently in use.
   ii. Analyse each system's advantages, disadvantages, possibilities, and dangers to provide a detailed picture of the varied array of cloud computing options available in the healthcare industry.
e. Evaluation of Data:
   i. Sort and analyse material from case studies, interviews, and literature using qualitative data analysis approaches.
   ii. Discover recurring themes, obstacles, and success factors to get a valuable understanding of the consequences of cloud-based healthcare systems.
f. Moral Aspects to Take into Account:
   i. Respect ethical standards at all times when conducting research, ensuring that interview subjects remain anonymous and confidential.
   ii. To achieve honesty and integrity in reporting, acknowledge any potential biases and limitations in the data-gathering process.
g. Validity and Trustworthiness:
   i. Verify the accuracy of the results by cross-referencing data from multiple sources, including case studies, literature, and interviews.
   ii. Ensure dependability by using standardized techniques for gathering data and maintaining a methodical approach throughout the study.
h. Data triangulation:
   i. Combine information from several sources to increase the validity of the conclusions.
   ii. Provide a comprehensive understanding of the study issue by integrating insights from case studies and interviews with information gleaned from the literature.

The flow of the methodology is presented in Fig. (**2**). Through the use of this comprehensive approach, the study aims to provide a thorough and nuanced examination of the deployment of cloud-based healthcare systems, connecting theoretical concepts with real-world experiences and insights from medical experts.

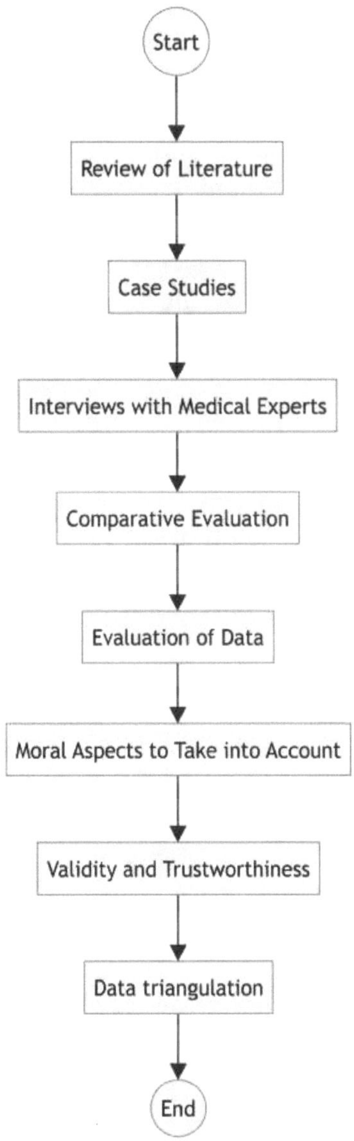

Fig. (2). Flow of the methodology.

ANALYSIS

The paper titled "Implementation of Cloud-Based Healthcare Systems" offers a thorough examination of how Information Technology (IT) applications have revolutionised the healthcare industry. The review of the literature delves into the background, advantages, challenges, and primary applications of cloud computing in the medical field. It demonstrates a significant change in the way healthcare is delivered, from scalable and interoperable cloud alternatives to traditional data management systems.

The paper's case studies offer insightful real-world examples of effective implementations, underscoring the importance of stakeholder participation and strategic planning. The stated difficulties—such as staff opposition and complex data migration—offer valuable insights to healthcare institutions considering cloud-based system adoption. The success criteria that have been identified, including solutions customised to meet the organisation's demands, help provide a more nuanced view of best practices in implementation.

Fig. (3) illustrates the diverse ways cloud computing is being utilized within the healthcare sector. The paper's observations are enhanced by interviews with healthcare practitioners, who offer a human perspective on the adoption of cloud-based systems. The significance of considering the human element in technology integration is shown by the focus on thorough training and change management. Professionals' positive comments about more efficient processes and better patient care provide strong proof of the observable advantages encountered in actual healthcare environments.

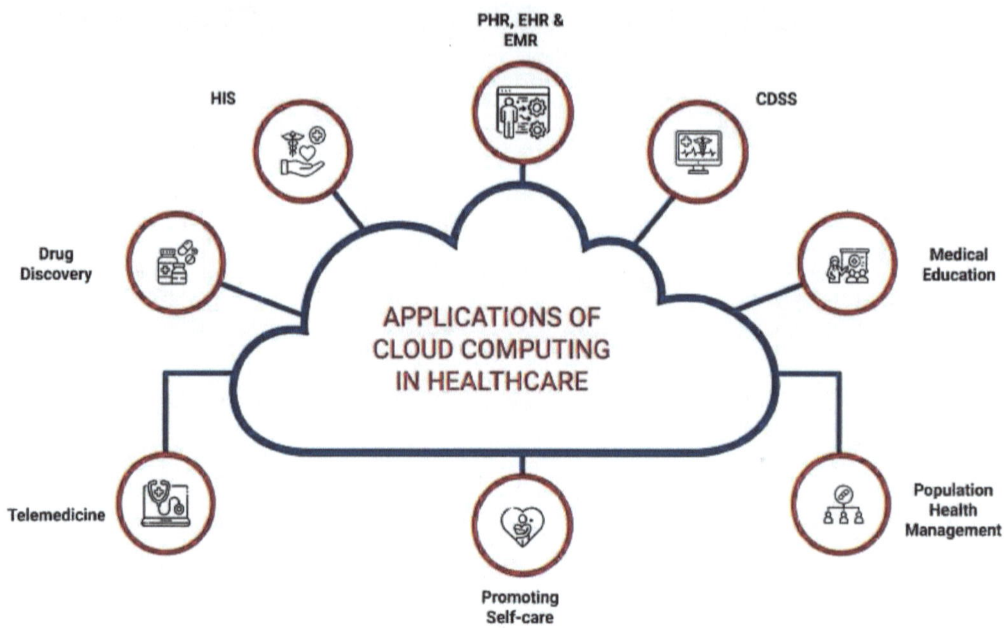

Fig. (3). Applications of cloud computing in healthcare.

The paper's comparative examination of several cloud-based healthcare systems makes a significant contribution by illuminating a varied environment with a range of advantages and disadvantages. To help healthcare organisations select solutions that align with their specific needs and goals, this section recognises the importance of understanding the unique characteristics of each system. Acknowledging the multiplicity of cloud solutions highlights the importance of customized deployment strategies, as opposed to a one-size-fits-all approach.

The report provides a comprehensive overview of the present state of cloud-based healthcare systems by synthesising data from various sources. Benefits, obstacles, and success factors identified provide insightful information for upcoming deployments, guiding healthcare organisations toward an IT-enabled, more patient-centered, and efficient model. The study opens the door for more developments in the field and makes a substantial contribution to the current conversation on the nexus between technology and healthcare.

Furthermore, the use of integrated data science approaches in cloud-based healthcare systems offers a distinct advantage over traditional, isolated methods. In comparison, earlier techniques primarily focused on solving individual issues, such as storage limitations, fragmented records, or remote access. Integrated data science, on the other hand, provides a holistic framework for real-time data processing, predictive analytics, and personalized care. This integration enables healthcare providers to extract actionable insights from diverse datasets, leading to faster diagnoses, optimized treatment strategies, and more effective resource allocation. Compared to siloed techniques reviewed in the literature, the integrated model significantly enhances clinical outcomes and decision-making efficiency.

FINDINGS

The results of the "Implementation of Cloud-Based Healthcare Systems" study demonstrate how the healthcare industry is undergoing a radical transformation as dynamic cloud solutions replace traditional data management methods. These discoveries include advantages such as enhanced data scalability and accessibility, balanced against drawbacks like reluctance to change and concerns about data security. It becomes clear that the influence on patient care is crucial, with improved communication and optimised operations. Interviews highlight the human element and the necessity of thorough training. The case studies emphasize the importance of strategic planning and stakeholder engagement as key success factors. The comparative study demonstrates how cloud options have a variety of strengths. Taken as a whole, these results traverse a challenging terrain, providing insights into a healthcare model transformed by technological advancements. Table **1** presents the Process Analysis in a cloud-based healthcare system.

Table 1. Process analysis in cloud-based healthcare system.

Aspect	Findings/Insights
Literature Review	• Evolution of cloud-based healthcare systems. • Benefits and challenges associated with implementation. • Key applications in healthcare.
Case Studies	• Successful implementations and outcomes. • Challenges faced and solutions adopted.
Interviews with Professionals	• Perspectives on challenges during implementation. • Perceived benefits and impact on healthcare operations.
Comparative Analysis	• Strengths, weaknesses, opportunities, and threats. • Diversity in cloud solutions in healthcare.
Data Analysis	• Identification of recurring themes and patterns. • Insights into implications of cloud-based systems.
Ethical Considerations	• Adherence to confidentiality and anonymity. • Acknowledgment of potential biases and limitations.
Validity and Reliability	• Cross-referencing information for validity. • Consistent data collection methods for reliability.
Triangulation of Data	• Corroboration of insights from multiple sources. • Well-rounded perspective on the research topic.

Development of Healthcare Systems: The study reveals a clear development in healthcare systems, characterised by a shift from traditional, regional data administration to the use of cloud-based solutions. This development underscores the industry's increasing awareness of the need for scalable, technologically advanced, and interoperable methods in healthcare delivery.

Cloud-Based System Advantages: The study identifies several significant advantages associated with the use of cloud-based healthcare systems. One key benefit that ensures real-time access to patient information is improved data accessibility. Furthermore, scalability and cost-effectiveness are emphasized, highlighting the potential of cloud solutions to alleviate conventional resource constraints in healthcare organizations.

Implementation Difficulties: The results highlight the challenges associated with implementing cloud-based healthcare solutions. Concerns about data security have surfaced as a major problem that must be carefully considered to satisfy privacy and compliance standards. Obstacles stemming from interoperability issues with current healthcare systems underscore the need for seamless integration strategies. The report also mentions a possible barrier to broad adoption: healthcare professionals' reluctance to adapt.

Applications of Cloud Computing: This study outlines the various ways cloud computing is being utilized in the medical field. Among the most important domains are Electronic Health Records (EHR), which provide secure, instantaneous access to patient data. One further important use that is becoming recognised is the integration of telemedicine services, which increases accessibility to healthcare and allows for remote consultations.

Effect on Patient Care: Research indicates that cloud-based healthcare systems have a significant impact on patient care. The study highlights the enhancement of individualized treatment plans, efficient processes, and improved professional communication. The results suggest that these systems support a patient-centric approach, which enhances health outcomes.

Human Variables in Implementation: Key human variables impacting the adoption of cloud-based technologies are revealed through interviews with healthcare professionals. The article acknowledges the value of thorough training and change management techniques in overcoming opposition and promoting an adaptive culture among medical personnel.

Success aspects in deployment: The case studies provided shed light on the essential success aspects for deploying a cloud-based healthcare system successfully. These consist of stakeholder interaction, strategy planning, and solution customization to match specific organizational requirements. These success characteristics offer important direction to other healthcare organisations considering the use of comparable technology.

Variability in Cloud Solutions: The comparative study highlights the variation in cloud-based medical systems. Every system has different strengths and limitations, which highlights the importance of customised implementation strategies. This research recognises that diverse healthcare organisations have distinct requirements and goals, and that a one-size-fits-all approach is not appropriate for them.

Data Security and Compliance: The study emphasizes the importance of addressing data security issues when implementing cloud-based healthcare solutions. It becomes clear that adhering to strict healthcare standards is essential, since strong security measures are required to protect patient data and preserve the accuracy of medical records.

Interoperability Difficulties: A common observation concerns the interoperability difficulties that arise when integrating cloud-based applications with the current healthcare infrastructure. This finding emphasizes how crucial it is for various healthcare platforms to collaborate and exchange data in a seamless manner to maximize the effectiveness of cloud solutions.

Technological Resistance: The study demonstrates that healthcare workers are not always open to adopting new technology. The discovery mentioned above highlights the need for focused approaches to address technological barriers, such as comprehensive training initiatives, to enable a more seamless shift to cloud-based services.

Impact on Administrative Efficiency: The use of cloud-based technologies is seen as a driver for improving administrative efficiency in healthcare organisations, independent of patient care. Healthcare workers can devote more time to patient-focused activities as a result of enhanced operational efficiency brought about by streamlined workflows, automated procedures, and better data management.

The adoption of cloud-based healthcare systems carries several significant managerial implications that extend beyond technical implementation. From an administrative standpoint, cloud computing offers healthcare managers enhanced visibility into system-wide operations, enabling real-time decision-making, improved coordination across departments, and optimized resource allocation. Cloud platforms facilitate scalable infrastructure planning, allowing the managers to adjust IT capacity as patient data volumes and service demands grow—without the need for significant capital expenditures.

In terms of policy and compliance, cloud integration facilitates maintaining regulatory alignment with frameworks such as HIPAA, GDPR, or national health data guidelines by providing secure and traceable data storage and access mechanisms. Managers can also utilize predictive analytics, supported by cloud-based data, to design targeted public health interventions or preventive care strategies based on regional or demographic trends.

Moreover, cloud systems promote interdepartmental collaboration and transparency by centralizing patient records and operational data. This empowers managers to monitor performance metrics, streamline reporting workflows, and facilitate quality assurance audits more effectively. As highlighted in the study's interviews and case studies, stakeholder engagement and training programs are crucial for smooth adoption, necessitating managerial foresight and leadership to foster organizational readiness and effective change management.

Ultimately, the strategic implementation of cloud-based solutions enables a shift from reactive to proactive healthcare management, aligning IT infrastructure with patient-centric service delivery, fiscal responsibility, and long-term sustainability in healthcare organizations.

CONCLUSION

The study on the "Implementation of Cloud-Based Healthcare Systems" leads the way towards a paradigm-shifting period in healthcare management. The combined results highlight a dramatic shift away from traditional data management paradigms and towards the adoption of cloud technologies, signifying a turning point in the development of healthcare informatics. The numerous benefits that have been demonstrated, including increased data accessibility, scalability, and global reach, underscore the critical role that cloud-based solutions play in advancing a more comprehensive, efficient, and patient-centered healthcare environment.

In the complex fabric of implementation, the study argues that it is crucial to address obstacles directly. Addressing concerns about data security, overcoming opposition from healthcare providers, and fostering interoperability with current systems have become priorities that require strategic focus. Despite their challenging nature, these issues are not insurmountable barriers, as the article provides insightful guidance on how to navigate these complexities skillfully.

Furthermore, the study emphasizes the importance of developing a robust cybersecurity framework as a prerequisite for implementing cloud-based healthcare systems. The dynamic and ever-evolving threat landscape demands constant attention to detail and flexible approaches to protect private patient data, guaranteeing its confidentiality and integrity. The promise of technological development becomes inextricably linked to the necessity of strengthening cybersecurity safeguards as healthcare organisations use cloud solutions.

In all of our thoughts, the relationship between cloud-based systems and patient care is crucial. These technologies enable more efficient workflows, customised treatment plans, and improved channels of communication between medical professionals. Insightful interviews highlight the human element, emphasizing the need for comprehensive training methods to facilitate the smooth integration of technology and foster cultural flexibility in healthcare organizations.

The case study success factors, such as stakeholder participation and strategic planning, provide helpful guidance to organisations starting similar implementation journeys. The array of cloud solutions, as demonstrated by comparative assessments, highlights the necessity of customised strategies designed to address the unique requirements of various healthcare settings.

In terms of the future, the merging of cloud-based systems with cutting-edge innovations like artificial intelligence and the Internet of Things heralds an exciting time ahead. The continuous digital transformation of healthcare is motivated by the possibility of further advances in data-driven decision-making, personalized medication, and predictive modeling. The results of this study reveal a compass that points the way towards overcoming obstacles and realising the full potential of cloud-based healthcare systems as the industry continues its unstoppable digital ascension. This journey sets the stage for a future in which patient-centered care and innovation will combine in novel and revolutionary ways, ushering in a new era of excellence in healthcare.

REFERENCES

[1] L.A. Tawalbeh, and S. Habeeb, "An integrated cloud-based healthcare system", *Proc. 5th Int. Conf. Internet of Things: Systems, Management Security (IoTSMS),* 2018pp. 268-273 Valencia, Spain. [http://dx.doi.org/10.1109/IoTSMS.2018.8554574.]

[2] S. Lakshmanachari, C. Srihari, A. Sudhakar, and P. Nalajala, "Design and implementation of cloud-based patient healthcare monitoring systems using IoT", *Proc. Int. Conf. Energy, Communications, Data Analytics, Soft Computing (ICECDS),* 2017pp. 3713-3717 Chennai, India. [http://dx.doi.org/10.1109/ICECDS.2017.8390157]

[3] P.E. Idoga, M. Toycan, H. Nadiri, and E. Çelebi, "Factors affecting the successful adoption of e-health cloud-based health system from healthcare consumers' perspective", *IEEE Access,* vol. 6, pp. 71216-71228, 2018. [http://dx.doi.org/10.1109/ACCESS.2018.2881489]

[4] S. Biswas, T. Akhter, M.S. Kaiser, and S.A. Mamun, "Cloud-based healthcare application architecture and electronic medical record mining: An integrated approach to improve healthcare system", *Proc. 17th Int. Conf. Comput. Inf. Technol. (ICCIT),* 2014pp. 286-291 Dhaka, Bangladesh. [http://dx.doi.org/10.1109/ICCITechn.2014.7073139]

[5] K.A. Parane, N.C. Patil, S.R. Poojara, and T.S. Kamble, "Cloud-based intelligent healthcare monitoring system", *Proc. Int. Conf. Issues Challenges Intell. Comput. Techn. (ICICT),* 2014pp. 697-701 Ghaziabad, India. [http://dx.doi.org/10.1109/ICICT.2014.6781324.]

[6] M. Parekh, and B. Saleena, "Designing a cloud-based framework for healthcare system and applying clustering techniques for region-wise diagnosis", *Procedia Comput. Sci.,* vol. 50, pp. 537-542, 2015. [http://dx.doi.org/10.1016/j.procs.2015.04.029]

[7] N.A. Azeez, and H.D. Iliyas, "Implementation of a 4-tier cloud-based architecture for collaborative health care delivery", *Nigerian Journal of Technological Development,* vol. 13, no. 1, pp. 17-25, 2016. [http://dx.doi.org/10.4314/njtd.v13i1.4]

[8] D.C. Wu, H.L. Lin, C.G. Cheng, C.P. Yu, and C.A. Cheng, "Improvement in healthcare quality of emergency department after the cloud-based system of medical information-exchange implementation", *Healthcare (Basel),* vol. 9, no. 8, p. 1032, 2021. [http://dx.doi.org/10.3390/healthcare9081032] [PMID: 34442169]

[9] P.T. Chen, and J.H. Chen, "Implementing cloud-based medical systems in hospitals and strategic implications", *Technol. Anal. Strateg. Manage.,* vol. 27, no. 2, pp. 198-218, 2015. [http://dx.doi.org/10.1080/09537325.2014.959483]

[10] R. Kavitha, E. Kannan, and S. Kotteswaran, "Implementation of cloud-based Electronic Health Record (EHR) for Indian healthcare needs", *Indian J. Sci. Technol.,* vol. 9, no. 3, pp. 1-5, 2016. [http://dx.doi.org/10.17485/ijst/2016/v9i3/86391]

CHAPTER 12

Enhancing Network Security through AI-Powered Anomaly Detection Using Generative Adversarial Networks

C. Satya Kumar[1,*], **Asha Sunki**[1], **Vinith Koppera**[1] and **Manish Hakeem**[1]

[1] *Department of Computer Science and Engineering, Computer Science and Engineering, Vardhaman College of Engineering, Hyderabad, India*

Abstract: Developments in communication technology have facilitated more data sharing in geographically dispersed settings, but they have also enlarged the attack surface, raising questions about network security. Research focuses on AI-based anomaly detection systems to improve Network Intrusion Detection Systems (NIDSs) in order to address this. However, data imbalance makes it more difficult for AI models to learn and effectively identify threats when legitimate traffic outnumbers malicious traffic. To balance data classes and enhance NIDS performance, suggested options include employing Generative Adversarial Networks (GANs) to produce artificial data that mimics small attack traffic. In order to guarantee that AI models acquire enough training data for both legitimate and malicious network traffic, the method includes GANs. Methods such as "voting classifier" (RF+AB+DT) and "stacking classifier" (LightGBM+DT) are used to improve the system's accuracy and resilience in detecting threats.

Keywords: Anomaly detection, Generative Adversarial Network (GAN), Network security, Network Intrusion Detection System (NIDS).

INTRODUCTION

Network topologies have changed drastically as 5G mobile communication technology has proliferated. This makes sending data across many networks easier. Data comes from gadgets, computers, and the IoT. This implies that network systems can handle more of these data types correctly [1]. Having more types of access points has, however, made the attack area bigger, leaving network systems open to possible dangers [2].

Also, the growing complexity and regularity of cyber-attacks make network systems even more vulnerable. As cyber-attack methods get more complicated,

* **Corresponding author C. Satya Kumar:** Department of Computer Science and Engineering, Computer Science and Engineering, Vardhaman College of Engineering, Hyderabad, India; E-mail: csatyakumar@gmail.com

Manoj Kumar, Sachin Kumar Gupta, Navnath Kale, Pramod Ganjewar & Sandeep Pande (Eds.)

it's even more important to have strong security steps [3]. Unfortunately, this has led to a lot of study being done on how to stop possible network threats.

Network threat identification is a major security challenge. This area has advanced with NIDS systems [4]. Recent research has largely focused on using AI to improve NIDS performance, resulting in considerable improvements [5]. The study first focused on improving NIDS utilizing Decision Trees (DTs) and support vector machines (SVMs) [6]. Since then, these attempts have included autoencoders [7], CNNs, and LSTM networks.

It's not easy to use these AI-based intruder detection systems in the real world, even though a lot of progress has been made in finding strange things [8]. A key issue is that network flow data is inherently uneven, with routine traffic being the bulk and malicious acts causing service breakdowns being very infrequent [9]. Furthermore, when it comes to negative conduct, the majority of the data is about well-known assaults, but certain sorts of attacks are still quite rare [10]. As a result, the problem with uneven data makes it harder for AI models to pick out the details of specific network risks. This lowers the accuracy of monitoring and leaves network systems open to attacks [11].

Because of these problems, researchers are still working on coming up with new ways to fix the data imbalance problem and make AI-based NIDS more reliable. These problems can be fixed to make AI-driven attack detection systems work better, which will make networks more resistant to new cyber dangers.

This research presents an innovative intrusion detection system that leverages Generative Adversarial Networks (GANs) to enhance anomaly detection in network traffic by addressing data imbalance—a common issue in real-world cybersecurity datasets. The proposed system integrates deep learning models (CNN, DNN, LSTM) with ensemble learning methods (Voting and Stacking classifiers) to boost detection accuracy and resilience. The model is rigorously evaluated across three prominent benchmark datasets—NSL-KDD, UNSW-NB15, and IoT-23—demonstrating exceptional performance, with ensemble methods achieving up to 99% accuracy. The study also contributes a detailed data preprocessing pipeline, including feature encoding, selection, and normalization, to optimize training and testing. Experimental results reveal that combining synthetic data generation with diverse classifier architectures significantly enhances intrusion detection capability. This approach not only improves model accuracy but also strengthens the generalizability of the detection system, paving the way for more secure and adaptive network environments.

LITERATURE SURVEY

Network intruder monitoring is an important part of protection that looks for illegal access, bad behaviour, and possible threats in network systems. As technology has evolved, especially with the development of 5G mobile communication and scattered networks, it has become more difficult to detect attacks on networks [12]. The complex and varied nature of modern cyber-attacks means that traditional entry detection methods often aren't enough to stop them. Because of this, academics have turned to DL and Artificial Intelligence (AI) to make Intrusion Detection Systems (IDSs) work better [13].

Gao *et al.* [14] suggested a new way to use semi-supervised learning to find network intrusions in computer systems that are based in the cloud. Both named and unmarked data are used in their method to improve the accuracy of recognition. Similarly, Alrawashdeh and Purdy [15] developed a live anomalous breach detection system using DL. This system employs deep learning models to detect anomalies in real-time network data.

Tang *et al.* [16] looked at how DL can be used for attack detection in software-defined networking (SDN) settings. They used a method that shows DL can effectively find network attacks in SDN systems.

Zhong *et al.* [17] looked into how big data-based DL systems could be used for breach detection. This showed how big data analytics could be used to improve detection skills. Haghighat and Li [18] suggested an intruder detection system that uses a voting-based neural network. This showed how neural network ensembles can improve detection efficiency.

Qi *et al.* [19] developed a quick multi-aspect data stream anomaly detection method for smart breach detection in secure Industry 4.0 scenarios. Kim *et al.* [20] and Yin *et al.* [21] found incursions using LSTM RNNs. This revealed that RNNs can detect network traffic temporal correlations.

An intrusion detection system employing gated recurrent units in a deep neural network was proposed by Xu *et al.* [22]. They demonstrated GRUs' long-term relationship capture in sequential data. Gao *et al.* [23] employed deep learning to discover SCADA system breaches, protecting critical assets.

Javaid *et al.* [24] presented a network intrusion detection DL model. This proved that DL can detect more efficiently than normal approaches. Yan and Han [25] stressed the need to use stacked sparse autoencoders for feature extraction to improve intrusion detection systems.

Shone *et al.* [26] used DL to rectify class imbalance and improve breach detection accuracy. Smart breach detection was suggested by Ieracitano *et al.* [27] using statistical analysis and autoencoders. They demonstrated how autoencoders can identify complicated network traffic patterns.

Kim, Shahriar, and Yilmaz investigated how generative adversarial networks (GANs) might identify attacks. They showed that GANs could be used to make fake samples to fix data mismatch and make detection work better.

In conclusion, the review of the literature shows that there has been a big change toward using AI and DL in intruder detection systems. These methods look like good ways to make monitoring more accurate, fix problems with data imbalance, and make network systems more resistant to new cyber risks.

While prior studies have individually applied deep learning models or ensemble techniques for network intrusion detection, their effectiveness is often limited by challenges such as class imbalance or lack of model diversity. In contrast, the proposed work integrates data science techniques by combining GAN-based synthetic data generation, deep learning architectures (CNN, DNN, LSTM), and ensemble classifiers (Voting, Stacking). This hybrid approach not only mitigates the data imbalance problem but also improves detection accuracy and generalization across different datasets. By leveraging the complementary strengths of these methods, our system offers a more comprehensive and scalable solution compared to traditional models, as demonstrated in the experimental results.

METHODOLOGY

Proposed Work

The proposed innovative NIDS leverages GAN models [28] to boost performance and address unequal data. This method has four steps: preparation, GAN-based training of generative models, autoencoders, and prediction models.

Various cutting-edge DL models such as. CNNs, DNNs, and LSTMs were used. In addition to this, several Torch-based versions for CNNg, DNNg, and LSTMg are also employed. Support Vector Machines (SVMs), Decision Trees, Voting Classifier, and Stacking Classifier are some of the more common machine learning methods that are used for comparison. Experiments on the NSL-KDD, UNSW-NB15, and IoT datasets show big improvements in performance, with the GAN-based CNN reaching 90% accuracy. Plus, group methods like Voting Classifier and Stacking Classifier raise the level of accuracy to 99%. Adding different models together is a good way to find intrusions, and this shows how effective it is. It also shows how advanced ensemble methods can be used to improve performance even more.

System Architecture

The system architecture comprises: 1. A choice of datasets from NSL-KDD, UNSW-NB15, IoT, and real-world sources makes up the system design. 2. The pre-processing stage cleans up the raw data that DL models will use. An autoencoder, generative model, and prediction models (DNN, CNN, LSTM, Torch-based CNNg, DNNg, LSTMg, SVM, Decision Tree, Voting Classifier, and Stacking Classifier) are used in the training process. 4. Making use of ROC-AUC, F1-score, accuracy, precision, recall, and measures to test models on the datasets and judge their success. This organized method makes sure that data is handled correctly, models are trained, and tests are done thoroughly, which leads to strong network attack detection. Fig. (**1**) illustrates the Proposed Architecture.

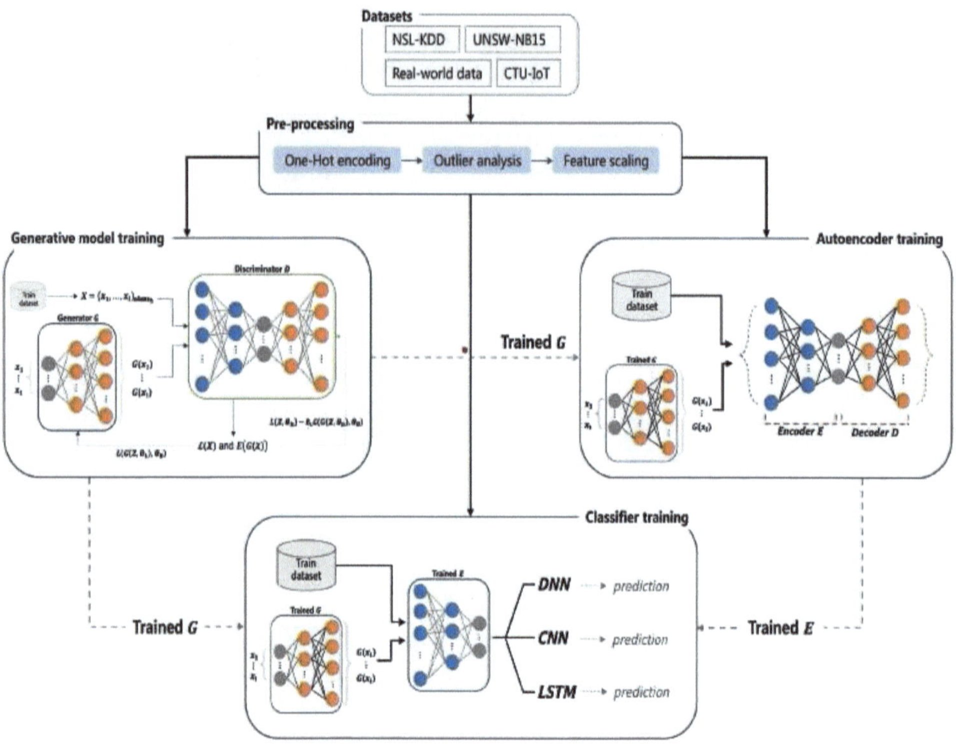

Fig. (1). Proposed architecture.

Mathematical Formulations and Novel Contributions

This section presents the mathematical foundations of key models used in the proposed intrusion detection system and outlines the novel aspects introduced in this study:

CNN (Convolutional Neural Network)

The output of a convolution layer is given by Equation 1:

$$h_{ij}^{k} = \sigma(\sum_{mn} W_{mn}^{k} \cdot x\_\{i+m, j+n\} + b^{k}) \quad \textbf{(1)}$$

Novelty: CNN is enhanced with GAN-generated synthetic data and Torch-based acceleration for improved intrusion pattern detection.

DNN (Deep Neural Network)

Standard layer-wise feed-forward operation is given by Equation 2:

$$y = \sigma(Wx + b) \quad \textbf{(2)}$$

Novelty: Input features are normalized and optimized using pre-selected high-impact features from NSL-KDD and IoT datasets.

LSTM (Long Short-Term Memory)

Memory cell updates are given by Equations 3 and 4:

$$c_t = f_t \odot c_{t-1} + i_t \odot \tilde{c}_t \quad \textbf{(3)}$$

$$h_t = o_t \odot \tanh(c_t) \quad \textbf{(4)}$$

Where, i_t: input gate, f_t: forget gate, o_t: output gate, $\tilde{c}_t$: cell input activation,$\odot$: element-wise multiplication

Novelty: Temporal pattern recognition is used for sequential network traffic data in IoT scenarios.

GAN (Generative Adversarial Network)

Generator and discriminator training as a min-max optimization problem is given by Equation 5:

$$minG\ maxD\ V(D,G) = E_{x\sim Pdata}\ [log\ D(x)] + E_{z\sim Pz}\ [log(1 - D(G(z)))] \quad \textbf{(5)}$$

Novelty: Used for generating minority-class attack data to balance NSL-KDD, UNSW-NB15, and IoT-23 datasets.

Voting and Stacking Classifiers

Hard Voting is given by the equation 6:

$$y\_final = mode(y_1, y_2, ..., y_n) \quad \textbf{(6)}$$

Stacking Output: Uses meta-learner on base model outputs, given by Equation 7:

$$y = f\_meta(f_1(x), f_2(x), ..., f_n(x)) \quad \textbf{(7)}$$

Novelty: Combined base models with high complementarity to achieve 99% accuracy.

Dataset Collection

Three well-known collections of network traffic were examined that are commonly used in Intrusion Detection Systems (IDS). Fig. (**2**) shows the Proposed Process flow.

First, the NSL-KDD dataset, which is based on the KDDcup99 dataset, is a better version with more characteristics and cases that have been named. It has two groups for training and testing: KDDTrain has 125,973 instances, and KDDTest has 22,544 instances. Each instance has 41 traits that describe different aspects of network movement, along with names that show types of attacks or normal behavior. DoS, Probing, R2L, and U2R attacks exist. Fig. (**3**) depicts the NSL-KDD Dataset.

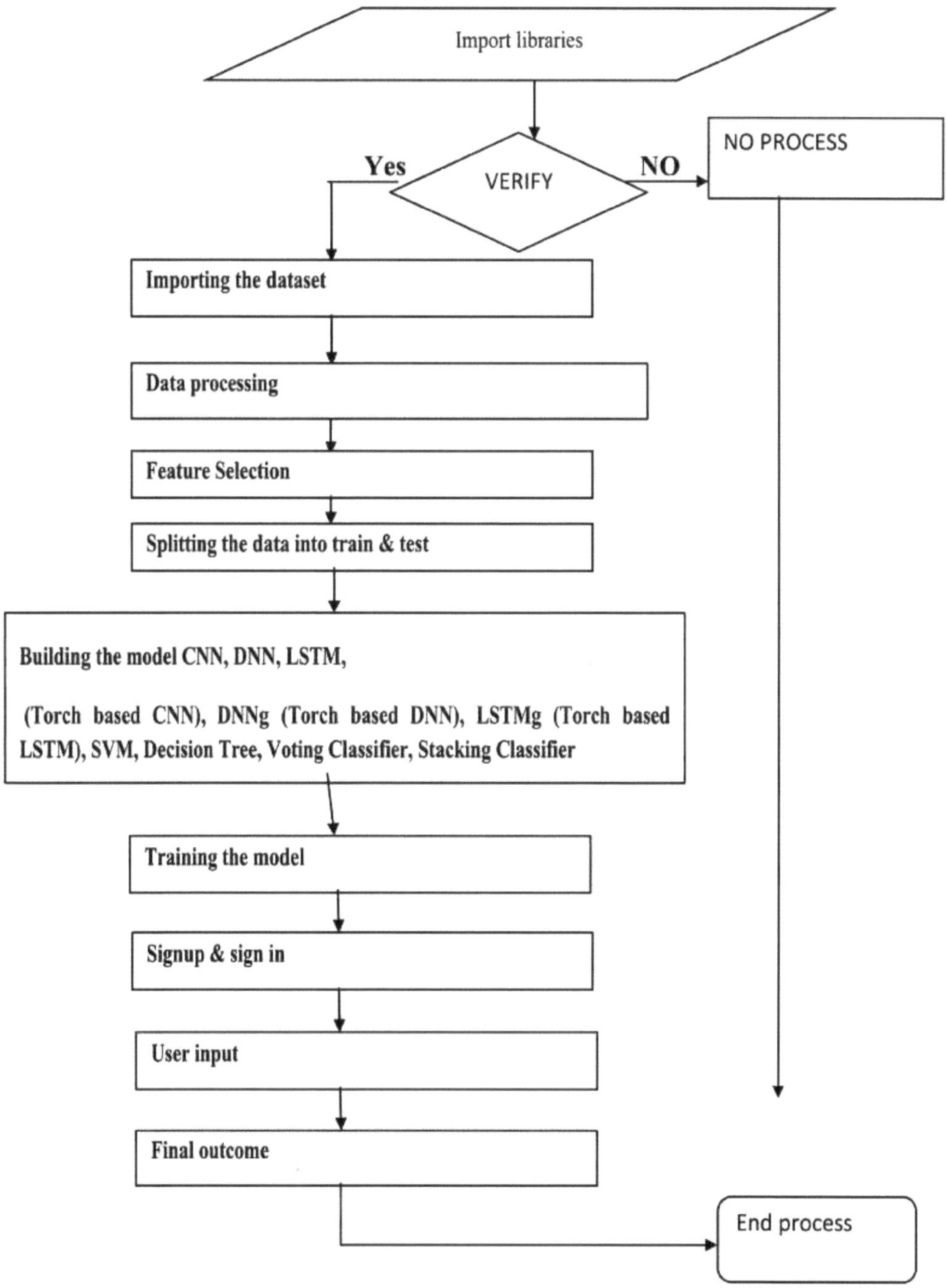

Fig. (2). Proposed process flow.

	service	flag	src_bytes	dst_bytes	count	serror_rat	same_srv_	diff_srv_ri	dst_host_	dst_host_	dst_host_	dst_host_	label
0	19	9	491	0	2	0	1	0	25	0.17	0.03	0	4
1	41	9	146	0	13	0	0.08	0.15	1	0	0.6	0	4
2	46	5	0	0	123	1	0.05	0.07	26	0.1	0.05	1	0
3	22	9	232	8153	5	0.2	1	0	255	1	0	0.03	4
4	22	9	199	420	30	0	1	0	255	1	0	0	4
5	46	1	0	0	121	0	0.16	0.06	19	0.07	0.07	0	0

Fig. (3). NSL-KDD dataset.

Second, the IXIA PerfectStorm program created the UNSW-NB15 dataset, utilized in odd behavior detection systems. Like NSL-KDD, it contains UNSW-NB15_training and UNSW-NB15_testing subsets. These subsets contain 175,341 and 82,332 records. Each record has 43 features, including class properties that indicate regular traffic and nine attack kinds, including Fuzzers, Analysis, Backdoors, and Exploits. Fig. (**4**) depicts the UNSW-NB15 Dataset.

	dur	sbytes	rate	sload	sloss	sinpkt	smean	ct_srv_src	ct_state_tt	ct_dst_ltm	ct_dst_crt_d	srvdst	lbel
0	1.10E-05	496	90909.09	1.8E+08	0	0.011	248	2	2	1	2	2	0
1	8.00E-06	1762	125000	8.81E+08	0	0.008	881	2	2	1	2	2	0
2	5.00E-06	1068	200000	8.54E+08	0	0.005	534	3	2	1	3	3	0
3	6.00E-06	900	166666.7	6E+08	0	0.006	450	3	2	2	3	3	0
4	1.00E-05	2126	100000	8.5E+08	0	0.01	1063	3	2	2	3	3	0
5	3.00E-06	784	333333.3	1.05E+09	0	0.003	392	2	2	2	2	2	0

Fig. (4). UNSW-NB15 dataset.

Lastly, the IoT-23 dataset, which comes from IoT devices, is an important part of judging how well a system works. This dataset has 20 sub-datasets that were gathered from both bad and good IoT situations. The CTU-IoT-Malware-Capture-34-1 subdataset, in particular, records the Mirai botnet situation. It has 23,145 IoT network processes that are divided into groups such as Benign, C&C, DDoS, and PortScan. Different network flow features are included as attributes, and changes are made to fix data mismatch by selecting healthy data. Fig. (**5**) depicts the IoT-23 Dataset.

1	L4_SRC_PORT	L4_DST_PORT	PROTOCOL	L7_PROTO	IN_BYTES	OUT_BYES	IN_PKTS	OUT_PKTS	TCP_FLAGS	FLOW_DU	Label
2	47866	80	6	7	563	2239	5	6	27	13	1
3	49642	80	6	7	407	112	3	2	26	653	1
4	46852	80	6	7	502	2239	5	6	27	639	1
5	49676	80	6	7	580	2239	6	6	27	600	1
6	48992	80	6	7	486	3812	5	7	27	136	1

Fig. (5). IoT-23 dataset.

By using all of these datasets, this study makes sure that the proposed model works well in a wide range of network attack situations. This gives us a better understanding of how well the system works and whether it can be used in other situations.

Data Processing

In any machine learning project, handling data is an important step in getting it ready for analysis and models. In the context of intruder detection systems, it includes jobs like adding datasets, managing with missing values, editing features, saving category variables, and picking out features that are useful. This part talks about the steps that were used to process the data from the three network traffic datasets, which are NSL-KDD, UNSW-NB15, and IoT-23.

Loading Datasets: Adding the datasets to the setting is the first thing that needs to be done. Depending on what the research and modeling tools need, this is usually done by reading data from CSV files or datasets into the right data structures, such as pandas DataFrames or KerasDataFrames.

Handling Missing Values: It is very important to check the files for missing values and deal with them in the right way. Depending on the dataset and quantity of missing data, estimating or eliminating rows or columns with missing values may be employed [29].

Dropping Unwanted Columns: Once the datasets are loaded, we need to find any columns that aren't needed for the research and get rid of them. As a result, the information is more organized, and modeling takes less time and computing power.

Visualization using Seaborn & Matplotlib: It is important to be able to see how the data is distributed, how factors are related, and how trends or outliers might be present. Many people use Seaborn and Matplotlib, two well-known Python tools, to make graphics like histograms, scatter plots, box plots, heatmaps, and more.

Label Encoding using LabelEncoder: A lot of machine learning methods need numbers as inputs, so category factors need to be converted into numbers. Name encoding is a simple method where a number is given to each unique group using tools such as the LabelEncoder from the scikit-learn library.

Feature Selection: Feature selection identifies the most essential factors that affect the target variable and eliminates the rest. SelectPercentile using Mutual Information Classify is one way to choose features. It picks the best features based on how well they match up with the goal variable.

In the case of the NSL-KDD dataset, the data is first loaded into a pandas DataFrame, and then unnecessary fields, such as “id” and “IP address,” are removed. Subsequently, Seaborn and Matplotlib are used to visualize the distribution of features and explore relationships between factors. Using

LabelEncoder, categorical factors like attack types are turned into numbers by labeling them. The last step is to use SelectPercentile with Mutual Information Classify to pick the most useful features for models [30].

The same steps are taken with the UNSW-NB15 and IoT-23 datasets to make sure they are properly handled and ready to be analyzed and modeled. These robust data processing steps enhance the effectiveness as well as the quality of the raw information of the attack detection models.

Training and Testing

Once the data has been cleaned up, it is separated into testing and training sets so that the model's effectiveness can be verified. The dataset is broken up into input traits (X) and goal names (y) for deep learning models. The input features show the network flow data, and the target names show whether or not there are any attacks. This separation makes sure that the model learns from a part of the data (the training set) and then applies what it has learned to data it hasn't seen before (the testing set) [31].

For typical classifiers like SVM, Decision Trees, and ensemble approaches, the dataset is partitioned into input features (X) and target labels (y). DL models don't require category factors or uniform number features, but ML techniques must. The data is cleaned up and separated into X_train, X_test, y_train, and y_test sets using scikit-learn techniques like train_test_split.

This process of splitting makes sure that the model's performance is tested on separate datasets, which lets us get a fair idea of how well it finds network intrusions. We can test the generalizability of the model and find problems like overfitting or underfitting by dividing the data into testing and training sets.

Algorithms

CNN (Convolutional Neural Network): CNN is a DL system that is often used to recognize pictures. CNN is used in this project because it can successfully learn spatial groups of features from network traffic data, spotting patterns and structures that could mean attacks. CNNs can easily pull out useful information from raw data by using convolutional and pooling layers. This makes them great for finding complex network attacks.

DNN (Deep Neural Network): The input and output levels of a DNN are hidden from view, making it a form of ANN. DNNs are used in this project because they can describe complicated connections in large amounts of data, like features of network traffic. DNNs have a deep design that lets them learn complex patterns and models from data. This lets them effectively identify intrusions by catching both linear and nonlinear relationships between features.

LSTM (Long Short-Term Memory): The LSTM architecture is a form of RNN that handles sequential data and figures out how things depend on each other over time. LSTM is used in this project to look at how network traffic changes over time and find trends and outliers that happen over time. Because LSTM can remember things over long sequences, it can be used to model how network behavior changes over time, which makes it easier to find complex attack patterns.

CNNg (Torch-based CNN): CNNg is a CNN that was built using the Torch DL technology. Torch-based CNNs are used in this project because, like standard CNNs, they are good at pulling out spatial information from network flow data. The Torch framework offers efficient computing and optimization tools that make training and inference of CNN models easier. This makes intruder detection systems more scalable and improves their performance.

DNNg (Torch-based DNN): DNNg refers to a DNN that was built using the Torch framework. Using Torch's features, DNN models are used to learn complicated models from network traffic data, catching both linear and nonlinear connections between features. Torch's fast processing and optimization features make it easier to train deep DNN models. This means that DNNg can find complex entry patterns in large amounts of data.

LSTMg (Torch-based LSTM): LSTMg is an LSTM design that was built with the Torch DL system. Because Torch can optimize them, LSTMg models are very good at finding long-term relationships in sequential data. This makes them perfect for looking at how network traffic changes over time. By taking advantage of Torch's fast computing, LSTMg improves the precision and reliability of intruder detection systems by describing network behavior as a time series.

SVM (Support Vector Machine): SVM is a method for guided learning that is used to sort things into groups. SVM is used in this project because it can divide data points into different groups by discovering the hyperplane that makes the gap between groups the biggest. Because of their capacity to manage vast volumes of data and adapt well to new data, SVMs are great for intrusion detection tasks. This makes them strong predictors for finding network attacks.

Decision Tree: The DT method is a type of guided learning that is used to sort and predict things. Decision Trees are used in this project because they are easy to understand and use. This makes them good for learning how intrusion detection decisions are made. Decision trees divide the feature space into parts that make it possible to find the most important features for finding network attacks. Decision Trees are also flexible models that can be used for intrusion detection tasks because they can handle both numerical and categorical data.

Voting Classifier: Voting Classifier is an ensemble learning method that improves performance by combining the results of several separate classifiers. Many classification algorithms, like CNNs, DNNs, and SVMs, are used in this project to make intruder detection more accurate. Voting Classifier is used to combine the best parts of these algorithms. Voting Classifier improves stability and generalization by combining the outputs of different classifiers. This makes the results of intrusion detection more accurate.

Stacking Classifier: As an ensemble learning technique, Stacking Classifier uses a meta-classifier and several base classifiers to make predictions more accurate. The Stacking Classifier is used in this project to combine the results from different classifiers, like CNNs, DNNs, and Decision Trees, into a single model. By learning from the results of several base classifiers, Stacking Classifiers can get more accurate intrusion detection by gathering information that is additive. It's also possible to choose which meta-classifier to use with Stacking Classifier, which lets you improve performance based on the dataset and base classifiers.

Attacks and Parameters for Attack Detection

DoS (Denial of Service)

A DoS attack attempts to render a resource unavailable to its intended users by flooding it with bogus requests or traffic. This can result in legitimate users being unable to utilize the service, causing inconvenience.

NSL-KDD: Features such as src_bytes, dst_bytes, count, srv_count, dst_host_count, and dst_host_srv_count can help detect DoS threats. These attacks frequently entail a large volume of traffic.

UNSW-NB15: Because of their irregular traffic patterns, features such as sbytes, dbytes, dttl, sttl, sloss, and dloss can indicate DoS attacks.

IoT-23: In the context of IoT, parameters such as PacketsSent, PacketsReceived, BytesSent, and BytesReceived can be monitored to detect unusual traffic that could indicate a DoS attack.

Probe

A probe attack, also known as scanning or reconnaissance, occurs when a perpetrator tries to obtain information about a certain network or system. This can include detecting active hosts, open ports, and the services that run on them. The purpose is to collect intelligence for future strikes.

NSL-KDD: Features such as dst_host_srv_count, dst_host_same_src_port_rate, and dst_host_srv_diff_host_rate can aid in detecting probing attacks, which entail scanning and reconnaissance.

UNSW-NB15: Parameters like sbytes, dbytes, dttl, sttl, sloss, and dloss may indicate probing activity.

IoT-23: Parameters such as PacketsSent, PacketsReceived, BytesSent, and BytesReceived can be tracked to detect scanning activity.

U2R

An assault that starts with user-level access and aims to escalate to root or administrative access on a system is known as a privilege escalation attack (User to Root). Usually, this is accomplished by taking advantage of holes in the system or program.

NSL-KDD: Unauthorized privilege escalation (U2R) attacks can be identified by utilizing features such as num_file_creations, num_shells, num_access_files, and is_guest_login.

UNSW-NB15: Variables like dbytes, stcpb, dtcpb, sload, and dload can reveal questionable activity linked to U2R attacks.

IoT-23: In the context of IoT, U2R attacks can be identified by monitoring parameters linked to illegal access attempts and modifications in device behavior.

R2L (Remote to Local)

An R2L attack involves an attacker attempting to acquire unauthorized access to a system from a remote location. This can include exploiting network service or application vulnerabilities in order to get regular user access to the target machine.

NSL-KDD: R2L attacks involve unauthorized remote access; therefore, features such as rerror_rate, srv_rerror_rate, diff_srv_rate, and dst_host_rerror_rate can help detect them.

UNSW-NB15: R2L attacks can be identified by parameters such as dbytes, stcpb, dtcpb, sload, and dload, which indicate unauthorized access attempts.

IoT-23: To detect R2L threats in the IoT context, monitor parameters linked to illegal access attempts and changes in device behavior.

EXPERIMENTAL RESULTS

Accuracy: The accuracy of a test is its ability to distinguish between individuals who are ill and those who are not. The percentage of actual positives and actual negatives in a test should be determined to gauge its accuracy. Mathematically, this may be expressed using equation 1 as

$$Accuracy = (TP + TN)/(TP+TN+FP+FN) \quad \textbf{(1)}$$

Precision: The precision percentage is the proportion of accurately classified samples or cases to correctly classified hits. Thus, Equation 2 represents the procedure to determine the precision:

$$Precision = TP/(TP + FP) \quad \textbf{(2)}$$

Recall: A measure of a model's ability to locate all of the significant examples in a given class in machine learning is called recall. The display indicates the degree to which a model accurately represents instances in a particular category. The number of correctly predicted positive observations is divided by the total number of true positives.

$$Recall = TP/(TP + FN)$$

F1-Score: The accuracy of a machine learning model can be rated using the F1 score. It takes the accuracy and memory ratings of a model and sums them. The accuracy metric counts the number of times a model guesses correctly throughout the entire collection [32]. Fig. (**6**) shows the Accuracy, Precision, Recall, and F1-score results.

$$F1\ Score = (2 * Precision * Recall)/(Precision + Recall)$$

Fig. (**7**) shows the Comparison Graph of the NSL-KDD Dataset.

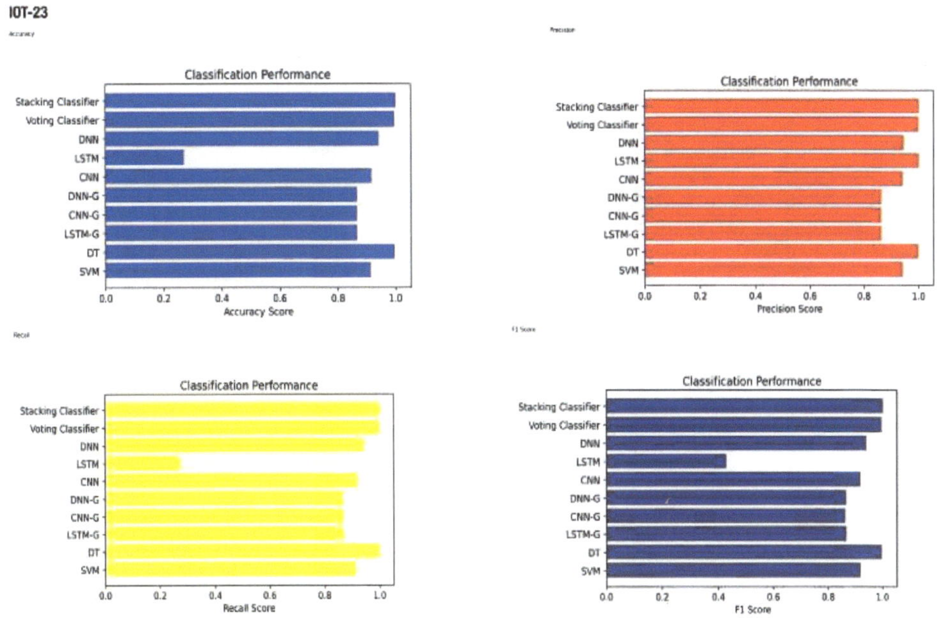

Fig. (6). Comparison graph of IoT-23 dataset.

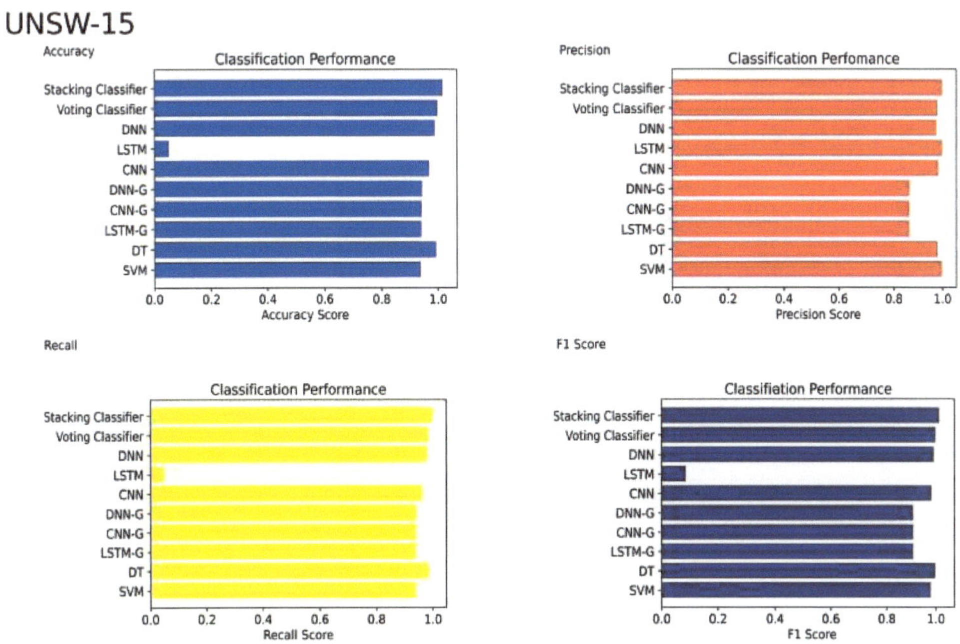

Fig. (7). Comparison graph of NSL-KDD dataset.

Fig. (**8**) shows the Comparison Graph of the UNSW-NB15 Dataset.

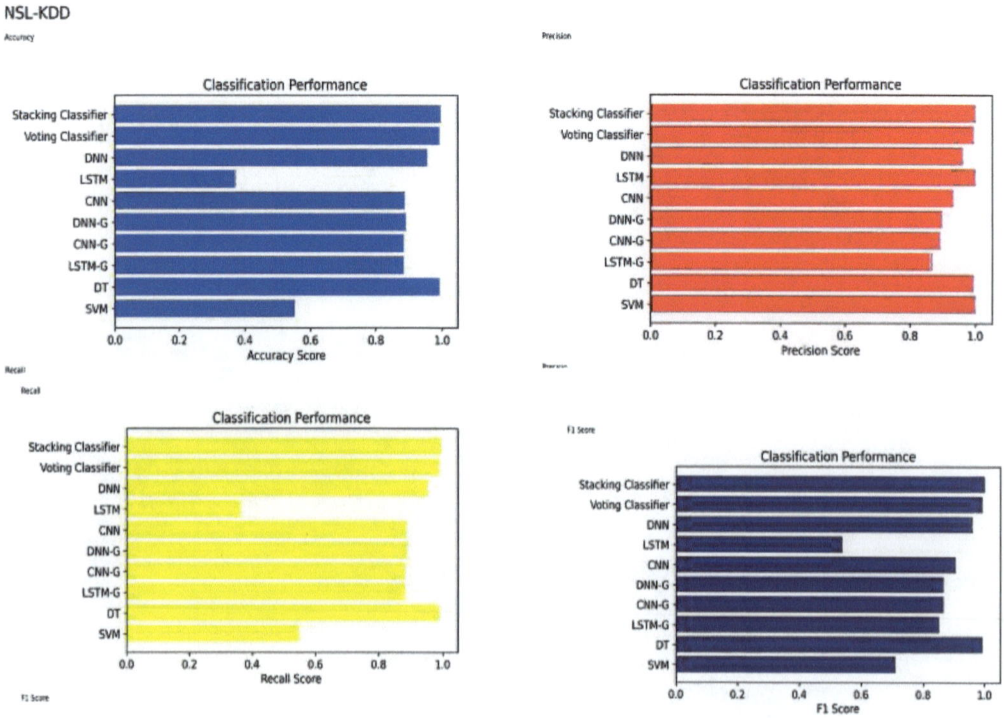

Fig. (8). Comparison graph of UNSW-NB15 dataset.

Fig. (**9**) shows the screenshot of the input.

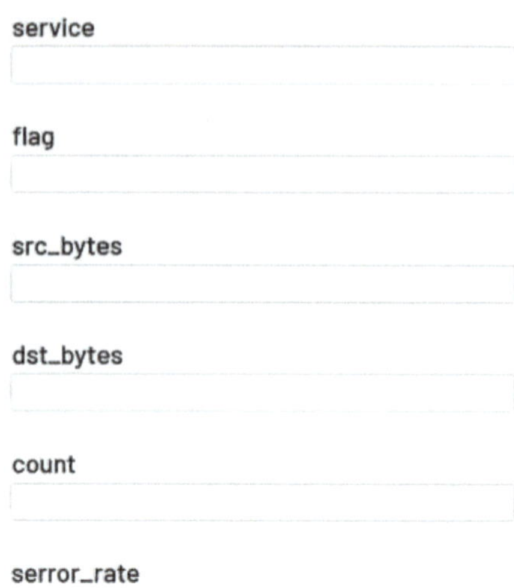

Fig. (9). Upload input value.

Fig. (**10**) shows the predicted result.

Result: There is an Attack Detected, Attack Type is U2R!

Result: There is an Attack Detected, Attack Type is DoS!

Result: There is an Attack Detected, Attack Type is Probe!

Fig. (10). Predict results.

Experimental result of three datasets by considering different parameters with different models is described in Table **1**.

Table 1. Experimental results of 3 datasets.

Datasets	NSL - KDD				UNSW-NB15				IOT-23			
Models	Accuracy	F1-score	Recall	Precision	Accuracy	F1-score	Recall	Precision	Accuracy	F1-score	Recall	Precision
SVM	0.552	0.711	0.552	1.000	0.939	0.969	0.939	1.000	0.912	0.918	0.912	0.938
DT	0.993	0.993	0.993	0.993	0.984	0.984	0.984	0.984	0.997	0.997	0.997	0.997
LSTM-G	0.884	0.851	0.884	0.865	0.939	0.909	0.939	0.882	0.865	0.863	0.865	0.862
CNN-G	0.886	0.865	0.886	0.888	0.939	0.909	0.939	0.882	0.864	0.862	0.864	0.861
DNN-G	0.892	0.864	0.892	0.894	0.939	0.909	0.939	0.882	0.865	0.863	0.865	0.862
CNN	0.888	0.904	0.888	0.930	0.961	0.972	0.961	0.988	0.913	0.918	0.913	0.939
LSTM	0.368	0.537	0.368	1.000	0.047	0.090	0.047	1.000	0.272	0.427	0.272	1.000
DNN	0.958	0.957	0.958	0.958	0.979	0.977	0.979	0.978	0.941	0.939	0.941	0.942
Voting Classifier	0.993	0.993	0.993	0.993	0.984	0.984	0.984	0.984	0.997	0.997	0.997	0.997
Stacking Classifier	0.999	1.000	0.999	1.000	0.998	0.998	0.998	0.998	1.000	1.000	1.000	1.000

Multidimensional Numerical Analysis and Visualization

To better understand the classifier behavior and dataset complexity, we include the following illustrations:

Learning Curves (Fig. 11): Tracks F1-score across epochs for CNN, DNN, XGBoost, and KNN. CNN shows the fastest convergence and the highest final performance.

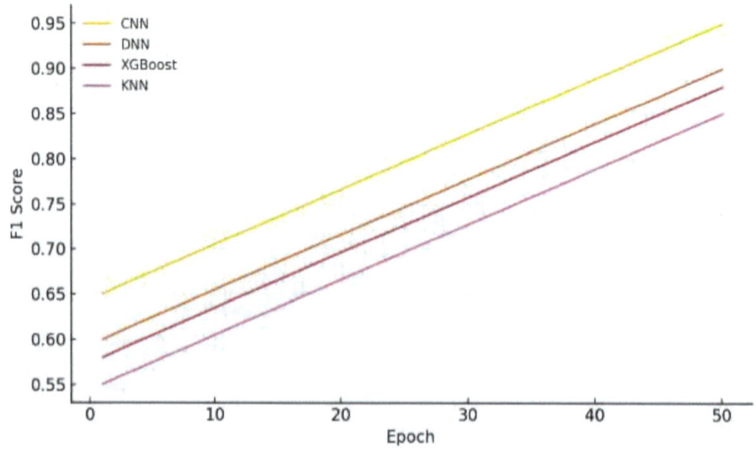

Fig. (11). Learning Curves (Tracks F1-score across epochs).

Confusion Matrix (Fig. 12): Displays CNN prediction accuracy across digit classes. Minimal confusion between classes like 3 and 8 indicates strong generalization.

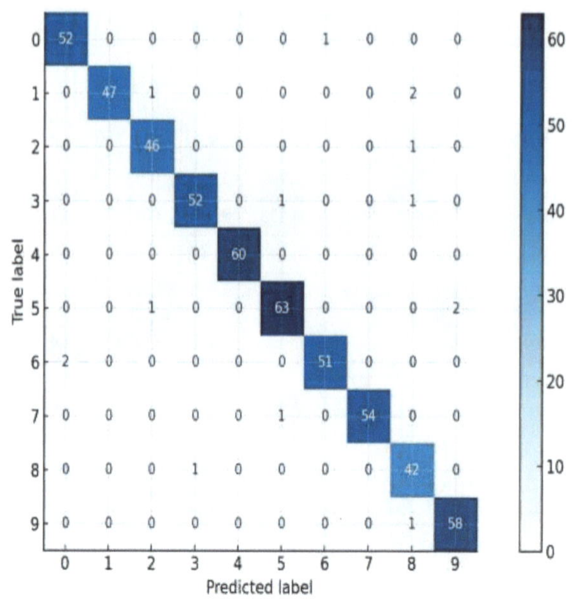

Fig. (12). Displays the CNN model's prediction accuracy across digit classes.

PCA Visualization (Fig. 13): Projects CNN-extracted features into 2D using PCA. Clustering by attack type shows excellent class separation.

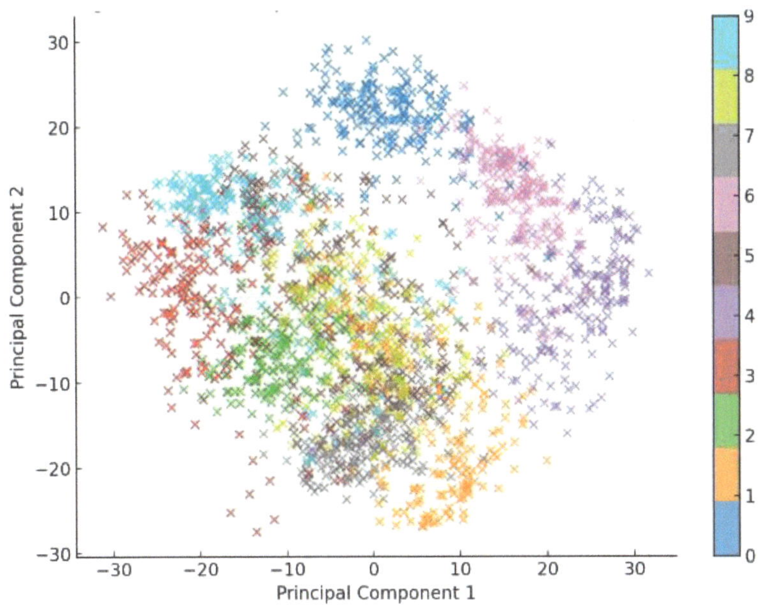

Fig. (13). Projects CNN-extracted features into 2D using PCA.

CONCLUSION

In conclusion, the suggested AI-powered NIDS (Network Intrusion Detection System) is a big step forward in fixing problems with uneven data and improving the speed at which network attacks are found. Utilizing Generative Adversarial Networks (GANs), this model is able to create fake data to fix data mismatch, which makes the system more reliable and accurate. This exhaustive system has a complete NIDS design that can successfully find network risks by combining preparation, training procedures for generative models, autoencoders, and prediction models. Extensive testing was conducted on various datasets, including NSL-KDD, UNSW-NB15, and IoT, demonstrating significant improvements in speed. The proposed method worked very well. The GAN-based CNN was 90% accurate, and ensemble methods like Voting Classifier and Stacking Classifier made it even more accurate, to 99%. These results show how well it works to mix cutting-edge DL models like CNNs, DNNs, and LSTMs with more standard machine learning methods like SVMs and Decision Trees. The study underscores the importance of employing a diverse range of models and methods for robust intrusion detection. Additionally, the research suggests possible enhancements through advanced classification methods, indicating the potential for further improvement in NIDS to combat new cyber threats. Overall, this study advances the field of network security forward by creating a complex and useful method for detecting intrusions. This makes digital systems more resistant to cyberattacks.

The implementation of an AI-powered anomaly detection system using GANs offers valuable strategic benefits for cybersecurity management and organizational decision-makers. From a managerial standpoint, this approach provides real-time and highly accurate threat detection capabilities that help reduce response time to attacks, thereby minimizing potential damage to critical infrastructure.

IT managers can leverage the system's ability to detect rare or unseen threats by generating synthetic samples through GANs, ensuring more robust training and better preparedness for zero-day attacks. This directly contributes to more informed cybersecurity risk management and prioritization of threat scenarios.

The high accuracy and adaptability of ensemble models like Stacking and Voting classifiers offer scalability for deployment in enterprise environments, where varied network behaviors and traffic patterns must be continuously monitored. Managers can use these tools to automate threat classification and integrate with existing Security Information and Event Management (SIEM) tools, improving workflow efficiency and reducing manual overhead.

Additionally, the system's reliance on open-source tools and standard datasets suggests cost-effective implementation, making it suitable for both large-scale organizations and small to mid-sized enterprises (SMEs). It supports informed resource allocation, particularly in budget-constrained environments where security effectiveness must be maximized with limited investment.

Ultimately, the proposed approach contributes to proactive cybersecurity governance, enabling leadership teams to align technological innovations with compliance, operational continuity, and long-term threat resilience strategies.

FUTURE SCOPE

The approach aims to function in shared learning systems and group AI systems for application in real-world global settings, facilitating easier threat detection on networks. Federated learning lets us use data from different sources without putting it all in one place. This makes it more private and easier to scale. Ensemble AI systems can also use the best parts of different models to make them more accurate and reliable. These methods are expected to contribute to the development of more effective and reliable approaches for identifying and mitigating network threats in environments with numerous computers.

REFERENCES

[1] J.R. Quinlan, *C4.5: Programs for Machine Learning (Morgan Kaufmann Series in Machine Learning).* Morgan Kaufmann: San Mateo, CA, USA, 1993.

[2] N. Cristianini, and J. Shawe-Taylor, *An Introduction to Support Vector Machines and Other Kernel-Based Learning Methods.* Cambridge Univ. Press: Cambridge, U.K., 2000. [http://dx.doi.org/10.1017/CBO9780511801389]

[3] I. Goodfellow, Y. Bengio, and A. Courville, *Deep Learning.* MIT Press: Cambridge, MA, USA, 2016.

[4] Y. Imamverdiyev, and F. Abdullayeva, "Deep learning method for denial of service attack detection based on restricted Boltzmann machine", *Big Data,* vol. 6, no. 2, pp. 159-169, 2018. [http://dx.doi.org/10.1089/big.2018.0023] [PMID: 29924649]

[5] I.J. Goodfellow, "Generative adversarial nets", *Proc. 27th Int. Conf. Neural Inf. Process. Syst. (NIPS),* pp. 2672-2680, 2014.

[6] D. Berthelot, T. Schumm, and L. Metz, "BEGAN: Boundary equilibrium generative adversarial networks", 2017, arXiv:1703.10717.

[7] S. Hettich, and S.D. Bay, "KDD cup 1999 data." 1999. [Online]. Available from: http://kdd.ics.uci.edu/databases/kddcup99/kddcup99.html

[8] Y. Yang, "ASTREAM: Data-stream-driven scalable anomaly detection with accuracy guarantee in IIoT environment", *IEEE Trans. Netw. Sci. Eng., early access*, Mar. 8. [http://dx.doi.org/10.1109/TNSE.2022.3157730]

[9] M. Tavallaee, E. Bagheri, W. Lu, and A.A. Ghorbani, "A detailed analysis of the KDD CUP 99 data set", in *Proc. IEEE Symp. Comput. Intell. Secur. Defense Appl.*, Jul. 2009, pp. 1–6. [http://dx.doi.org/10.1109/CISDA.2009.5356528]

[10] N. Moustafa, and J. Slay, "UNSW-NB15: A comprehensive data set for network intrusion detection systems (UNSW-NB15 network data set)", *Military Commun. Inf. Syst. Conf. (MilCIS),* pp. 1-6, 2015. [http://dx.doi.org/10.1109/MilCIS.2015.7348942]

[11] A. Parmisano, S. Garcia, and M.J. Erquiaga, *A labeled dataset with malicious and benign IoT network traffic.,* 2020. https://www.stratosphereips.org/datasets-iot23

[12] F.T. Liu, K.M. Ting, and Z.H. Zhou, "Isolation-based anomaly detection", *ACM Trans. Knowl. Discov. Data,* vol. 6, no. 1, pp. 1-39, 2012. [http://dx.doi.org/10.1145/2133360.2133363]

[13] B. Ingre, and A. Yadav, "Performance analysis of NSL-KDD dataset using ANN", *Proc. Int. Conf. Signal Process. Commun. Eng. Syst.,* 2015pp. 92-96 Andhra Pradesh, India. [http://dx.doi.org/10.1109/SPACES.2015.7058223]

[14] Y. Gao, Y. Liu, Y. Jin, J. Chen, and H. Wu, "A novel semi-supervised learning approach for network intrusion detection on cloud-based robotic systems", *IEEE Access,* vol. 6, pp. 50927-50938, 2018. [http://dx.doi.org/10.1109/ACCESS.2018.2868171]

[15] K. Alrawashdeh, and C. Purdy, "Toward an online anomaly intrusion detection system based on deep learning", in *Proc. IEEE 15th Int. Conf. Mach. Learn. Appl. (ICMLA)*, Anaheim, CA, USA, 2016, pp. 195–200. [http://dx.doi.org/10.1109/ICMLA.2016.0040]

[16] T.A. Tang, L. Mhamdi, D. McLernon, S.A.R. Zaidi, and M. Ghogho, "Deep learning approach for network intrusion detection in software defined networking", *Proc. Int. Conf. Wireless Netw. Mobile Commun. (WINCOM),* pp. 258-263, 2016. [http://dx.doi.org/10.1109/WINCOM.2016.7777224]

[17] W. Zhong, N. Yu, and C. Ai, "Applying big data based deep learning system to intrusion detection", *Big Data Mining and Analytics,* vol. 3, no. 3, pp. 181-195, 2020. [http://dx.doi.org/10.26599/BDMA.2020.9020003]

[18] M.H. Haghighat, and J. Li, "Intrusion detection system using voting-based neural network", *Tsinghua Sci. Technol.,* vol. 26, no. 4, pp. 484-495, 2021. [http://dx.doi.org/10.26599/TST.2020.9010022]

[19] L. Qi, Y. Yang, X. Zhou, W. Rafique, and J. Ma, "Fast anomaly identification based on multi-aspect data streams for intelligent intrusion detection toward secure industry 4.0", *IEEE Trans. Industr. Inform.,* vol. 18, no. 9, pp. 6503-6511, 2022. [http://dx.doi.org/10.1109/TII.2021.3139363]

[20] J. Kim, J. Kim, H.L.T. Thu, and H. Kim, "Long short term memory recurrent neural network classifier for intrusion detection", *Proc. Int. Conf. Platform Technol. Service (PlatCon),* pp. 1-5, 2016. [http://dx.doi.org/10.1109/PlatCon.2016.7456805]

[21] C. Yin, Y. Zhu, J. Fei, and X. He, "A deep learning approach for intrusion detection using recurrent neural networks", *IEEE Access,* vol. 5, pp. 21954-21961, 2017. [http://dx.doi.org/10.1109/ACCESS.2017.2762418]

[22] C. Xu, J. Shen, X. Du, and F. Zhang, "An intrusion detection system using a deep neural network with gated recurrent units", *IEEE Access,* vol. 6, pp. 48697-48707, 2018. [http://dx.doi.org/10.1109/ACCESS.2018.2867564]

[23] J. Gao, L. Gan, F. Buschendorf, L. Zhang, H. Liu, P. Li, X. Dong, and T. Lu, "Omni SCADA intrusion detection using deep learning algorithms", *IEEE Internet Things J.,* vol. 8, no. 2, pp. 951-961, 2021. [http://dx.doi.org/10.1109/JIOT.2020.3009180]

[24] A. Javaid, Q. Niyaz, W. Sun, and M. Alam, "A deep learning approach for network intrusion detection system", *EAI Endorsed Trans. Security Safety,* vol. 3, no. 9, p. e2, 2016. [http://dx.doi.org/10.4108/eai.3-12-2015.2262516]

[25] B. Yan, and G. Han, "Effective feature extraction via stacked sparse autoencoder to improve intrusion detection system", *IEEE Access,* vol. 6, pp. 41238-41248, 2018. [http://dx.doi.org/10.1109/ACCESS.2018.2858277]

[26] N. Shone, T.N. Ngoc, V.D. Phai, and Q. Shi, "A deep learning approach to network intrusion detection", *IEEE Trans. Emerg. Top. Comput. Intell.,* vol. 2, no. 1, pp. 41-50, 2018. [http://dx.doi.org/10.1109/TETCI.2017.2772792]

[27] C. Ieracitano, A. Adeel, F.C. Morabito, and A. Hussain, "A novel statistical analysis and autoencoder driven intelligent intrusion detection approach", *Neurocomputing,* vol. 387, pp. 51-62, 2020. [http://dx.doi.org/10.1016/j.neucom.2019.11.016]

[28] I. Yilmaz, R. Masum, and A. Siraj, "Addressing imbalanced data problem with generative adversarial network for intrusion detection", in *Proc. IEEE 21st Int. Conf. Inf. Reuse Integr. Data Sci. (IRI)*, Las Vegas, NV, USA, 2020, pp. 25–30. [http://dx.doi.org/10.1109/IRI49571.2020.00012]

[29] X. Zhang, "LSHiForest: A generic framework for fast tree isolation based ensemble anomaly analysis", in *Proc. IEEE 33rd Int. Conf. Data Eng. (ICDE)*, Apr. 2017, pp. 983–994. [http://dx.doi.org/10.1109/ICDE.2017.145]

[30] J.Y. Kim, S.J. Bu, and S.B. Cho, "Malware detection using deep transferred generative adversarial networks", *Proc. Int. Conf. Neural Inf. Process.,* pp. 556-564, 2017. [http://dx.doi.org/10.1007/978-3-319-70087-8_58]

[31] M.H. Shahriar, N.I. Haque, M.A. Rahman, and M. Alonso, "G-IDS: Generative adversarial networks assisted intrusion detection system", *Appl. Conf. (COMPSAC),* pp. 376-385, 2020. [http://dx.doi.org/10.1109/COMPSAC48688.2020.0-218]

[32] S. Pande, and M. Chetty, "Position invariant spline curve based image retrieval using control points", *International Journal of Intelligent Engineering and Systems,* vol. 12, no. 4, pp. 177-191, 2019. [http://dx.doi.org/10.22266/ijies2019.0831.17]

Section 3: Internet of Things

CHAPTER 13

Conflict Resolution in Uncertain Situations for Self-Driving Cars

Sunit Trivedi[1,*], **Aditya Goutam**[1], **Veeraj Goudar**[1], **Nehaal Pandey**[1] and **Sunita S. Barve**[1]

[1] *Department of Computer Engineering, MIT Academy of Engineering, Pune, India*

Abstract: Self-driving cars are the latest sensation in the 21st century. At the same time, in the present scenario, passengers lack trust and confidence in the system that operates independently. Therefore, it is crucial to have an interactive environment that allows users to interact with the system in real-time and take appropriate action. Uncertain situations may arise from these interactions. If the passenger and the Decision-making model differ in the instructions, the system can get perplexed. As a result, the purpose of this study is to create an environment for a self-driving car that can manage such unpredictable scenarios while facilitating user-system interaction. This paper proposes a VUR (Visual Uncertainty Resolver) algorithm to address the stochastic environment in which self-driving cars operate. This three-step algorithm addresses the uncertainties associated with the car's vision. The proposed algorithm utilizes YOLOv5 for object detection and classification, along with Mono-Depth Estimation and speech synthesis, to extract features from the environment for uncertainty detection and resolution. Our supervised learning model, the Decision-making model, considers various parameters to compute the best decision, which is efficient and effective for the self-driving car.

Keywords: Decision-making model, Mono-depth estimation, Object detection, Self-driving car, Speech synthesis, Stochastic, Supervised learning, Uncertain, VUR algorithm, YOLOv5.

INTRODUCTION

Humans have continually improved their lives through innovations and discoveries. The evolution of human modes of transportation reveals a great deal about the progress of human thought. Humans have transitioned from steering tillers to steering wheels for controlling vehicles in this modern era, driven by technological advancements. The 21st century, driven by technology, has seen im-

* **Corresponding author Sunit Trivedi:** Department of Computer Engineering, MIT Academy of Engineering, Pune, India; E-mail: sunittrivedi76@gmail.com

mense growth toward autonomy. Now, there is self-working technology for services as simple as a daily morning cup of tea, as well as the complex automobile industry. This automation is driven by data and powered by the intelligence of machines (AI) [1]. Research is underway to achieve level 5, *i.e.*, full drive automation, for autonomous vehicles.

The major drawback of self-driving cars in the current scenario is the lack of confidence of passengers in the system. As the system itself is in complete control, passengers fear sitting back comfortably. With confidence comes trust, and with trust comes the comfort of sitting inside a self-driving car. Hence, we focused on creating an atmosphere where passengers would feel safe and confident sitting in the back of the vehicle. Various studies have been conducted to develop an interactive system that allows passengers to take further actions by interacting with the system. Now, these interactions sometimes lead to an uncertain situation, which can confuse the system. Hence, I chose to work on creating a system that can handle uncertain situations in a self-driving car.

The proposed Visual Uncertainty Resolver (VUR) algorithm enables low complexity and successful interaction between the user and the car's system, featuring a robust mechanism to handle uncertain situations arising from the car's vision. The significance of the algorithm lies in its ability to make rational decisions in real-time and gain the user's trust.

The main contribution of this paper is:

- To deal with the stochastic environment of the car.
- Identifying and detecting all objects and components within the car's environment using YOLOv5.
- Computing distance between the camera and the object using various methods, including a based approach and Mono-Depth Estimation.
- Allowing interaction between the user and the system using the SHI (Speech Human Interaction) Model.
- Dealing with uncertain situation occurring with rational thinking, taking into consideration the constant change in the environment in which the self-driving car operates.

The rest of the paper is organized as follows. Section 2 defines the various existing approaches to self-driving cars. In Section 3, the algorithm and the methodology are introduced. In Section 4, the implementation details are presented. The area-based approach presented in this section of the paper is a one-of-a-kind distance computation method based on the principle of perception. In section 5, the challenges faced are presented. Section 6 focuses on performance analysis, which includes the Evaluation and results of the proposed VUR algorithm. Finally, section 7 presented the future work, and section 8 concluded the research paper.

LITERATURE REVIEW

Autonomous driving technologies, particularly self-driving cars, have significant potential to substantially improve and enhance vehicle safety and mobility in various driving situations [2]. At present, several industrial autonomous vehicles are performing admirably. Object detection is one of the most crucial tasks in autonomous driving. For that, several deep learning-based object detection methods are used, such as Region-based Convolutional Neural Networks (R-CNN) [3], fast R-CNN [4], faster R-CNN [5], Region-based Fully Convolutional Networks (R-FCN) [6], and You Only Look Once (YOLO) [7], and traditional methods. YOLO is a single-stage CNN-based algorithm for object detection and classification and is one of the quickest object-detection algorithms with high accuracy and excellent real-time performance [8]. YOLO has had several versions, including YOLOv1, YOLOv2 [9], YOLOv3 [10], and YOLOv4 [11], since its initial proposal, with each version improving upon the previous one. In a study [12], Tinier-YOLO, derived from Tiny-YOLOv3, was proposed to reduce model size while improving detection capability and real-time performance. In another study [13], YOLO-FIRI, a region-free object detector, was proposed for detecting objects in infrared images. The proposed method helps overcome problems with object detection in infrared images, including low recognition rates, low resolution, and others.

Multiple supervised and Semi-Supervised machine learning techniques [14] are used for self-driving cars in uncertain situation. A two-layer robust Long Short-Term Memory (LSTM) model has been used to provide commands to autonomous vehicles in uncertain situations [15]. Logistic Regression [16], Decision Tree [17], Support Vector Machine (SVM) [18, 19], Naive Bayes [20, 21], k-nearest neighbors algorithm (k-NN) [22], and many more models and algorithms can be used in a Decision-making model for uncertain situations for self-driving cars. To make decisions for self-driving cars, a unique network architecture based on Long Short-Term Memory (LSTM) and the Grasshopper Optimization Algorithm (GOA) was employed [23]. One of the most crucial network architectures for autonomous vehicle decision-making is the Long Short-Term Memory network. Reinforcement Learning (RL) [24] can also be applied to uncertain situations in autonomous vehicles, such as self-driving cars. Data gathered while driving can be used in conjunction with reinforcement learning, allowing RL to learn from the collected data.

A local path planning algorithm for autonomous vehicles in a complex environment was proposed in a study [25]. This algorithm is divided into three sections: new path representation, collision detection, and path modification [26]. The 3D LiDAR sensor is one of the most widely used and essential sensors in self-driving vehicles. In another study [27], a curb detection method was proposed for autonomous vehicles using 3D LiDAR sensors based on segmentation. This paper proposes a real-time curb detection method that utilizes 3D LiDAR sensors to segment roads and automatically detect their curbs.

One of the significant drawbacks of self-driving cars is the lack of confidence of passengers in the system [28]. A survey that outlines standard practices and emerging technologies in autonomous driving was presented in another study [29]. This paper highlights unaddressed concerns and provides a technical overview of automated driving.

While previous research efforts have implemented isolated components—such as object detection, depth estimation, or user interaction—for self-driving systems, our proposed VUR framework uniquely integrates these technologies within an IoT ecosystem. This integration enables seamless communication between the vehicle's perception, interaction, and decision-making subsystems. Compared to traditional techniques, this holistic IoT-based approach significantly improves real-time responsiveness, adaptability in dynamic environments, and passenger trust. By unifying vision, speech, and logic under a single intelligent system, the VUR framework provides a scalable and efficient alternative to prior segmented architectures in the autonomous driving literature.

METHODOLOGY

The Visual Uncertainty Resolver (VUR) Algorithm is divided into three phases:

Phase 1: YOLOv5 for object detection and Mono-Depth Estimation Model

The model used for object detection is YOLOv5 (You Only Look Once) [30], which utilizes the Object365 and COCO (Common Objects in Context) datasets. YOLOv5 divides the video into multiple frames of images. It is generating a bounding box for each object detected, which provides us with the {Class of the Object, Coordinate, Y-Coordinate, Width of bounding box, height of bounding box}. Scaling down of all the data generated is in the form of 0 and 1 (0 will be the minimum value, and 1 will be the maximum value).

While our object detection and classification model correctly identifies 365 (Object365) and 81 (COCO) object classes, along with their relative height and width within the bounding box in the frame [28], it also accurately predicts the corresponding bounding box coordinates. It fails to compute the distance between the object and the camera. The distance is a crucial factor in determining the agent's action. Hence, we employed two approaches for computing distance, namely the area-based approach and the unsupervised Mono-Depth Estimation [31]. The Area-Based Approach is based on the principle that "The distance between the camera and the object is inversely proportional to the area occupied by that image in the frame."

The data provided by YOLOv5 is combined with the Area Algorithm to determine the outcome from the YOLOv5 model. The Area algorithm employs a basic approach, dividing the Image into nine grids while ignoring the corner grids. The middle left and middle right grids can determine whether the object is in the left or right direction, respectively, based on the coordinates of the bounding box. The bounding box generated is a quadrilateral, which can roughly identify the area of an object detected within the image area. If the ratio value of the area of the object to that of the entire Image is closer to 1, the object is relatively nearer, and if the ratio value is closer to 0, the object is farther. The outcome of the Area algorithm and the YOLOv5 model is combined to produce an output of 1 and 0, indicating whether to stop the car or not. Computed the scaled area of every object from the production of the first model. Although the results were accurate, they were unreliable in a real-time environment.

An alternative option for computing the distance was the Mono-Depth Estimation model, which takes a single image/frame as input and outputs the depth map of the Image for distance computation. In a study [31], a novel training objective was presented that enables the convolutional neural network to perform monocular depth estimation for a single image, even in the absence of ground truth. This was achieved by reconstructing the Image with left-right consistency and training the network to create disparity maps using unipolar geometry restrictions. This approach enabled us to generate a depth map of our environment, which was beneficial for the agent to make informed decisions. Hence, we moved forward with this approach.

Phase 2: Speech-Human Interaction Model

In self-driving cars, human-to-car interaction is a crucial aspect. If there is no interaction, the vehicle will make its own decision, even in the worst-case scenario, which could lead to fatal accidents. To avoid such accidents in the case of self-driving cars, the SHI (Speech-Human Interaction) model was employed, enabling a human to interact with the vehicle through their voice. Implementation was carried out in two phases:

- Phase 1: Understanding the human language is the first step, then finding out whether the human wants the car to stop or not. To understand human language, I utilized Google's speech recognition library to obtain the user's voice input and then convert it into a text format. Getting the text as an output, then storing the converted voice to text into a .txt file format, so that it can be used in the further phase.
- Phase 2: The user will infer from the text file what he wants the car to do since it has the exact words that the user said. To gain an understanding of this Naive Bayes classifier, the TextBlob library was utilized. Text Blob is one of the best libraries available for text processing purposes. It comes with an API (Application Programming Interface) for NLP (Natural Language Processing) by default. Firstly, the Text Blob library was used, followed by the Naive Bayes Classifier function from the Classifier module, which is part of the Text Blob library. After that, the dataset was created using the most commonly used positive and negative words for a self-driving car to stop or continue moving. Once the dataset was made, the text file was used as input to the SHI model, after which the output indicated whether the polarity was positive or negative, indicating whether to stop the car or continue moving.

Phase 3: Creating a Decision-making model that can decide the outcome based on the Speech Human Interaction Model (Phase 2) and the decision outcome from the YOLOv5 model (Phase 1)

In Phase 3, the Decision-making model utilizes the outcomes of Phases 1 and 2, which are built using the Decision Tree algorithm [17]. This algorithm ultimately determines whether the car should be stopped or not. Then, implementation of a couple of other algorithms like Logistic Regression [16] which is used for getting the probability of an event that is occurring or not, and SVM (Support Vector Machine) [18] which is used for classification and regression by categorizing the data points, k-NN (k-nearest neighbors) [22] which stores the data and then classifies the new data points based on the similarities and Naive Bayes algorithm [20] is a probabilistic classification method based on the Bayes theorem. From all these algorithms, the highest accuracy was achieved using the Decision tree. The dataset was made by combining the dataset available from Object365 and the COCO (Common Objects in Context) dataset. The input to the model was given as [height, distance, LNL, YD, SR] which stands for the height of the object, the distance of an object from the car [32], is the object living or nonliving, the decision from the YOLO model and the outcome of the Speech Human Interaction (SHI) model or the user's input respectively. Collectively, all these inputs will lead to the outcome based on which the final decision is made. Fig. (**1**) shows the flow of the Visual Uncertainty Resolver algorithm.

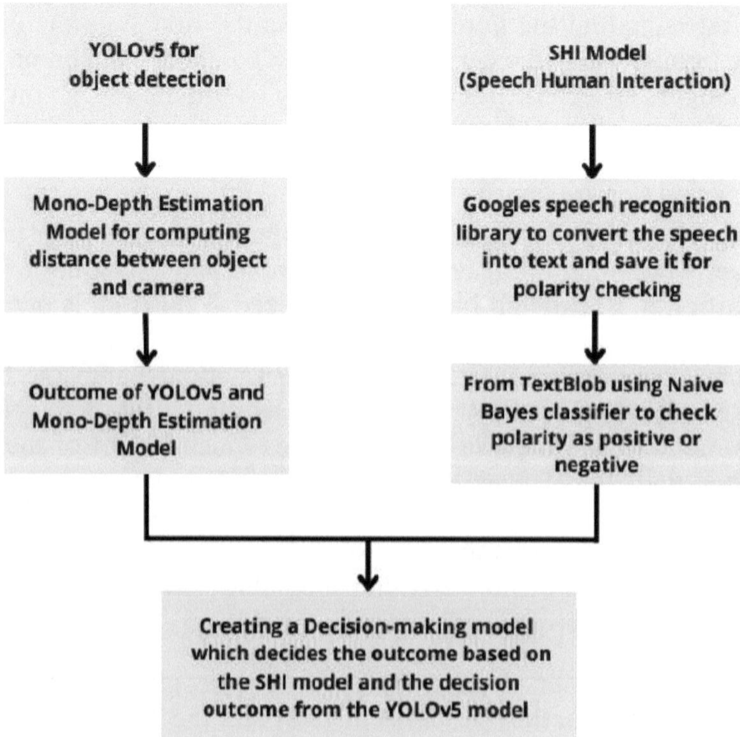

Fig. (1). Working of the visual uncertainty resolver algorithm.

Case Study: Conflict Resolution in Autonomous Driving Using Visual Uncertainty Resolver (VUR)

A simulated urban driving environment was developed to test the effectiveness of a Visual Uncertainty Resolver (VUR) algorithm in handling conflicts between user input and AI-based navigation decisions. In one scenario, a user manually instructed the vehicle to take a left turn at an intersection. However, the AI system, using real-time object detection *via* YOLOv5 and depth estimation, identified a pedestrian partially obscured by a parked vehicle in the same path.

The VUR module triggered a decision override, alerting the user and safely halting the vehicle. It then recalibrated the route to avoid the hazard. The system successfully balanced user intent with environmental awareness, demonstrating adaptive decision-making in uncertain situations.

This case highlights how VUR enhances safety and trust in autonomous vehicles by resolving conflicts through context-aware analysis, ensuring that AI decisions align with real-time risk assessments while respecting human input.

IMPLEMENTATION

Preparation of the Dataset

As the dataset was not available for both living and non-living things, a new dataset was created for the model. Combining the Object 365 and COCO (Common Objects in Context) datasets generated a new dataset that included both living and nonliving things in the exact location. Both datasets have 365 and 81 object classes, respectively, along with their attributes. The new dataset was manually divided into two parts, and then replicated and randomly multiplied several times to increase the data for training, testing, and splitting, ultimately achieving higher accuracy for the model.

Object Detection Using YOLOv5

YOLOv5 utilizes a single neural network to process an entire image and identify objects by generating a bounding box around each object, along with its corresponding confidence score, in real-time with very high accuracy. While implementing the YOLO model, the objects identified from the frames in the

Videos were appended to a CSV file containing the class of the object, its coordinates, width, and height. When evaluated on the COCO and Object365 datasets, the YOLOv5 can classify a total of 446 distinct objects in a frame.

The result difference before and after implementing the YOLOv5 model is that the model has successfully identified most of the objects visible in the frame in Fig. (**2b**), which enhances the Decision-making model. Conversely, in (Figs. **3a** and **3b**), where the false object has been detected, which is a painting of a human on the wall with a high confidence score, this affects the Decision-making model.

Fig. (2a). Before implementation of the YOLOv5 model.

Fig. (2b). After implementation of the YOLOv5 model.

Fig. (3a). Before implementation of the YOLOv5 model.

Fig. (3b). After implementation of the YOLOv5 model.

Computing the Distance between the Camera and Object using the Mono-Depth Estimation Model

Used an unsupervised Mono-Depth Estimation model, which takes input from a single frame and returns a depth map and a NumPy array. The NumPy array identifies the distance of a living or non-living being placed within a particular coordinate range. Depth estimation for a single image was achieved by reconstructing the Image with left-right consistency and training the network to create disparity maps using epipolar geometry restrictions. This approach helped generate a depth map of the environment, which was beneficial for the agent to make informed decisions. (Figs. **4a** and **4b**) show the use of the Mono-depth estimation model for object identification purposes.

Fig. (4a). Image used for implementation of the mono-depth estimation model.

Fig. (4b). After implementation of the mono-depth estimation model.

Decision-making Model

A Decision-Making Model (DMM) that would take five input parameters (Human Decision, YOLO Decision, Living or Non-Living Being, Height, and Width). Here, the decision-making model employed supervised learning models, including Logistic Regression, Decision Trees, Support Vector Machines, and k-Nearest Neighbors. The DMM employs a Decision Tree, which is a widely used method for categorization and prediction. A Decision Tree is a tree structure that resembles a flowchart, where an internal node represents a test of an attribute, each branch represents the test result, and each leaf node (terminal node) represents the class label.

The different formulae used for the algorithms mentioned above are mentioned below:

- Logistic Regression: It maps predicted values to probabilities using the sigmoid function given in equation 1.

$$E(T,X) = \sum_{\propto X}^{n} \quad P(c)E(c) \tag{1}$$

- Decision Tree: Entropy measures the randomness of the information being processed. The representation of the entropy of multiple attributes is given by equation 2.

$$f(x) = \frac{1}{1+e^{-x}} \tag{2}$$

where T denotes the current state, X denotes the selected attribute, and P denotes the probability of an event in a particular state.

Information gain is a statistical property that measures how successfully a specific attribute distinguishes training instances according to their intended categorization, as per equation 3.

$$Information\_Gain = Entropy\ (before) - \sum_{i=0}^{k} \quad Entropy\ (j,\ after) \tag{3}$$

where "before" refers to the dataset before the split, K refers to the number of subsets produced by the split, and (j, after) refers to the subset j after the split.

The Gini index is a cost function that is used to evaluate splits in a dataset, given in equation 4.

$$Gini = 1 - \sum_{i=1}^{c} \quad (Pi)^2 \tag{4}$$

Where p denotes the probability of an event occurring in a particular state.

Support Vector Machine: Prediction using kernels given in equation 5

$$w^T \Phi(x) = (\sum \alpha_n y_n \Phi(x_n))^T \Phi(x) => \sum \alpha_n y_n \Phi^T(x_n)\Phi(x) => \sum \alpha_n y_n k(x_n, x) \quad \textbf{(5)}$$

Anytime when asked to predict a test feature vector x, which is essentially $w^T\Phi(x)$ is mapped to a complex $\Phi(x)$.

Then, using the duals, modify it such that the prediction is wholly independent of the complex feature basis Φ. And it is further predicted using kernels.

As a result, the conclusion was that there was no need for a sophisticated basis to describe non-separable data adequately, and the kernel suffices.

K-nearest neighbors algorithm: Minkowski distance as per equation 6:

$$D(x,y) = \sqrt[p]{\sum_d |x_d - y_d|p} \quad \textbf{(6)}$$

Where x and y denote the points between which the distance is to be calculated, and p is a variable that can have a value ranging from zero to infinity.

CHALLENGES FACED

Processing Speed of the Object Detection Algorithm

Two-stage algorithms, such as R-CNN and Faster R-CNN, are relatively slow and can take up to a second per frame for object detection and classification. The optimum processing speed requirement should be as low as possible. Hence, we decided to go with the single-stage CNN-based YOLOv5 algorithm, which processes at a speed of 30 FPS. It identifies 365 (dataset: Object365) plus an additional 81 (dataset: COCO) object classes along with their attributes.

Accuracy of Depth Estimation Model

The first approach to calculating the distance between the camera and the object was based on area. The Area-based approach was based on the principle that the distance between the camera and the object is inversely proportional to the area covered by the object in the frame. This was a less accurate measure as it failed to give the exact distance between the two. Hence, shifted to stereo image input-based disparity map generation and depth map computation. The main challenge here was the requirement for two stereo frame inputs for processing. Since all was based on a single camera frame input, I decided to overlook this approach. Finally, settled on unsupervised single-frame Mono-Depth Estimation for depth map computation, which returns a NumPy array and a depth map.

Preparation of the Dataset

The Decision-making model utilizes a Decision Tree algorithm for prediction, requiring a dataset to predict the value, which in this case applies to both living and nonliving things. It is not available on the internet, so the dataset was created by combining the COCO and Object365 datasets. After doing so, it distinguished between living and non-living as it was merged.

Use of YOLOv5

Knowing that the YOLOv5 model was designed for processing images only, it was a challenge to convert the dashcam video into multiple frames and then pass them to the YOLOv5 model frame by frame.

Naming of Attributes

Moving forward in the process, the CSV file generated after image processing contained only data, not the names of the attributes. Therefore, it was necessary to manually identify the contents of each column and name them accordingly.

PERFORMANCE ANALYSIS

Evaluation and Comparison of Various Decision-making Models

Since no dataset was available, we generated one randomly by combining the Object365 and COCO datasets. To achieve a higher accuracy rate for the model, we multiplied the random dataset several times to create a larger dataset. The Evaluation of the results can be done by measuring the accuracy rate.

Here, various models, including Logistic Regression, Decision Trees, Support Vector Machines, Naive Bayes, and k-Nearest Neighbors algorithms, were used for the Decision-making model. From the results mentioned below, it is evident that the Decision Tree achieved the highest accuracy rate.

The accuracy rate of the Decision-making model is as follows:

- Logistic regression (52.6%)
- Decision Tree (57.3%)
- Support Vector Machine (50.3%)

- k-nearest neighbors algorithm (51%)
- Naive Bayes (48.6%)

The accuracy rate will vary due to the random dataset generated each time, as shown in Fig. (**5**).

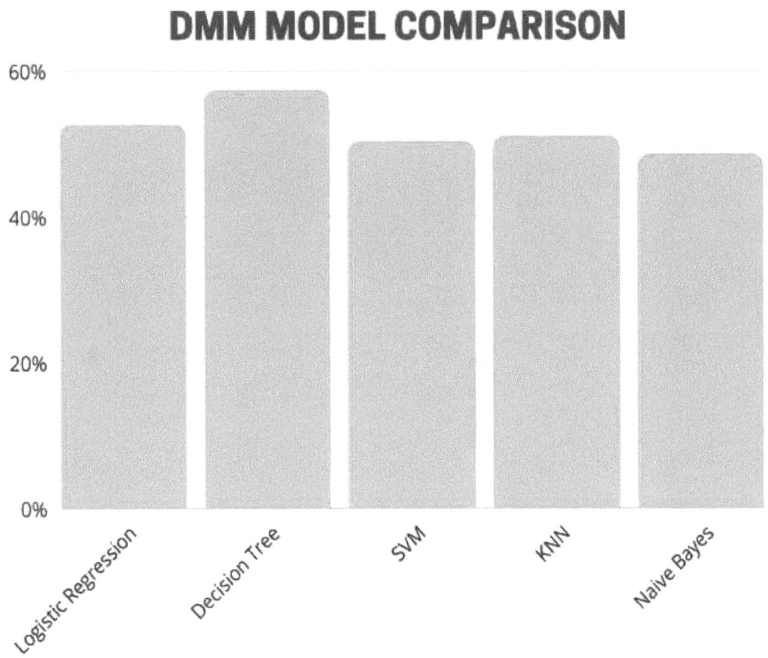

Fig. (5). Comparison of various models based on accuracy rate.

RESULTS

The execution of the Visual Uncertainty Resolver (VUR) Algorithm is successful, achieving a 57.3% accuracy rate compared to the Decision Tree. The prediction for the self-driving car was made by the Decision-making model, which considered both the decision from YOLOv5 and the human's decision. The supervised learning models are used, which impose certain constraints on the self-driving car.

CONCLUSION

In this paper, a proposal for conflict resolution in uncertain situations for self-driving cars is presented, based on the Visual Uncertainty Resolver (VUR) Algorithm. The Visual Uncertainty Resolver Algorithm comprises three phases: YOLOv5 for object detection, a Mono-Depth Estimation model for computing the distance between any object and the camera, a SHI (Speech-Human Interaction) model for human interaction with the self-driving car, and a Decision-making model. Implemented different models such as Logistic Regression, Decision Tree, Support Vector Machine, Naive Bayes, and k-nearest neighbors' algorithm for the Decision-making model. The results verify that the highest accuracy rate of 57.3% was achieved using the Decision Tree, and the uncertainty of the decision for the self-driving car was determined by the Decision-making model, which considered both the decision from the YOLOv5 model and the SHI model. Additionally, Reinforcement Learning can be used to enhance the accuracy and functionality of the algorithm.

Considering all aspects, it can be concluded that with the help of the decision-making model, the system will be able to make the best possible optimal decision to deal with uncertain situations. Through this paper, the proposed algorithm aims to increase the user's trust in autonomous vehicles and enhance their confidence in the system by creating an interactive environment between the car and the passenger.

The implementation of the Visual Uncertainty Resolver (VUR) algorithm in autonomous vehicles introduces several key implications for automotive industry managers, deployment strategists, and public safety regulators.

From an operational management perspective, integrating VUR into the autonomous driving software stack enables more reliable decision-making in ambiguous or unpredictable scenarios. This can enhance route safety and passenger confidence—both of which are crucial for the broader commercial adoption of self-driving technology. Fleet managers can leverage the improved interaction mechanisms between human passengers and the vehicle to enhance user experience and reduce incident response time.

For automotive engineering managers, the modular structure of the VUR—comprising YOLOv5 for object detection, Mono-Depth Estimation for spatial analysis, and the Speech-Human Interaction (SHI) model for real-time user feedback—provides a framework for systematically validating and iterating AI decision-making modules before deployment. The design supports hardware agnosticism and flexibility, which is critical when deploying solutions across different vehicle platforms.

In terms of strategic planning and policy alignment, the human-in-the-loop interaction modeled by SHI addresses concerns related to ethical and legal accountability in autonomous systems. Managers and regulatory planners can use these features to comply with emerging transportation safety standards and human oversight requirements (*e.g.*, ISO 26262, UNECE WP.29).

Finally, the decision-making performance results, while currently achieving modest accuracy (57.3% with Decision Tree), provide a scalable starting point for data-driven performance benchmarking and continuous improvement pipelines—allowing product managers and AI system evaluators to track, refine, and deploy AI decision logic in a controlled, safety-critical environment.

FUTURE WORK

In future work, some exciting options were discovered. But most important will be trying Reinforcement learning as the next objective.

REFERENCES

[1] I. Yaqoob, L.U. Khan, S.M.A. Kazmi, M. Imran, N. Guizani, and C.S. Hong, "Autonomous driving cars in smart cities: recent advances, requirements, and challenges", *IEEE Netw,* vol. 34, no. 1, pp. 174-181, 2020.
[http://dx.doi.org/10.1109/MNET.2019.1900120]

[2] W. Wang, W. Zhang, and D. Zhao, "Understanding V2V driving scenarios through traffic primitives", 2018 Online: http://arxiv.org/abs/1807.10422

[3] R. Girshick, J. Donahue, T. Darrell, and J. Malik, "Rich feature hierarchies for accurate object detection and semantic segmentation", in *Proc. IEEE Conf. Comput. Vis. Pattern Recognit.*, Jun. 2014, pp. 580–587.
[http://dx.doi.org/10.1109/CVPR.2014.81]

[4] R. Girshick, "Fast R-CNN", in *Proc. IEEE Int. Conf. Comput. Vis. (ICCV)*, Dec. 2015, pp. 1440–1448.
[http://dx.doi.org/10.1109/ICCV.2015.169]

[5] S. Ren, K. He, R. Girshick, and J. Sun, "Faster R-CNN: Towards real-time object detection with region proposal networks", *in Proc. Adv. Neural Inf. Process. Syst,* pp. 91-99, 2015.

[6] J. Dai, Y. Li, K. He, and J. Sun, "R-FCN: Object detection *via* region-based fully convolutional networks", *in Proc. Adv. Neural Inf. Process. Syst,* pp. 379-387, 2016.

[7] J. Redmon, S. Divvala, R. Girshick, and A. Farhadi, "You only look once: Unified, real-time object detection", in Proc. IEEE Conf. Comput. Vis. Pattern Recognit. (CVPR), Jun. 2016, pp. 779–788.
[http://dx.doi.org/10.1109/CVPR.2016.91]

[8] B. R. Vignesh, D. Sandhip Kumar, V. Gokul, and R. Priya, "Object detection YOLO-v4 based smart car system with an integrated virtual assistant", *J. Phys.: Conf. Ser.,,* vol. 1916, 2021.
[http://dx.doi.org/10.1088/1742-6596/1916/1/012047]

[9] J. Redmon, and A. Farhadi, "YOLO9000: Better, faster, stronger", 2017, arXiv:1612.08242. [Online]. Available from: https://arxiv.org/abs/1612.08242
[http://dx.doi.org/10.1109/CVPR.2017.690]

[10] J. Redmon, and A. Farhadi, "YOLOv3: An incremental improvement", 2018, arXiv:1804.02767. [Online]. Available from: http://arxiv.org/abs/1804.02767

[11] A. Bochkovskiy, C-Y. Wang, and H-Y.M. Liao, "YOLOv4: Optimal speed and accuracy of object detection", 2020, arXiv:2004.10934. [Online]. Available from: http://arxiv.org/abs/2004.10934

[12] W. Fang, L. Wang, and P. Ren, "Tinier-YOLO: A real-time object detection method for constrained environments", *IEEE Access,* vol. 8, pp. 1935-1944, 2020.
[http://dx.doi.org/10.1109/ACCESS.2019.2961959]

[13] S. Li, Y. Li, Y. Li, M. Li, and X. Xu, "YOLO-FIRI: Improved YOLOv5 for infrared image object detection", *IEEE Access,* vol. 9, pp. 141861-141875, 2021.

[http://dx.doi.org/10.1109/ACCESS.2021.3120870]

[14] M.Y. Raut, and S.S. Barve, "A semi-automated review classification system based on supervised machine learning", 2017 *1st International Conference on Intelligent Systems and Information Management (ICISIM)*, 2017, pp. 127-133. [http://dx.doi.org/10.1109/ICISIM.2017.8122162]

[15] T. Deruyttere, V. Milewski, and M.F. Moens, "Giving commands to a self-driving car: How to deal with uncertain situations?", *Eng. Appl. Artif. Intell,* vol. 103, p. 104257, 2021. [http://dx.doi.org/10.1016/j.engappai.2021.104257]

[16] D. Dingen, M. van't Veer, P. Houthuizen, E.H.J. Mestrom, E.H.H.M. Korsten, A.R.A. Bouwman, and J. van Wijk, "RegressionExplorer: Interactive Exploration of Logistic Regression Models with Subgroup Analysis", *IEEE Trans. Vis. Comput. Graph,* vol. 25, no. 1, pp. 246-255, 2019. [http://dx.doi.org/10.1109/TVCG.2018.2865043] [PMID: 30222573]

[17] A. Navada, A.N. Ansari, S. Patil, and B.A. Sonkamble, "Overview of use of decision tree algorithms in machine learning", 2011 *IEEE Control and System Graduate Research Colloquium*, 2011, pp. 37-42. [http://dx.doi.org/10.1109/ICSGRC.2011.5991826]

[18] Y. Yang, J. Li, and Y. Yang, "The research of the fast SVM classifier method", 2015 *12th International Computer Conference on Wavelet Active Media Technology and Information Processing (ICCWAMTIP)*, 2015, pp. 121-124. [http://dx.doi.org/10.1109/ICCWAMTIP.2015.7493959]

[19] S.S. Deulkar, and S.S. Barve, "Feature-based Fruit Quality Grading System using Support Vector Machine", 2018 *3rd IEEE International Conference on Recent Trends in Electronics, Information & Communication Technology (RTEICT)*, 2018, pp. 2367-2372. [http://dx.doi.org/10.1109/RTEICT42901.2018.9012384]

[20] F-J. Yang, "An Implementation of Naive Bayes Classifier", *2018 International Conference on Computational Science and Computational Intelligence (CSCI),* pp. 301-306, 2018. [http://dx.doi.org/10.1109/CSCI46756.2018.00065]

[21] P.D. Ganjewar, S. Barani, and S.J. Wagh, "Data reduction using incremental Naive Bayes Prediction (INBP) in WSN", *2015 International Conference on Information Processing (ICIP),* pp. 398-403, 2015. [http://dx.doi.org/10.1109/INFOP.2015.7489415]

[22] M. Cococcioni, F. Rossi, E. Ruffaldi, and S. Saponara, "Novel Arithmetics to Accelerate Machine Learning Classifiers in Autonomous Driving Applications", 2019 *26th IEEE International Conference on Electronics, Circuits and Systems (ICECS)*, 2019, pp. 779-782. [http://dx.doi.org/10.1109/ICECS46596.2019.8965031]

[23] Y. Shi, Y. Li, J. Fan, T. Wang, and T. Yin, "A novel network architecture of decision-making for self-driving vehicles based on long short-term memory and grasshopper optimization algorithm", *IEEE Access,* vol. 8, pp. 155429-155440, 2020. [http://dx.doi.org/10.1109/ACCESS.2020.3019048]

[24] Z. Cao, S. Xu, H. Peng, D. Yang, and R. Zidek, "Confidence-aware reinforcement learning for self-driving cars", *IEEE Trans. Intell. Transp. Syst.* in press

[25] U. Lee, S. Yoon, H. Shim, P. Vasseur, and C. Demonceaux, "Local path planning in a complex environment for self-driving car", *IEEE Trans. Control Syst. Technol,* vol. 15, 2014.

[26] K. Khade, V. Gadget, H. Patil, and S. Velankar, "Autonomous Electric Vehicle Using Ultrasonic Sensor Skirt Approach", 2018 *3rd International Conference for Convergence in Technology (I2CT)*, Pune, India, 2018, pp. 1-6. [http://dx.doi.org/10.1109/I2CT.2018.8529387]

[27] Y. Zhang, J. Wang, X. Wang, and J.M. Dolan, "Segmentation-based curb detection method for self-

driving via a 3D-LiDAR sensor", *IEEE Trans. Intell. Transp. Syst,* vol. 19, no. 12, pp. 3981-3991, 2018.
[http://dx.doi.org/10.1109/TITS.2018.2789462]

[28] A. K. Amuda, and A. B. Adeyemo, *Customers Churn Prediction in Financial Institution Using Artificial Neural Network,* 2019.

[29] E. Yurtsever, J. Lambert, A. Carballo, and K. Takeda, "A survey of autonomous driving: Common practices and emerging technologies", *IEEE Access,* vol. 8, pp. 58443-58469, 2020.
[http://dx.doi.org/10.1109/ACCESS.2020.2983149]

[30] I.S. Isa, M.S.A. Rosli, U.K. Yusof, M.I.F. Maruzuki, and S.N. Sulaiman, "Optimizing the Hyperparameter Tuning of YOLOv5 for Underwater Detection", *IEEE Access,* vol. 10, pp. 52818-52831, 2022.
[http://dx.doi.org/10.1109/ACCESS.2022.3174583]

[31] C. Godard, O. Mac Aodha, and G.J. Brostow, "Unsupervised Monocular Depth Estimation with Left-Right Consistency", 2017, arXiv:1609.03677v3. [Online].
[http://dx.doi.org/10.1109/CVPR.2017.699]

[32] Z. AsghariVarzaneh, M. Shanbehzadeh, and H. Kazemi-Arpanahi, "Prediction of successful aging using ensemble machine learning algorithms," *BMC Med. Inform. Decis. Mak*, 2022.
[http://dx.doi.org/10.1186/s12911-022-02001-6]

CHAPTER 14

Security and Privacy Preserving in Cloud Computing Using IoT

Vivek Talnikar[1], **Monika Dangore**[2], **Anita Mahajan**[3], **Vanita Kshirsagar**[4], **Yogesh Mali**[5,*] and **Vishal Borate**[6]

[1] *Department of Computer Engineering, Annasaheb Dange College of Engineering & Technology, Ashta, India*

[2] *Department of Computer Engineering, Marathwada Mitramandal's Institute of Technology, Pune, India*

[3] *Department of Computer Engineering, Ajeenkya D. Y. Patil School of Engineering, Pune, India*

[4] *Department of Computer Engineering, Dr. D. Y. Patil Institute of Technology, Pune, India*

[5] *Department of Computer Engineering, G.H Raisoni College of Engineering and Management, Pune, India*

[6] *Department of Computer Engineering, Dr. D. Y. Patil Colleges of Engineering & Innovation, Talegaon, Pune, India*

Abstract: The Web of Clinical Things (WCT) coordinates the medical care industry with the Web of Things (WoT) environment. It enables the creation, collection, transmission, and analysis of clinical data through IoT integration. These IoT networks comprise various medical services, IT frameworks, clinical sensors, and management software. The IoMT enhances the medical care framework by creating a seamless, open, integrated, and reliable system. Nonetheless, ensuring secure verification in IoMT is challenging due to the diverse communication environment of various IoMT devices. Although various examinations have investigated potential IoMT device authentication techniques, more work is required, especially in client validation, to develop long-term IoMT solutions. Secret key administration remains one of the significant challenges in this specific circumstance. This paper presents an IoMT-related electronic passwordless verification strategy that is quick, powerful, and secure. To achieve cross-stage similarity, it integrates a version of FIDO2/WebAuthn, one of the latest standards for passwordless authentication. This streamlines the process of obtaining and further developing client accreditations while maintaining compliance with regulations. The paper also assesses the delays in IoMT gadget verification and enrollment processes. Results and reproductions demonstrate how the proposed framework can achieve rapid validation on cloud servers with minimal enrollment and approval processes, regardless of device types.

* **Corresponding author Yogesh Mali:** Department of Computer Engineering, G.H Raisoni College of Engineering and Management, Pune, India; E-mail: yogesh.mali@raisoni.net

Manoj Kumar, Sachin Kumar Gupta, Navnath Kale, Pramod Ganjewar & Sandeep Pande (Eds.)

Keywords: Authentication, DAA algorithm, ECC, IoMT, Online login.

INTRODUCTION

The IoMT has significantly transformed the medical services landscape by utilizing clinical hardware connected to the Internet to enable remote connections between patients and healthcare providers [1]. IoMT gadgets collect clinical data from patients and provide it to healthcare experts for review to identify diseases earlier. In IoMT, patient information security is of the utmost concern. The principal level of safety in IoMT is element validation [2]. The substance might be the client, an IoMT device, any smart device, and so on. Be that as it may, IoMT verification is a challenging task due to the variety of devices and limited resource availability. The most widely used method of gadget validation currently is password verification. This methodology, however, could have a couple of imperfections. Due to the widespread use of passwords in advanced stages, phishing attempts sometimes involve mimicking legitimate sites [3]. To ensure client security and protection, it is essential to reduce dependence on secret phrase-based authentication for access to online services [4]. By moving confirmation to the gadget instead of exchanging accreditations through the Web, the password-less validation approach modifies the fundamental security design.

The Coronavirus pandemic has indeed underscored the importance of intelligent medical care benefits that provide remote anticipation, diagnosis, and therapy [5]. The concept of "brilliant medical care" encompasses something beyond mere mechanical promotion and advancements in the medical services industry. Clients often use the same passwords across multiple sites, making them vulnerable to man-in-the-middle attacks and easy for attackers to compromise.

Secret key passages through human collaboration and various secret phrase recollections become tedious and costly assignments [6]. Putting away passwords in the data set does not guarantee the security of clients' information. Clients are seeking universal authentication to streamline their daily routines while maintaining the highest level of safety and organizational protection [7].

Fig. (**1**) illustrates the time it takes to break a password based on its strength [8]. On average, people spend just over 15 minutes per week entering and resetting their passwords. In contrast to a while back, 74% of respondents reported being more concerned about the security and protection of their information. Secret word-based gadgets are especially vulnerable to phishing attacks, where attackers trick users into revealing their credentials, thereby compromising security. Malware, keyloggers, or other malicious software can steal passwords from clients' devices, compromising the entire IoMT ecosystem. Assailants can also take advantage of human weaknesses, persuading victims to disclose passwords or other sensitive information. A few IoT and clinical gadgets have limited input options, making it challenging to implement our strategies effectively. In the event of a security breach, it may require significant investment to identify unauthorized access, allowing attackers to cause harm or access sensitive data before being detected.

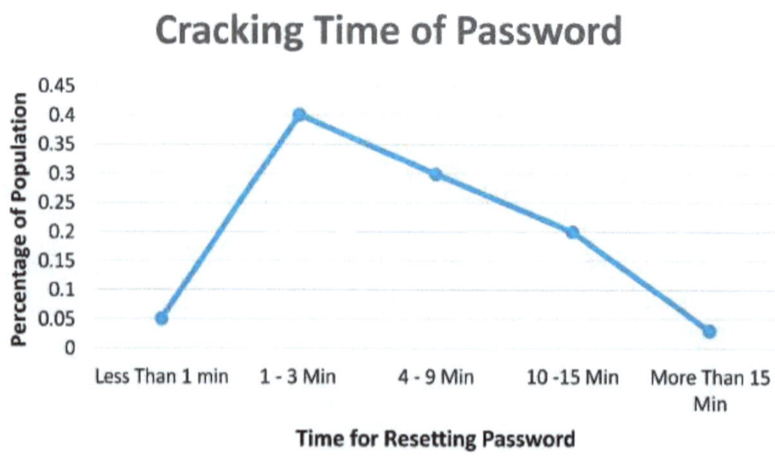

Fig. (1). Breaking season of passwords.

In this paper, we propose a passwordless, security-saving verification strategy that involves a single passkey to authenticate various devices in an IoMT environment. To facilitate cross-stage similarity, we rely on the FIDO2 standard, which utilizes public key cryptography. Gadgets that are enlisted and verified with the FIDO2/WebAuthn convention use passkeys for this cycle. The authenticator checks QR codes to produce passkeys, which are then used to make marks. The FIDO2 standard is a web-based authentication framework that enables users to authenticate themselves to servers using an electronic device known as an authenticator.

Furthermore, we inspected the time expected for enrollment and confirmation utilizing FIDO2/WebAuthn and passkeys, which eliminate password-based verification and reduce the need for human interaction, even during the initial login across different platforms.

The remainder of the paper is organized as follows: Segment 2 covers related work. Segment 3 examines the issue definition. In Segment 4, we present the proposed technique, which retains itemized data for the FIDO2/WebAuthn standard and the ECDAA algorithm. At long last, in Segment 6, we examine the outcomes, followed by the conclusion in Segment 7.

This paper proposes a novel passwordless and privacy-preserving authentication system for the Internet of Medical Things (IoMT) using the FIDO2/WebAuthn protocol and QR code–based passkey mechanisms. The system addresses significant challenges in IoMT authentication—such as credential theft, phishing, and cross-platform interoperability—by enabling secure, user-friendly verification without relying on traditional passwords. The key innovation lies in allowing users to authenticate multiple devices using a single passkey, managed securely through a trusted platform module and delivered *via* QR codes. The authentication workflow integrates Elliptic Curve Cryptography–based Direct Anonymous Attestation (ECC-DAA) to further protect identity privacy during device registration and login. Performance evaluation across various IoMT devices shows minimal authentication delays, demonstrating practical feasibility. This architecture enhances security, reduces user burden, and significantly improves trust in cloud-enabled medical IoT systems.

RELATED WORK

The previous writing has recommended various IoT validation plans; nonetheless, there aren't many passwordless answers to be found. This segment covers the different strategies employed for validating and approving IoT devices.

The trap strategy combined with a fog computing facility is a method for securing patients' medical big data (MBD) in the healthcare cloud, as described in [9]. It acts as a secondary layer, storing decoy MBDs (DMBDs) to mislead attackers into thinking they have accessed real MBDs (OMBDs). Reference [10] proposes a method for sharing clinical records in the cloud that safeguards patient protection. It parcels the clinical dataset in light of the qualities of clinical records, addressing the various aspects of clinical information with different security concerns.

In a paper [11], a framework confirmation convention is recommended that approves the organization's gadgets without storing information in memory. Truly Unclonable Capabilities (PUFs) are used to assign a unique identity to every device, providing secure validation when data is sent to the server. Another paper [12] presents a gadget confirmation convention for an IoMT gadget network that enhances system security and strengthens the network against various attacks. This convention can be utilized regardless of the specialized strategy between the end device and the server, as no data about the device is stored on the server, thereby eliminating the need for the framework.

RFID innovation, which is energy-efficient, compact, and increasingly complex, now plays a key role in providing the actual layer to IoT in personalized healthcare within intelligent environments. Another paper [13] investigates the high-level utilization of RFID in body-driven frameworks for gathering information, such as temperature, humidity, and various gases, from the client's living environment. The secure ECC-based validation, approval, and key administration for remote sensor networks in 5G-coordinated IoMT [14] offers a robust and effective system. A Paper [15] examines a zero-information approach to creating one-time schemes that safely recover the novel identifier and the Equipment Media Access Control key, enhancing device authentication. However, as One-Time Keys (OTKs) can be reused and stored on user devices, energy efficiency research is noted for its strong data recovery abilities. Still, it falls short of fully addressing security issues.

An alternative undertaking recommended in [16] proposes involving the Application as a Help and Two-Element Confirmation to eliminate the complexity of qualification checks in a server-based framework. For impersonation episodes, the framework shows its solidarity [17]. This biometric authentication-driven approach restricts access to several web-based services. Online-based information capacity is vulnerable to interruptions and attacks.

The question of well-being is examined in a study [18], which proposes a framework for multifaceted confirmation and numerous login controls to check clients' characters. Strategies for cryptography are employed to prevent information leaks, and techniques for encoding are used to avoid data leaks. To recognize noxious clients, recommended approaches and systems have exhibited critical discovery rates and misdirecting ready rates [19].

Another study in [20] presented late PUF-based gadget validation and permitted move frameworks with multiple layers of confirmation to secure the server safely. In a multifaceted, verifier-driven FIDO application structure, the client's device functions as the authenticator. This framework is utilized to establish secure connections between IoT devices and other systems, ensuring reliable communication [21].

While various approaches, such as PUFs, biometric authentication, RFID systems, and one-time keys, have contributed significantly to securing IoMT environments, they each suffer from limitations, including hardware dependency, high computational cost, privacy risks, or a lack of cross-platform compatibility. In contrast, the proposed integrated IoT solution leverages the FIDO2/WebAuthn protocol combined with ECC-DAA and QR code–based passkeys, offering a lightweight, scalable, and platform-independent mechanism. This approach not only eliminates the risk of credential reuse and phishing attacks but also ensures multi-device operability without compromising user privacy—an aspect where many traditional schemes fall short. Furthermore, our solution minimizes latency and supports faster device enrollment and authentication, as demonstrated in the performance evaluation. This positions our method as a more practical and forward-compatible alternative for secure medical IoT ecosystems.

PROBLEM STATEMENT

IoMT gadgets can connect to the cloud through any PC or device in an open wireless network. Notwithstanding, while dealing with delicate clinical information in the IoMT setting, a few security concerns emerge, including the following:

To start with, if malevolent cyberattacks manage to commandeer clinical sensors connected to an individual's body, this could result in erroneous data collection and possibly jeopardize the patient's well-being. Second, unsafe hacks might uncover private clinical and patient data. Third, IoMT gadgets frequently rely on low-power clinical sensors worn on the body; however, the convention being used may be too complicated for everyday use or continuous support due to the need for constant monitoring.

A robust and direct passwordless verification framework for IoMT devices is crucial to prevent information breaches and man-in-the-middle attacks, ensuring secure, cross-platform device authentication.

WORKING MODULE

This segment covers the utilization of distributed computing and FIDO2 to authenticate IoMT devices while maintaining their security, as detailed in [22]. FIDO2 provides phishing-safe verification elements for Web of Clinical Things (IoMT) devices, making them more widely available. Utilizing the JavaScript Programming interface, which permits sites to associate with authenticators and perform cryptography with public key declarations, Fig. (**2**) shows how validation gadgets can interface with clients.

The proposed framework utilizes cloud-based innovation for multi-stage, secure IoMT validation, employing Multi-Factor Authentication (MFA) or passkeys. By using passkeys, IoMT gadgets situated at the edge layer can be validated without requiring a username or password. Passkeys resolve the cross-stage interoperability issue while also supporting multi-device management.

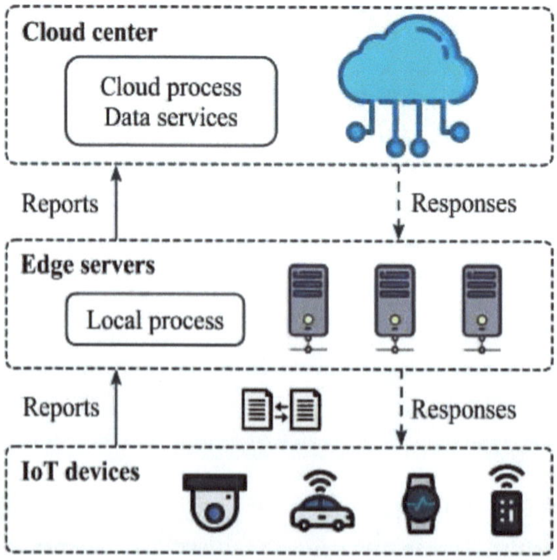

Fig. (2). The security protecting the verification of IoT utilizing distributed computing.

The technique comprises four parts: (a) a Confided in Outsider (TTP), (b) a WebAuthn structure, (c) an Android telephone, and (d) a fast reaction (QR) code. To produce passkeys for authenticators (for example, IoMT gadgets like smartwatches, glucose monitors, and Android phones), the operating system (Windows 11) is integrated with the WebAuthn Programming Interface and a web crawler supported by FIDO that generates QR codes. Android phones are considered versatile platforms for validating intelligent IoT devices.

A camera-based authenticator scans a short QR code to establish login credentials for device verification. These gadgets store a set of values known as a public-private key pair, which is specific to a particular client, site, or security supplier. During the sign-up process, the client supplies the site with their public key. Each time the client attempts to sign in, the device provides proof of ownership, confirmed by the client's unique key. Simultaneously, the Application affirms that it is utilizing the public key supplied during the join process, demonstrating that the client actually owns the corresponding private key.

A client's gadget or framework can communicate with an authenticator using the Client-to-Authenticator Protocol 1 (CTAP1) [23]. This considers the utilization of both interior and external authenticators, such as those integrated into computers or handheld devices, for PC applications and web services that utilize the Web Authentication (WebAuthn) standard established by the W3C.

IoMT gadgets can communicate with other devices *via* Bluetooth (BLE) without requiring certification on each site they visit. While validating on a web-based platform or with a trusted third-party where the verification tool has been approved, a WebAuthn login is used. The associated gadget selects to sign in using credentials, such as a freely available key [24]. The site page requires several keys to test the verifier, and the client agrees to the use of the key, either orally or through an electronic method. The validation interaction confirms the site's URL. If the URL matches the encoded key pair, the authenticator responds by creating a signature, which is confirmed using the confidential key. The site then checks the computerized signature using the publicly accessible key assigned to the client and the specialist organization during enrollment.

If both the reaction and the mark are substantial, the individual is permitted to sign in. For authenticator approval, the recently referenced Elliptic Curve Digital Signature Algorithm (ECDSA) calculation [25] is applied. The proposed arrangement uses a protected passkey conveyed through a QR code to upgrade security. The following segment frames the direct course of the proposed arrangement [26].

WORKING PROCESS OF THE PROPOSED ALGORITHM

We have adopted the FIDO2-QRCode confirmation convention, which utilizes passkeys to provide multi-factor authentication credentials generated by A Trusted Platform Module (TPM). In light of our assessment of the most recent FIDO standard, FIDO2/WebAuthn, this approach upgrades gadget security [27].

The proposed protection safeguarding verification of IoT utilizing a distributed computing component displayed in Fig. (**3**) contains the following advances:

- *Di* begins the enlistment cycle for a client *QR* authenticator present in the cloud. A client initiates the verification interaction by interfacing their record to the application supplier (web Programming interface on the door, similar to any PC or server), which is also known as a trusted third party.
- In response to a solicitation from the client, an irregular token is made as a code. It will only become open after one of the security endorsements for the cell phone or tablet, such as an individual ID number, fingerprint, or face recognition, has been set up. The program engineer could offer a FIDO login measure that portrays the characteristics expected to validate the feature.
- After the Passage application supplier has confirmed the security certifications of (an IoMT gadget), a nonce, or the acknowledged declaration, which has an end, is also remembered. To provide multi-device qualifications, it is stored in the cell phone as Passkeys. We assume that the confidential stage in the cell phone and entryway is in effect.

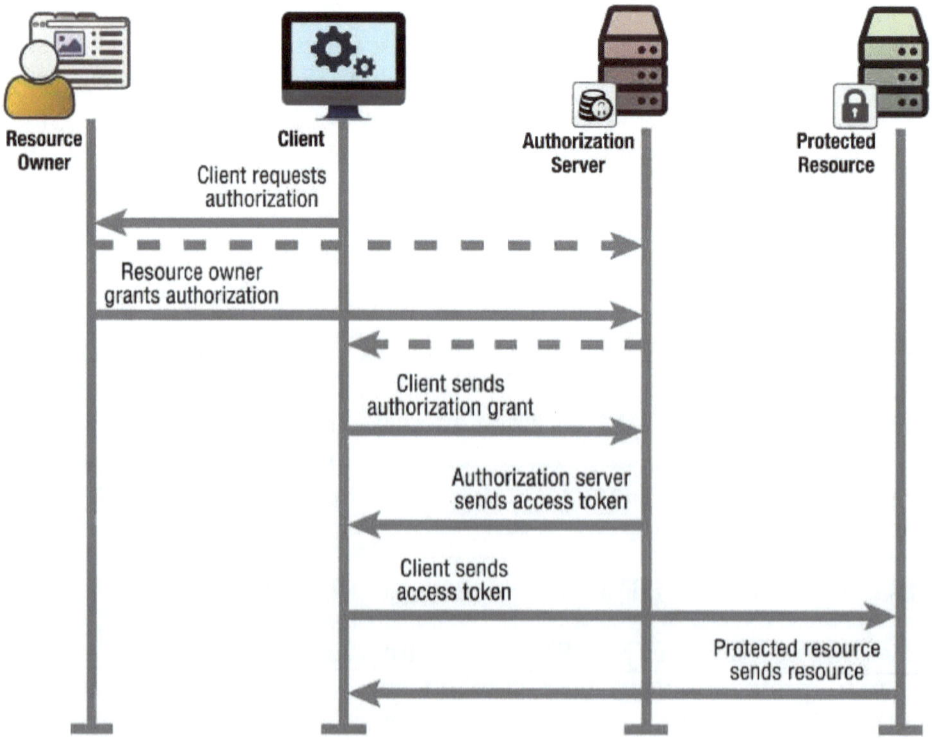

Fig. (3). Protection saving secret wordless validation.

In this way, after three phases, the enlistment technique is done.

- After enrollment, Passkeys are kept on the client's device as a secret key instead of on a cloud server [28].
- The sign-in process is then begun, which likewise sends a confirmation solicitation to the user, who then advances it to the validation server. The verification server approves the answer.
- After the confirmation reaction has been given, a message affirming verification is sent to the clients' versatile devices [29].

Mathematical Innovation and Cryptographic Formulation

The security of the proposed password-less authentication system is based on Elliptic Curve Cryptography (ECC) and Direct Anonymous Attestation (DAA). The mathematical novelty lies in the use of ECDAA to ensure both authentication and user anonymity.

Let the elliptic curve over a finite field be defined by:

$Y^2 = x^3 + ax + b \bmod p$

Where p is a prime, and a, b ϵ Zp, define the curve.

Each IoMT device generates a private key ddd and computes its public key:

$Q=d{\bullet}G$

where G is the base point on the curve.

For ECDAA-based anonymous signatures:

A signature $\sigma = (R, s)$ is generated such that:

$R=k{\bullet}G$, $s=k+h{\bullet}d \bmod n$

where k is a random nonce, and h is the hash of the message and public key.

This scheme is combined with QR-code–based key distribution, enabling passkeys to be transmitted securely without credential reuse. This hybrid model of ECDAA and WebAuthn overcomes platform dependence and supports cross-device federated authentication—a core novelty of the system.

RESULT AND DISCUSSION

In this segment, we break down the consequences of the proposed protection saving confirmation for IoMT inside a distributed computing climate [30].

Execution Assessment

We researched the care and management of four distinct IoMT devices for enrollment and confirmation on an internet-based service or Trusted Third Party (TTP), integrated with a FIDO server, to assess the practicality of our proposed approach. Every gadget was subjected to different tests, and the typical results were still up in the air and being surveyed. Passkeys work on the check cycle, making confirmation quicker and less dependent on client communication [31].

Fig. (**4**) outlines the enrollment time recorded for the four IoMT devices, each with different specifications. These IoMT gadgets are used as authenticators, and the time consumed during enrollment varies depending on the gadget and its attributes [32]. The enrollment cycle is directed on the cloud server, and it is evident that virtually all devices require some investment to enroll, with only minor variations. The most extreme time taken for enrollment by an IoMT gadget is 576 milliseconds, which occurs during the initial enrollment when the gadget uses its passkey [33].

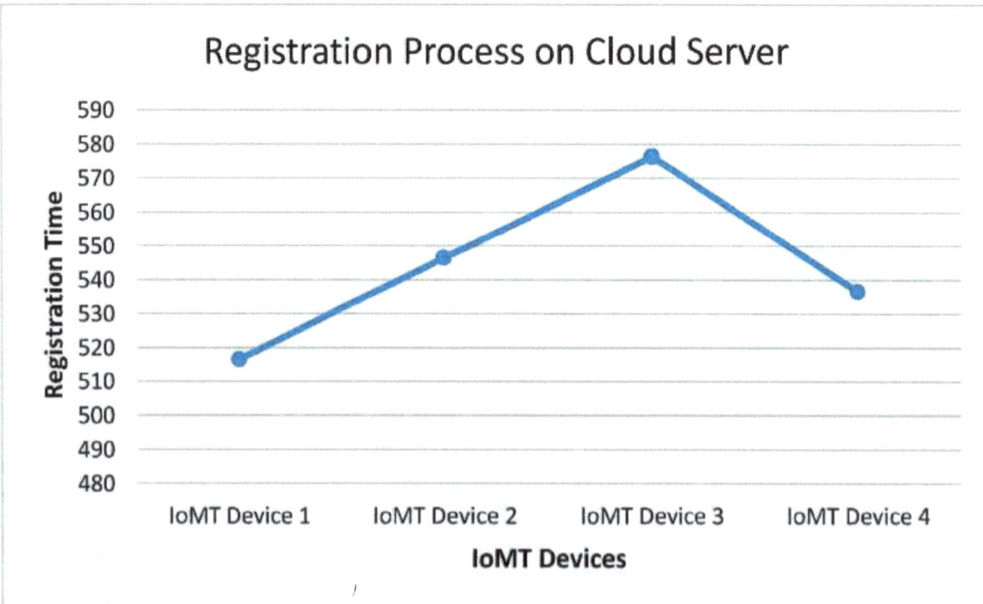

Fig. (4). Enlistment interaction on cloud server.

To avoid the need to enroll each gadget with a client account multiple times, multi-gadget validation continues to be used with passkeys [34]. In contrast to other ExtraF Models, multi-stage confirmation with adaptability and similarity is possible using passkeys. Cryptographic keys play a crucial role in preventing replay attacks, where attackers attempt to reuse captured authentication information [35]—the one—of—a—kind confidential key forestalls such attempts. The combination of FIDO2's cryptographic keys and biometric factors in smartwatch authentication provides a robust security system. This reconciliation of solid cryptographic principles and exceptional biometric features reinforces the validation process, ensuring that only authorized clients and devices can access sensitive information and services on the smartwatch [36].

Fig. (**5**) outlines the verification delay for each IoMT device with the trusted third party (TTP) following the enrollment cycle for each of the four IoMT devices. It is observed that the time taken for confirmation is, for the most part, not exactly the time expected for enrollment. In the Direct Anonymous Attestation (DAA) conspiracy, the public key is coordinated, and only the certified client is confirmed by the cycle. None of the gadgets takes more than 538 milliseconds to complete the server-side validation. The validation time for every gadget is also impacted by the underlying design or details of the gadgets, resulting in variations in verification times across different gadgets.

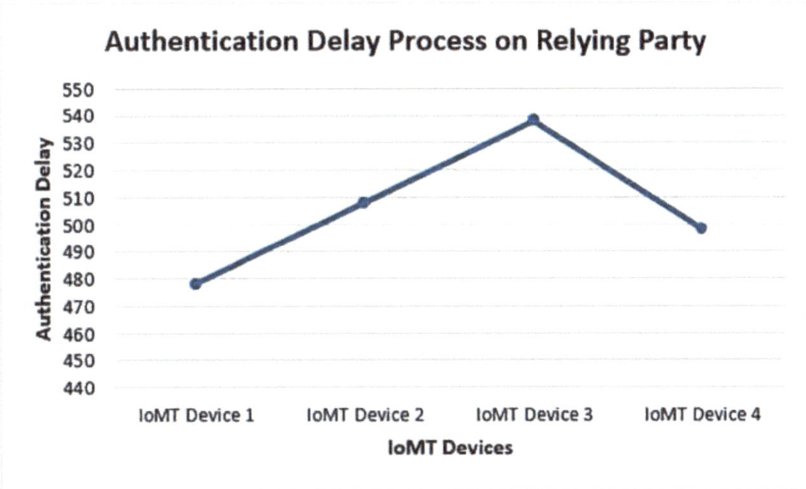

Fig. (5). Verification cycle on the depending party.

Performance Analysis with Multidimensional Visualization

To better analyze the scalability and security efficiency of the proposed scheme, the following multidimensional results are provided:

Device-wise Authentication vs. Enrollment Time

A comparative bar chart (Fig. **6**) illustrates the performance of different IoMT devices during enrollment and authentication. Despite hardware differences, all devices show authentication times under 540 ms.

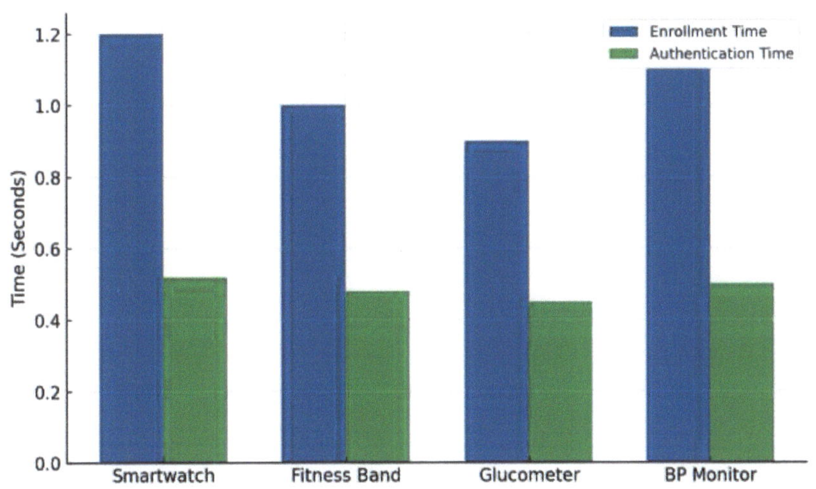

Fig. (6). Enrollment *vs* authentication time across IoMT devices.

Security Efficiency vs. Credential Type

Fig. (7) presents a grouped bar chart comparing password-based and passwordless (FIDO2) methods for average latency, security breach rate (simulated), and user interaction steps. FIDO2 significantly reduces latency and eliminates the risks associated with credential reuse.

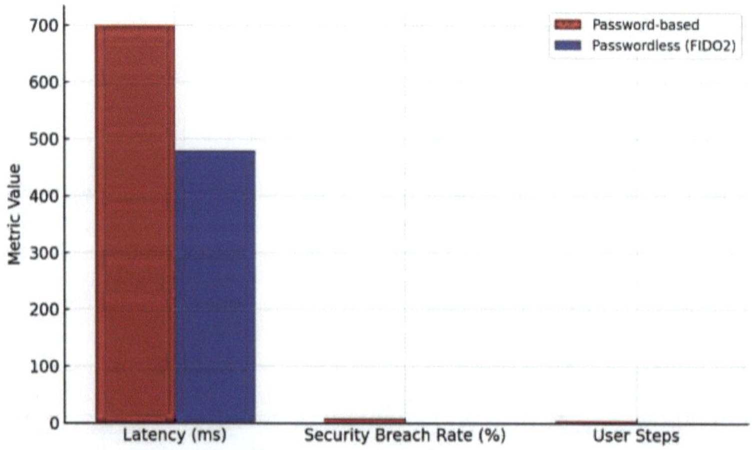

Fig. (7). Password *vs*. passwordless authentication metrics.

2D Visualization of Enrollment and Verification Metrics

Figure Z visualizes the enrollment time and verification time across devices using a 2D scatter plot, allowing for the observation of proportional relationships and hardware sensitivity.

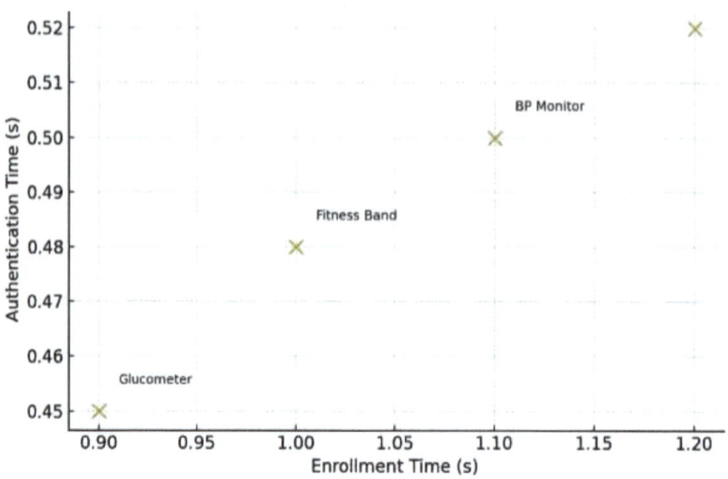

Fig. (8). 2D view of enrollment *vs* authentication times.

CONCLUSION

The improvement of a vigorous IoMT-based framework to safeguard the secrecy of basic and delicate patient information has become progressively useful, particularly with the new ascent and widespread reception of IoMT, especially during the Coronavirus pandemic. It has been observed that most IoMT safety efforts are ineffective against various threats, including quantum attacks. In this way, to safeguard clients' information and personalities, the verification framework should be reinforced. In this review, we investigated the FIDO2 convention-based passwordless validation arrangement, offering cross-platform functionality. The authenticator (an Android phone) generated QR codes to create passkeys that enable multi-device authentication features.

Different IoMT devices were enrolled and verified on the FIDO Server to assess the performance of the FIDO2 enrollment and verification processes. Our work likewise covered the Elliptic-Curve Cryptography-Direct Unknown Confirmation (ECC-DAA) approach, which portrays a security component to verify different IoMT gadgets in a cloud environment.

The Direct Unknown Verification approach, which also maintains the client's sent message and ID with the TTP, ensures the client's privacy. Contrasted with competing conventions, FIDO2/WebAuthn stands out due to its fast enrollment and verification processes, even with low client involvement and standard computing resources.

The proposed FIDO2/WebAuthn-based passwordless authentication framework holds significant implications for managers and decision-makers in the domains of healthcare IT and cloud security. Reducing reliance on traditional password-based systems lowers the administrative overhead associated with password resets, phishing mitigation, and user credential management. The use of passkeys across multiple IoMT devices enhances operational efficiency and minimizes downtime in clinical settings. This approach also supports cross-platform interoperability, allowing seamless integration of new devices without repeated credential provisioning. Moreover, the robust privacy-preserving cryptographic mechanisms help ensure compliance with healthcare data protection regulations such as HIPAA or GDPR. Collectively, these outcomes enable healthcare managers to make informed decisions regarding technology deployment, cybersecurity investment, and IT workforce training, ultimately improving patient safety, system usability, and trust in connected medical systems.

Future upgrades will include adding extra gadgets as authenticators to create various keys for FIDO2 multi-stage validation. Furthermore, we intend to develop an assessment framework to highlight the FIDO2 standard's simplicity and identify any security vulnerabilities.

REFERENCES

[1] P.B. More, A.N. Jadhav, I. Khatik, S. Singh, V.K. Borate, and Y.K. Mali, "Sign Language Recognition Using Hand Gestures", In: *2024 3rd International Conference for Advancement in Technology (ICONAT)* GOA, India, 2024, pp. 1-5. [http://dx.doi.org/10.1109/ICONAT61936.2024.10774685]

[2] Y. Mali, M.E. Pawar, A. More, S. Shinde, V. Borate, and R. Shirbhate, "Improved Pin Entry Method to Prevent Shoulder Surfing Attacks", In: *2023 14th International Conference on Computing Communication and Networking Technologies (ICCCNT)* Delhi, India, 2023, pp. 1-6. [http://dx.doi.org/10.1109/ICCCNT56998.2023.10306875]

[3] Y.K. Mali, and A. Mohanpurkar, "Advanced pin entry method by resisting shoulder surfing attacks", *2015 International Conference on Information Processing (ICIP),* pp. 37-42, 2015.Pune, India [http://dx.doi.org/10.1109/INFOP.2015.7489347]

[4] S.A. Nalawade, R. Pattnaik, S. Kadam, P.P. Lodha, Y.K. Mali, and V.K. Borate, "Smart Contract System with Blockchain Capability for Improving Supply Chain Management", In: *2024 3rd International Conference for Advancement in Technology (ICONAT)* GOA, India, 2024, pp. 1-7. [http://dx.doi.org/10.1109/ICONAT61936.2024.10774955]

[5] S.P. Patil, S.Y. Zurange, A.A. Shinde, M.M. Jadhav, Y.K. Mali, and V. Borate, "Upgrading Energy Productivity in Urban City Through Neural Support Vector Machine Learning for Smart Grids", In: *2024 15th International Conference on Computing Communication and Networking Technologies (ICCCNT)* Kamand, India, 2024, pp. 1-5. [http://dx.doi.org/10.1109/ICCCNT61001.2024.10724069]

[6] S. Modi, M. Modi, V. Alone, A. Mohite, V.K. Borate, and Y.K. Mali, "Smart shopping trolley Using Arduino UNO", In: *2024 15th International Conference on Computing Communication and Networking Technologies (ICCCNT)* Kamand, India, 2024, pp. 1-6. [http://dx.doi.org/10.1109/ICCCNT61001.2024.10725524]

[7] U. Mehta, S. Chougule, R. Mulla, V. Alone, V.K. Borate, and Y.K. Mali, "Instant Messenger Forensic System", In: *2024 15th International Conference on Computing Communication and Networking Technologies (ICCCNT)* Kamand, India, 2024, pp. 1-6. [http://dx.doi.org/10.1109/ICCCNT61001.2024.10724367]

[8] P. Shimpi, B. Balinge, T. Golait, S. Parthasarathi, C.J. Arunima, and Y. Mali, "Job Crafter - The One-Stop Placement Portal", In: *2024 15th International Conference on Computing Communication and Networking Technologies (ICCCNT)* Kamand, India, 2024, pp. 1-8. [http://dx.doi.org/10.1109/ICCCNT61001.2024.10725010]

[9] V. Ingale, B. Wankar, K. Jadhav, T. Adedoja, V.K. Borate, and Y.K. Mali, "AI-powered solutions and technological integration are revolutionizing healthcare for easily accessible and efficient medical care", In: *2024 15th International Conference on Computing Communication and Networking Technologies (ICCCNT)* Kamand, India, 2024, pp. 1-6. [http://dx.doi.org/10.1109/ICCCNT61001.2024.10725646]

[10] U. Mulani, V. Nandgaonkar, R. Mulla, S. Sonavane, V.K. Borate, and Y.K. Mali, "Smart Contract System with Blockchain Capability for Improved Supply Chain Management Traceability and Transparency", In: *2024 15th International Conference on Computing Communication and Networking Technologies (ICCCNT)* Kamand, India, 2024, pp. 1-7. [http://dx.doi.org/10.1109/ICCCNT61001.2024.10723871]

[11] S. Sonawane, U. Mulani, D.S. Gaikwad, A. Gaur, V.K. Borate, and Y.K. Mali, "Blockchain and Web3.0 based NFT Marketplace", In: *2024 15th International Conference on Computing Communication and Networking Technologies (ICCCNT)* Kamand, India, 2024, pp. 1-6.

[http://dx.doi.org/10.1109/ICCCNT61001.2024.10724420]

[12] P. Mandale, S. Modi, M.M. Jadhav, S.S. Khawate, V.K. Borate, and Y.K. Mali, "Investigation of different techniques on digital actual frameworks toward distributed denial of services attack", In: *2024 15th International Conference on Computing Communication and Networking Technologies (ICCCNT)* Kamand, India, 2024, pp. 1-6. [http://dx.doi.org/10.1109/ICCCNT61001.2024.10725776]

[13] D. Sengupta, S.A. Nalawade, L. Sharma, M.S.J. Kakade, V.K. Borate, and Y.K. Mali, "Enhancing file security using hybrid cryptography", In: *2024 15th International Conference on Computing Communication and Networking Technologies (ICCCNT)* Kamand, India, 2024, pp. 1-8. [http://dx.doi.org/10.1109/ICCCNT61001.2024.10724120]

[14] A. More, S. Khane, D. Jadhav, H. Sahoo, and Y.K. Mali, "Auto-shield: IoT-based OBD application for car health monitoring", In: *2024 15th International Conference on Computing Communication and Networking Technologies (ICCCNT)* Kamand, India, 2024, pp. 1-10. [http://dx.doi.org/10.1109/ICCCNT61001.2024.10726186]

[15] U.H. Wanaskar, M. Dangore, D. Raut, R. Shirbhate, V.K. Borate, and Y.K. Mali, "A method for re-identifying subjects in video surveillance using deep neural network fusion", In: *2024 15th International Conference on Computing Communication and Networking Technologies (ICCCNT)* Kamand, India, 2024, pp. 1-4. [http://dx.doi.org/10.1109/ICCCNT61001.2024.10726255]

[16] A. More, O.L. Ramishte, S.K. Shaikh, S. Shinde, and Y.K. Mali, "Chain-checkmate: Chess game using blockchain", In: *2024 15th International Conference on Computing Communication and Networking Technologies (ICCCNT)* Kamand, India, 2024, pp. 1-7. [http://dx.doi.org/10.1109/ICCCNT61001.2024.10725572]

[17] J.D. Palkar, C.H. Jain, K.P. Kashinath, A.O. Vaidya, V.K. Borate, and Y.K. Mali, "Machine learning approach for human brain counselling", In: *2024 15th International Conference on Computing Communication and Networking Technologies (ICCCNT)* Kamand, India, 2024, pp. 1-8. [http://dx.doi.org/10.1109/ICCCNT61001.2024.10723852]

[18] M. Dangore, S. Modi, S. Nalawade, U. Mehta, V.K. Borate, and Y.K. Mali, "Revolutionizing sport education with AI", In: *2024 15th International Conference on Computing Communication and Networking Technologies (ICCCNT)* Kamand, India, 2024, pp. 1-8. [http://dx.doi.org/10.1109/ICCCNT61001.2024.10724009]

[19] M. Dangore, D. Bhaturkar, K.M. Bhale, H.M. Jadhav, V.K. Borate, and Y.K. Mali, "Applying random forest for iot systems in industrial environments", In: *2024 15th International Conference on Computing Communication and Networking Technologies (ICCCNT)* Kamand, India, 2024, pp. 1-7. [http://dx.doi.org/10.1109/ICCCNT61001.2024.10725751]

[20] A. More, S.R. Shinde, P.M. Patil, D.S. Kane, Y.K. Mali, and V.K. Borate, "Advancements in early detection of lung cancer using YOLOv7", In: *2024 5th International Conference on Smart Electronics and Communication (ICOSEC)* Trichy, India, 2024, pp. 1739-1746. [http://dx.doi.org/10.1109/ICOSEC61587.2024.10722534]

[21] A.O. Vaidya, M. Dangore, V.K. Borate, N. Raut, Y.K. Mali, and A. Chaudhari, "Deep Fake Detection for Preventing Audio and Video Frauds Using Advanced Deep Learning Techniques", In: *2024 IEEE Recent Advances in Intelligent Computational Systems* RAICS: Kothamangalam, Kerala, India, 2024, pp. 1-6. [http://dx.doi.org/10.1109/RAICS61201.2024.10689785]

[22] S. Sawardekar, R. Mulla, S. Sonawane, A. Shinde, V. Borate, and Y.K. Mali, (2025). "Application of Modern Tools in Web 3.0 and Blockchain to Innovate the Healthcare System." In: Rawat, S., Kumar, A., Raman, A., Kumar, S., Pathak, P. (eds) *Proceedings of Third International Conference on Computational Electronics for Wireless Communications. ICCWC 2023.* Lecture Notes in Networks and Systems, vol 962. Springer, Singapore. [http://dx.doi.org/10.1007/978-981-97-1946-4_2]

[23] S. Modi, Y. Mali, R. Kotwal, V. Kisan Borate, P. Khairnar, and A. Pathan, Hand Gesture Recognition and Real-Time Voice Translation for the Deaf and Dumb.*Semantic Intelligence. ISIC 2023. Lecture Notes in Electrical Engineering.,* S. Jain, N. Mihindukulasooriya, V. Janev, C.M. Shimizu, Eds., vol. Vol. 1258. Springer: Singapore, 2024. [http://dx.doi.org/10.1007/978-981-97-7356-5_35]

[24] A. Bhongade, S. Dargad, A. Dixit, Y.K. Mali, B. Kumari, and A. Shende, Cyber Threats in Social Metaverse and Mitigation Techniques.*Smart Systems: Innovations in Computing. SSIC 2023. Smart Innovation, Systems and Technologies.,* A.K. Somani, A. Mundra, R.K. Gupta, S. Bhattacharya, A.P. Mazumdar, Eds., vol. Vol. 392. Springer: Singapore, 2024. [http://dx.doi.org/10.1007/978-981-97-3690-4_34]

[25] Y. Mali, and T. Upadhyay, "Fraud Detection in Online Content Mining Relies on the Random Forest Algorithm", *SciWaveBulletin,* vol. 1, no. 3, pp. 13-20, 2023. [http://dx.doi.org/10.61925/SWB.2023.1302]

[26] Hrushikesh Kale, Kartik Aswar, and Dr Yogesh Mali Kisan Yadav, "Attendance Marking using Face Detection", *International Journal of Advanced Research in Science, Communication and Technology,* pp. 417-424, .

[27] F. Inamdar, D. Ojha, C.J. Ojha, and D.Y. Mali, "Job Title Predictor System", *International Journal of Advanced Research in Science. Tongxin Jishu,* pp. 457-463, 2024.

[28] S. Jagdale, P. Takale, P. Lonari, S. Khandre, and Y. Mali, "Crime Awareness and Registration System", *Int. J. Sci. Res. Sci. Technol.,* vol. 5, no. 8, 2020.

[29] S. Modi, Y. Mali, L. Sharma, P. Khairnar, D.S. Gaikwad, and V. Borate, A Protection Approach for Coal Miners' Safety Helmet Using IoT.*Semantic Intelligence. ISIC 2023. Lecture Notes in Electrical Engineering.,* S. Jain, N. Mihindukulasooriya, V. Janev, C.M. Shimizu, Eds., vol. Vol. 1258. Springer: Singapore, 2024. [http://dx.doi.org/10.1007/978-981-97-7356-5_30]

[30] Y.K. Mali, L. Sharma, K. Mahajan, F. Kazi, P. Kar, and A. Bhogle, "Application of CNN Algorithm on X-Ray Images in COVID-19 Disease Prediction", *2023 IEEE International Carnahan Conference on Security Technology (ICCST),* pp. 1-6, 2023.Pune, India [http://dx.doi.org/10.1109/ICCST59048.2023.10726852]

[31] S. Modi, "Automated Attendance Monitoring System for Cattle through CCTV", *Rev. Electrón. Vet.,* vol. 25, no. 1, pp. 1025-1034, 2024. [http://dx.doi.org/10.69980/redvet.v25i1.724]

[32] Y. Mali, and V. Chapte, "Grid-based authentication system", *International Journal of Advanced Research in Computer Science and Management Studies,* vol. 2, no. 10, pp. 93-99, 2014.

[33] R. Asreddy, A. Shingade, N. Vyavhare, A. Rokde, and Y. Mali, "A Survey on Secured Data Transmission Using RSA Algorithm and Steganography", *International Journal of Scientific Research in Computer Science Engineering and Information Technology (IJSRCSEIT)*, vol. 4, no. 8, pp. 159-162, September-October 2019, ISSN 2456–3307.

[34] J. Pathak, N. Sakore, R. Kapare, A. Kulkarni, and Prof. Yogesh Mali, "Mobile Rescue Robot", *International Journal of Scientific Research in Computer Science Engineering and Information Technology (IJSRCSEIT)*, vol. 4, no. 8, pp. 10-12, September-October 2019, ISSN 2456–3307.

[35] P. Lonari, S. Jagdale, S. Khandre, P. Takale, and P.Y. Mali, "Crime Awareness and Registration System", *International Journal of Scientific Research in Computer Science Engineering and Information Technology (IJSRCSEIT)*, vol. 8, no. 3, pp. 287-298, May-June 2021, ISSN 2456–3307.

[36] Y. Mali and N. Sawant, "Smart Helmet for Coal Mining", *International Journal of Advanced Research in Science Communication and Technology (IJARSCT)*, vol. 3, no. 1, February 2023.

SUBJECT INDEX

Manoj Kumar, Sachin Kumar Gupta, Navnath Kale, Pramod Ganjewar & Sandeep Pande (Eds.)

F

G

H

I

K

L

M

N

O

P

R

S

T

V

W

X

Y

www.ingramcontent.com/pod-product-compliance
Lightning Source LLC
LaVergne TN
LVHW070948210926
848482LV00002B/133
* 9 7 9 8 8 9 8 8 1 4 7 3 1 *